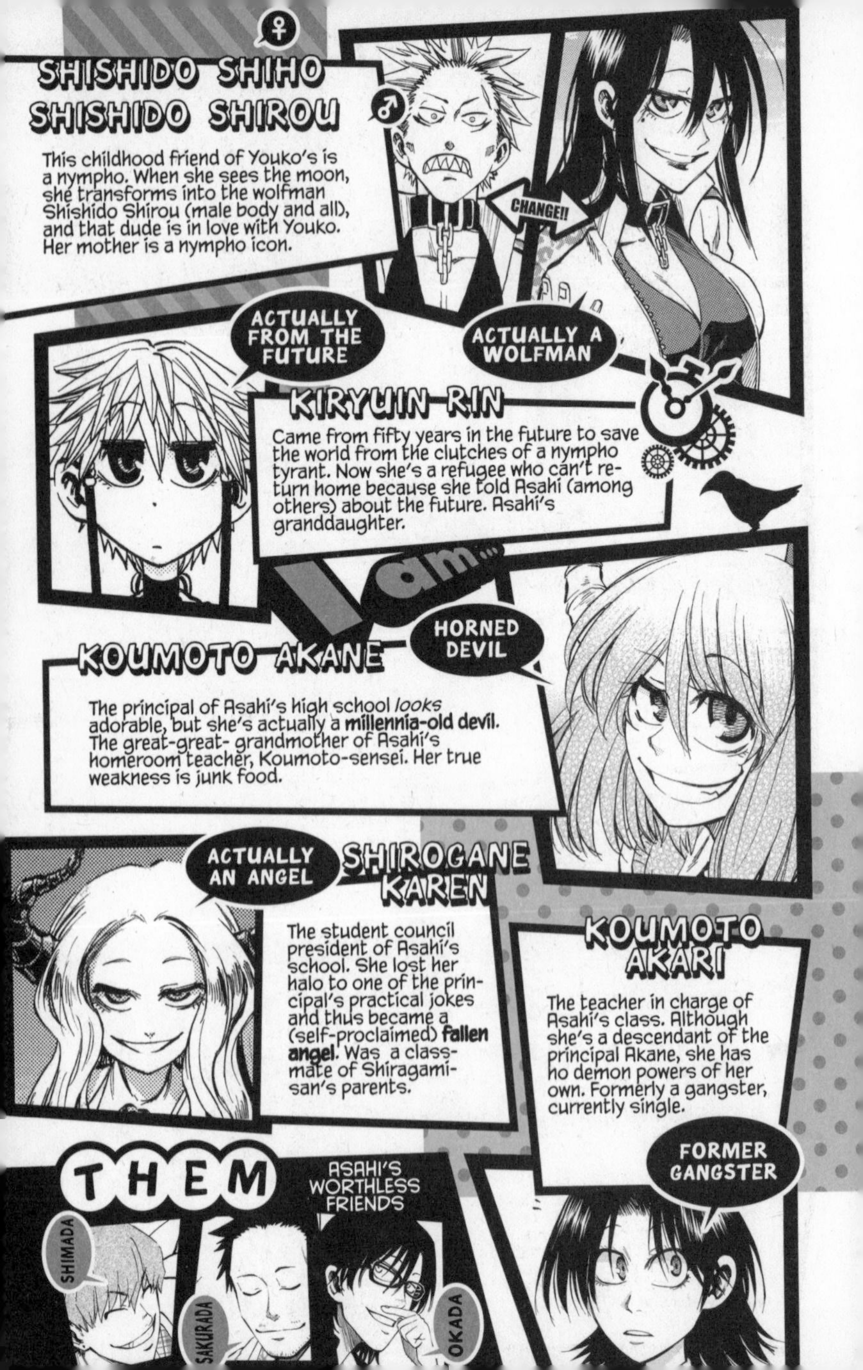

♀
SHISHIDO SHIHO
♂
SHISHIDO SHIROU
This childhood friend of Youko's is a nympho. When she sees the moon, she transforms into the wolfman Shishido Shirou (male body and all), and that dude is in love with Youko. Her mother is a nympho icon.
CHANGE!!
ACTUALLY A WOLFMAN
ACTUALLY FROM THE FUTURE
KIRYUIN RIN
Came from fifty years in the future to save the world from the clutches of a nympho tyrant. Now she's a refugee who can't return home because she told Asahi (among others) about the future. Asahi's granddaughter.
I am...
HORNED DEVIL
KOUMOTO AKANE
The principal of Asahi's high school *looks* adorable, but she's actually a **millennia-old devil.** The great-great- grandmother of Asahi's homeroom teacher, Koumoto-sensei. Her true weakness is junk food.
SHIROGANE KAREN
ACTUALLY AN ANGEL
The student council president of Asahi's school. She lost her halo to one of the principal's practical jokes and thus became a (self-proclaimed) **fallen angel**. Was a classmate of Shiragami-san's parents.
KOUMOTO AKARI
The teacher in charge of Asahi's class. Although she's a descendant of the principal Akane, she has no demon powers of her own. Formerly a gangster, currently single.
FORMER GANGSTER
THEM
ASAHI'S WORTHLESS FRIENDS
OKADA
SAKURADA
SHIMADA

SEVEN SEAS ENTERTAINMENT PRESENTS

My Monster Secret
"Actually, I am..."

story and art by Eiji Masuda

VOLUME 11

TRANSLATION
Alethea and Athena Nibley

ADAPTATION
Rebecca Scoble

LETTERING AND LAYOUT
Annaliese Christman

LOGO DESIGN
Karis Page

COVER DESIGN
Nicky Lim

PROOFREADER
Shanti Whitesides
Danielle King

ASSISTANT EDITOR
Jenn Grunigen

PRODUCTION ASSISTANT
CK Russell

PRODUCTION MANAGER
Lissa Pattillo

EDITOR IN CHIEF
Adam Arnold

PUBLISHER
Jason DeAngelis

JITSUHA WATASHIHA Volume 11
© EIJI MASUDA 2015
Originally published in Japan in 2015 by Akita Publishing Co., Ltd.
English translation rights arranged with Akita Publishing Co., Ltd.
through TOHAN CORPORATION, Tokyo.

No portion of this book may be reproduced or transmitted in any form without
written permission from the copyright holders. This is a work of fiction. Names,
characters, places, and incidents are the products of the author's imagination
or are used fictitiously. Any resemblance to actual events, locales, or persons,
living or dead, is entirely coincidental.

Seven Seas books may be purchased in bulk for promotional, educational, or
business use. Please contact your local bookseller or the Macmillan Corporate
and Premium Sales Department at 1-800-221-7945, extension 5442, or by
e-mail at MacmillanSpecialMarkets@macmillan.com.

Seven Seas and the Seven Seas logo are trademarks of
Seven Seas Entertainment, LLC. All rights reserved.

ISBN: 978-1-626928-06-0

Printed in Canada

First Printing: June 2018

10 9 8 7 6 5 4 3 2 1

FOLLOW US ONLINE: www.sevenseasentertainment.com

READING DIRECTIONS

This book reads from *right to left*, Japanese style.
If this is your first time reading manga, you start
reading from the top right panel on each page and
take it from there. If you get lost, just follow the
numbered diagram here. It may seem backwards at
first, but you'll get the hang of it! Have fun!!

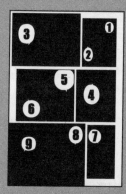

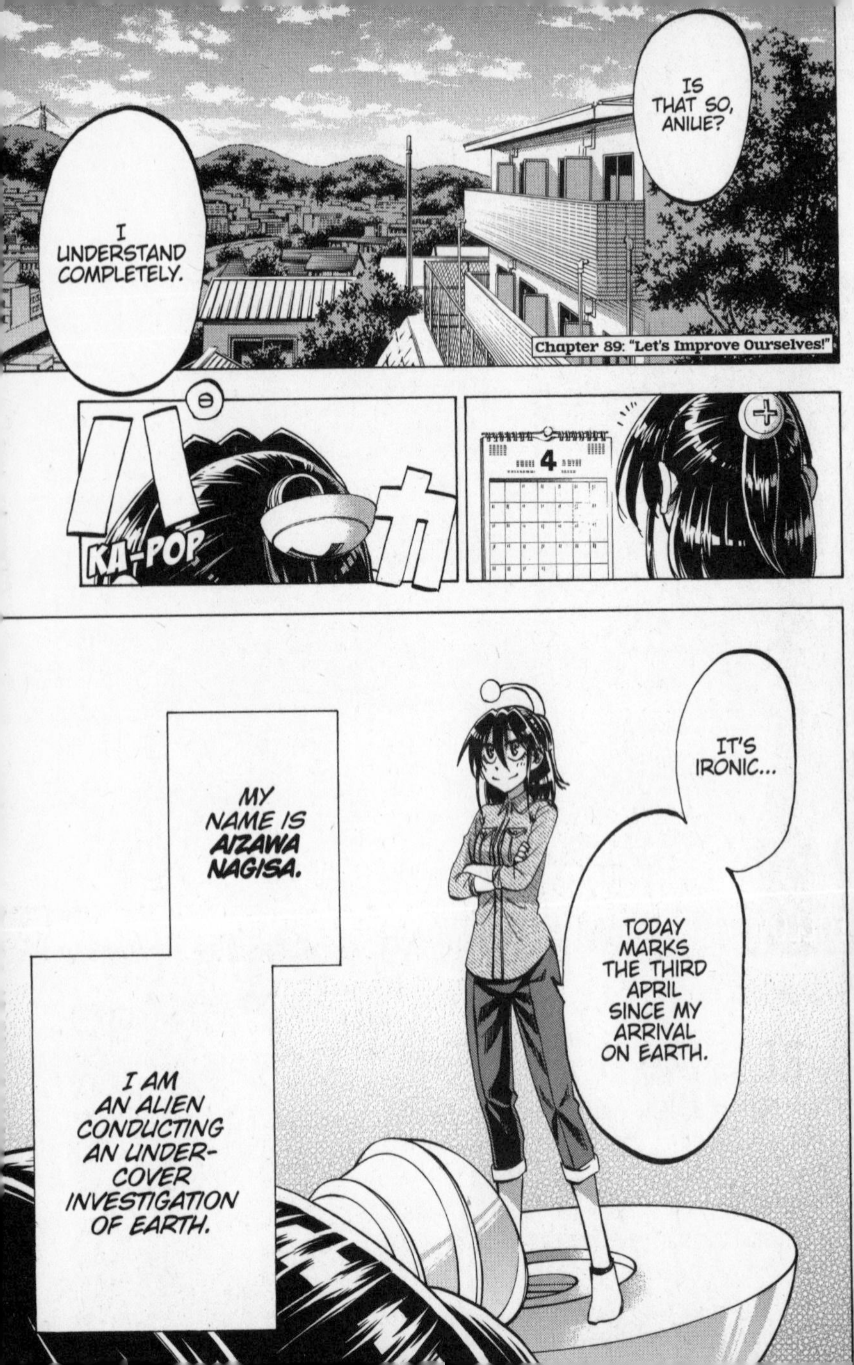
IS THAT SO, ANIUE?
I UNDERSTAND COMPLETELY.
Chapter 89: "Let's Improve Ourselves!"
KA-POP
IT'S IRONIC...
TODAY MARKS THE THIRD APRIL SINCE MY ARRIVAL ON EARTH.
MY NAME IS AIZAWA NAGISA.
I AM AN ALIEN CONDUCTING AN UNDER-COVER INVESTIGATION OF EARTH.

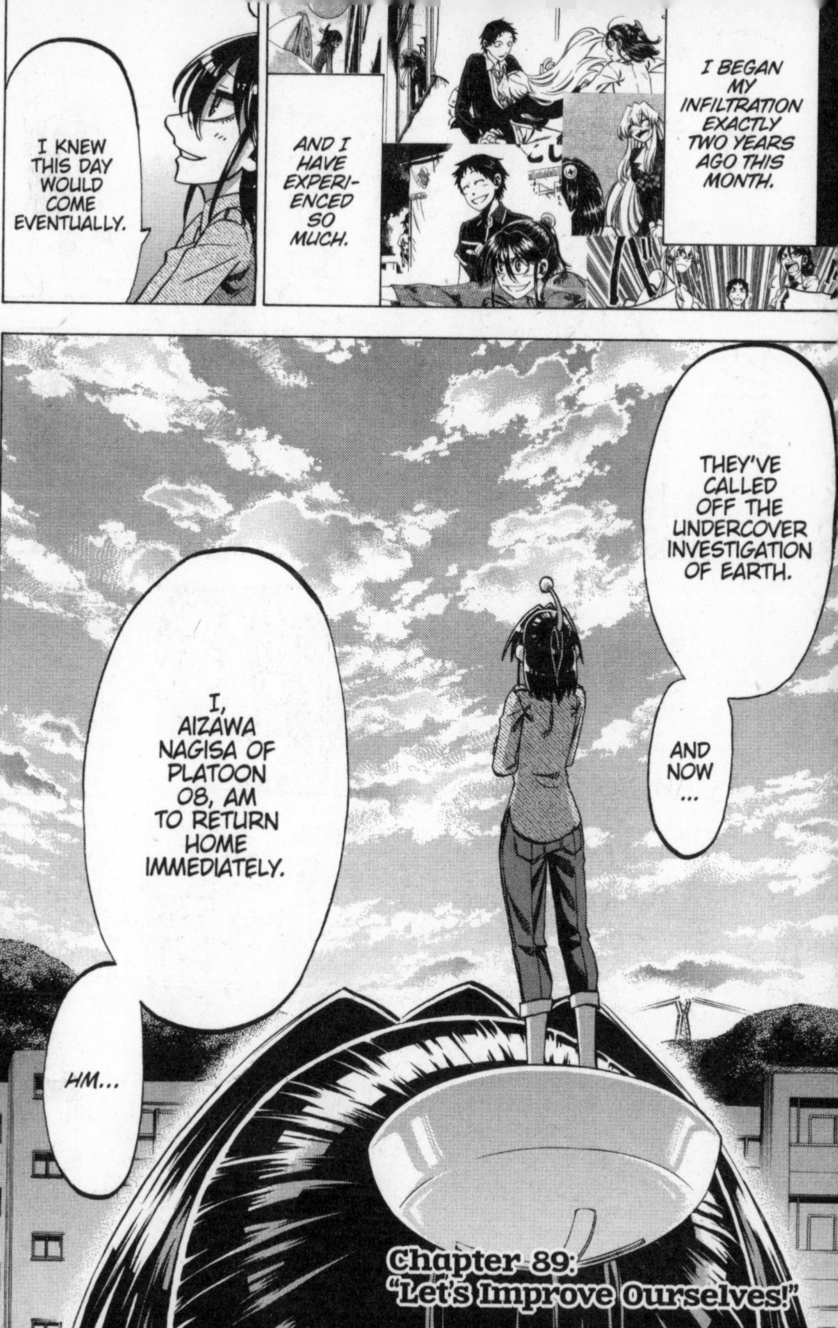
I BEGAN MY INFILTRATION EXACTLY TWO YEARS AGO THIS MONTH.
AND I HAVE EXPERIENCED SO MUCH.
I KNEW THIS DAY WOULD COME EVENTUALLY.
THEY'VE CALLED OFF THE UNDERCOVER INVESTIGATION OF EARTH.
AND NOW ...
I, AIZAWA NAGISA OF PLATOON 08, AM TO RETURN HOME IMMEDIATELY.
HM...
Chapter 89: "Let's Improve Ourselves!"

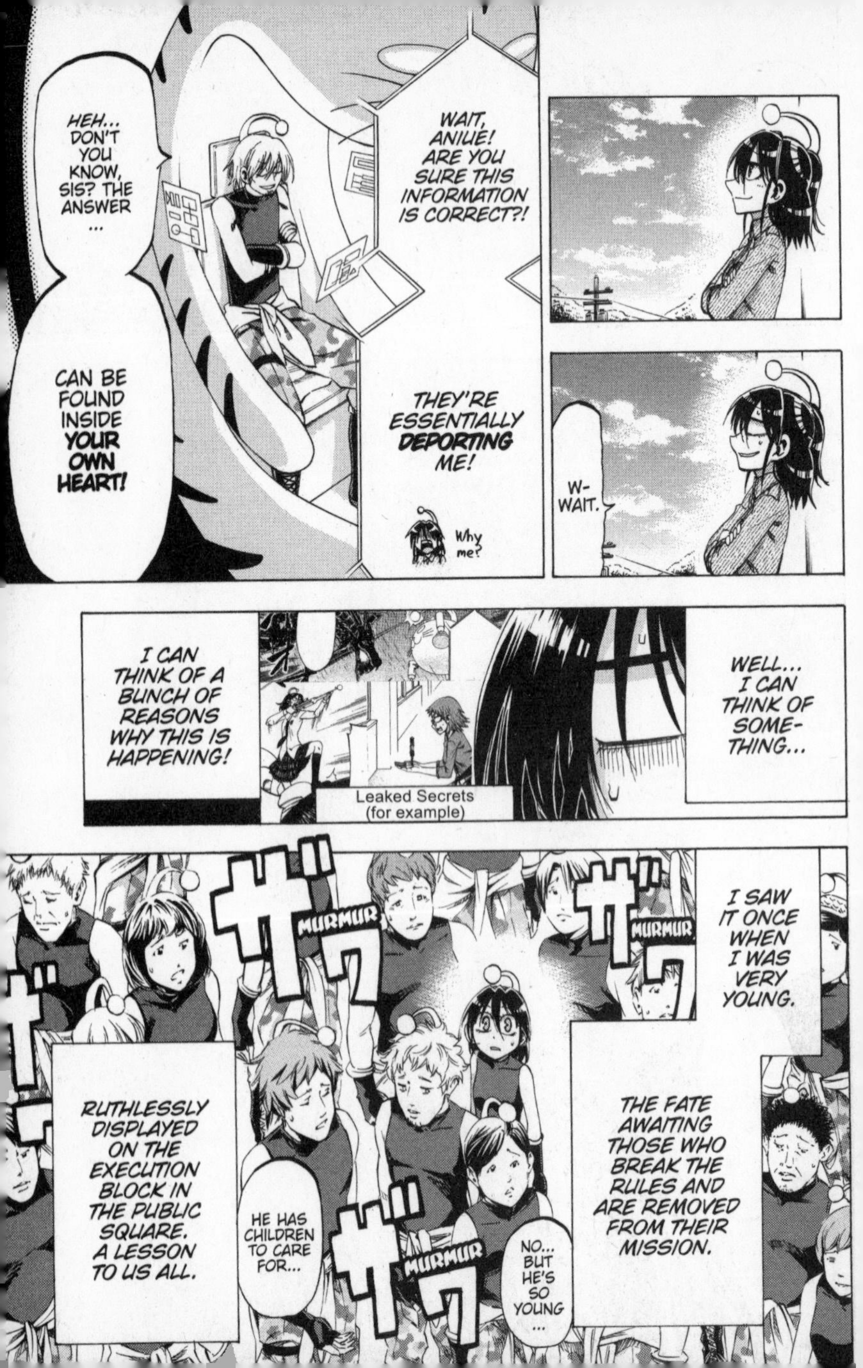
W- WAIT.
WAIT, ANIUE! ARE YOU SURE THIS INFORMATION IS CORRECT?!
THEY'RE ESSENTIALLY DEPORTING ME!
Why me?
HEH... DON'T YOU KNOW, SIS? THE ANSWER ...
CAN BE FOUND INSIDE YOUR OWN HEART!
WELL... I CAN THINK OF SOME-THING...
I CAN THINK OF A BUNCH OF REASONS WHY THIS IS HAPPENING!
Leaked Secrets (for example)
I SAW IT ONCE WHEN I WAS VERY YOUNG.
THE FATE AWAITING THOSE WHO BREAK THE RULES AND ARE REMOVED FROM THEIR MISSION.
ザワ
MURMUR
ザワ
MURMUR
NO... BUT HE'S SO YOUNG ...
HE HAS CHILDREN TO CARE FOR...
ザワ
MURMUR
RUTHLESSLY DISPLAYED ON THE EXECUTION BLOCK IN THE PUBLIC SQUARE. A LESSON TO US ALL.

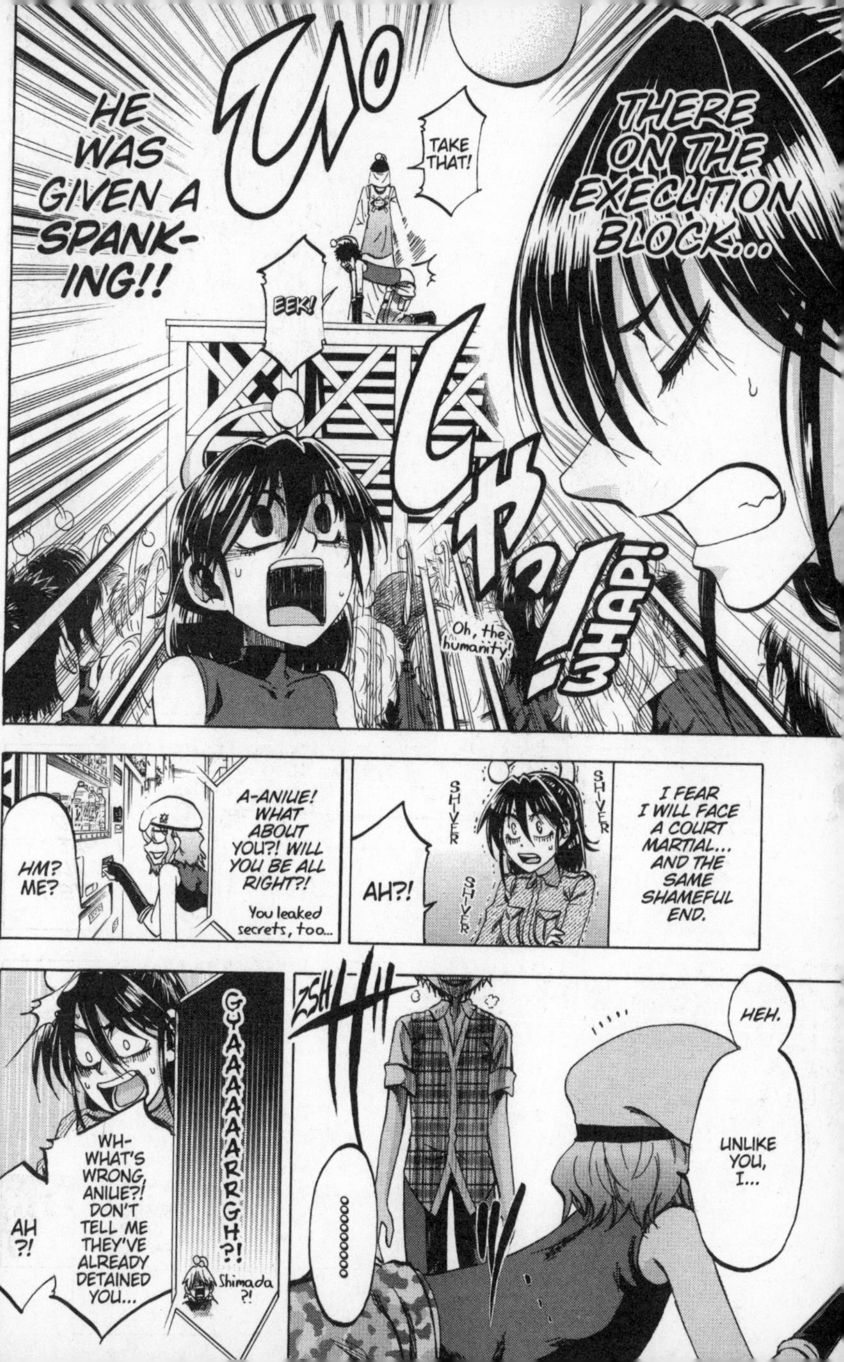
THERE ON THE EXECUTION BLOCK...
TAKE THAT!
EEK!
HE WAS GIVEN A SPANK-ING!!
WHAP!
Oh, the humanity!
I FEAR I WILL FACE A COURT MARTIAL... AND THE SAME SHAMEFUL END.
SHIVER
SHIVER
SHIVER
AH?!
A-ANIUE! WHAT ABOUT YOU?! WILL YOU BE ALL RIGHT?!
You leaked secrets, too...
HM? ME?
HEH.
UNLIKE YOU, I...
ZSHHH
GYAAAAAARRGH?!
Shimada ?!
WH-WHAT'S WRONG, ANIUE?! DON'T TELL ME THEY'VE ALREADY DETAINED YOU...
AH ?!

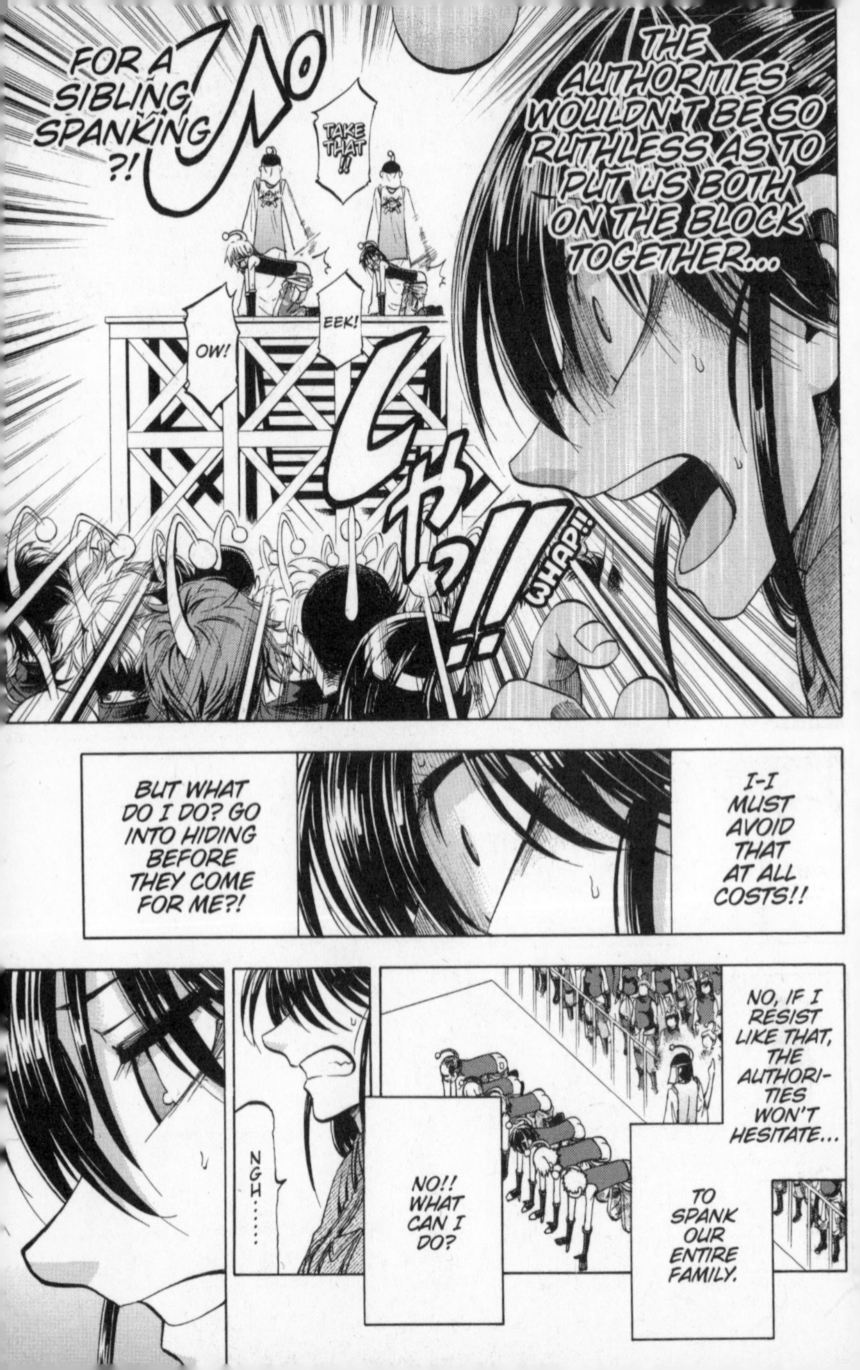
THE AUTHORITIES WOULDN'T BE SO RUTHLESS AS TO PUT US BOTH ON THE BLOCK TOGETHER...
FOR A SIBLING SPANKING?!
NO
TAKE THAT!!
EEK!
OW!
WHAP!!
I-I MUST AVOID THAT AT ALL COSTS!!
BUT WHAT DO I DO? GO INTO HIDING BEFORE THEY COME FOR ME?!
NO, IF I RESIST LIKE THAT, THE AUTHORITIES WON'T HESITATE...
TO SPANK OUR ENTIRE FAMILY.
NO!! WHAT CAN I DO?
NGH......

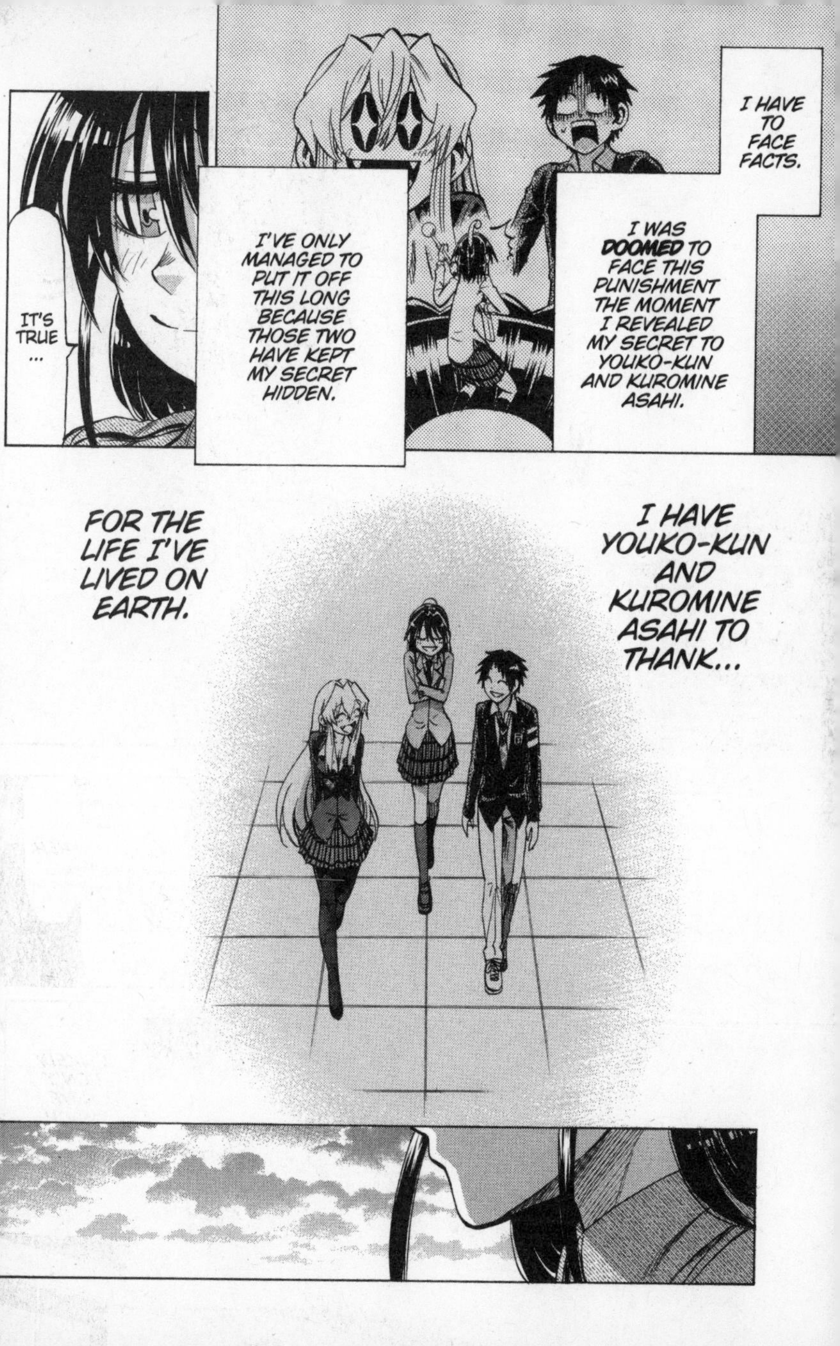
I HAVE TO FACE FACTS.
I WAS **DOOMED** TO FACE THIS PUNISHMENT THE MOMENT I REVEALED MY SECRET TO YOUKO-KUN AND KUROMINE ASAHI.
I'VE ONLY MANAGED TO PUT IT OFF THIS LONG BECAUSE THOSE TWO HAVE KEPT MY SECRET HIDDEN.
IT'S TRUE ...
I HAVE YOUKO-KUN AND KUROMINE ASAHI TO THANK...
FOR THE LIFE I'VE LIVED ON EARTH.

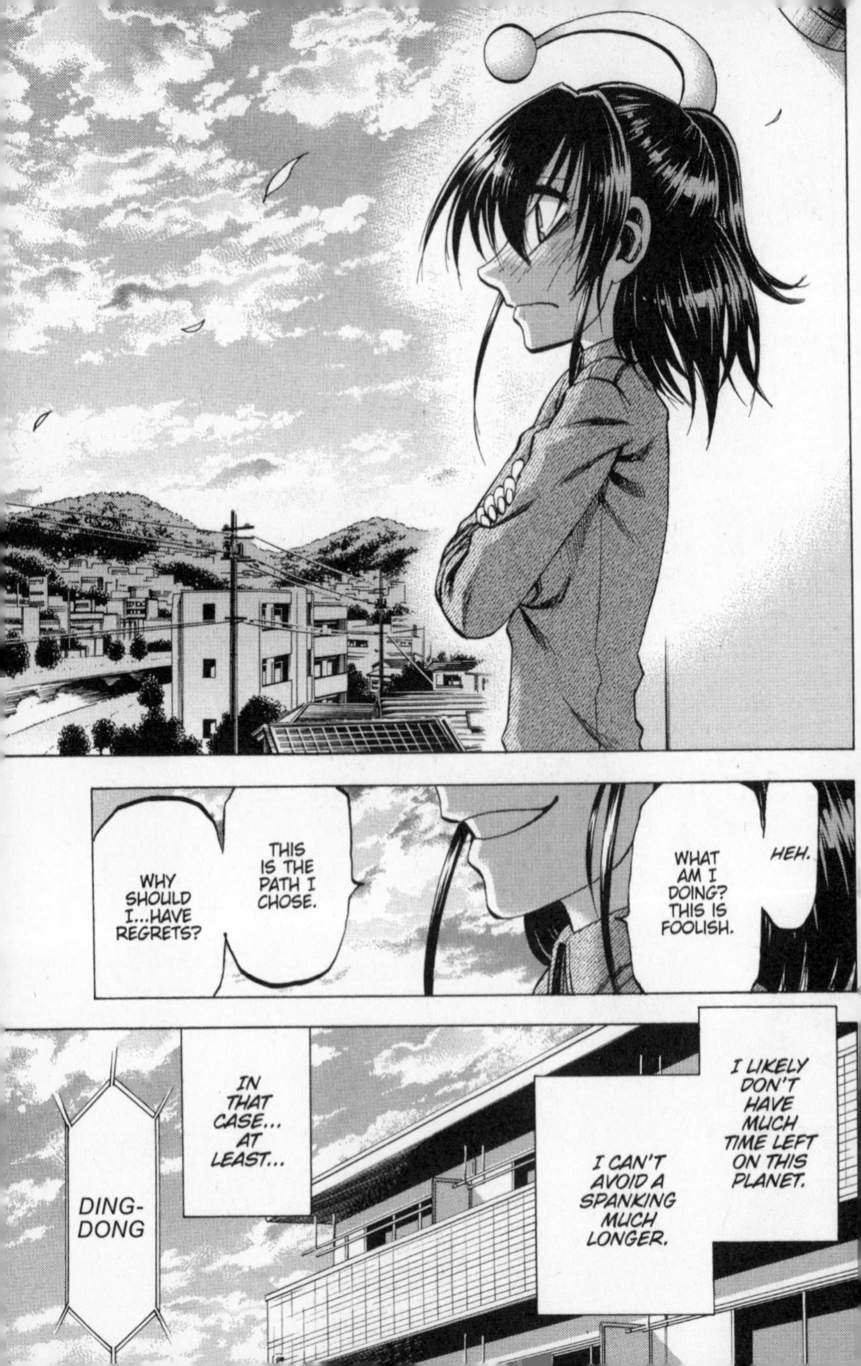
HEH.
WHAT AM I DOING? THIS IS FOOLISH.
THIS IS THE PATH I CHOSE.
WHY SHOULD I...HAVE REGRETS?
I LIKELY DON'T HAVE MUCH TIME LEFT ON THIS PLANET.
I CAN'T AVOID A SPANKING MUCH LONGER.
IN THAT CASE... AT LEAST...
DING-DONG

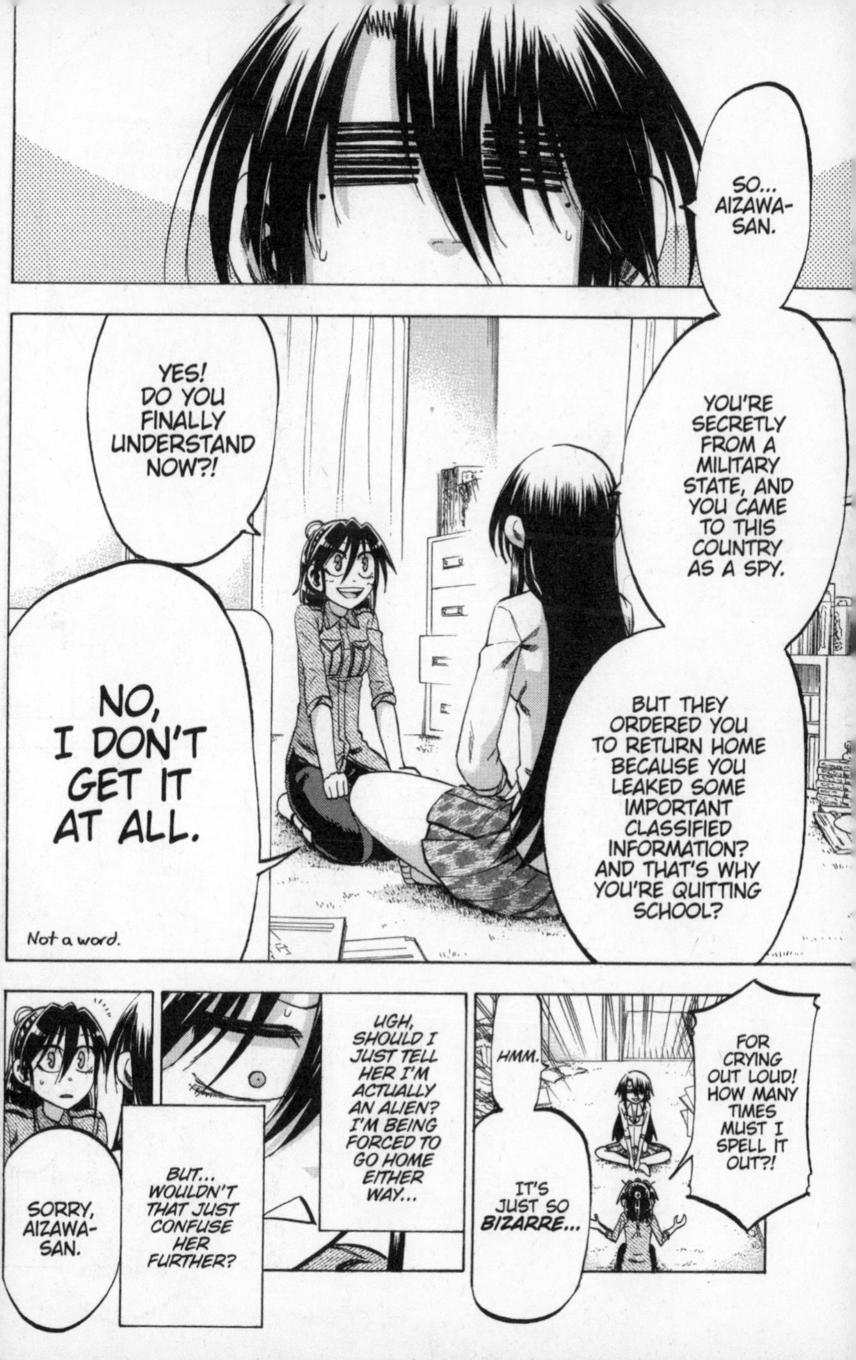
SO... AIZAWA-SAN.
YOU'RE SECRETLY FROM A MILITARY STATE, AND YOU CAME TO THIS COUNTRY AS A SPY.
BUT THEY ORDERED YOU TO RETURN HOME BECAUSE YOU LEAKED SOME IMPORTANT CLASSIFIED INFORMATION? AND THAT'S WHY YOU'RE QUITTING SCHOOL?
YES! DO YOU FINALLY UNDERSTAND NOW?!
NO, I DON'T GET IT AT ALL.
Not a word.
FOR CRYING OUT LOUD! HOW MANY TIMES MUST I SPELL IT OUT?!
HMM.
IT'S JUST SO BIZARRE...
UGH, SHOULD I JUST TELL HER I'M ACTUALLY AN ALIEN? I'M BEING FORCED TO GO HOME EITHER WAY...
BUT... WOULDN'T THAT JUST CONFUSE HER FURTHER?
SORRY, AIZAWA-SAN.

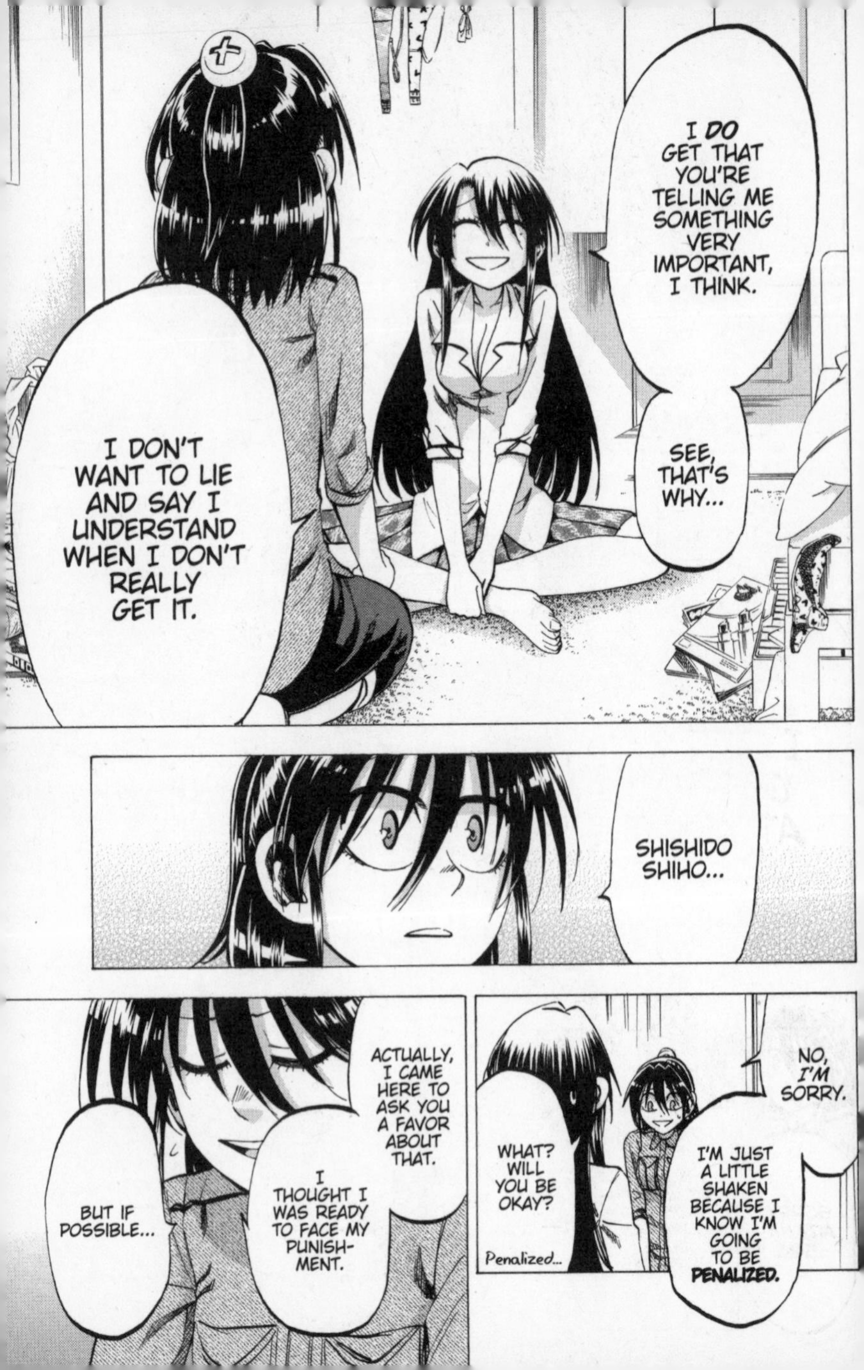
I DO GET THAT YOU'RE TELLING ME SOMETHING VERY IMPORTANT, I THINK.
SEE, THAT'S WHY...
I DON'T WANT TO LIE AND SAY I UNDERSTAND WHEN I DON'T REALLY GET IT.
SHISHIDO SHIHO...
NO, I'M SORRY.
I'M JUST A LITTLE SHAKEN BECAUSE I KNOW I'M GOING TO BE PENALIZED.
WHAT? WILL YOU BE OKAY?
Penalized...
ACTUALLY, I CAME HERE TO ASK YOU A FAVOR ABOUT THAT.
I THOUGHT I WAS READY TO FACE MY PUNISH-MENT.
BUT IF POSSIBLE...

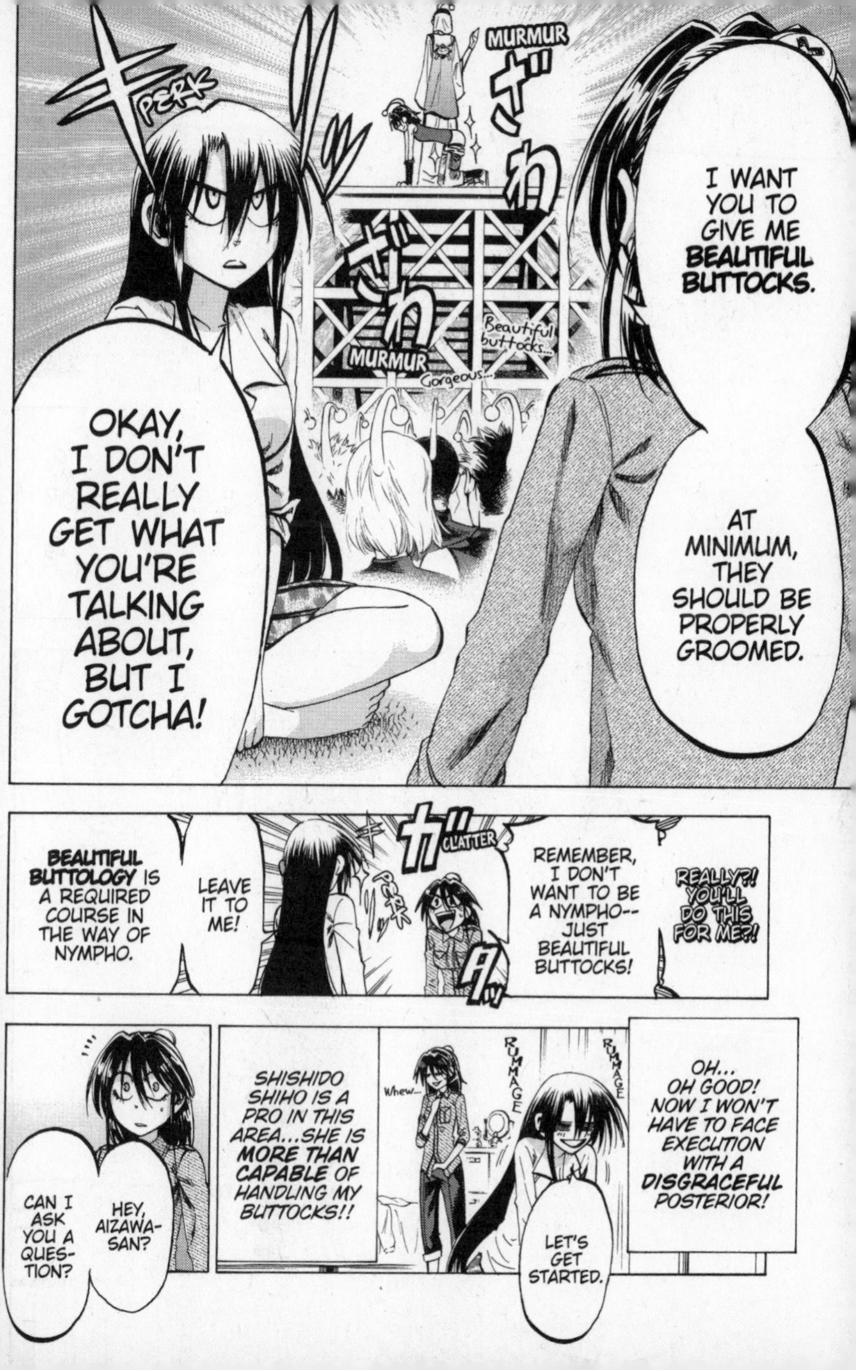
I WANT YOU TO GIVE ME **BEAUTIFUL BUTTOCKS.**
AT MINIMUM, THEY SHOULD BE PROPERLY GROOMED.
MURMUR
ざわ
ざわ
MURMUR
Beautiful buttocks...
Gorgeous...
PERK
OKAY, I DON'T REALLY GET WHAT YOU'RE TALKING ABOUT, BUT I GOTCHA!
REALLY?! YOU'LL DO THIS FOR ME?!
REMEMBER, I DON'T WANT TO BE A NYMPHO-- JUST BEAUTIFUL BUTTOCKS!
CLATTER
PERK
LEAVE IT TO ME!
BEAUTIFUL BUTTOLOGY IS A REQUIRED COURSE IN THE WAY OF NYMPHO.
OH... OH GOOD! NOW I WON'T HAVE TO FACE EXECUTION WITH A **DISGRACEFUL** POSTERIOR!
RUMMAGE
RUMMAGE
LET'S GET STARTED.
Whew...
SHISHIDO SHIHO IS A PRO IN THIS AREA...SHE IS **MORE THAN CAPABLE** OF HANDLING MY BUTTOCKS!!
HEY, AIZAWA-SAN?
CAN I ASK YOU A QUES-TION?

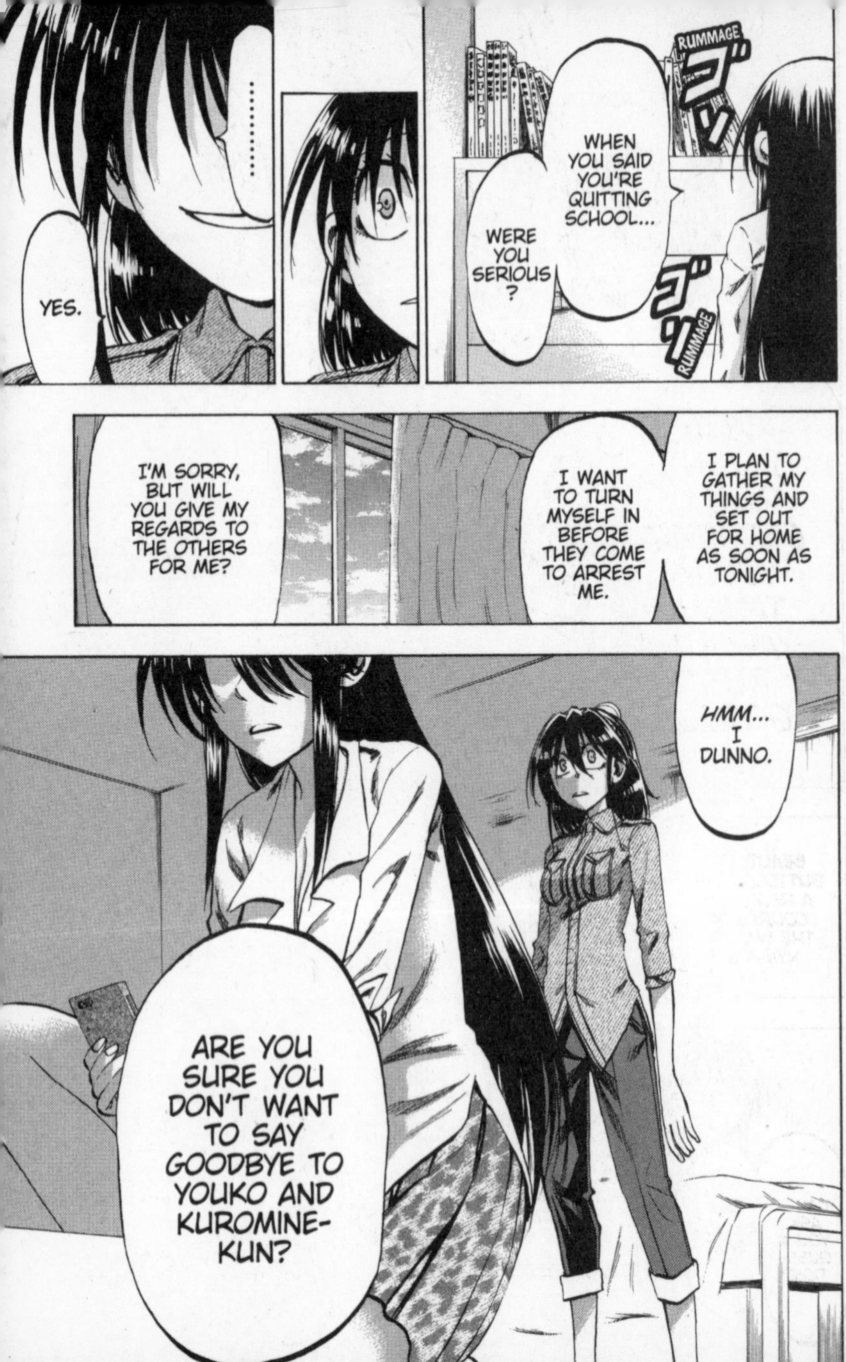
RUMMAGE
WHEN YOU SAID YOU'RE QUITTING SCHOOL...
WERE YOU SERIOUS?
RUMMAGE
......
YES.
I PLAN TO GATHER MY THINGS AND SET OUT FOR HOME AS SOON AS TONIGHT.
I WANT TO TURN MYSELF IN BEFORE THEY COME TO ARREST ME.
I'M SORRY, BUT WILL YOU GIVE MY REGARDS TO THE OTHERS FOR ME?
HMM... I DUNNO.
ARE YOU SURE YOU DON'T WANT TO SAY GOODBYE TO YOUKO AND KUROMINE-KUN?

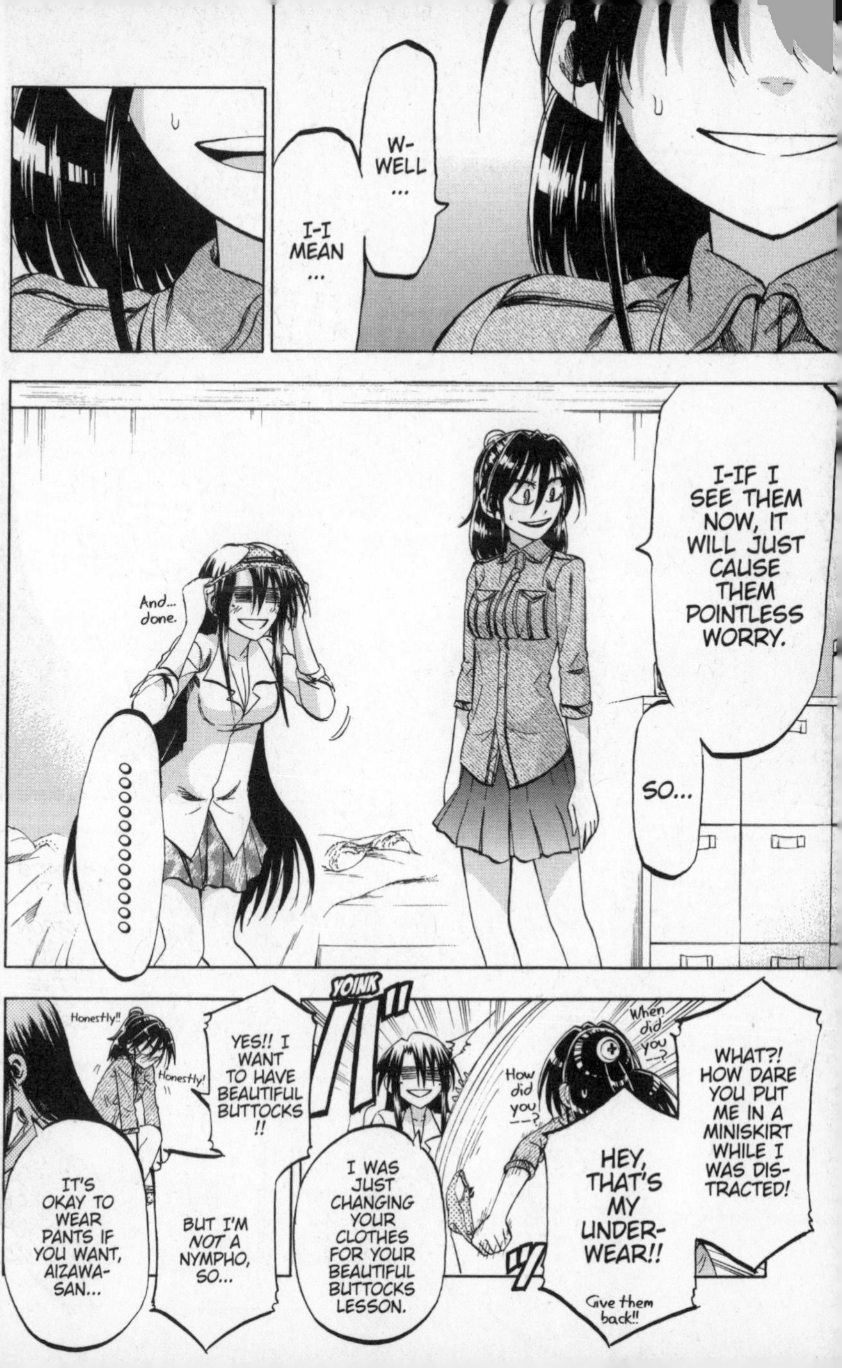
W-WELL ...
I-I MEAN ...
I-IF I SEE THEM NOW, IT WILL JUST CAUSE THEM POINTLESS WORRY.
SO...
And... done.
WHAT?! HOW DARE YOU PUT ME IN A MINISKIRT WHILE I WAS DIS-TRACTED!
When did you --?
HEY, THAT'S MY UNDER-WEAR!!
Give them back!!
How did you --?
YOINK
I WAS JUST CHANGING YOUR CLOTHES FOR YOUR BEAUTIFUL BUTTOCKS LESSON.
YES!! I WANT TO HAVE BEAUTIFUL BUTTOCKS !!
BUT I'M *NOT* A NYMPHO, SO...
Honestly!!
Honestly!
IT'S OKAY TO WEAR PANTS IF YOU WANT, AIZAWA-SAN...

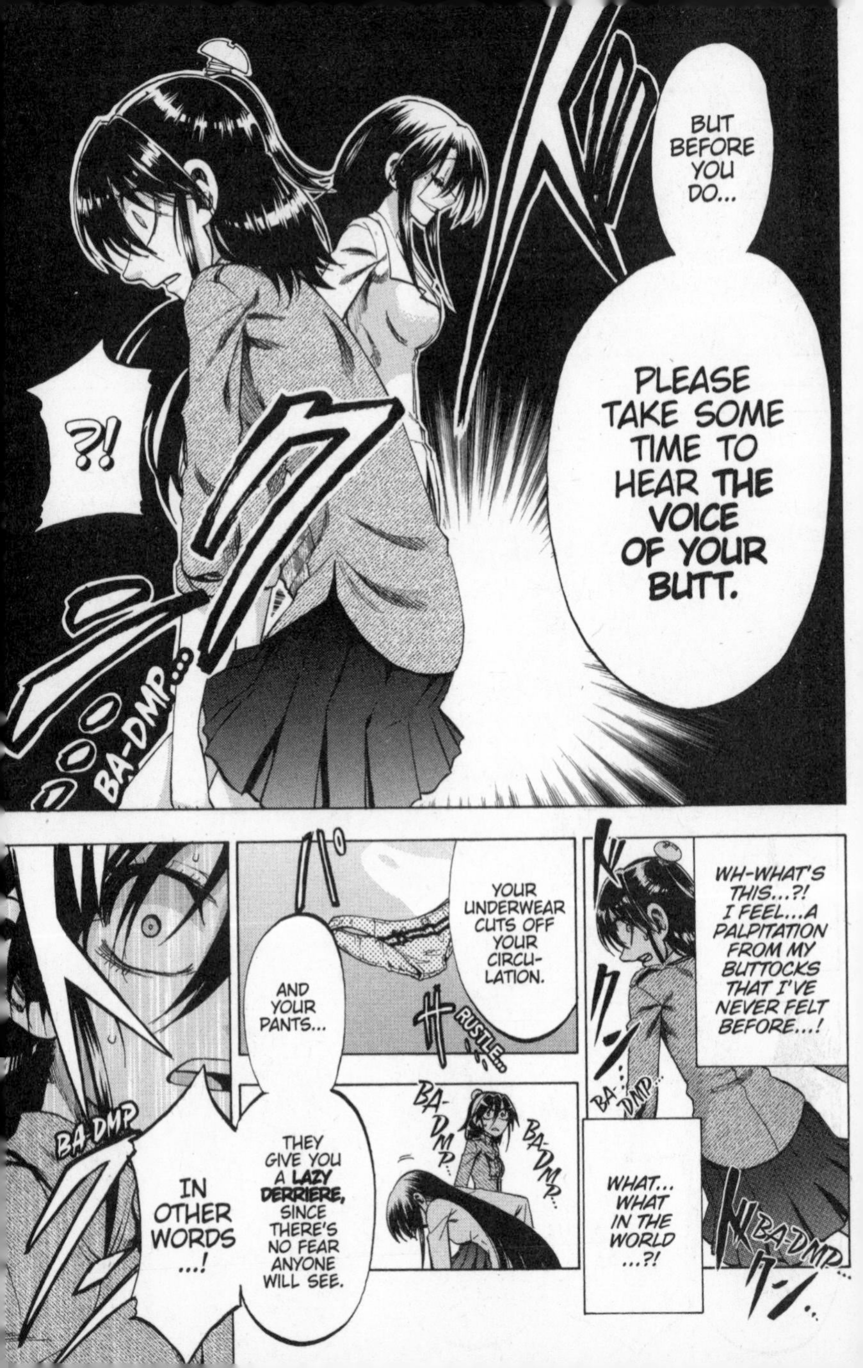
BUT BEFORE YOU DO...
PLEASE TAKE SOME TIME TO HEAR THE VOICE OF YOUR BUTT.
?!
BA-DMP...
WH-WHAT'S THIS...?! I FEEL...A PALPITATION FROM MY BUTTOCKS THAT I'VE NEVER FELT BEFORE...!
BA-DMP...
BA-DMP...
WHAT... WHAT IN THE WORLD ...?!
YOUR UNDERWEAR CUTS OFF YOUR CIRCULATION.
RUSTLE...
AND YOUR PANTS...
BA-DMP...
BA-DMP...
THEY GIVE YOU A **LAZY DERRIERE,** SINCE THERE'S NO FEAR ANYONE WILL SEE.
BA-DMP
IN OTHER WORDS ...!

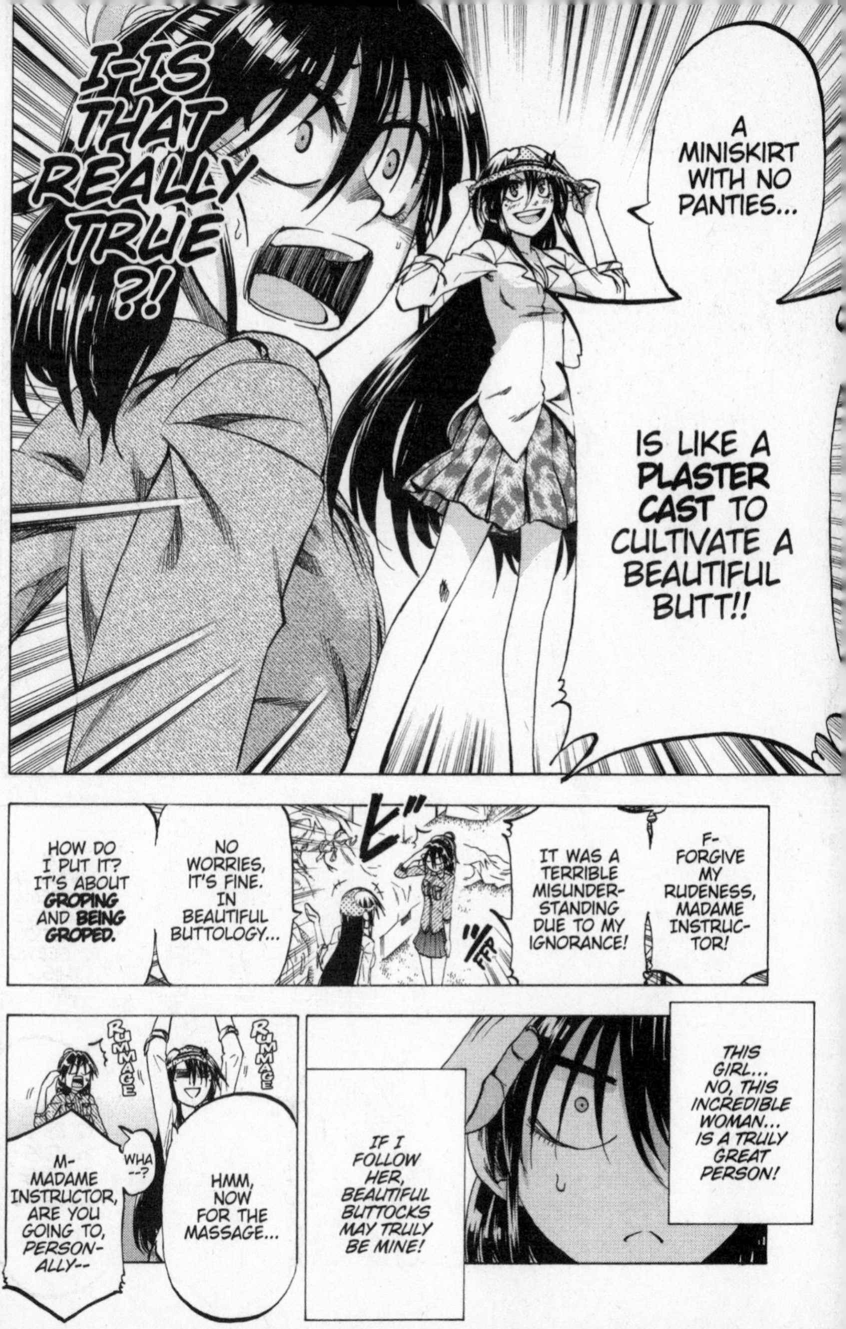
A MINISKIRT WITH NO PANTIES...
IS LIKE A **PLASTER CAST** TO CULTIVATE A BEAUTIFUL BUTT!!
I-IS THAT REALLY TRUE?!
F-FORGIVE MY RUDENESS, MADAME INSTRUCTOR!
IT WAS A TERRIBLE MISUNDERSTANDING DUE TO MY IGNORANCE!
NO WORRIES, IT'S FINE. IN BEAUTIFUL BUTTOLOGY...
HOW DO I PUT IT? IT'S ABOUT **GROPING** AND **BEING GROPED.**
THIS GIRL... NO, THIS INCREDIBLE WOMAN... IS A TRULY GREAT PERSON!
IF I FOLLOW HER, BEAUTIFUL BUTTOCKS MAY TRULY BE MINE!
RUMMAGE
RUMMAGE
HMM, NOW FOR THE MASSAGE...
WHA--?
M-MADAME INSTRUCTOR, ARE YOU GOING TO, PERSONALLY--

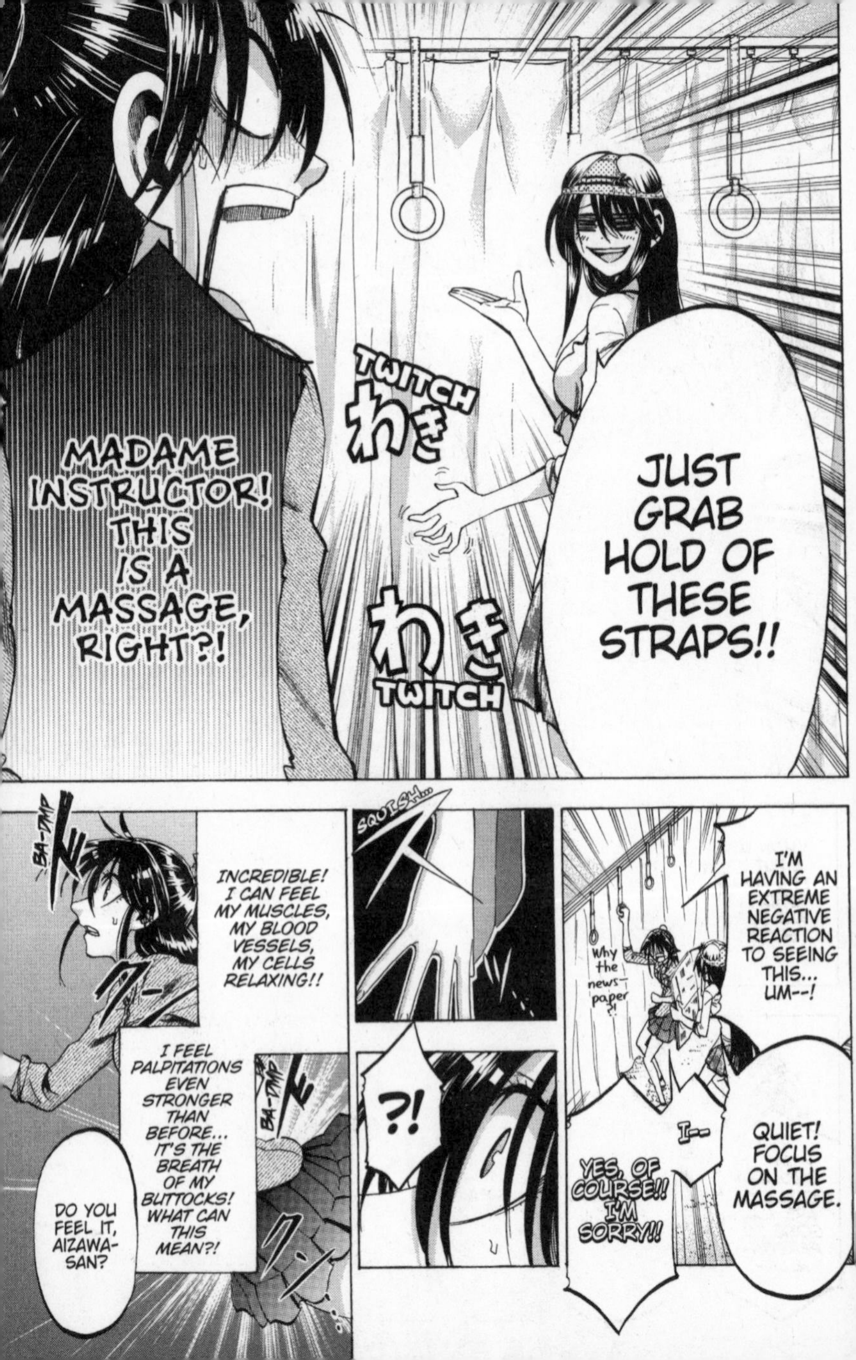
JUST GRAB HOLD OF THESE STRAPS!!
TWITCH
わき
わき
TWITCH
MADAME INSTRUCTOR! THIS IS A MASSAGE, RIGHT?!
I'M HAVING AN EXTREME NEGATIVE REACTION TO SEEING THIS... UM--!
Why the news-paper?!
QUIET! FOCUS ON THE MASSAGE.
I--
YES, OF COURSE!! I'M SORRY!!
SQUISH...
?!
INCREDIBLE! I CAN FEEL MY MUSCLES, MY BLOOD VESSELS, MY CELLS RELAXING!!
BA-DMP
I FEEL PALPITATIONS EVEN STRONGER THAN BEFORE... IT'S THE BREATH OF MY BUTTOCKS! WHAT CAN THIS MEAN?!
BA-DMP
DO YOU FEEL IT, AIZAWA-SAN?

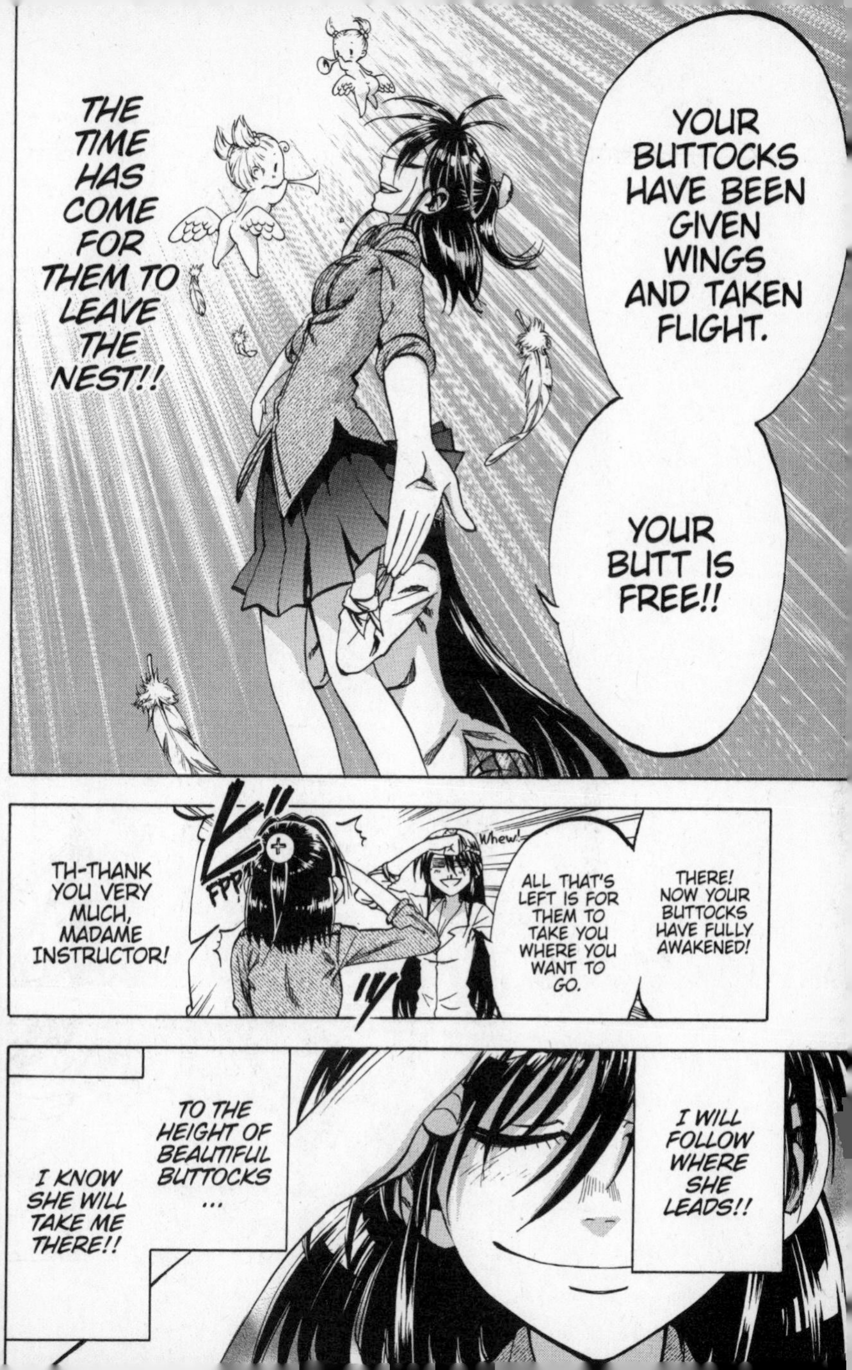
YOUR BUTTOCKS HAVE BEEN GIVEN WINGS AND TAKEN FLIGHT.
YOUR BUTT IS FREE!!
THE TIME HAS COME FOR THEM TO LEAVE THE NEST!!
THERE! NOW YOUR BUTTOCKS HAVE FULLY AWAKENED!
ALL THAT'S LEFT IS FOR THEM TO TAKE YOU WHERE YOU WANT TO GO.
Whew!
FPP
TH-THANK YOU VERY MUCH, MADAME INSTRUCTOR!
I WILL FOLLOW WHERE SHE LEADS!!
TO THE HEIGHT OF BEAUTIFUL BUTTOCKS ...
I KNOW SHE WILL TAKE ME THERE!!

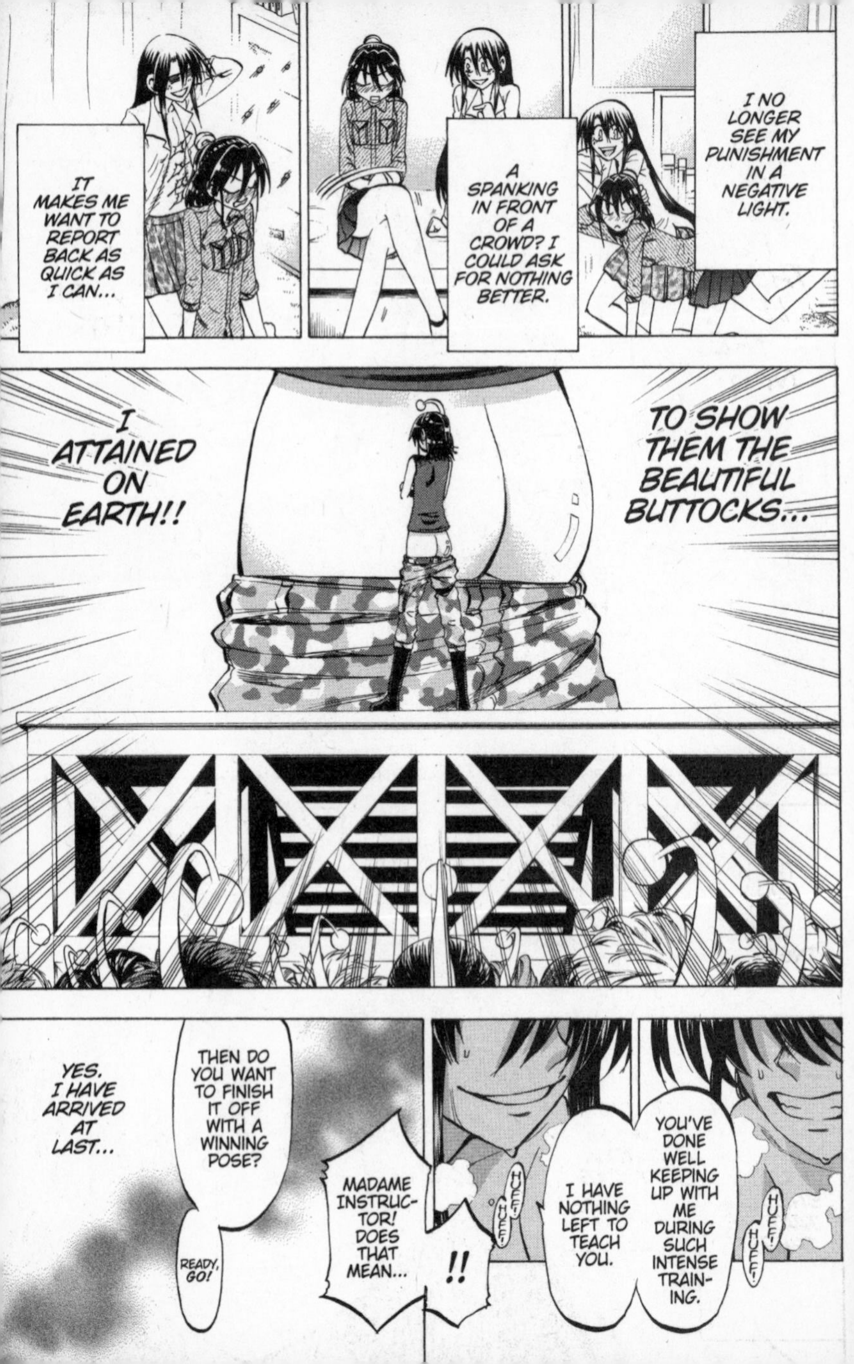
I NO LONGER SEE MY PUNISHMENT IN A NEGATIVE LIGHT.
A SPANKING IN FRONT OF A CROWD? I COULD ASK FOR NOTHING BETTER.
IT MAKES ME WANT TO REPORT BACK AS QUICK AS I CAN...
TO SHOW THEM THE BEAUTIFUL BUTTOCKS...
I ATTAINED ON EARTH!!
HUFF! HUFF!
YOU'VE DONE WELL KEEPING UP WITH ME DURING SUCH INTENSE TRAIN-ING.
I HAVE NOTHING LEFT TO TEACH YOU.
HUFF! HUFF!
!!
MADAME INSTRUC-TOR! DOES THAT MEAN...
THEN DO YOU WANT TO FINISH IT OFF WITH A WINNING POSE?
YES. I HAVE ARRIVED AT LAST...
READY, GO!

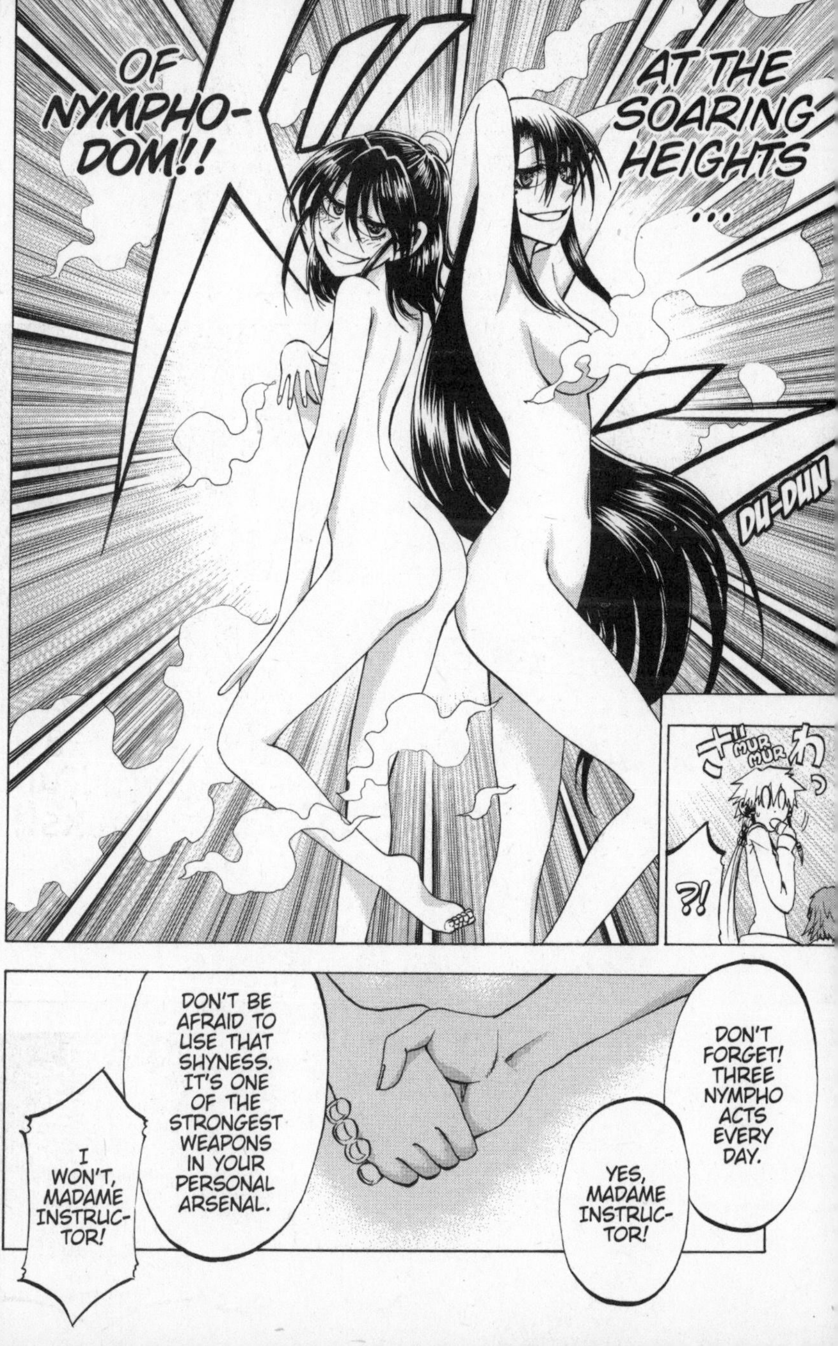
AT THE SOARING HEIGHTS...
OF NYMPHO-DOM!!
DU-DUN
ざわ
MUR MUR
?!
DON'T FORGET! THREE NYMPHO ACTS EVERY DAY.
YES, MADAME INSTRUCTOR!
DON'T BE AFRAID TO USE THAT SHYNESS. IT'S ONE OF THE STRONGEST WEAPONS IN YOUR PERSONAL ARSENAL.
I WON'T, MADAME INSTRUCTOR!

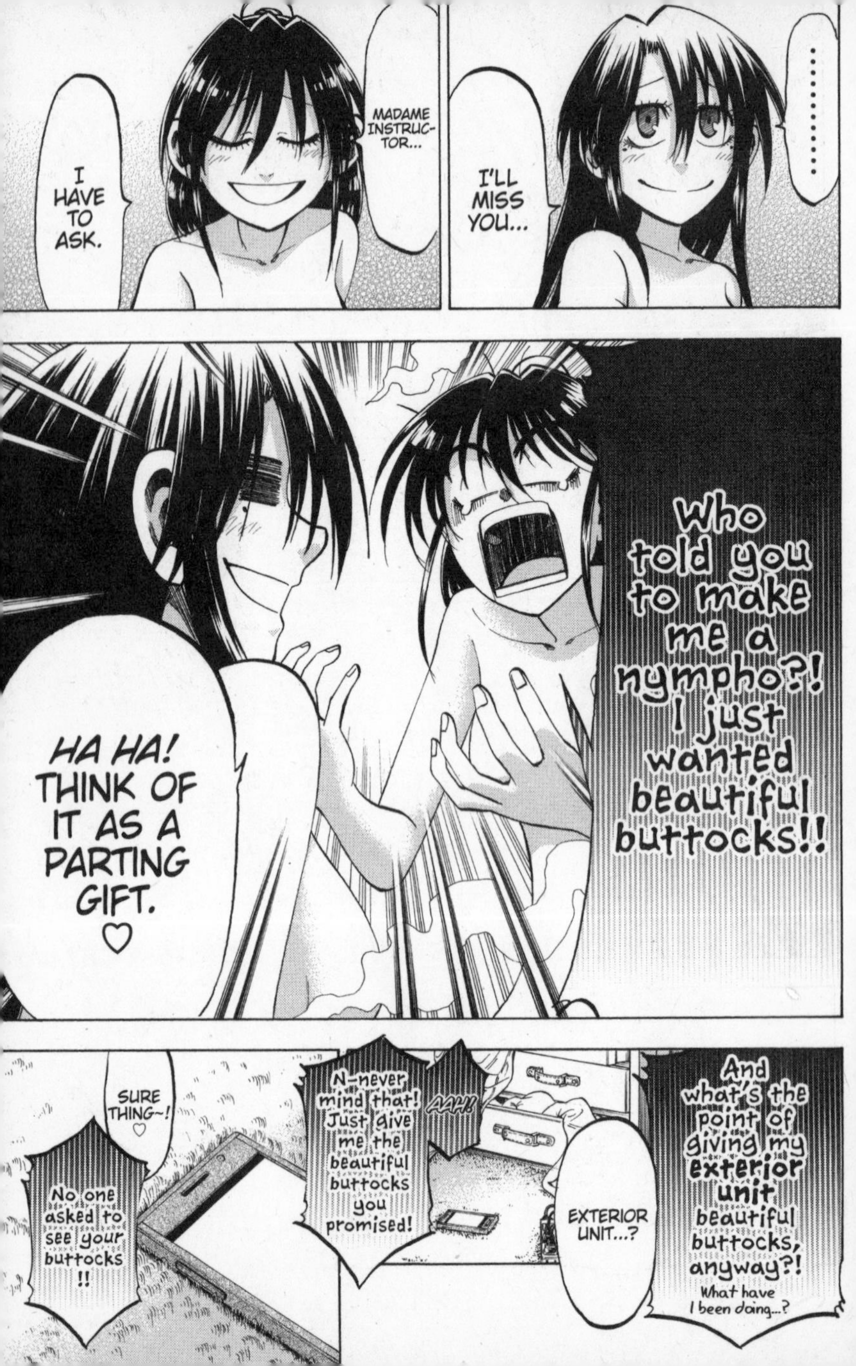
……
I'LL MISS YOU...
MADAME INSTRUCTOR...
I HAVE TO ASK.
Who told you to make me a nympho?! I just wanted beautiful buttocks!!
HA HA! THINK OF IT AS A PARTING GIFT. ♡
And what's the point of giving my exterior unit beautiful buttocks, anyway?!
What have I been doing...?
EXTERIOR UNIT...?
AAH!
N-never mind that! Just give me the beautiful buttocks you promised!
SURE THING~! ♡
No one asked to see your buttocks !!

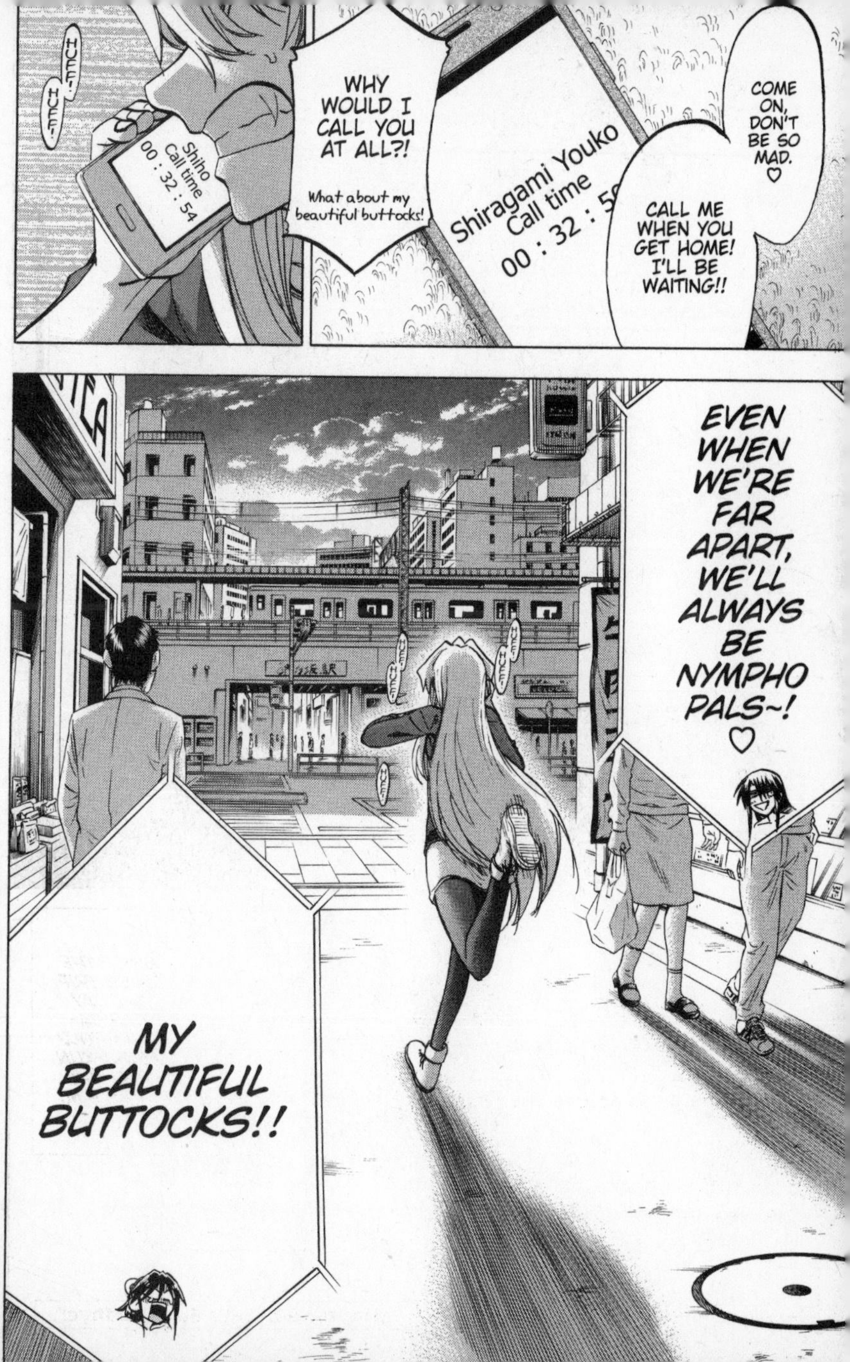
COME ON, DON'T BE SO MAD. ♡
CALL ME WHEN YOU GET HOME! I'LL BE WAITING!!
Shiragami Youko
Call time
00 : 32 : 5
WHY WOULD I CALL YOU AT ALL?!
What about my beautiful buttocks!
Shiho
Call time
00 : 32 : 54
HUFF! HUFF!
EVEN WHEN WE'RE FAR APART, WE'LL ALWAYS BE NYMPHO PALS~! ♡
HUFF HUFF
HUFF HUFF
HUFF
MY BEAUTIFUL BUTTOCKS!!

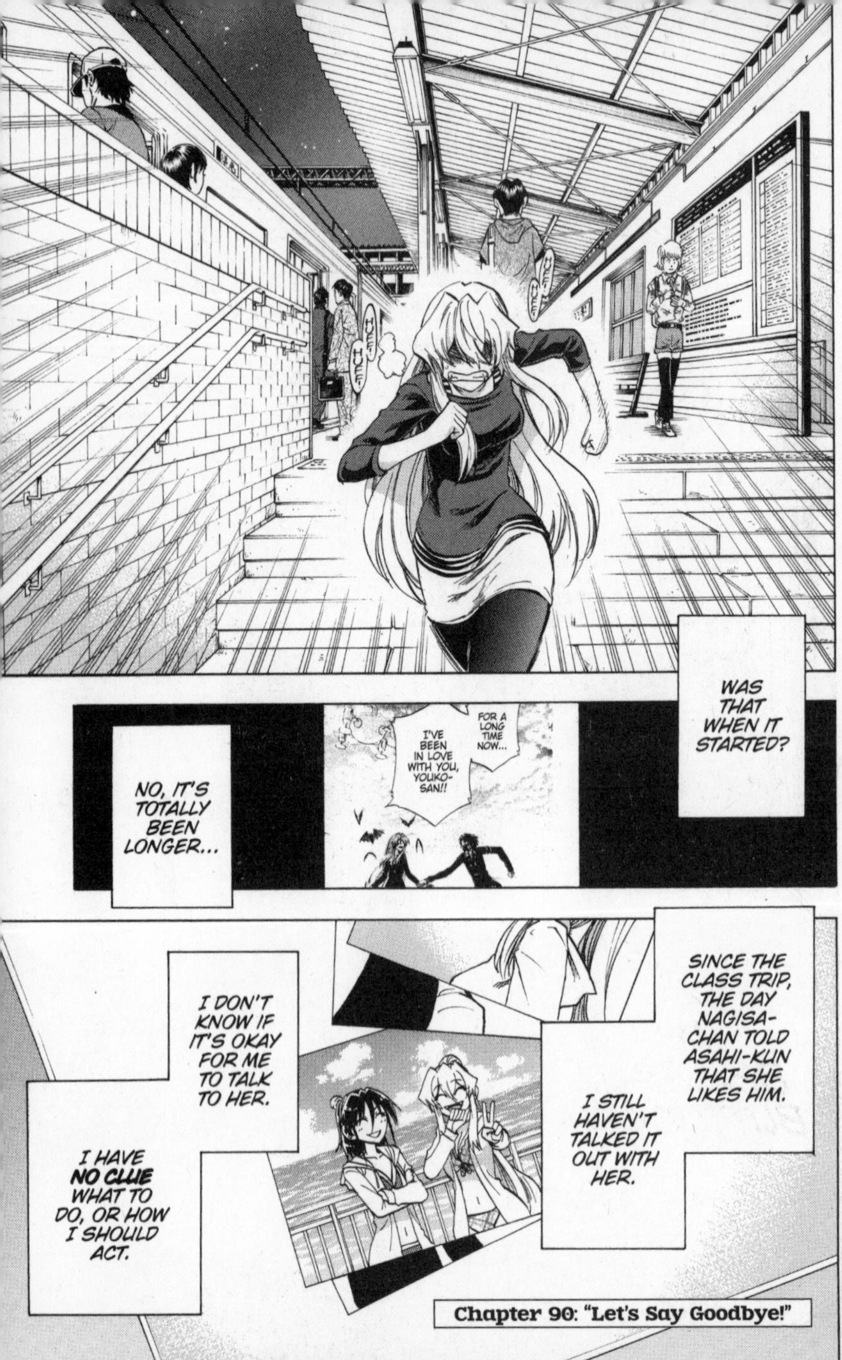
HUFF
HUFF
HUFF
HUFF
WAS THAT WHEN IT STARTED?
FOR A LONG TIME NOW...
I'VE BEEN IN LOVE WITH YOU, YOUKO-SAN!!
NO, IT'S TOTALLY BEEN LONGER...
SINCE THE CLASS TRIP, THE DAY NAGISA-CHAN TOLD ASAHI-KUN THAT SHE LIKES HIM.
I STILL HAVEN'T TALKED IT OUT WITH HER.
I DON'T KNOW IF IT'S OKAY FOR ME TO TALK TO HER.
I HAVE **NO CLUE** WHAT TO DO, OR HOW I SHOULD ACT.

Chapter 90: "Let's Say Goodbye!"

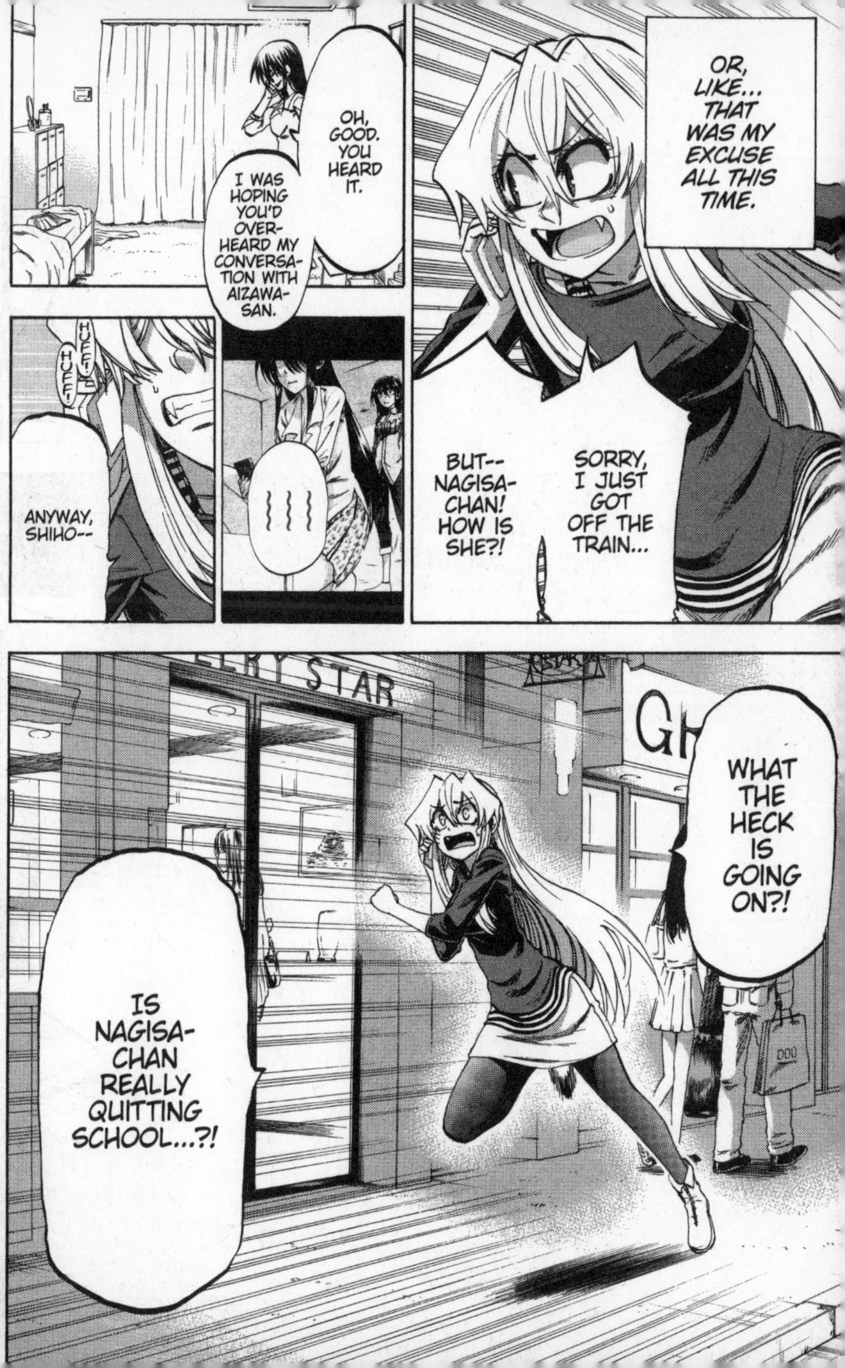
OR, LIKE... THAT WAS MY EXCUSE ALL THIS TIME.
SORRY, I JUST GOT OFF THE TRAIN...
BUT-- NAGISA-CHAN! HOW IS SHE?!
OH, GOOD. YOU HEARD IT.
I WAS HOPING YOU'D OVER-HEARD MY CONVERSA-TION WITH AIZAWA-SAN.
HUFF! HUFF!
ANYWAY, SHIHO--
WHAT THE HECK IS GOING ON?!
IS NAGISA-CHAN REALLY QUITTING SCHOOL...?!

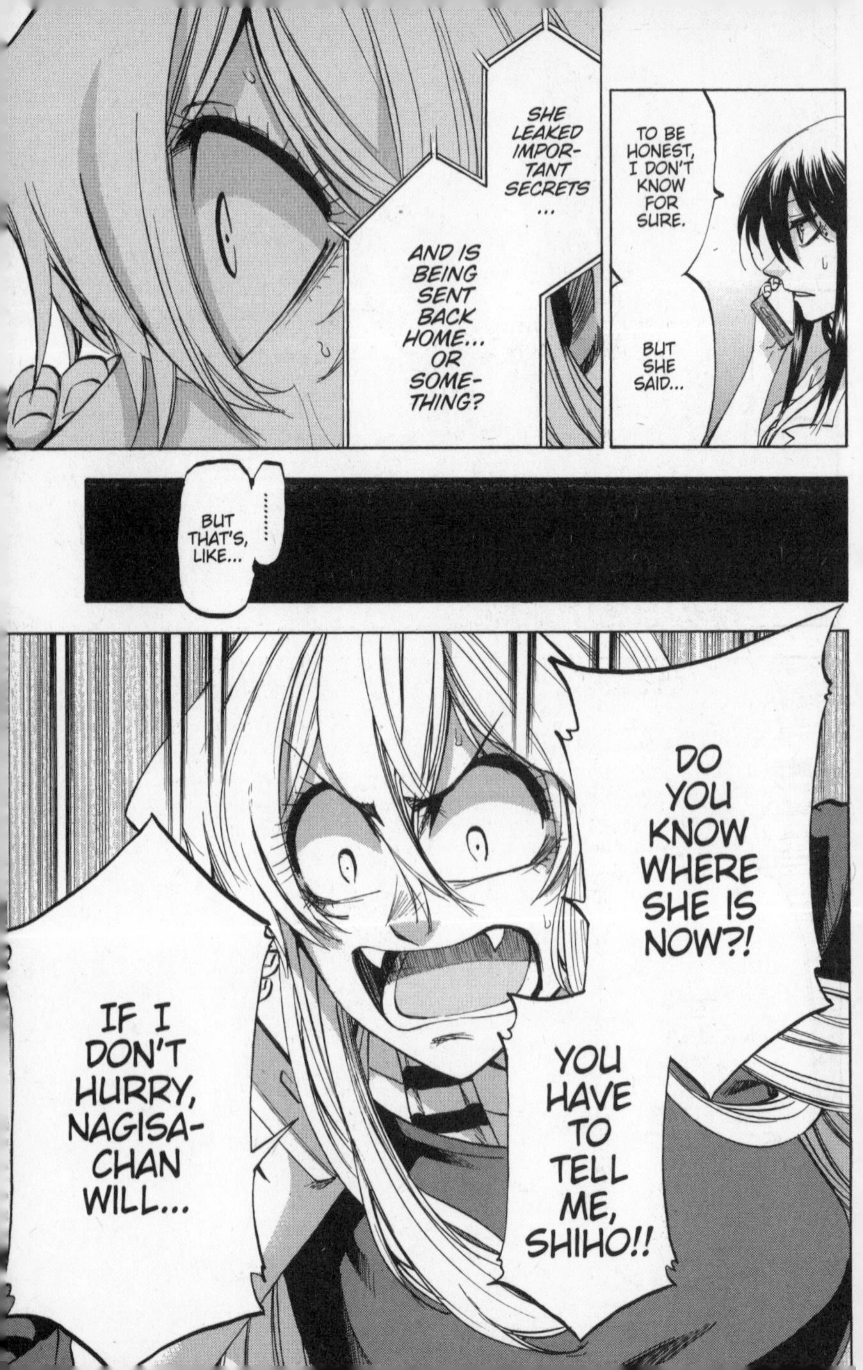
TO BE HONEST, I DON'T KNOW FOR SURE.
BUT SHE SAID...
SHE LEAKED IMPORTANT SECRETS...
AND IS BEING SENT BACK HOME... OR SOMETHING?
......
BUT THAT'S, LIKE...
DO YOU KNOW WHERE SHE IS NOW?!
YOU HAVE TO TELL ME, SHIHO!!
IF I DON'T HURRY, NAGISA-CHAN WILL...

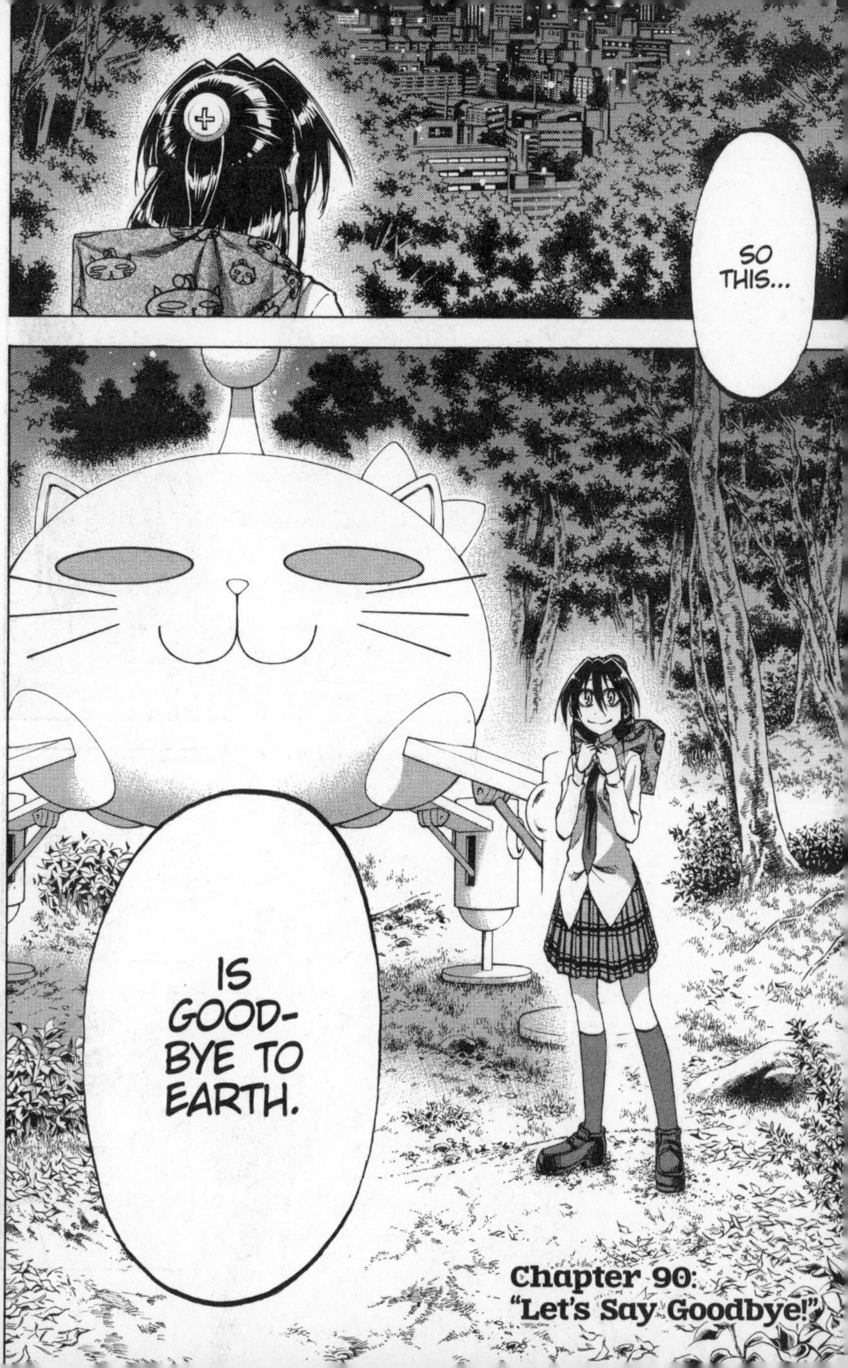
SO THIS...
IS GOOD-BYE TO EARTH.

Chapter 90: "Let's Say Goodbye!"

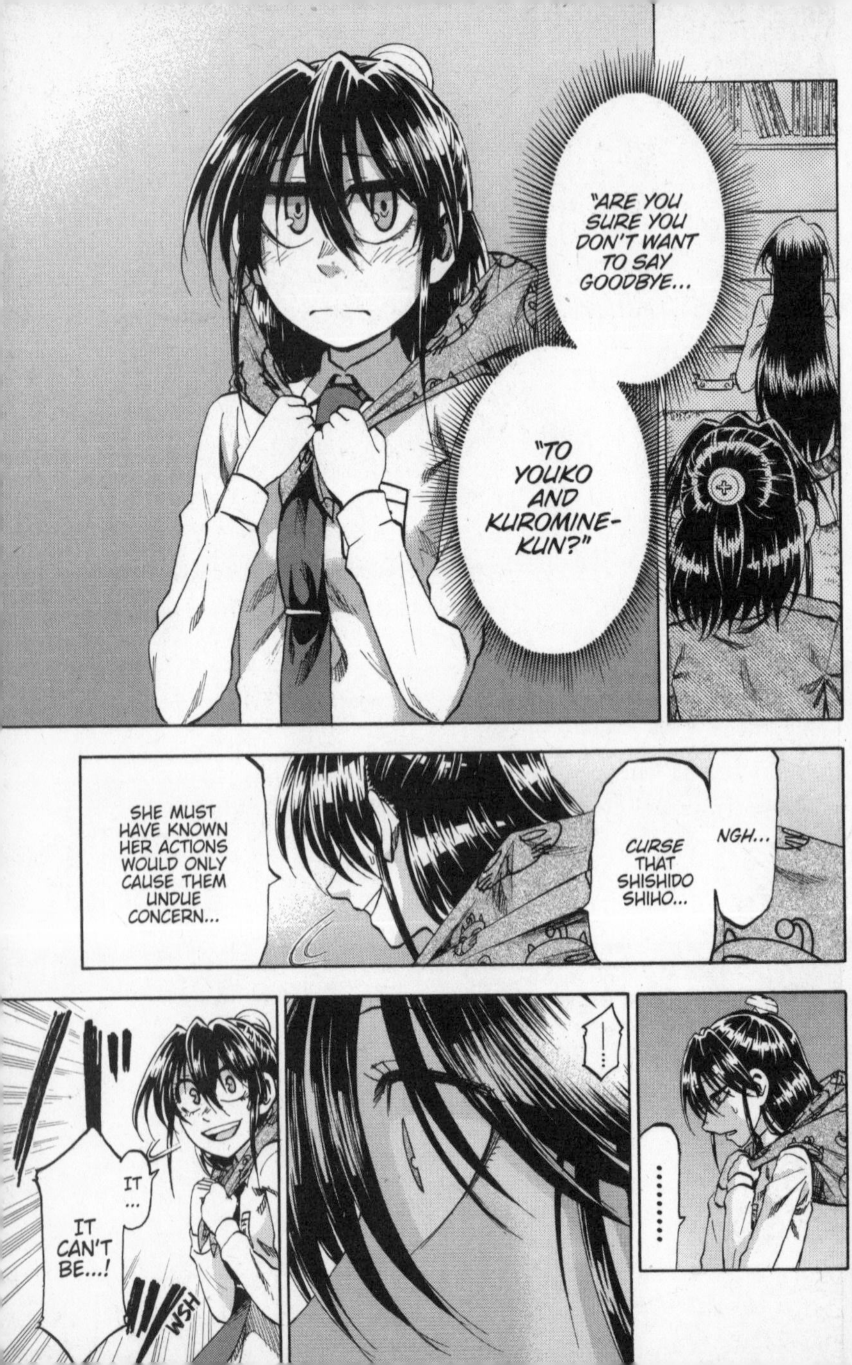
"ARE YOU SURE YOU DON'T WANT TO SAY GOODBYE...
"TO YOUKO AND KUROMINE-KUN?"
NGH...
CURSE THAT SHISHIDO SHIHO...
SHE MUST HAVE KNOWN HER ACTIONS WOULD ONLY CAUSE THEM UNDUE CONCERN...
....
!......
IT...
IT CAN'T BE...!
WSH

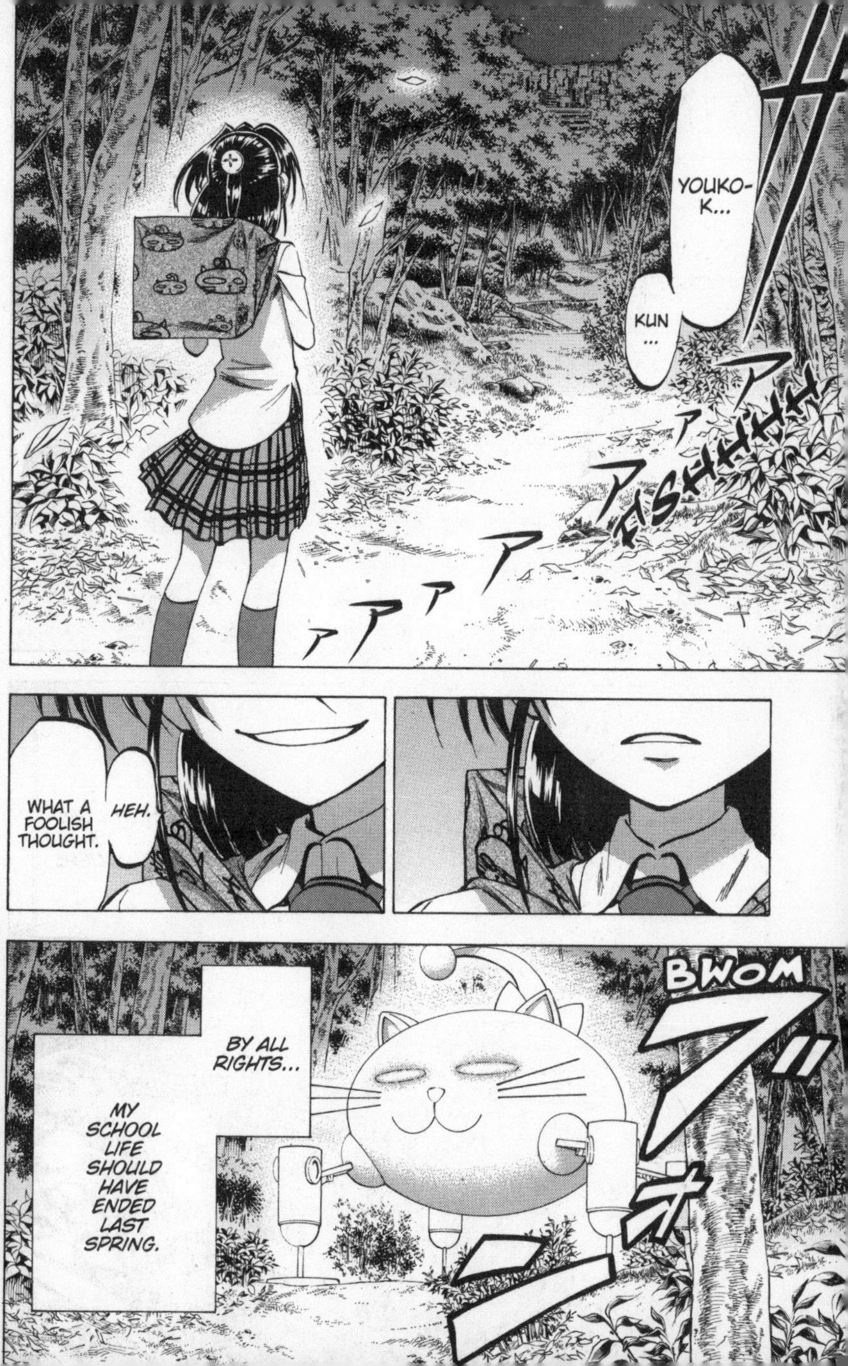
YOUKO-K...
KUN...
FASHHHH
HEH.
WHAT A FOOLISH THOUGHT.
BWOM
BY ALL RIGHTS...
MY SCHOOL LIFE SHOULD HAVE ENDED LAST SPRING.

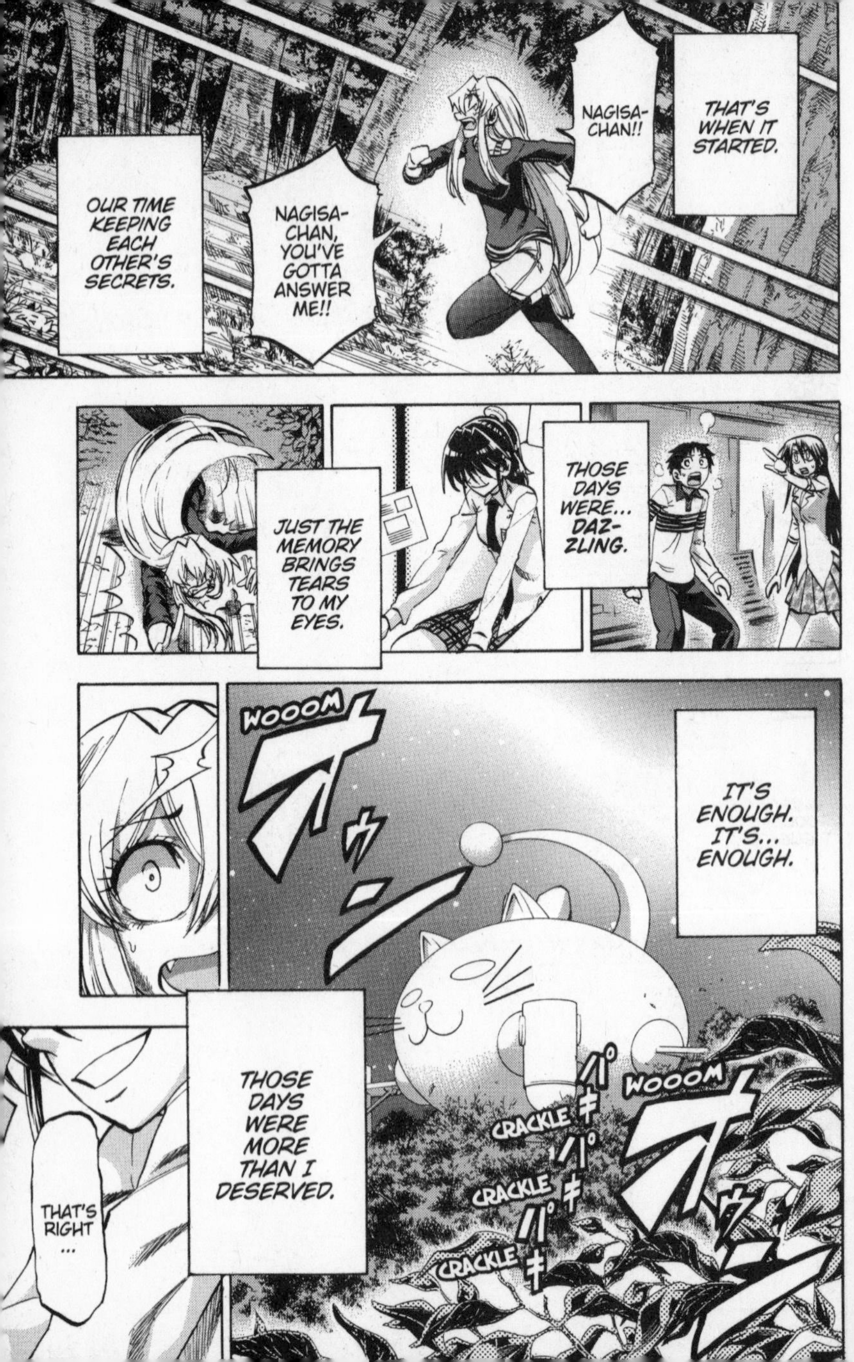
THAT'S WHEN IT STARTED.
NAGISA-CHAN!!
NAGISA-CHAN, YOU'VE GOTTA ANSWER ME!!
OUR TIME KEEPING EACH OTHER'S SECRETS.
THOSE DAYS WERE... DAZ-ZLING.
JUST THE MEMORY BRINGS TEARS TO MY EYES.
IT'S ENOUGH. IT'S... ENOUGH.
WOOOM
WOOOM
CRACKLE
CRACKLE
CRACKLE
THOSE DAYS WERE MORE THAN I DESERVED.
THAT'S RIGHT ...

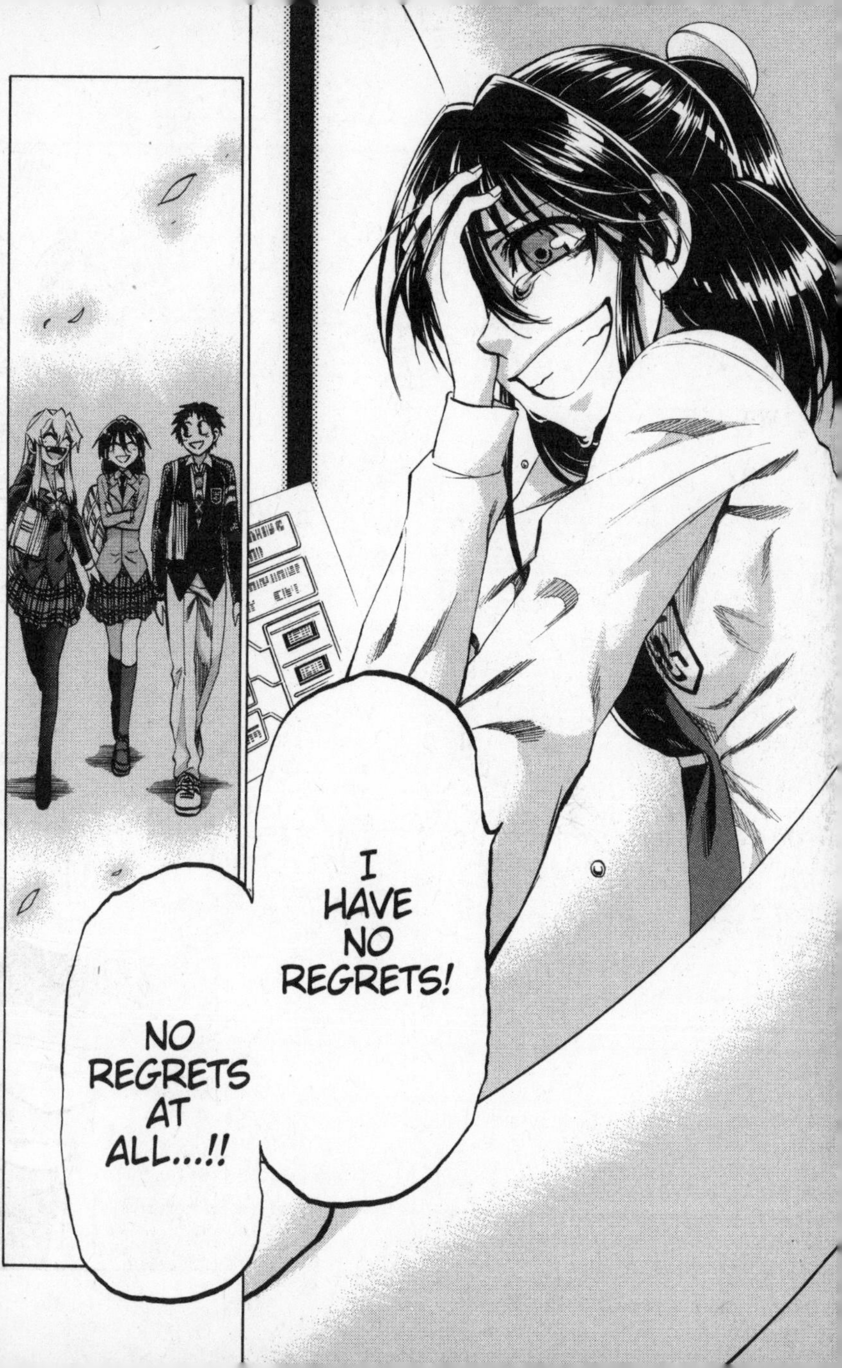
I HAVE NO REGRETS!
NO REGRETS AT ALL...!!

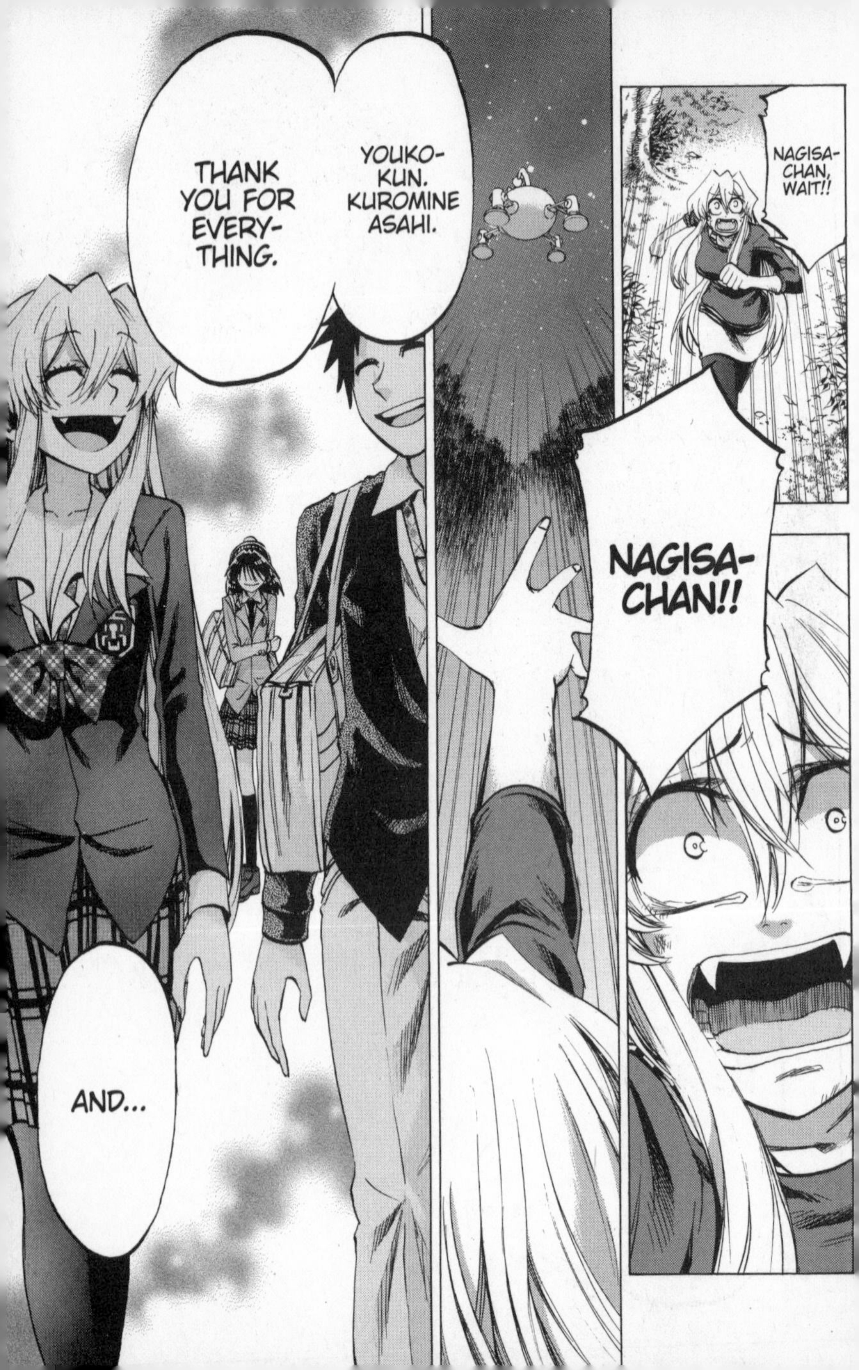
NAGISA-CHAN, WAIT!!
NAGISA-CHAN!!
YOUKO-KUN. KUROMINE ASAHI.
THANK YOU FOR EVERYTHING.
AND...

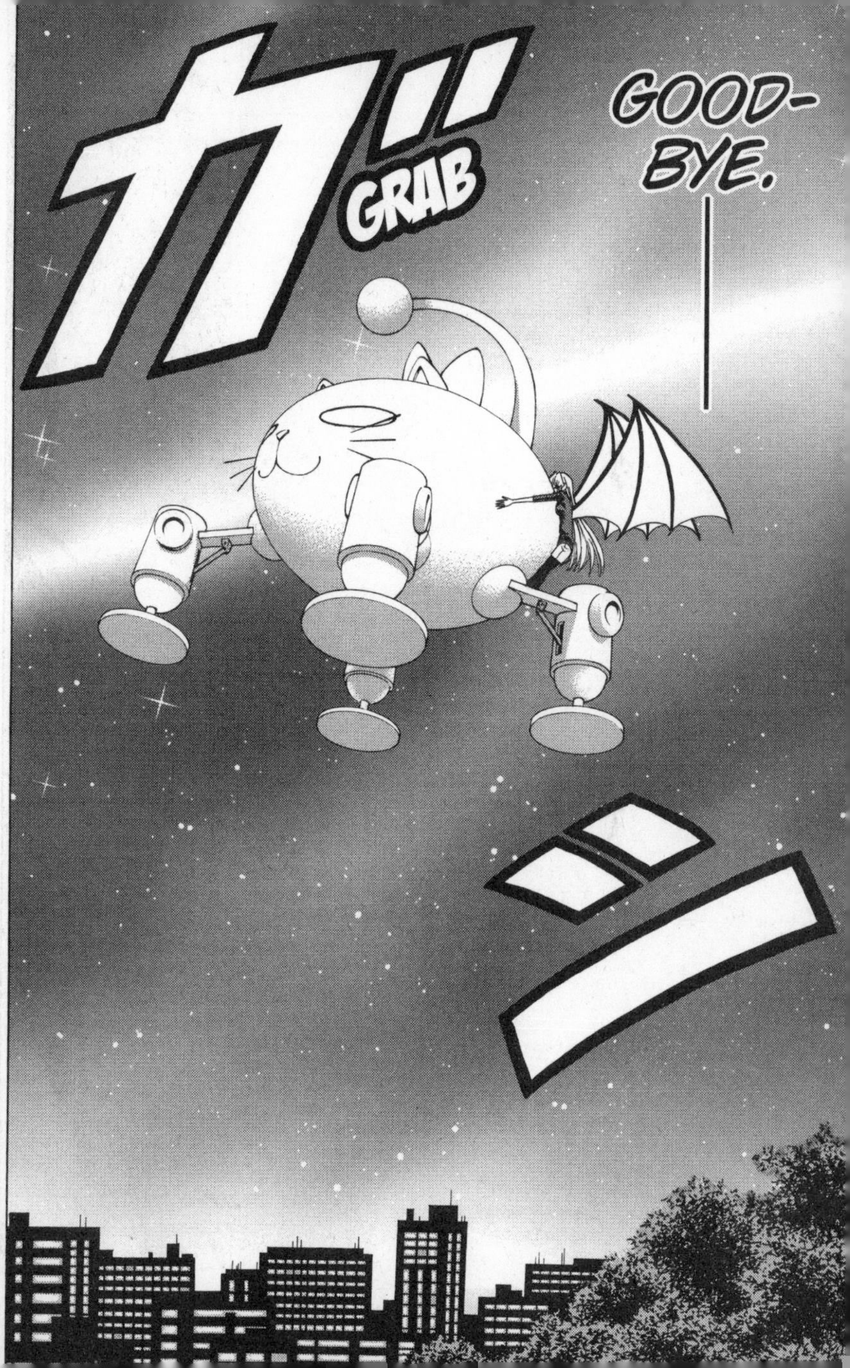
GOOD-BYE.
カッ
GRAB

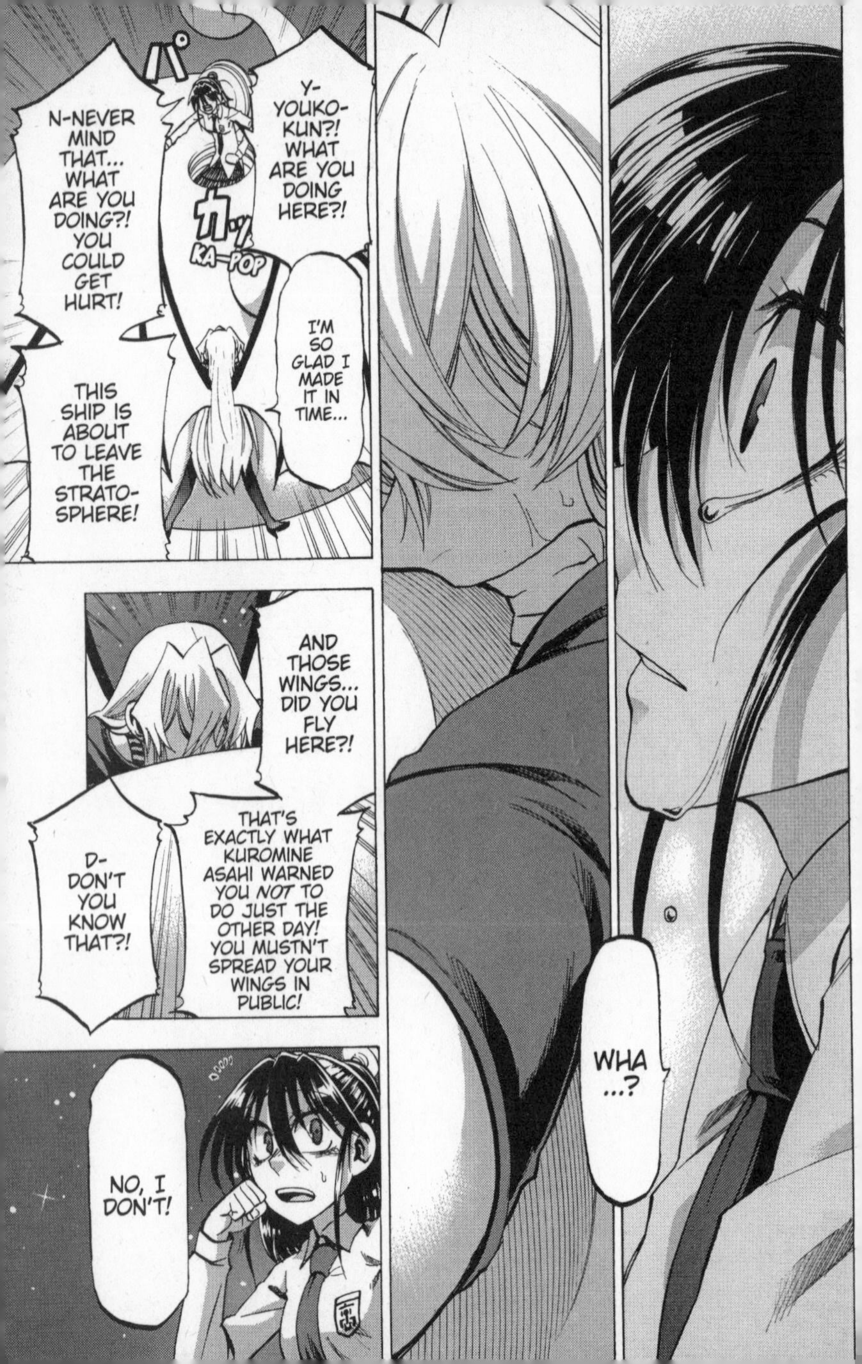
WHA ...?
Y-YOUKO-KUN?! WHAT ARE YOU DOING HERE?!
I'M SO GLAD I MADE IT IN TIME...
KA-POP
N-NEVER MIND THAT... WHAT ARE YOU DOING?! YOU COULD GET HURT!
THIS SHIP IS ABOUT TO LEAVE THE STRATO-SPHERE!
AND THOSE WINGS... DID YOU FLY HERE?!
THAT'S EXACTLY WHAT KUROMINE ASAHI WARNED YOU *NOT* TO DO JUST THE OTHER DAY! YOU MUSTN'T SPREAD YOUR WINGS IN PUBLIC!
D-DON'T YOU KNOW THAT?!
NO, I DON'T!

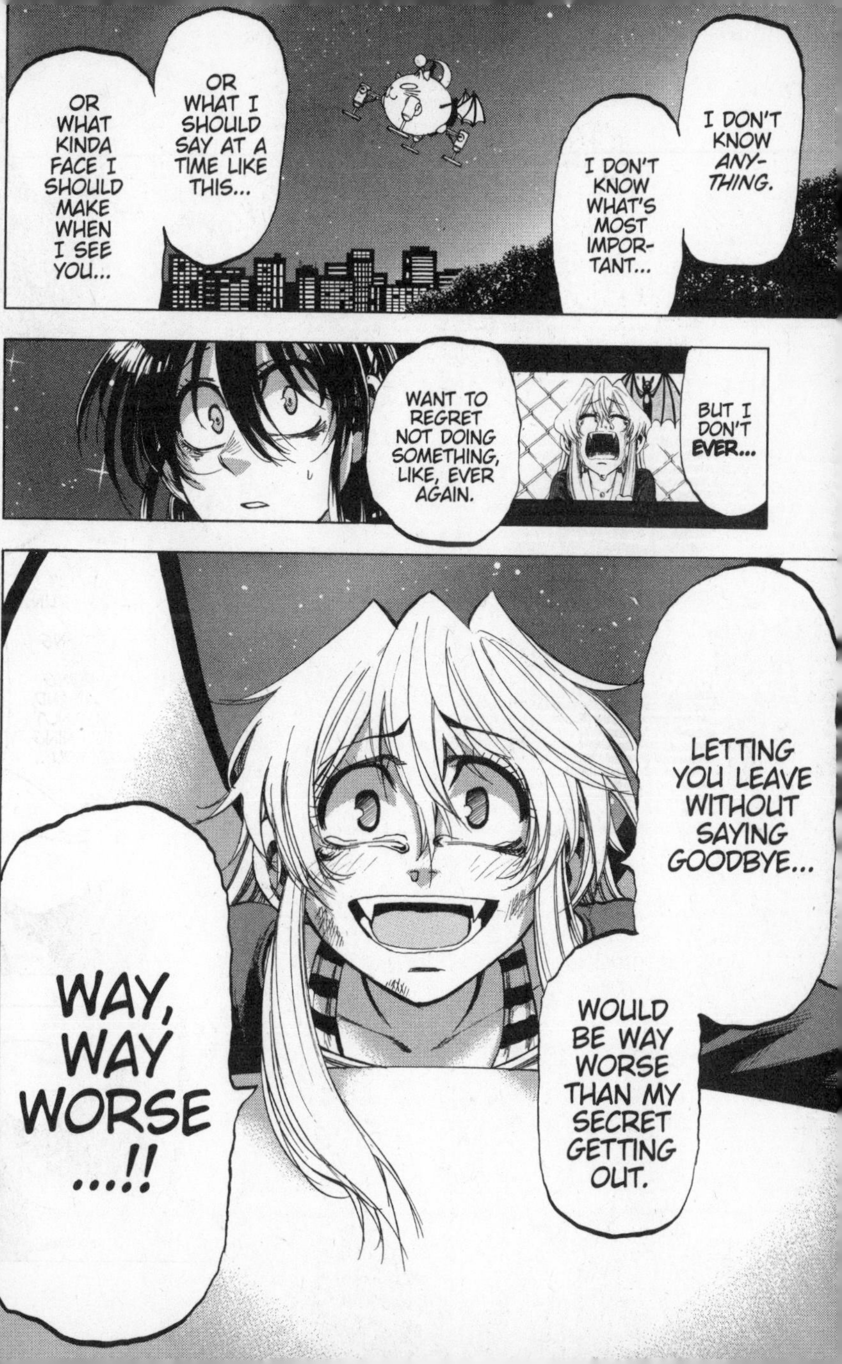
I DON'T KNOW *ANYTHING*.
I DON'T KNOW WHAT'S MOST IMPORTANT...
OR WHAT I SHOULD SAY AT A TIME LIKE THIS...
OR WHAT KINDA FACE I SHOULD MAKE WHEN I SEE YOU...
BUT I DON'T **EVER...**
WANT TO REGRET NOT DOING SOMETHING, LIKE, EVER AGAIN.
LETTING YOU LEAVE WITHOUT SAYING GOODBYE...
WOULD BE WAY WORSE THAN MY SECRET GETTING OUT.
WAY, WAY WORSE ...!!

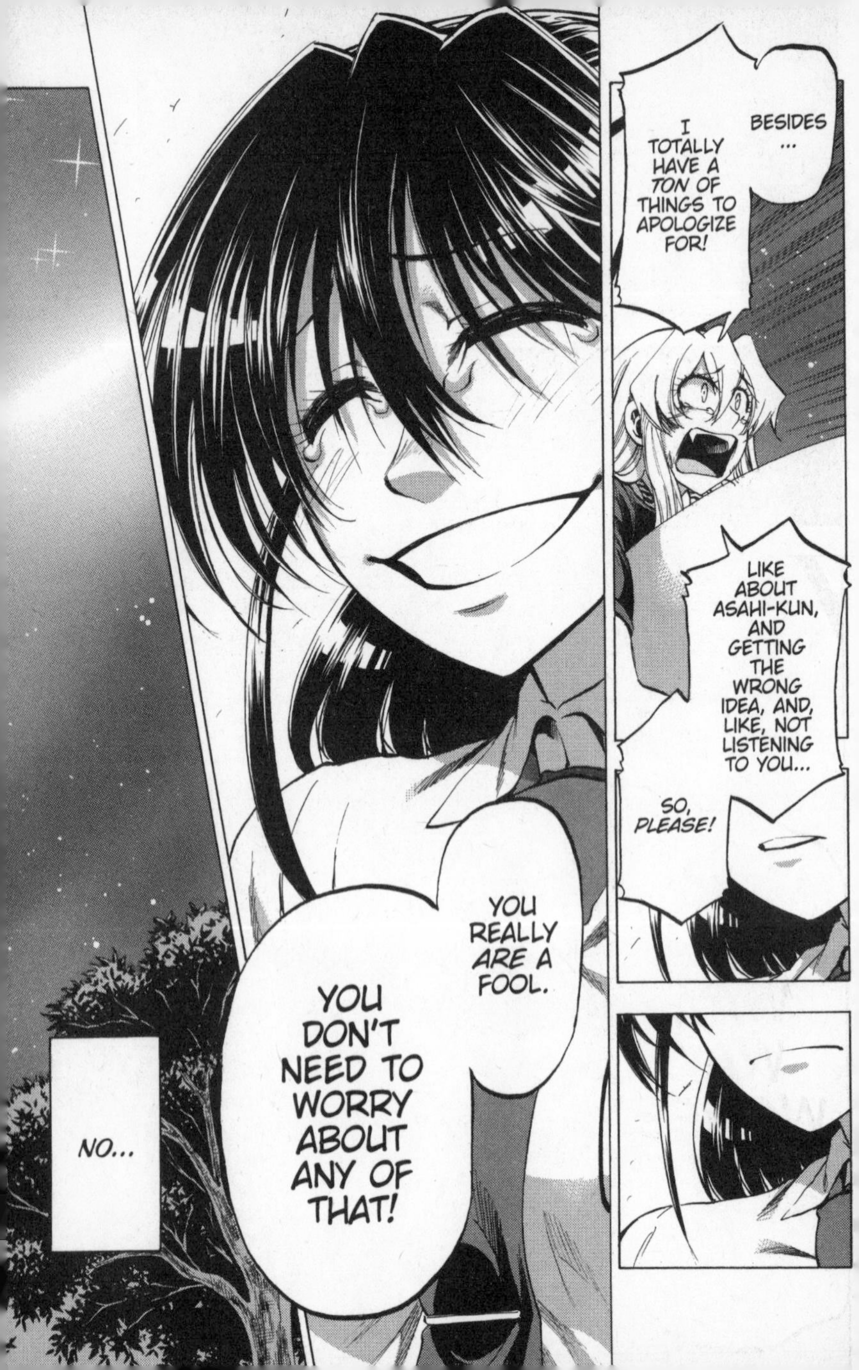
BESIDES...
I TOTALLY HAVE A *TON* OF THINGS TO APOLOGIZE FOR!
LIKE ABOUT ASAHI-KUN, AND GETTING THE WRONG IDEA, AND, LIKE, NOT LISTENING TO YOU...
SO, *PLEASE!*
YOU REALLY *ARE* A FOOL.
YOU DON'T NEED TO WORRY ABOUT ANY OF THAT!
NO...

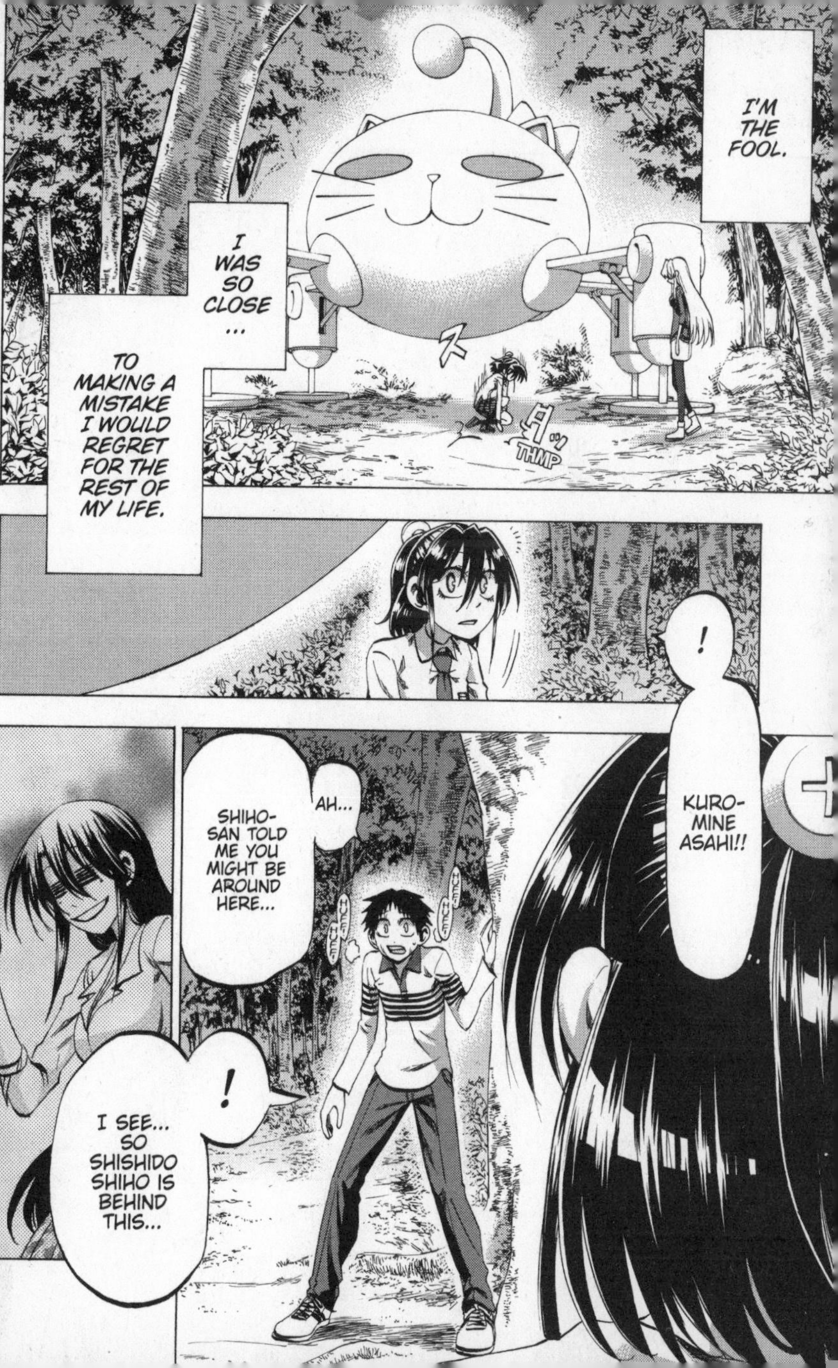
I'M THE FOOL.
I WAS SO CLOSE ...
TO MAKING A MISTAKE I WOULD REGRET FOR THE REST OF MY LIFE.
THMP
!
KURO-MINE ASAHI!!
AH...
SHIHO-SAN TOLD ME YOU MIGHT BE AROUND HERE...
HUFF HUFF
HUFF HUFF
!
I SEE... SO SHISHIDO SHIHO IS BEHIND THIS...

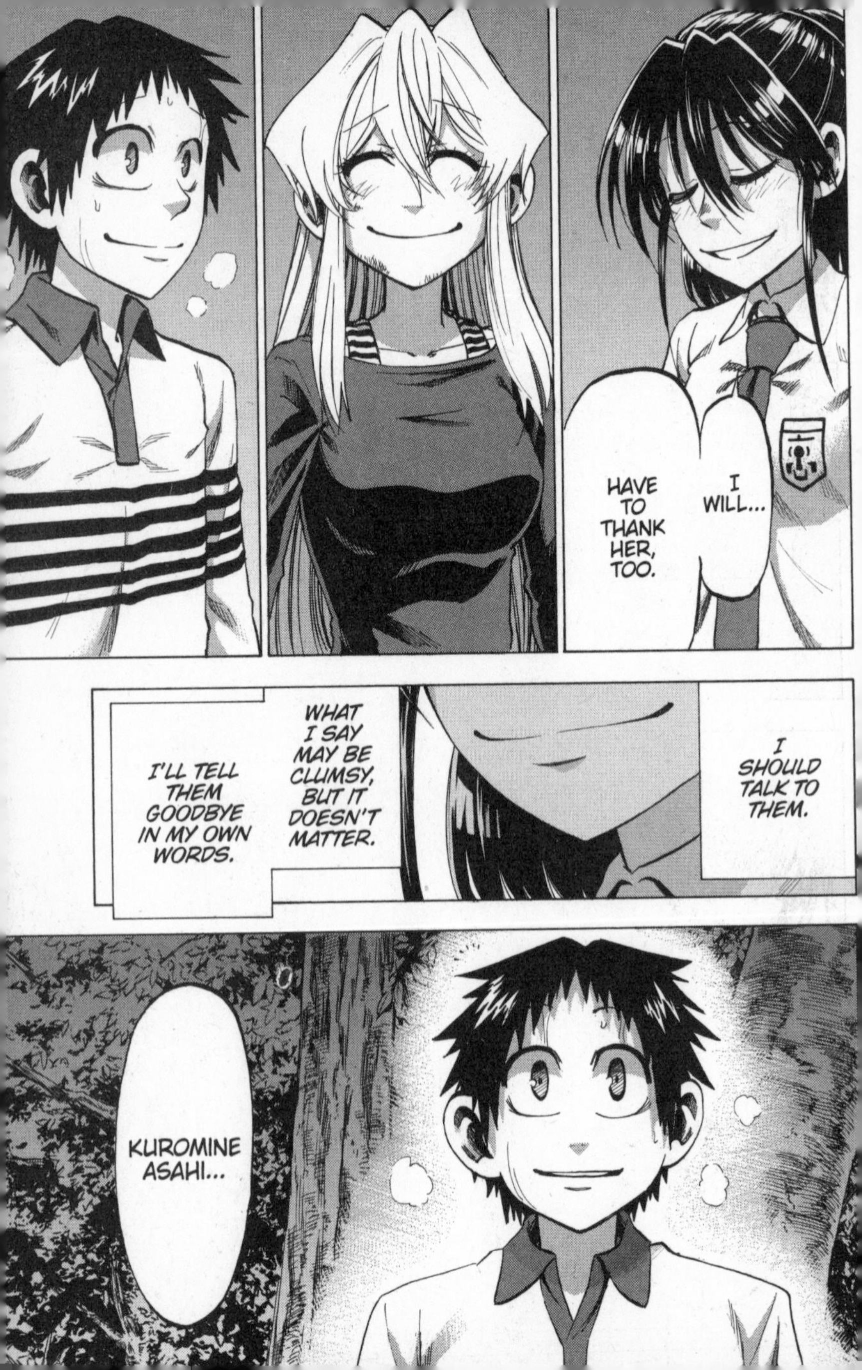
I WILL...
HAVE TO THANK HER, TOO.
I SHOULD TALK TO THEM.
WHAT I SAY MAY BE CLUMSY, BUT IT DOESN'T MATTER.
I'LL TELL THEM GOODBYE IN MY OWN WORDS.
KUROMINE ASAHI...

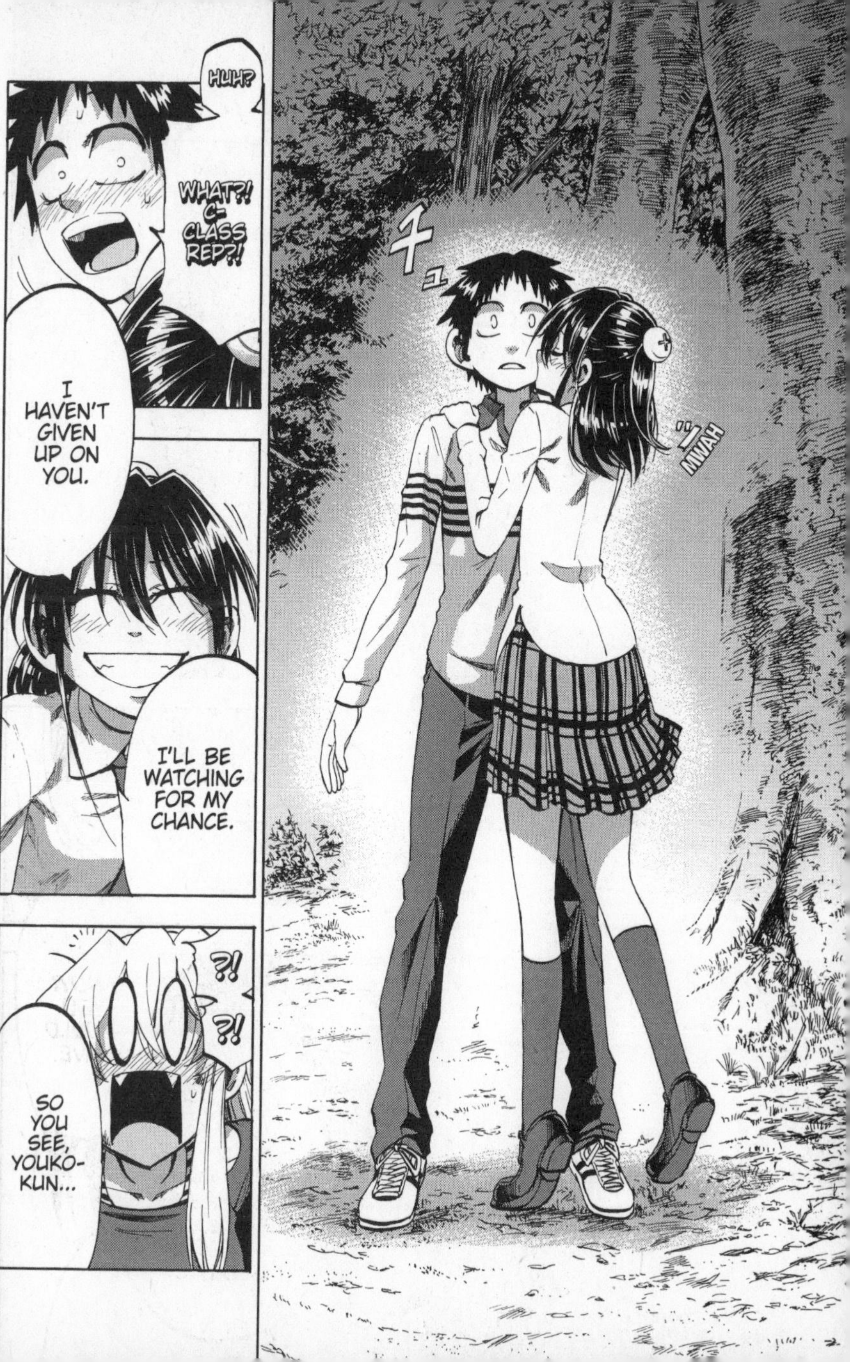
チュ
MWAH
HUH?
WHAT?! C-CLASS REP?!
I HAVEN'T GIVEN UP ON YOU.
I'LL BE WATCHING FOR MY CHANCE.
?!
?!
SO YOU SEE, YOUKO-KUN...

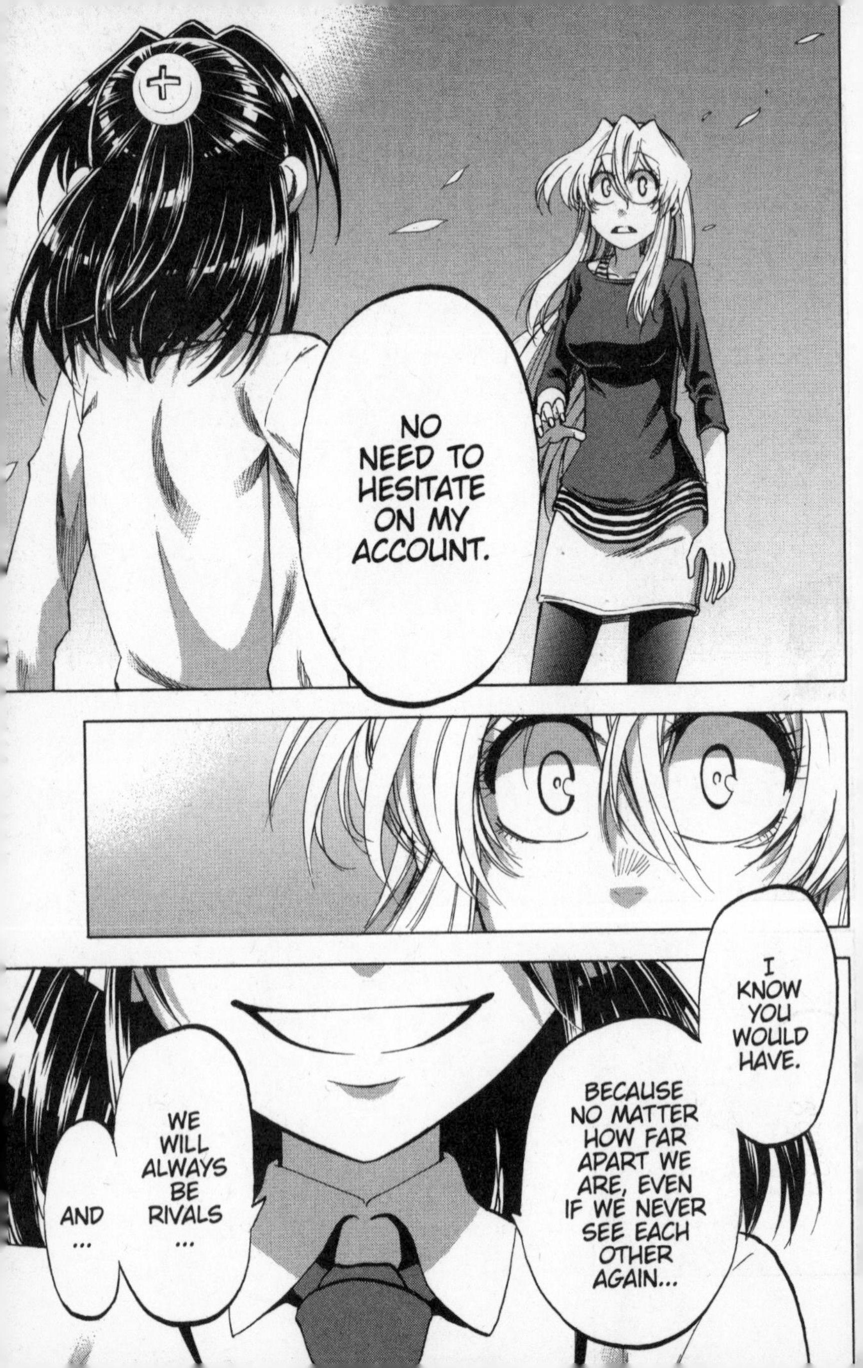
NO NEED TO HESITATE ON MY ACCOUNT.
I KNOW YOU WOULD HAVE.
BECAUSE NO MATTER HOW FAR APART WE ARE, EVEN IF WE NEVER SEE EACH OTHER AGAIN...
WE WILL ALWAYS BE RIVALS ...
AND ...

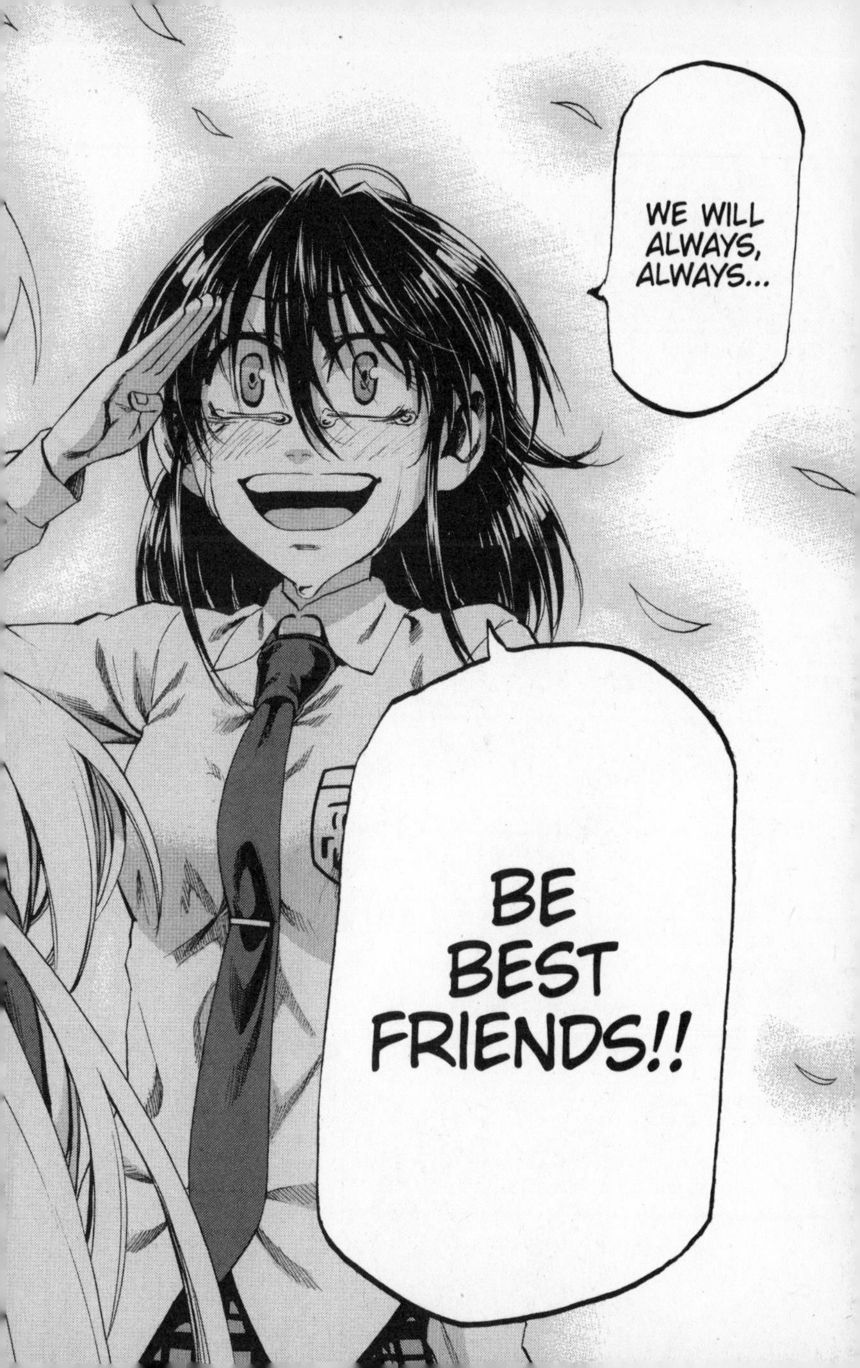
WE WILL ALWAYS, ALWAYS...
BE BEST FRIENDS!!

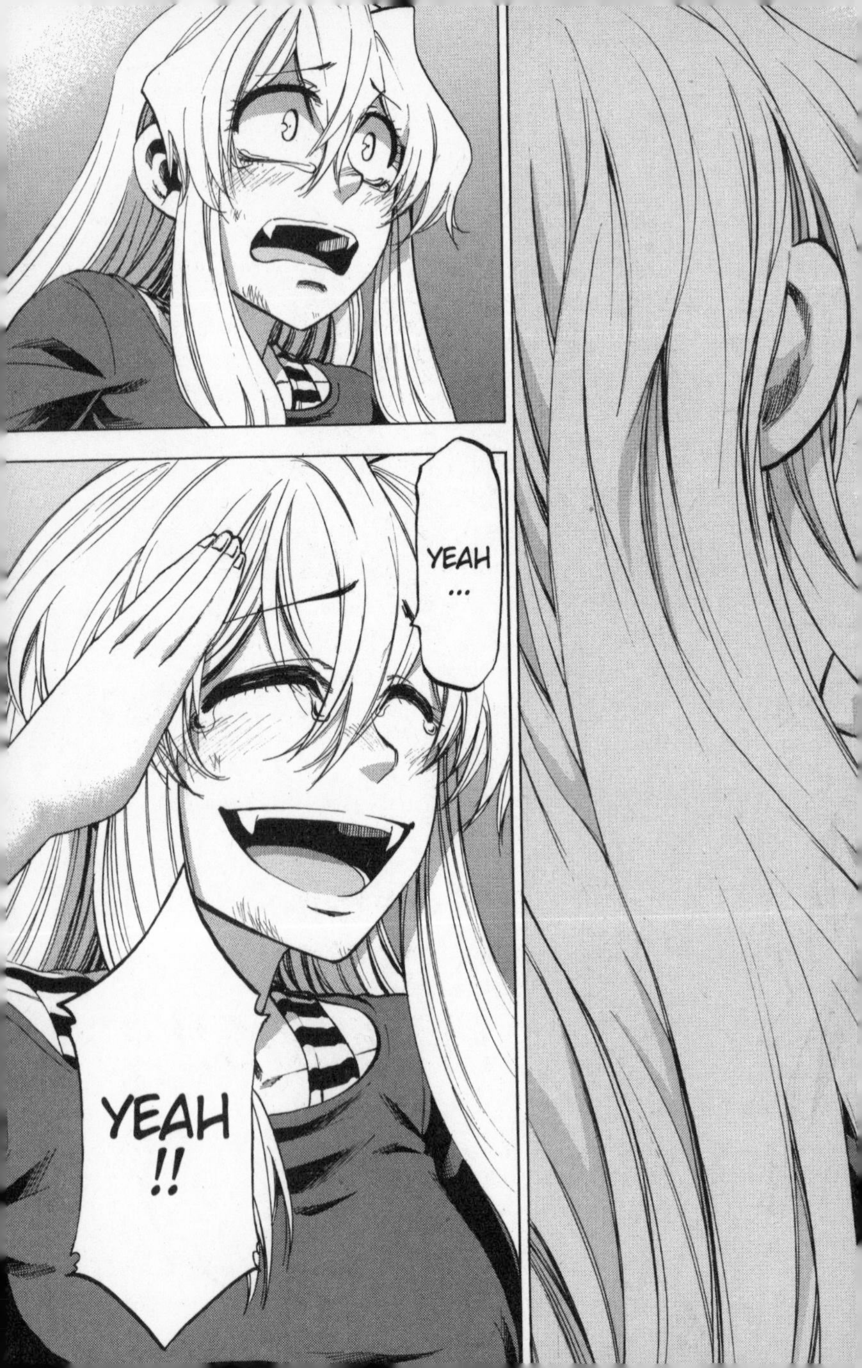
YEAH ...
YEAH !!

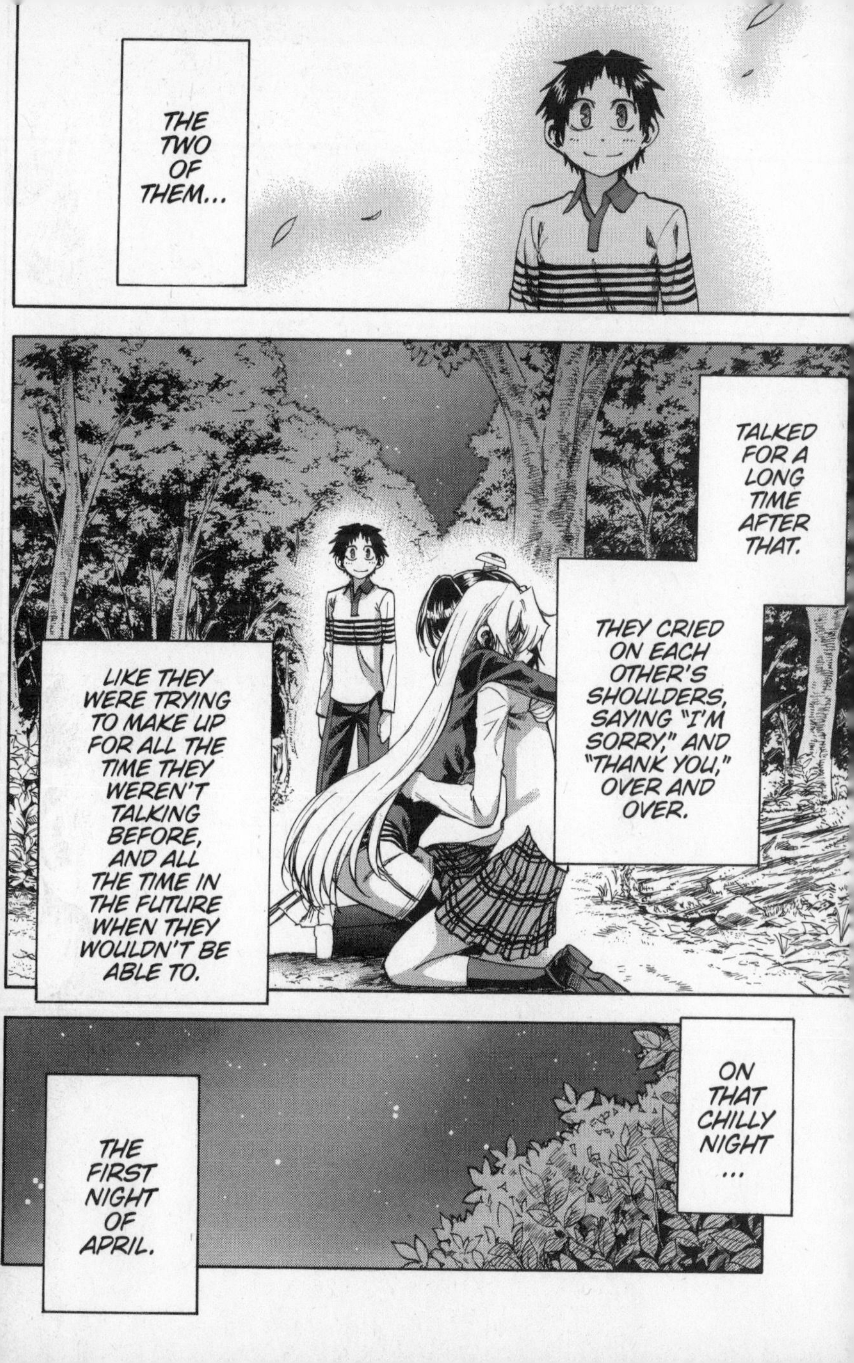
THE TWO OF THEM…
TALKED FOR A LONG TIME AFTER THAT.
THEY CRIED ON EACH OTHER'S SHOULDERS, SAYING "I'M SORRY," AND "THANK YOU," OVER AND OVER.
LIKE THEY WERE TRYING TO MAKE UP FOR ALL THE TIME THEY WEREN'T TALKING BEFORE, AND ALL THE TIME IN THE FUTURE WHEN THEY WOULDN'T BE ABLE TO.
ON THAT CHILLY NIGHT…
THE FIRST NIGHT OF APRIL.

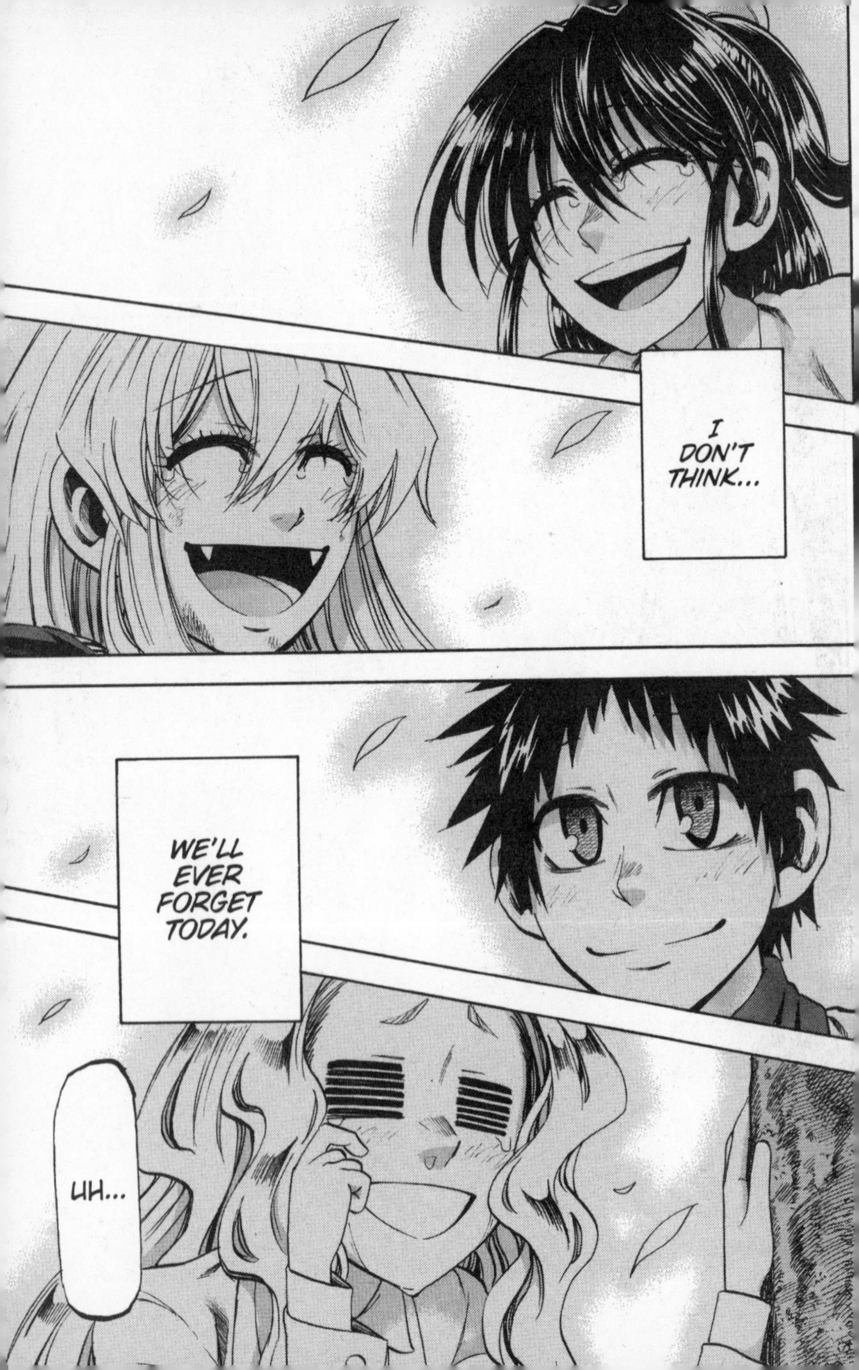
I DON'T THINK...
WE'LL EVER FORGET TODAY.
UH...

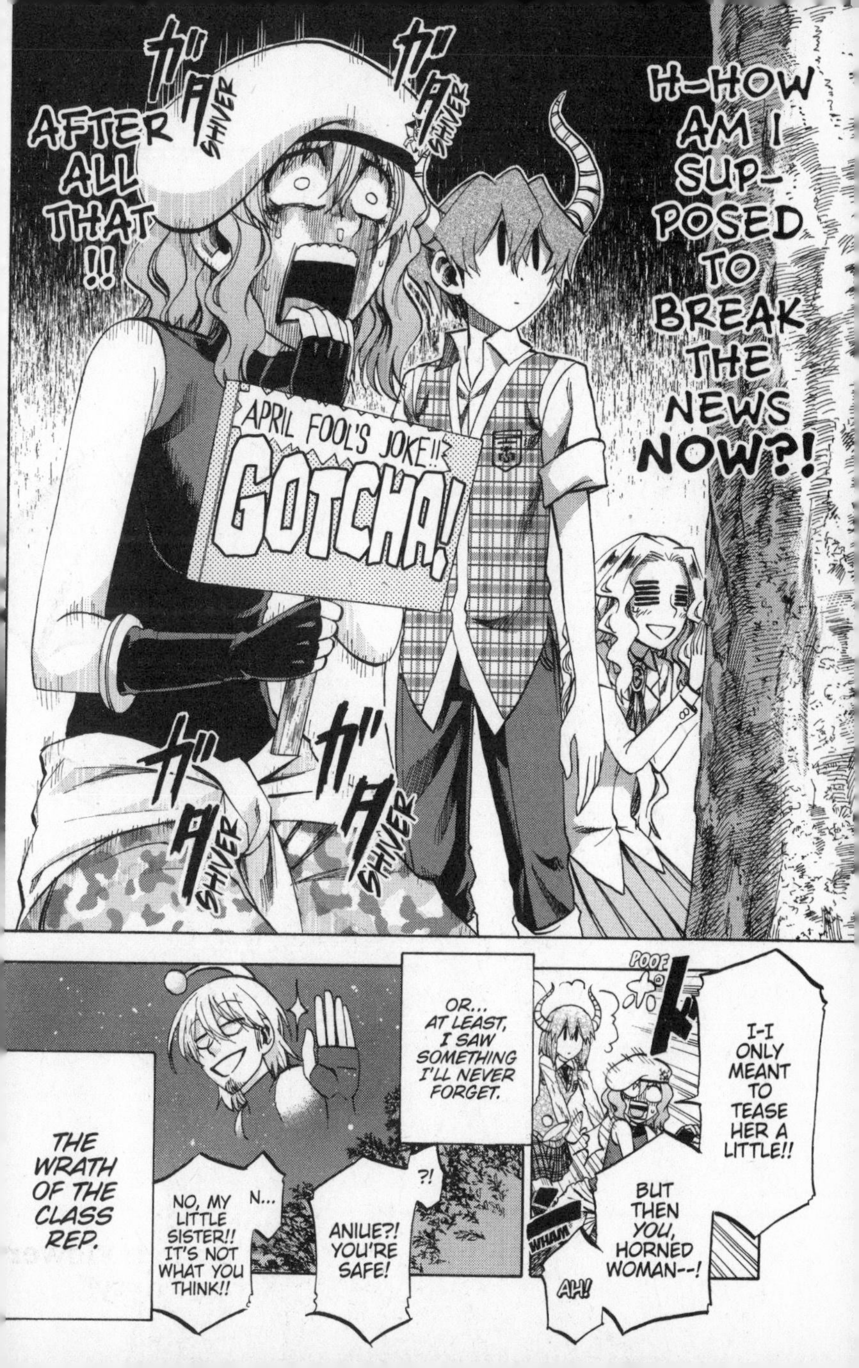
H-HOW AM I SUP-POSED TO BREAK THE NEWS NOW?!
ガタ
SHIVER
AFTER ALL THAT!!
ガタ
SHIVER
APRIL FOOL'S JOKE!!
GOTCHA!
ガタ
SHIVER
ガタ
SHIVER
POOF
I-I ONLY MEANT TO TEASE HER A LITTLE!!
OR... AT LEAST, I SAW SOMETHING I'LL NEVER FORGET.
BUT THEN YOU, HORNED WOMAN--!
WHAM
AH!
?!
ANIUE?! YOU'RE SAFE!
N...
NO, MY LITTLE SISTER!! IT'S NOT WHAT YOU THINK!!
THE WRATH OF THE CLASS REP.

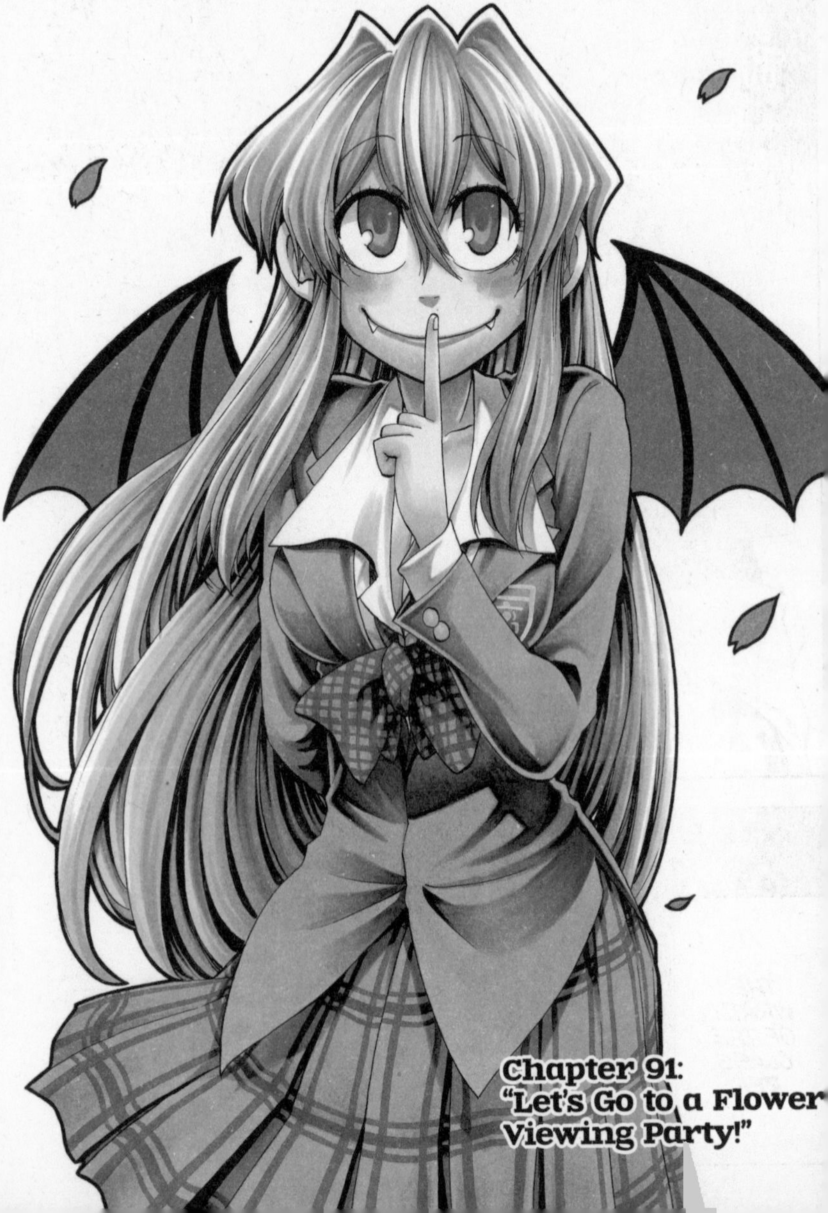
Chapter 91:
"Let's Go to a Flower Viewing Party!"

TOP SECRET

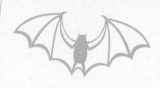

My Monster Secret 11

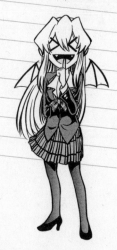

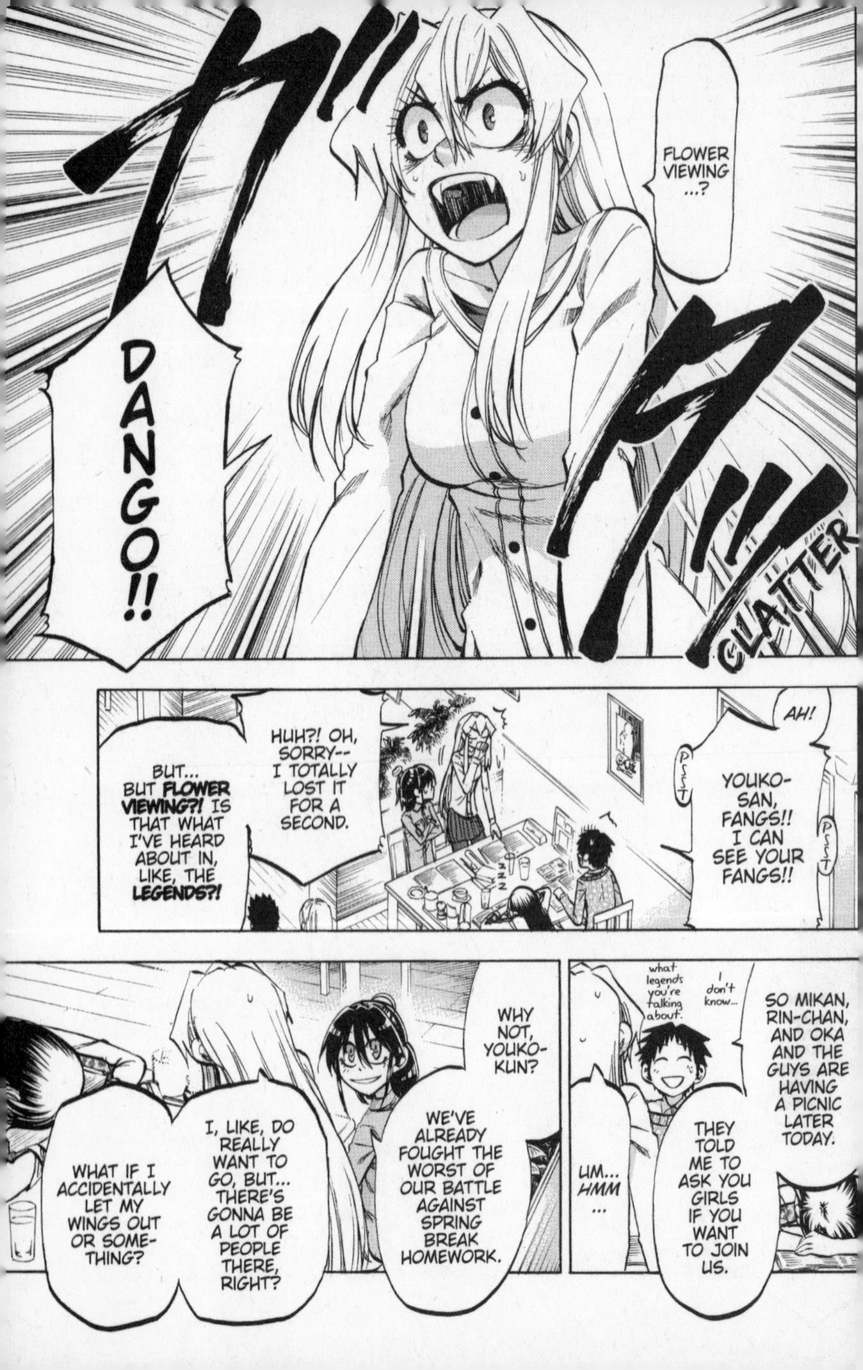
FLOWER VIEWING ...?
DANGO!!
CLATTER
AH!
YOUKO-SAN, FANGS!! I CAN SEE YOUR FANGS!!
PSST
PSST
HUH?! OH, SORRY-- I TOTALLY LOST IT FOR A SECOND.
BUT... BUT **FLOWER VIEWING?!** IS THAT WHAT I'VE HEARD ABOUT IN, LIKE, THE **LEGENDS?!**
SO MIKAN, RIN-CHAN, AND OKA AND THE GUYS ARE HAVING A PICNIC LATER TODAY.
THEY TOLD ME TO ASK YOU GIRLS IF YOU WANT TO JOIN US.
I don't know...
what legends you're talking about.
UM... *HMM* ...
WHY NOT, YOUKO-KUN?
WE'VE ALREADY FOUGHT THE WORST OF OUR BATTLE AGAINST SPRING BREAK HOMEWORK.
I, LIKE, DO REALLY WANT TO GO, BUT... THERE'S GONNA BE A LOT OF PEOPLE THERE, RIGHT?
WHAT IF I ACCIDENTALLY LET MY WINGS OUT OR SOME-THING?

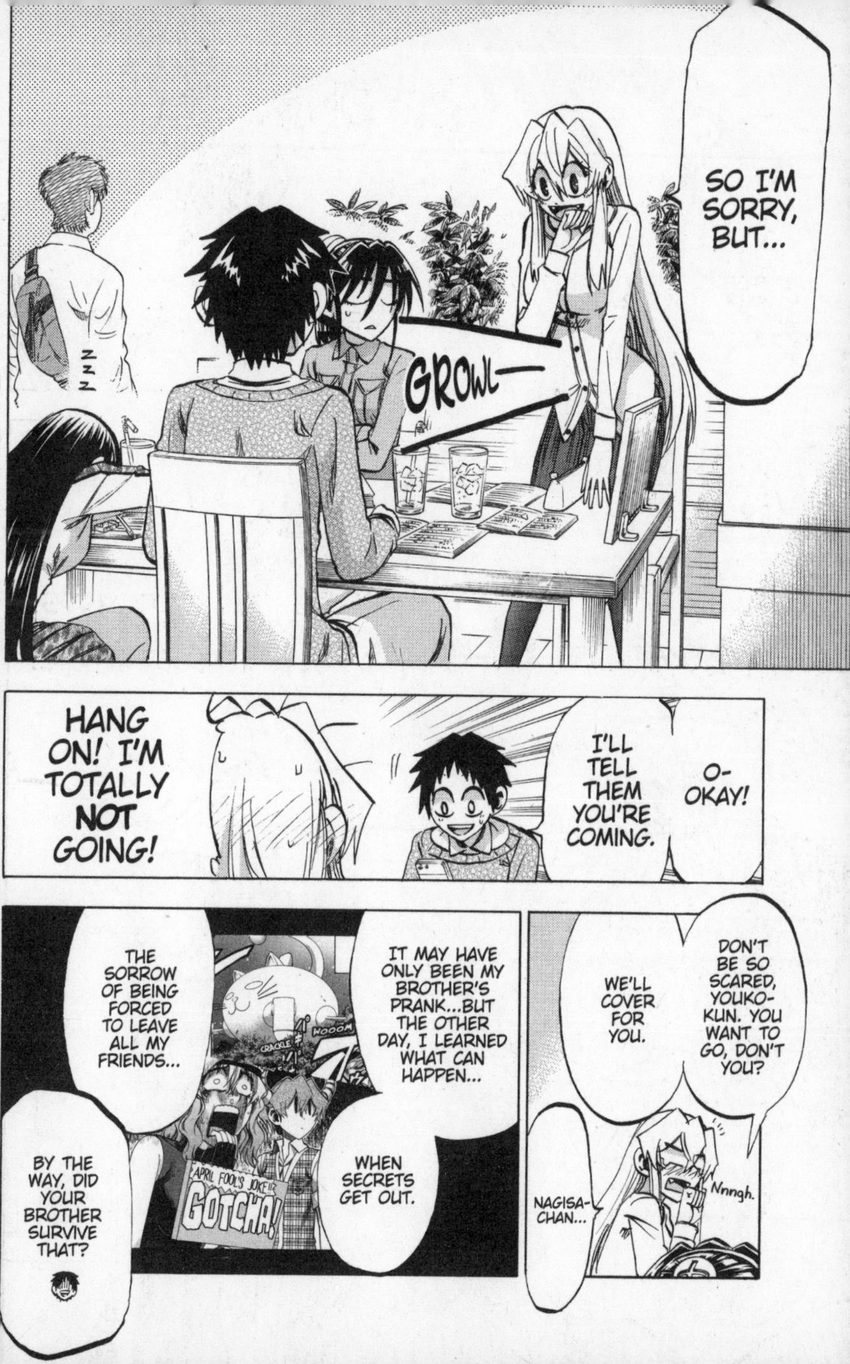
SO I'M SORRY, BUT...
GROWL—
Z Z Z
O-OKAY!
I'LL TELL THEM YOU'RE COMING.
HANG ON! I'M TOTALLY NOT GOING!
DON'T BE SO SCARED, YOUKO-KUN. YOU WANT TO GO, DON'T YOU?
WE'LL COVER FOR YOU.
Nnngh.
NAGISA-CHAN...
IT MAY HAVE ONLY BEEN MY BROTHER'S PRANK...BUT THE OTHER DAY, I LEARNED WHAT CAN HAPPEN...
THE SORROW OF BEING FORCED TO LEAVE ALL MY FRIENDS...
WOOOM
CRACKLE
APRIL FOOL'S JOKE!!
GOTCHA!
WHEN SECRETS GET OUT.
BY THE WAY, DID YOUR BROTHER SURVIVE THAT?

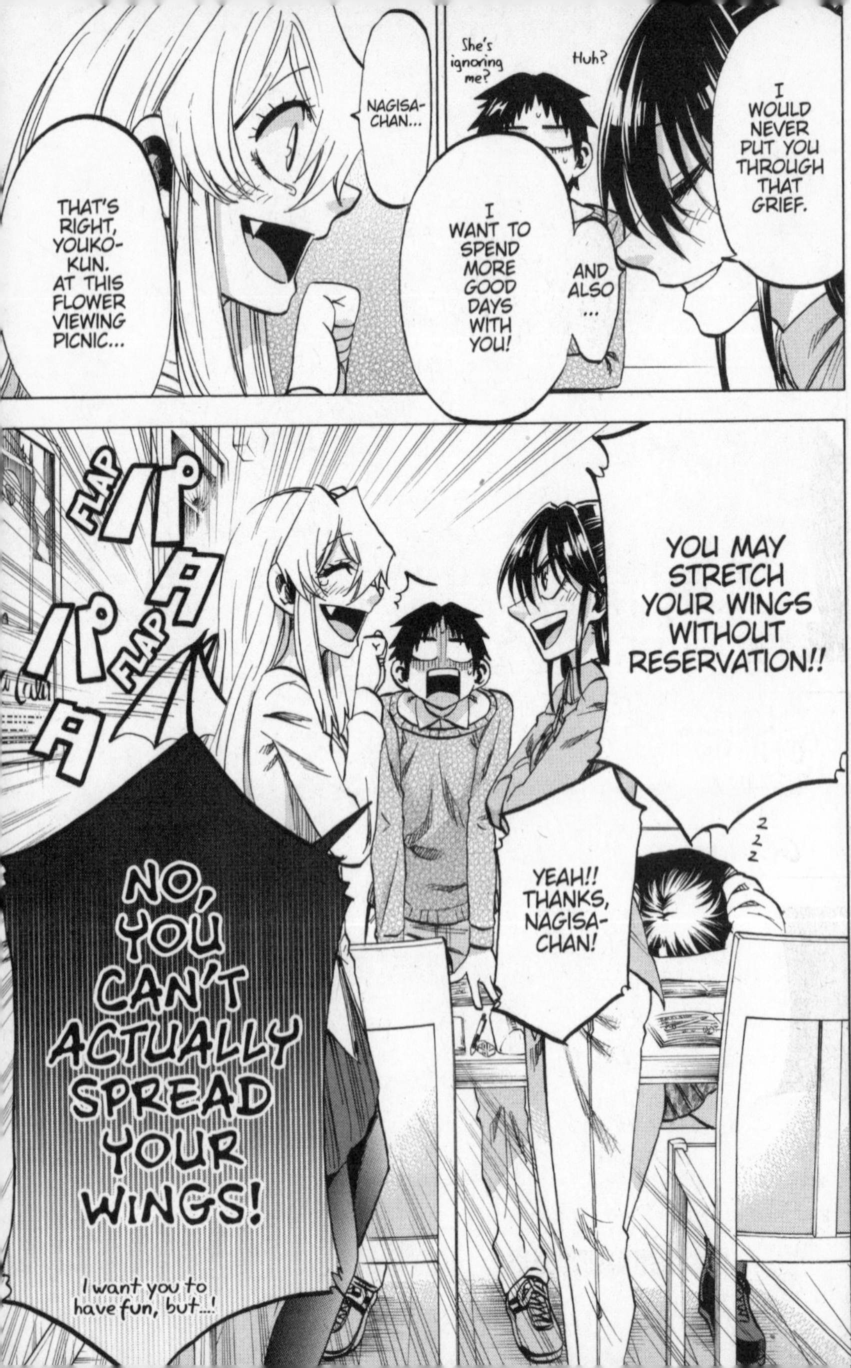
I WOULD NEVER PUT YOU THROUGH THAT GRIEF.
Huh?
She's ignoring me?
AND ALSO...
I WANT TO SPEND MORE GOOD DAYS WITH YOU!
NAGISA-CHAN...
THAT'S RIGHT, YOUKO-KUN. AT THIS FLOWER VIEWING PICNIC...
YOU MAY STRETCH YOUR WINGS WITHOUT RESERVATION!!
z z z
YEAH!! THANKS, NAGISA-CHAN!
パタ FLAP
パタ FLAP
NO, YOU CAN'T ACTUALLY SPREAD YOUR WINGS!
I want you to have fun, but...!

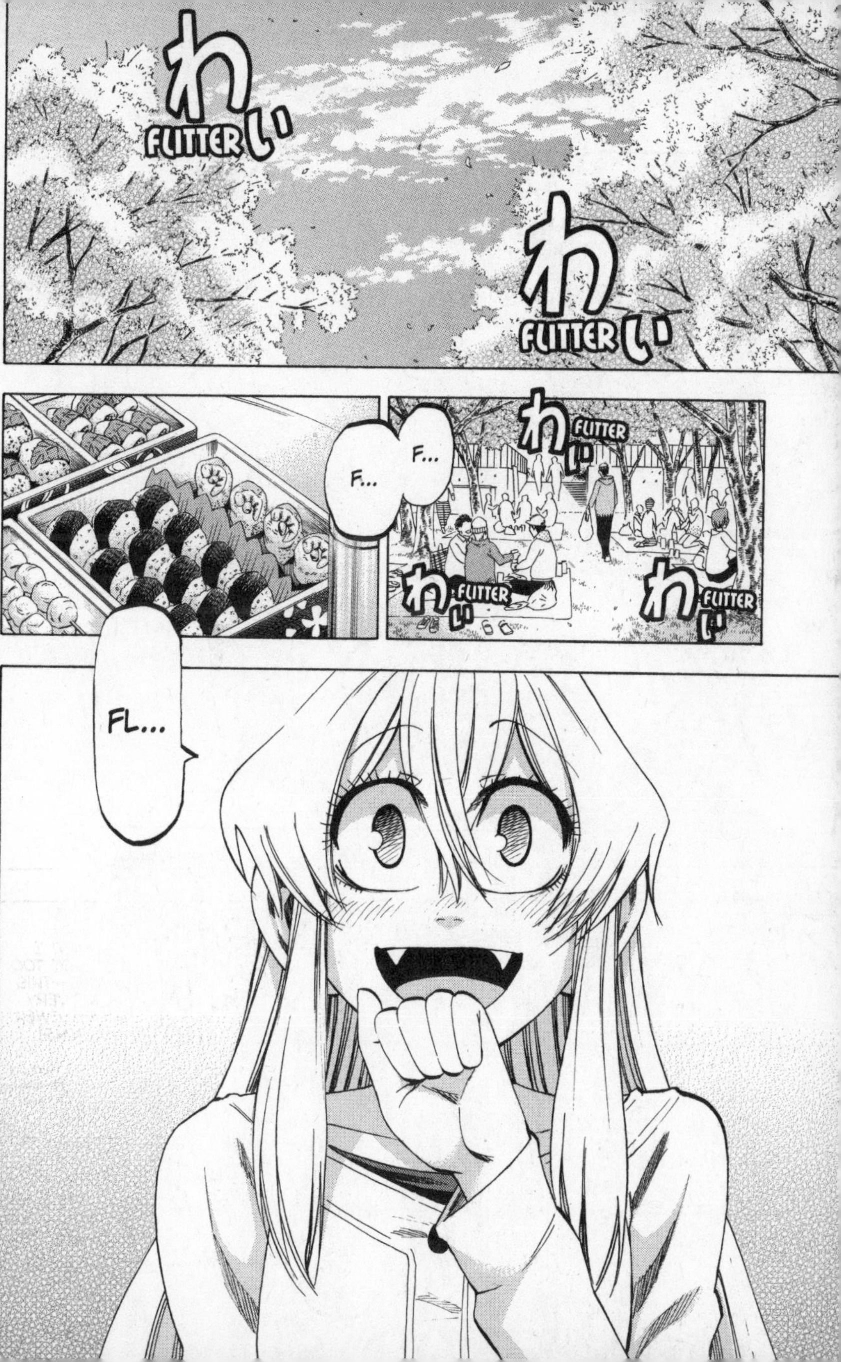

わ FLITTER い
わ FLITTER い
わ FLITTER い
わ FLITTER い
わ FLITTER い
F...
F...
FL...

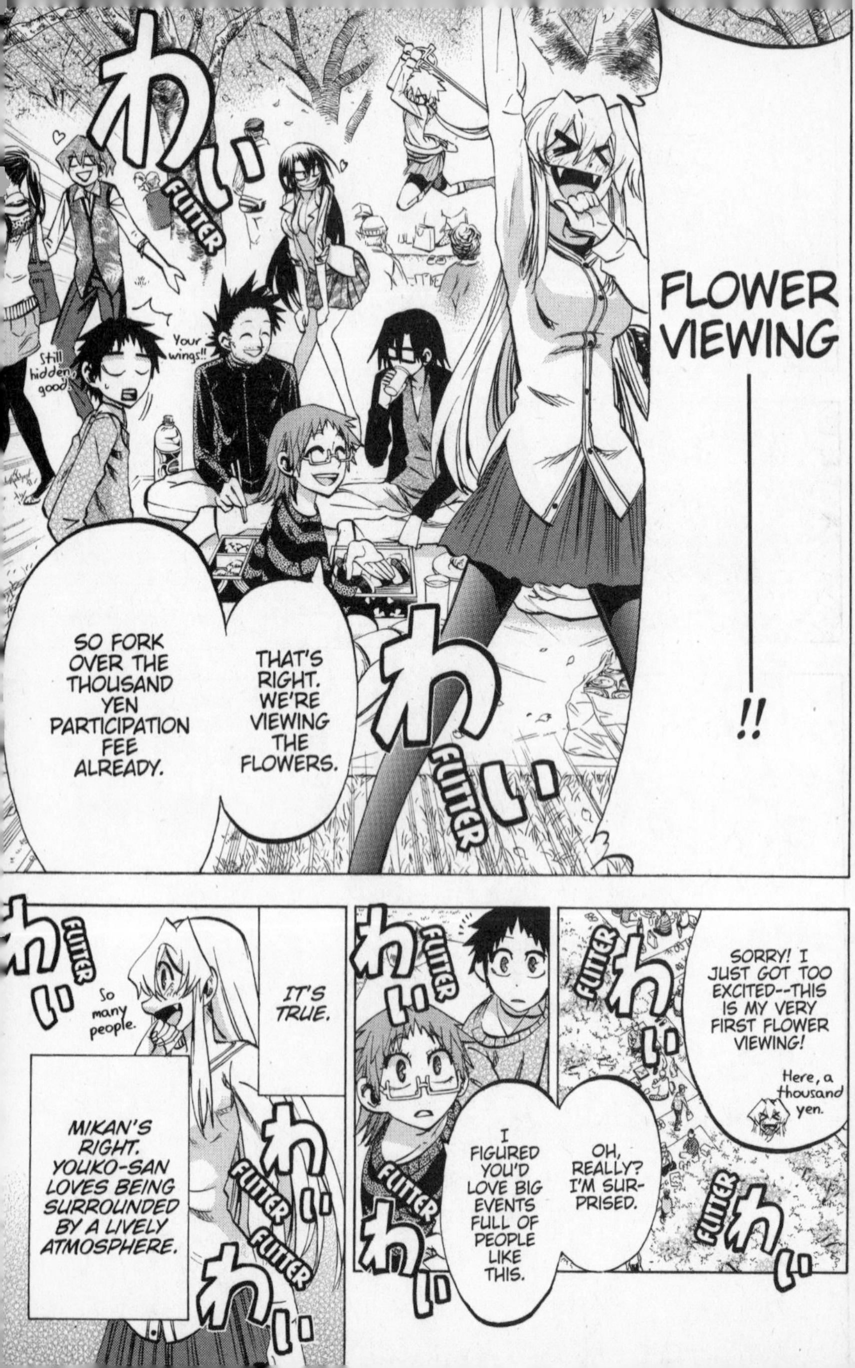
FLOWER VIEWING
!!
わい
FLUTTER
わい
FLUTTER
Your wings!!
Still hidden good.
THAT'S RIGHT. WE'RE VIEWING THE FLOWERS.
SO FORK OVER THE THOUSAND YEN PARTICIPATION FEE ALREADY.
SORRY! I JUST GOT TOO EXCITED--THIS IS MY VERY FIRST FLOWER VIEWING!
Here, a thousand yen.
FLUTTER
わい
FLUTTER
わい
OH, REALLY? I'M SUR-PRISED.
I FIGURED YOU'D LOVE BIG EVENTS FULL OF PEOPLE LIKE THIS.
FLUTTER
わい
FLUTTER
わい
IT'S TRUE.
So many people.
FLUTTER
わい
MIKAN'S RIGHT. YOUKO-SAN LOVES BEING SURROUNDED BY A LIVELY ATMOSPHERE.
FLUTTER
わい
FLUTTER
わい

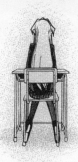

LAST SPRING...

YOUKO-SAN SPENT ALL HER TIME ALONE, KEEPING HER SECRET.

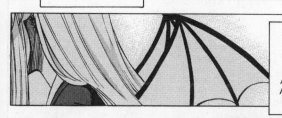

SHE'S A VAMPIRE.

AND THAT SECRET KEPT HER ISOLATED.

Thanks!

WE'RE NOT OUT OF THE WOODS YET.

BUT SEEING YOUKO-SAN LETTING LOOSE, SURROUNDED BY FRIENDS...

IS BETTER THAN FLOWERS, BETTER THAN FOOD. IT'S THE BEST PART OF THE WHOLE PICNIC.

わ
FLITTER

わ
FLITTER

わ
FLITTER

わ
FLITTER

わ
FLITTER

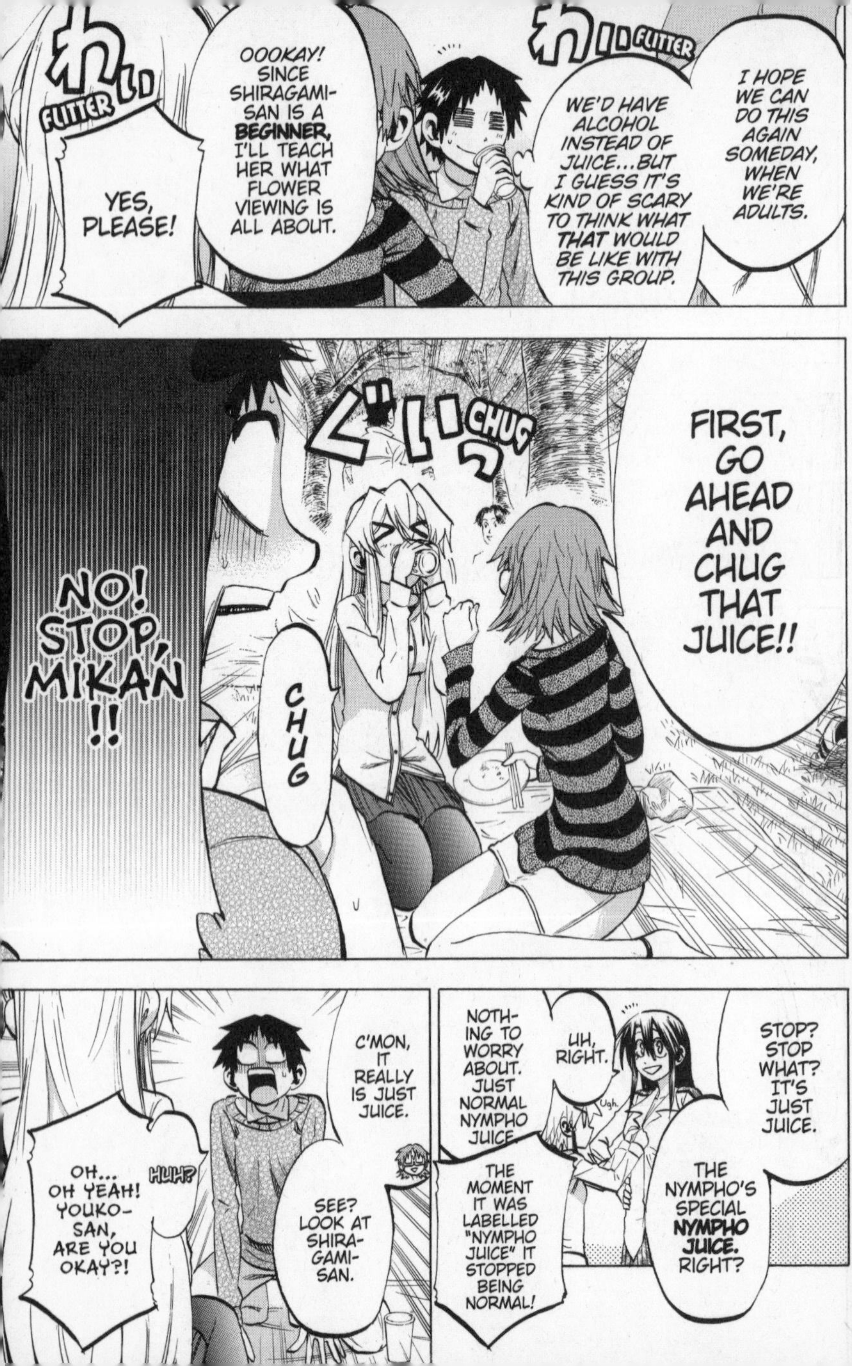
I HOPE WE CAN DO THIS AGAIN SOMEDAY, WHEN WE'RE ADULTS.
FLUTTER
WE'D HAVE ALCOHOL INSTEAD OF JUICE...BUT I GUESS IT'S KIND OF SCARY TO THINK WHAT THAT WOULD BE LIKE WITH THIS GROUP.
OOOKAY! SINCE SHIRAGAMI-SAN IS A BEGINNER, I'LL TEACH HER WHAT FLOWER VIEWING IS ALL ABOUT.
FLUTTER
YES, PLEASE!
FIRST, GO AHEAD AND CHUG THAT JUICE!!
CHUG
CHUG
NO! STOP, MIKAN!!
STOP? STOP WHAT? IT'S JUST JUICE.
UH, RIGHT.
NOTHING TO WORRY ABOUT. JUST NORMAL NYMPHO JUICE.
THE NYMPHO'S SPECIAL NYMPHO JUICE. RIGHT?
Ugh.
THE MOMENT IT WAS LABELLED "NYMPHO JUICE" IT STOPPED BEING NORMAL!
C'MON, IT REALLY IS JUST JUICE.
SEE? LOOK AT SHIRAGAMI-SAN.
HUH?
OH... OH YEAH! YOUKO-SAN, ARE YOU OKAY?!

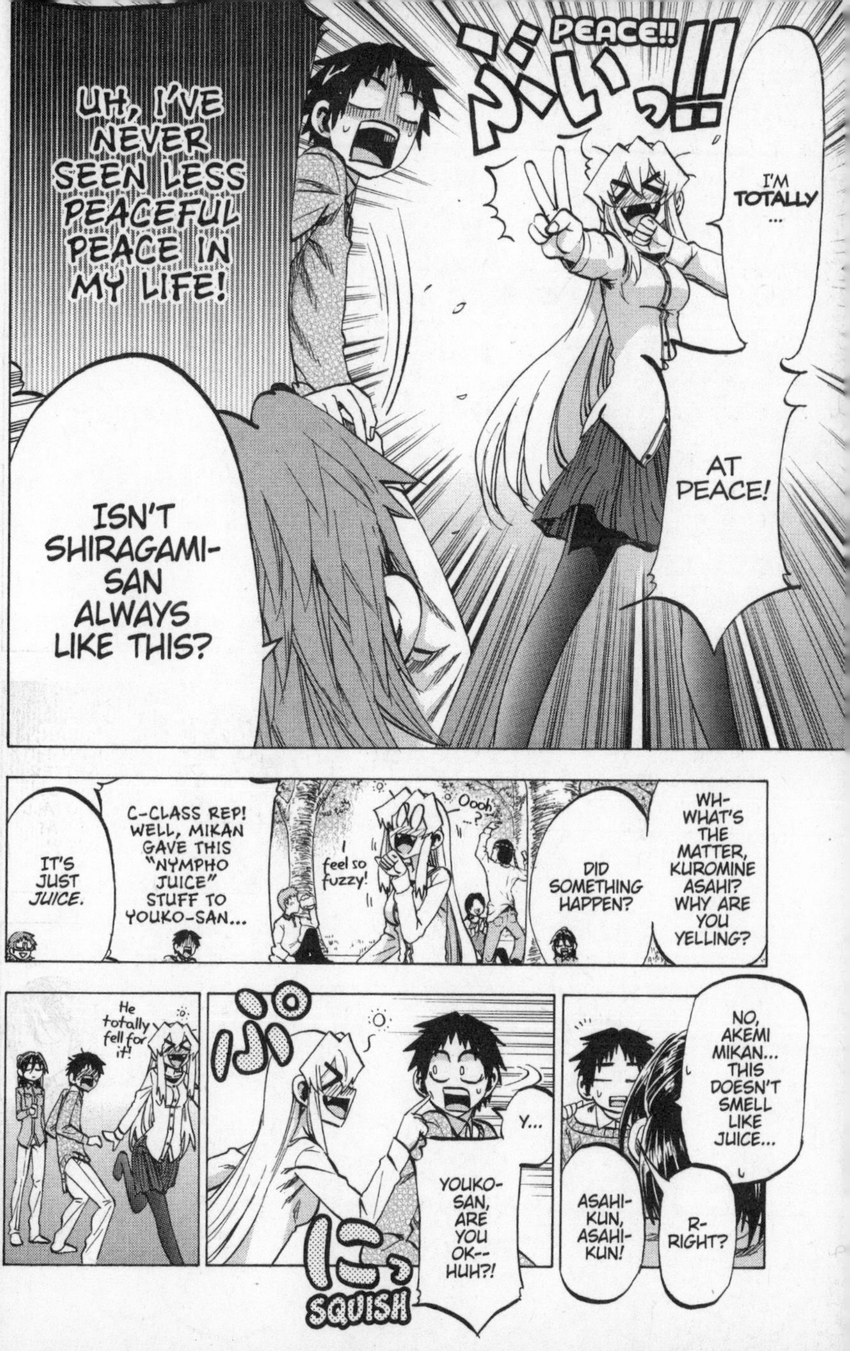
I'M TOTALLY ... AT PEACE!
PEACE!!
UH, I'VE NEVER SEEN LESS PEACEFUL PEACE IN MY LIFE!
ISN'T SHIRAGAMI-SAN ALWAYS LIKE THIS?
WH-WHAT'S THE MATTER, KUROMINE ASAHI? WHY ARE YOU YELLING?
DID SOMETHING HAPPEN?
Oooh ...?
I feel so fuzzy!
C-CLASS REP! WELL, MIKAN GAVE THIS "NYMPHO JUICE" STUFF TO YOUKO-SAN...
IT'S JUST JUICE.
NO, AKEMI MIKAN... THIS DOESN'T SMELL LIKE JUICE...
R-RIGHT?
ASAHI-KUN, ASAHI-KUN!
Y...
YOUKO-SAN, ARE YOU OK--HUH?!
ぷにっ
SQUISH
He totally fell for it!

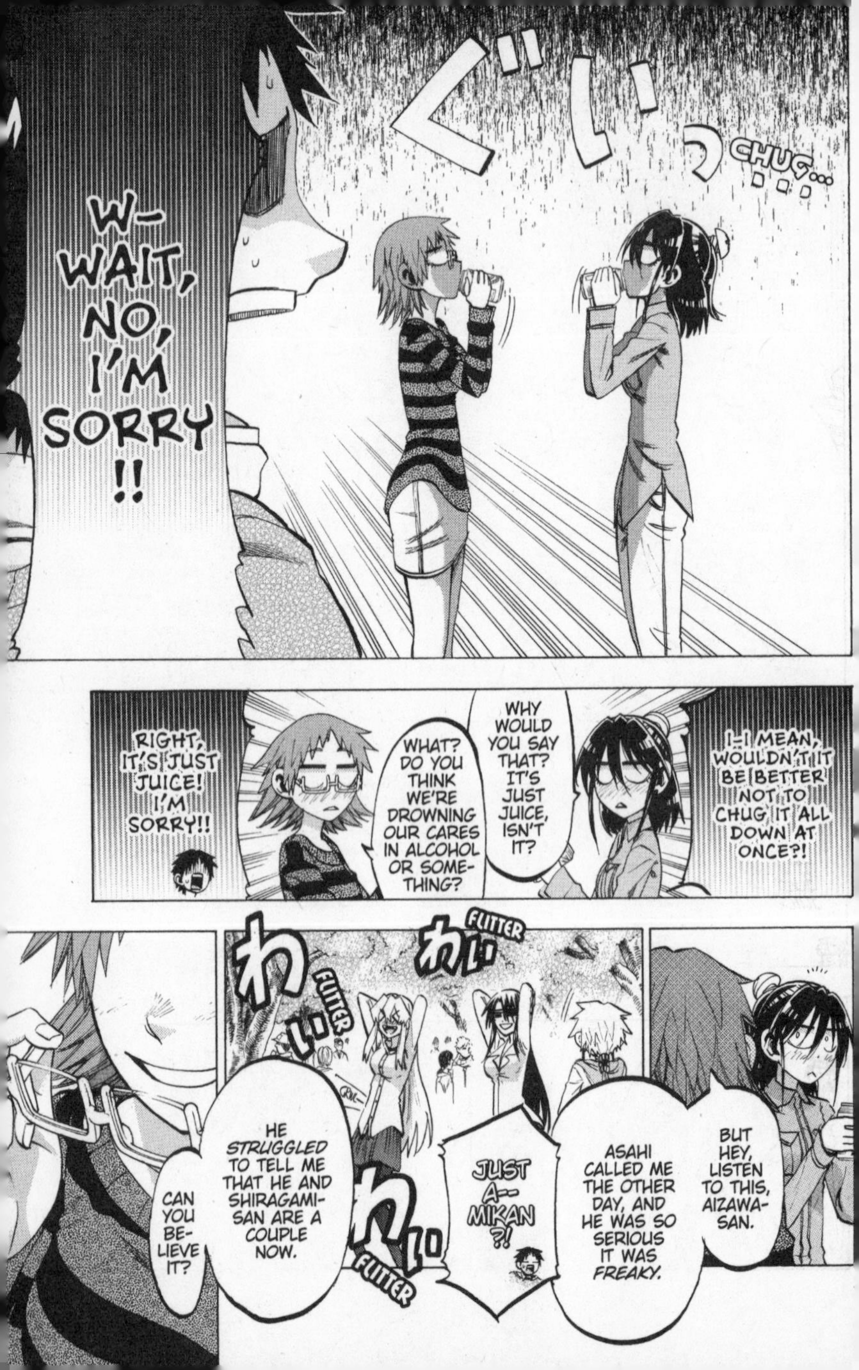
ぐいっ
CHUG...
W-WAIT, NO, I'M SORRY!!
I-I MEAN, WOULDN'T IT BE BETTER NOT TO CHUG IT ALL DOWN AT ONCE?!
WHY WOULD YOU SAY THAT? IT'S JUST JUICE, ISN'T IT?
WHAT? DO YOU THINK WE'RE DROWNING OUR CARES IN ALCOHOL OR SOMETHING?
RIGHT, IT'S JUST JUICE! I'M SORRY!!
BUT HEY, LISTEN TO THIS, AIZAWA-SAN.
わい FLITTER
わい FLITTER
ASAHI CALLED ME THE OTHER DAY, AND HE WAS SO SERIOUS IT WAS *FREAKY*.
JUST A-- MIKAN ?!
わい FLITTER
HE STRUGGLED TO TELL ME THAT HE AND SHIRAGAMI-SAN ARE A COUPLE NOW.
CAN YOU BELIEVE IT?

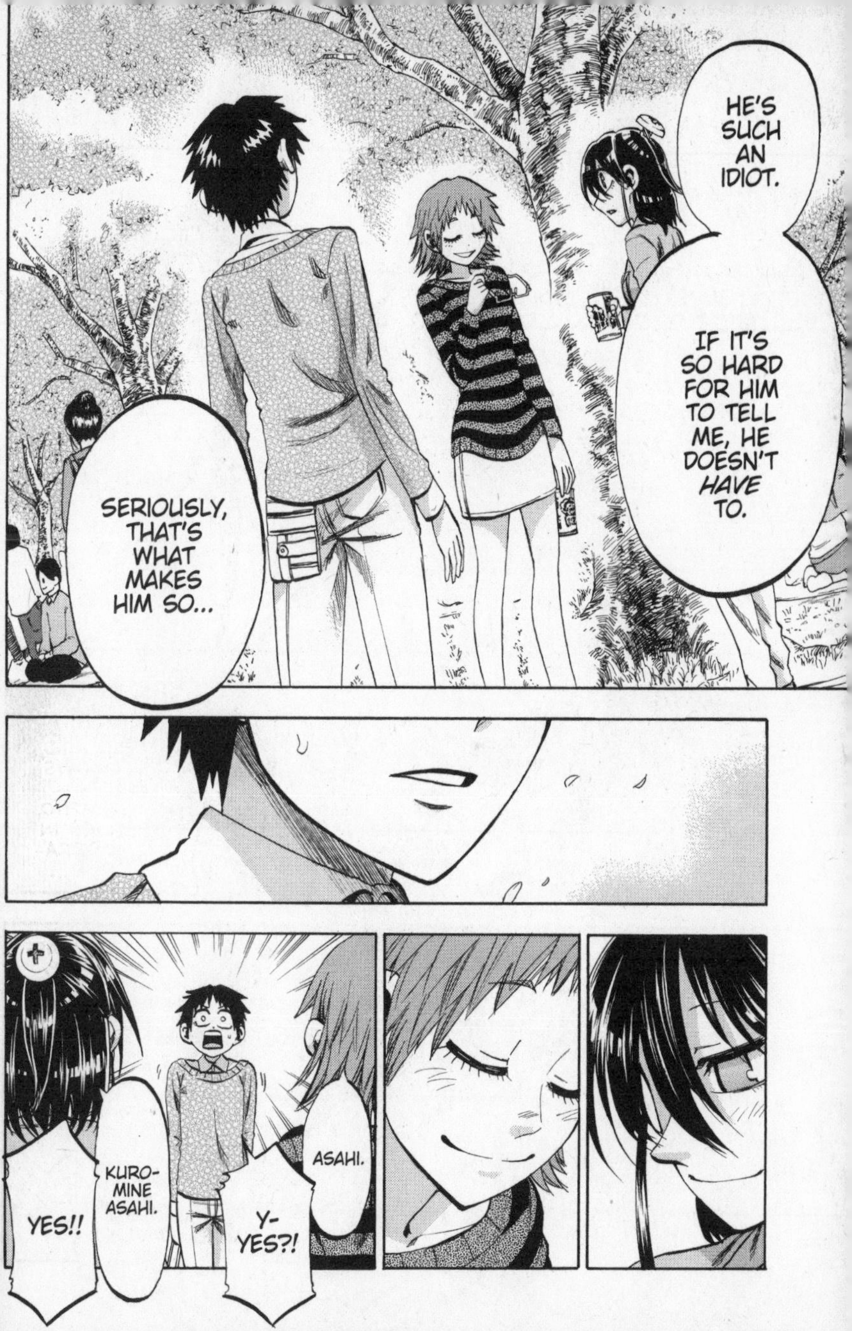
HE'S SUCH AN IDIOT.
IF IT'S SO HARD FOR HIM TO TELL ME, HE DOESN'T *HAVE* TO.
SERIOUSLY, THAT'S WHAT MAKES HIM SO...
ASAHI.
Y-YES?!
KURO-MINE ASAHI.
YES!!

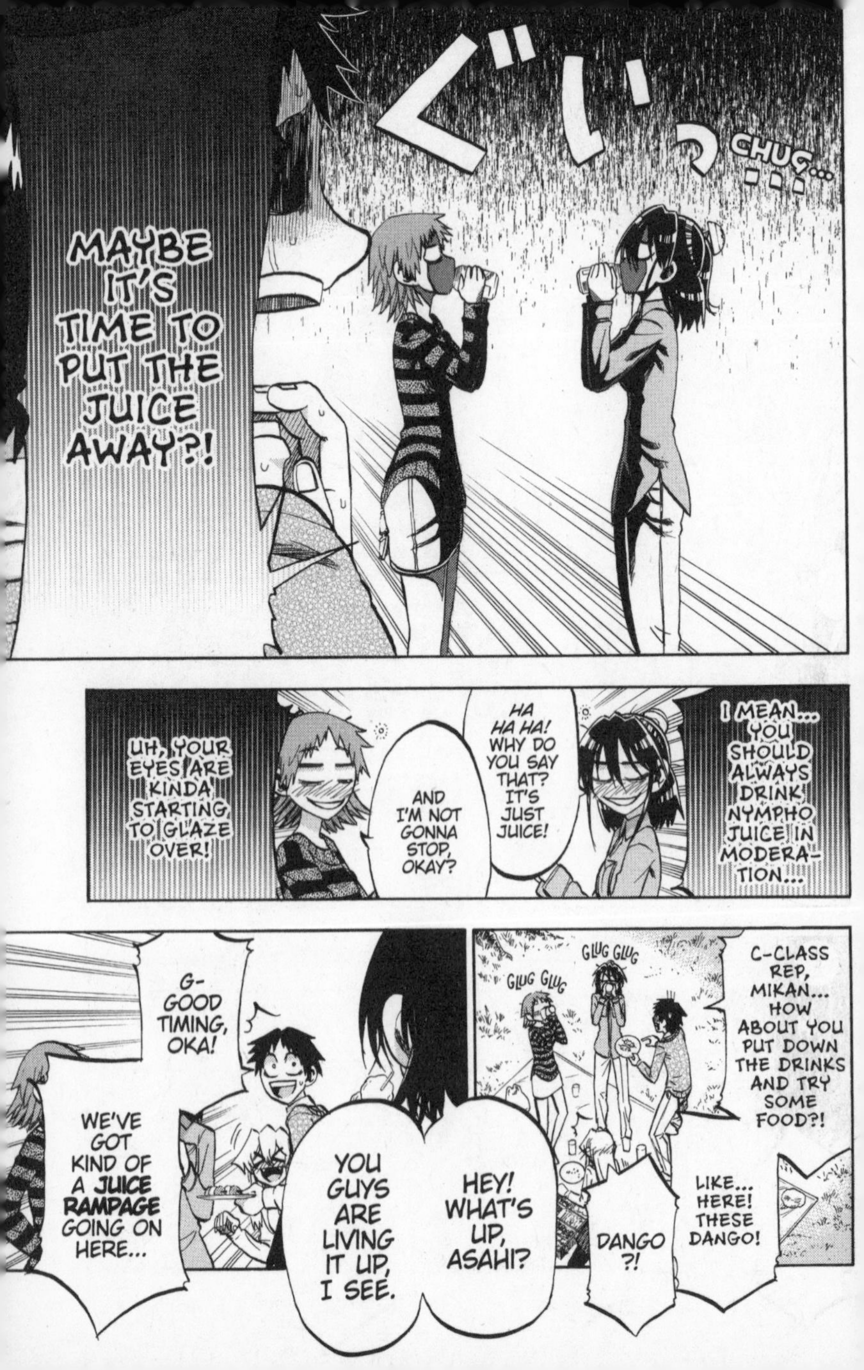
ぐびっ
CHUG...
MAYBE IT'S TIME TO PUT THE JUICE AWAY?!
I MEAN... YOU SHOULD ALWAYS DRINK NYMPHO JUICE IN MODERA-TION...
HA HA HA! WHY DO YOU SAY THAT? IT'S JUST JUICE!
AND I'M NOT GONNA STOP, OKAY?
UH, YOUR EYES ARE KINDA STARTING TO GLAZE OVER!
GLUG GLUG
GLUG GLUG
C-CLASS REP, MIKAN... HOW ABOUT YOU PUT DOWN THE DRINKS AND TRY SOME FOOD?!
LIKE... HERE! THESE DANGO!
DANGO?!
G-GOOD TIMING, OKA!
HEY! WHAT'S UP, ASAHI?
YOU GUYS ARE LIVING IT UP, I SEE.
WE'VE GOT KIND OF A **JUICE RAMPAGE** GOING ON HERE...

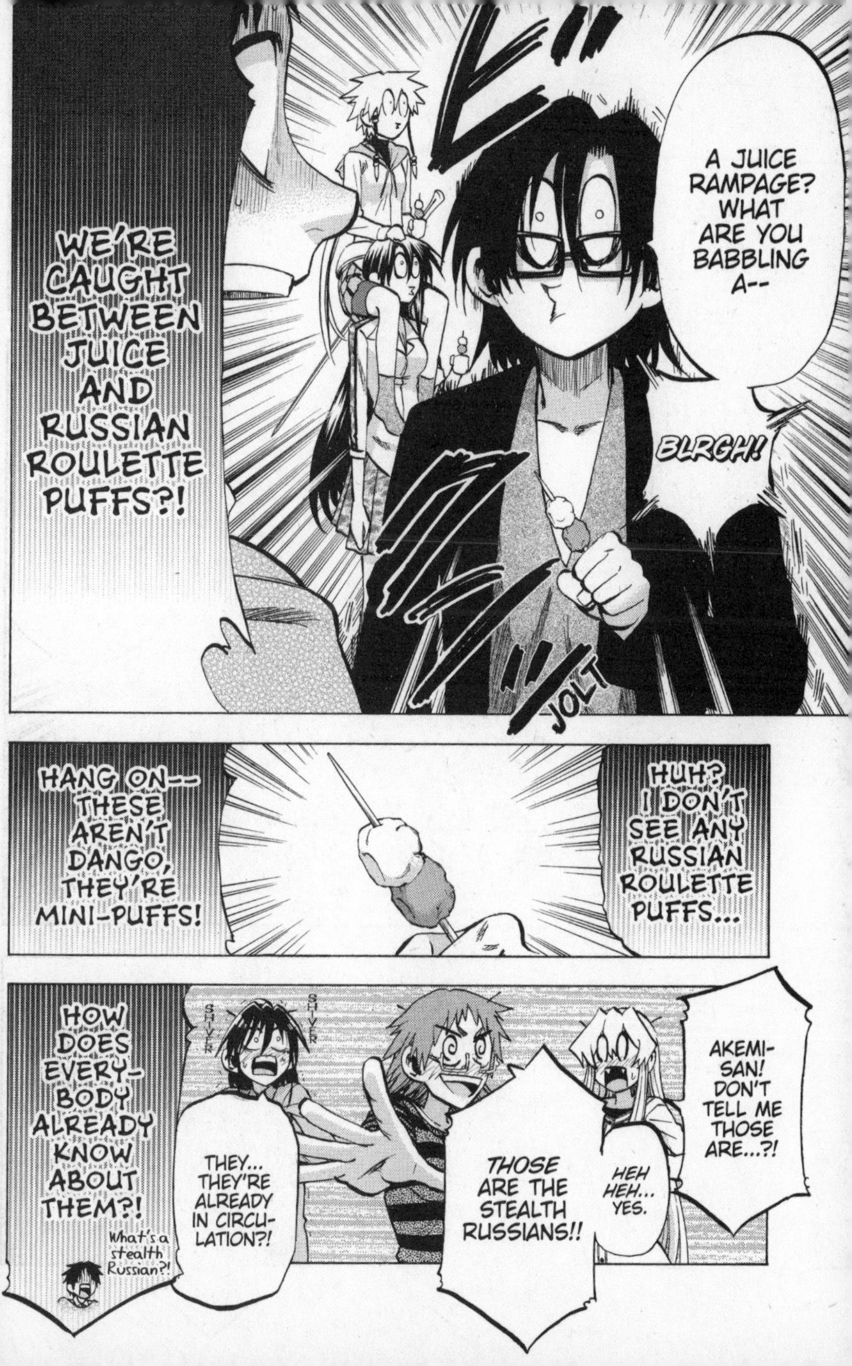
A JUICE RAMPAGE? WHAT ARE YOU BABBLING A--
BLRGH!
WE'RE CAUGHT BETWEEN JUICE AND RUSSIAN ROULETTE PUFFS?!
JOLT
HUH? I DON'T SEE ANY RUSSIAN ROULETTE PUFFS...
HANG ON-- THESE AREN'T DANGO, THEY'RE MINI-PUFFS!
AKEMI-SAN! DON'T TELL ME THOSE ARE...?!
HEH HEH... YES.
THOSE ARE THE STEALTH RUSSIANS!!
SHIVER
SHIVER
THEY... THEY'RE ALREADY IN CIRCULATION?!
HOW DOES EVERYBODY ALREADY KNOW ABOUT THEM?!
What's a stealth Russian?!

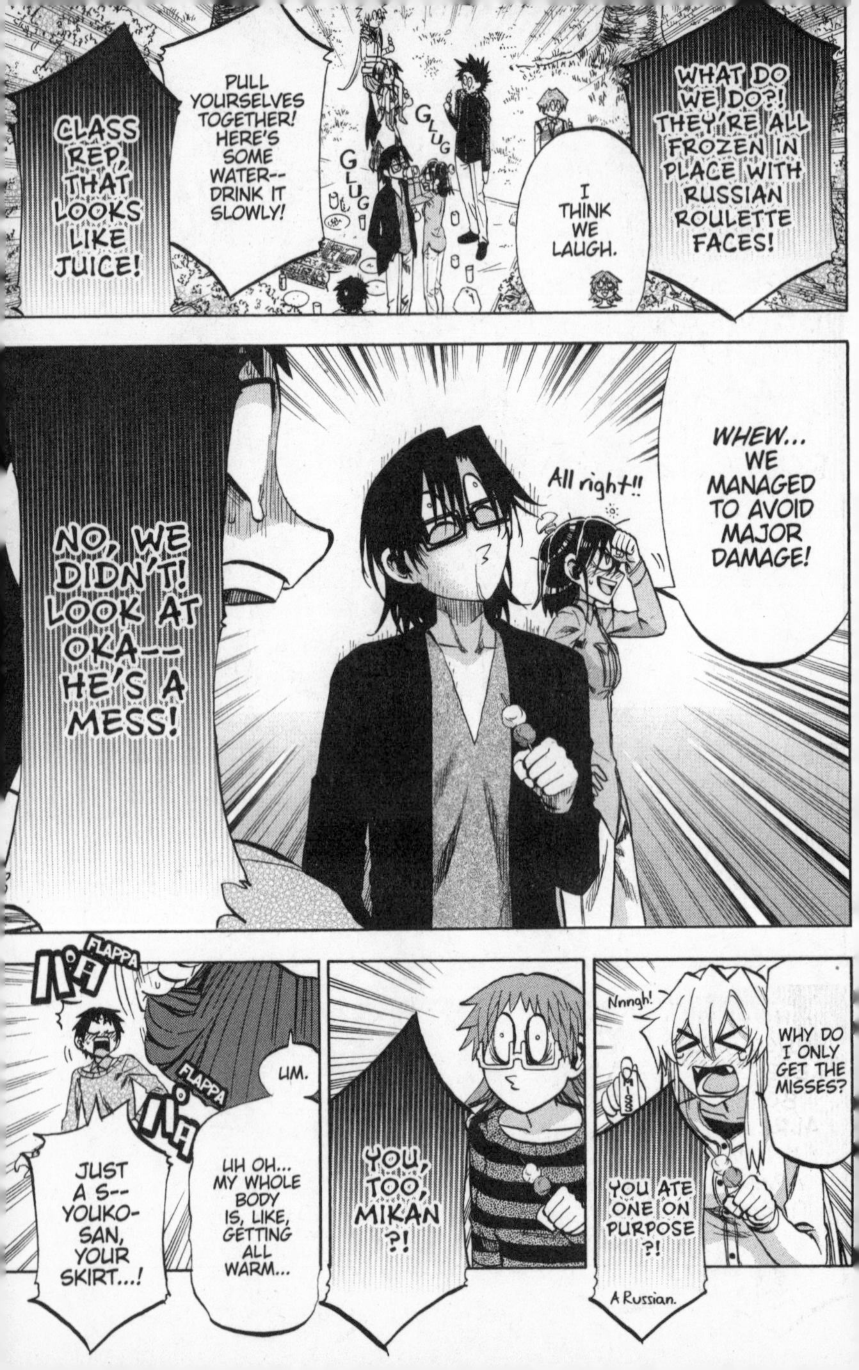
WHAT DO WE DO?! THEY'RE ALL FROZEN IN PLACE WITH RUSSIAN ROULETTE FACES!
I THINK WE LAUGH.
GLUG
GLUG
PULL YOURSELVES TOGETHER! HERE'S SOME WATER-- DRINK IT SLOWLY!
CLASS REP, THAT LOOKS LIKE JUICE!
WHEW... WE MANAGED TO AVOID MAJOR DAMAGE!
All right!!
NO, WE DIDN'T! LOOK AT OKA-- HE'S A MESS!
Nnngh!
WHY DO I ONLY GET THE MISSES?
MISS
YOU ATE ONE ON PURPOSE?!
A Russian.
UM.
YOU, TOO, MIKAN?!
FLAPPA
FLAPPA
UH OH... MY WHOLE BODY IS, LIKE, GETTING ALL WARM...
JUST A S-- YOUKO-SAN, YOUR SKIRT...!

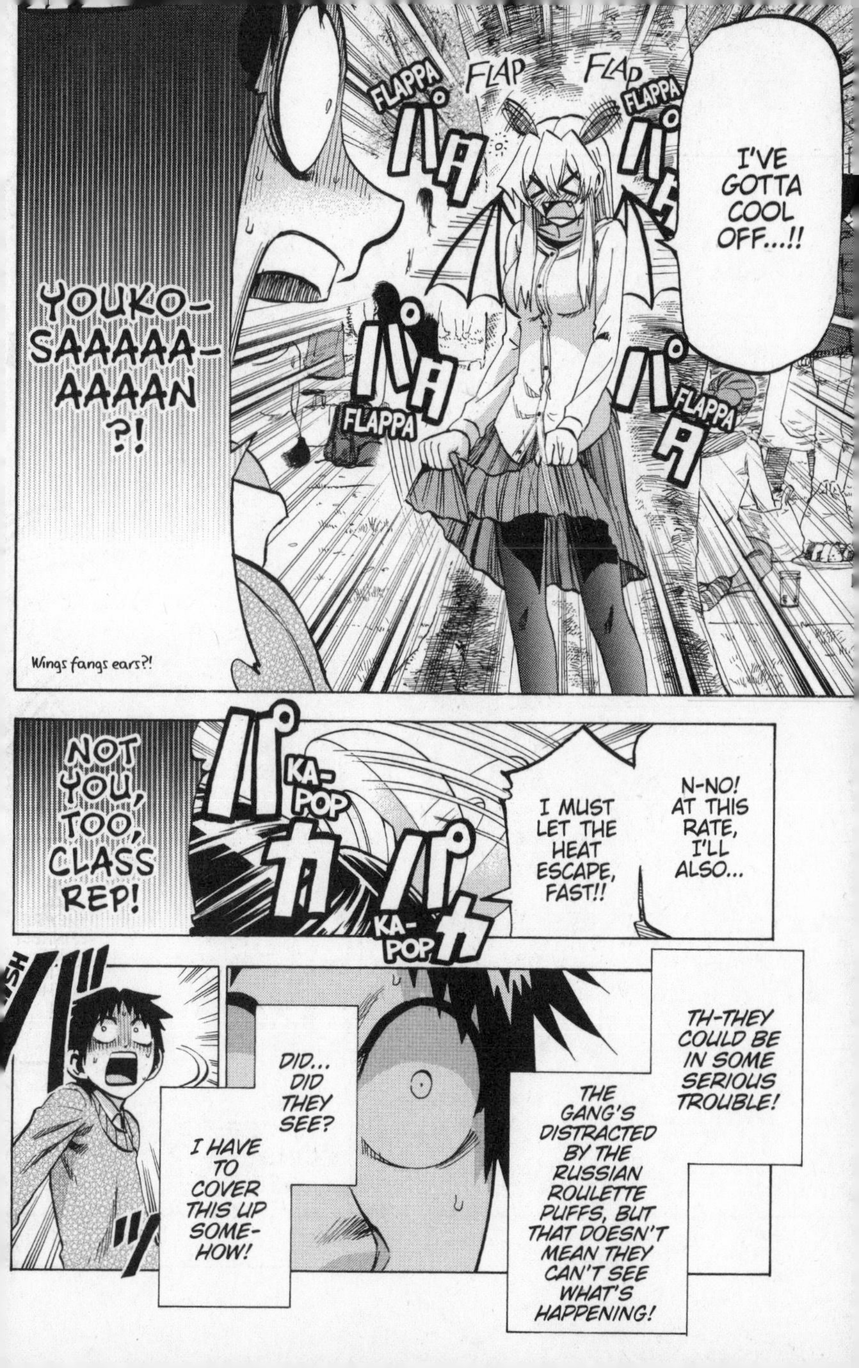
I'VE GOTTA COOL OFF...!!
FLAPPA
FLAP
FLAP
FLAPPA
FLAPPA
FLAPPA
YOUKO-SAAAAAA-AAAAN?!
Wings fangs ears?!
N-NO! AT THIS RATE, I'LL ALSO...
I MUST LET THE HEAT ESCAPE, FAST!!
KA-POP
KA-POP
NOT YOU, TOO, CLASS REP!
TH-THEY COULD BE IN SOME SERIOUS TROUBLE!
THE GANG'S DISTRACTED BY THE RUSSIAN ROULETTE PUFFS, BUT THAT DOESN'T MEAN THEY CAN'T SEE WHAT'S HAPPENING!
DID... DID THEY SEE?
I HAVE TO COVER THIS UP SOME-HOW!

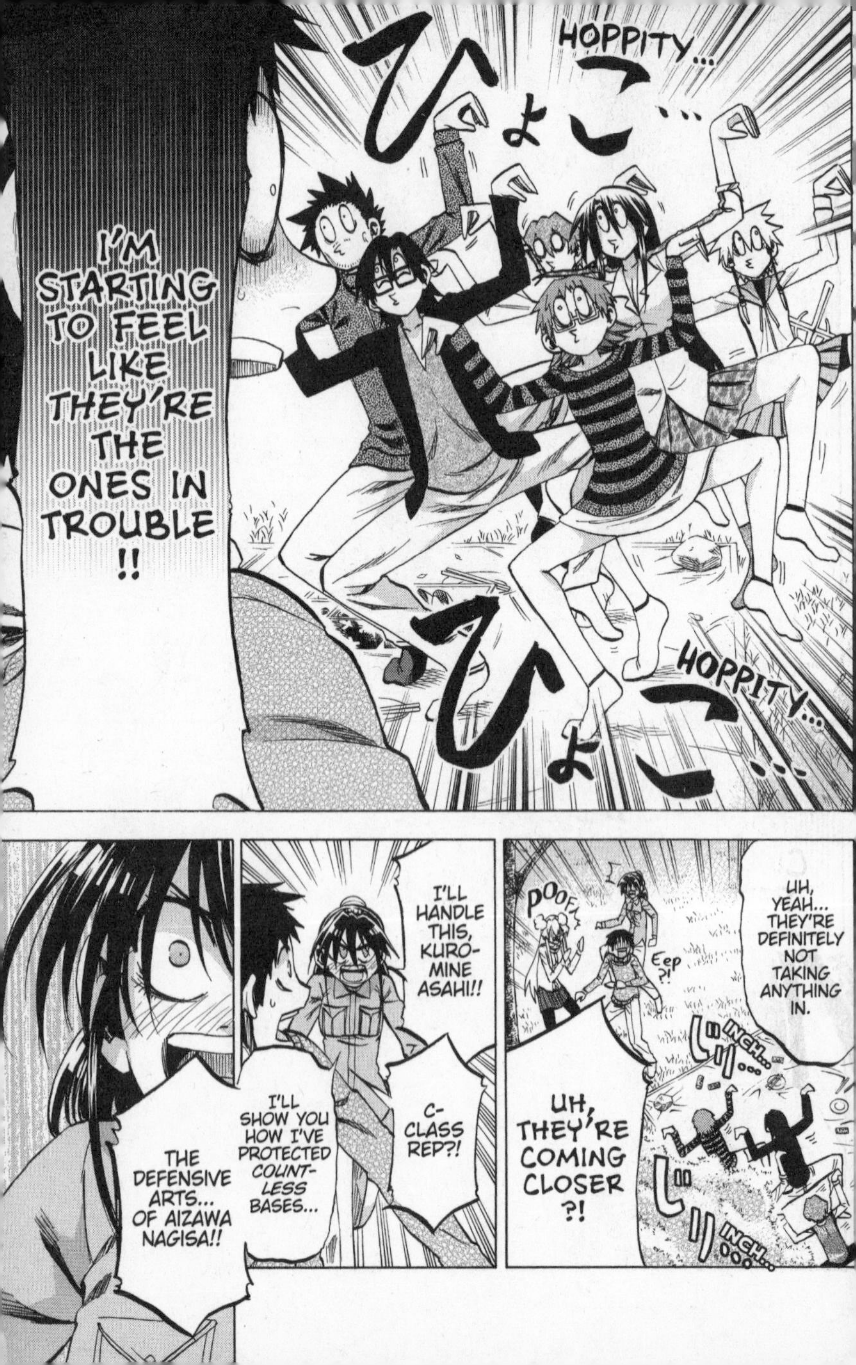

HOPPITY...
ひょこ…
HOPPITY...
ひょこ…
I'M STARTING TO FEEL LIKE THEY'RE THE ONES IN TROUBLE!!
UH, YEAH... THEY'RE DEFINITELY NOT TAKING ANYTHING IN.
POOF!
Eep?!
INCH...
UH, THEY'RE COMING CLOSER?!
INCH...
I'LL HANDLE THIS, KUROMINE ASAHI!!
C-CLASS REP?!
I'LL SHOW YOU HOW I'VE PROTECTED COUNTLESS BASES...
THE DEFENSIVE ARTS... OF AIZAWA NAGISA!!

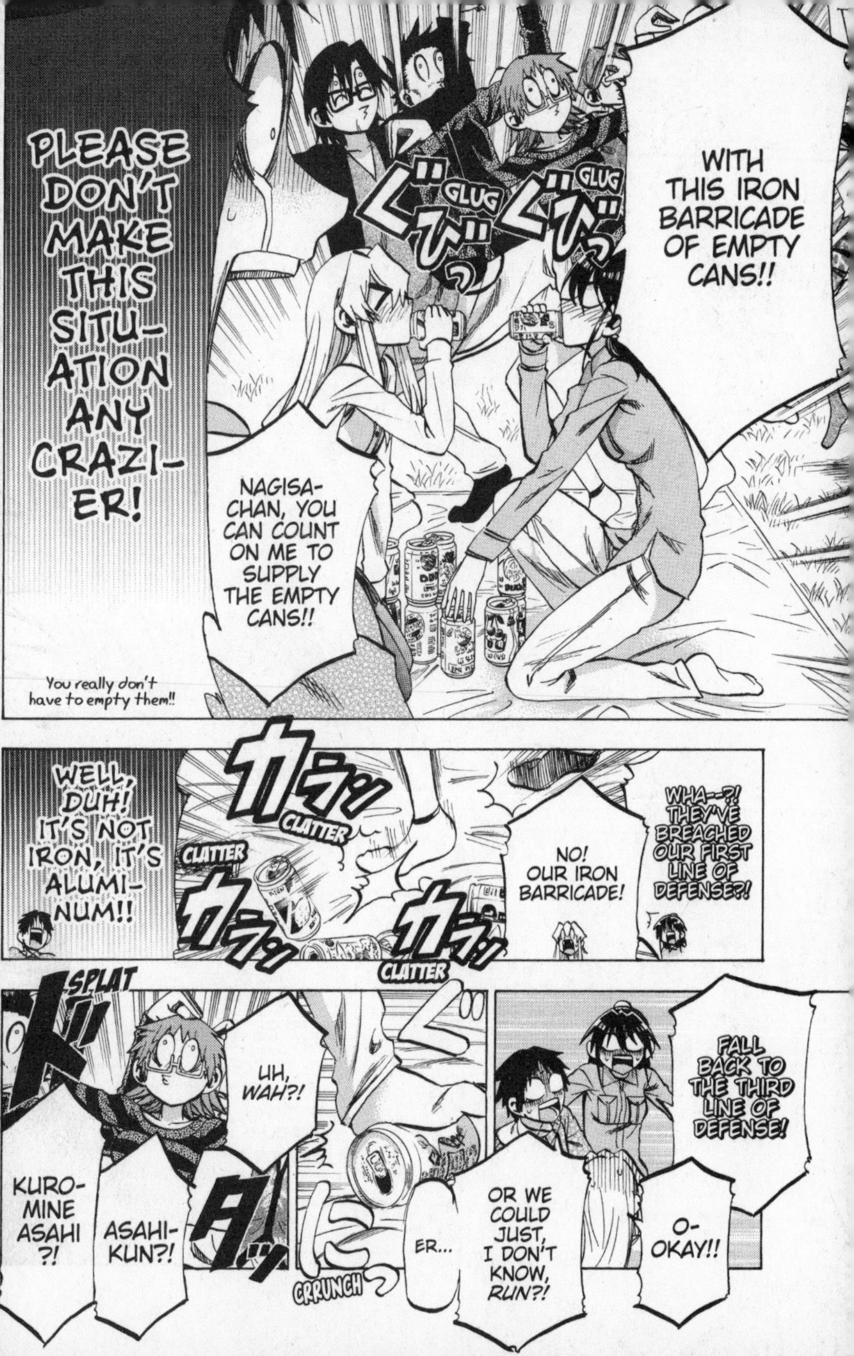
WITH THIS IRON BARRICADE OF EMPTY CANS!!
GLUG
GLUG
NAGISA-CHAN, YOU CAN COUNT ON ME TO SUPPLY THE EMPTY CANS!!
PLEASE DON'T MAKE THIS SITU-ATION ANY CRAZI-ER!
You really don't have to empty them!!
WHA--?! THEY'VE BREACHED OUR FIRST LINE OF DEFENSE?!
NO! OUR IRON BARRICADE!
CLATTER
CLATTER
CLATTER
WELL, DUH! IT'S NOT IRON, IT'S ALUMI-NUM!!
FALL BACK TO THE THIRD LINE OF DEFENSE!
O-OKAY!!
OR WE COULD JUST, I DON'T KNOW, RUN?!
ER...
UH, WAH?!
CRRUNCH
ASAHI-KUN?!
KURO-MINE ASAHI ?!
SPLAT

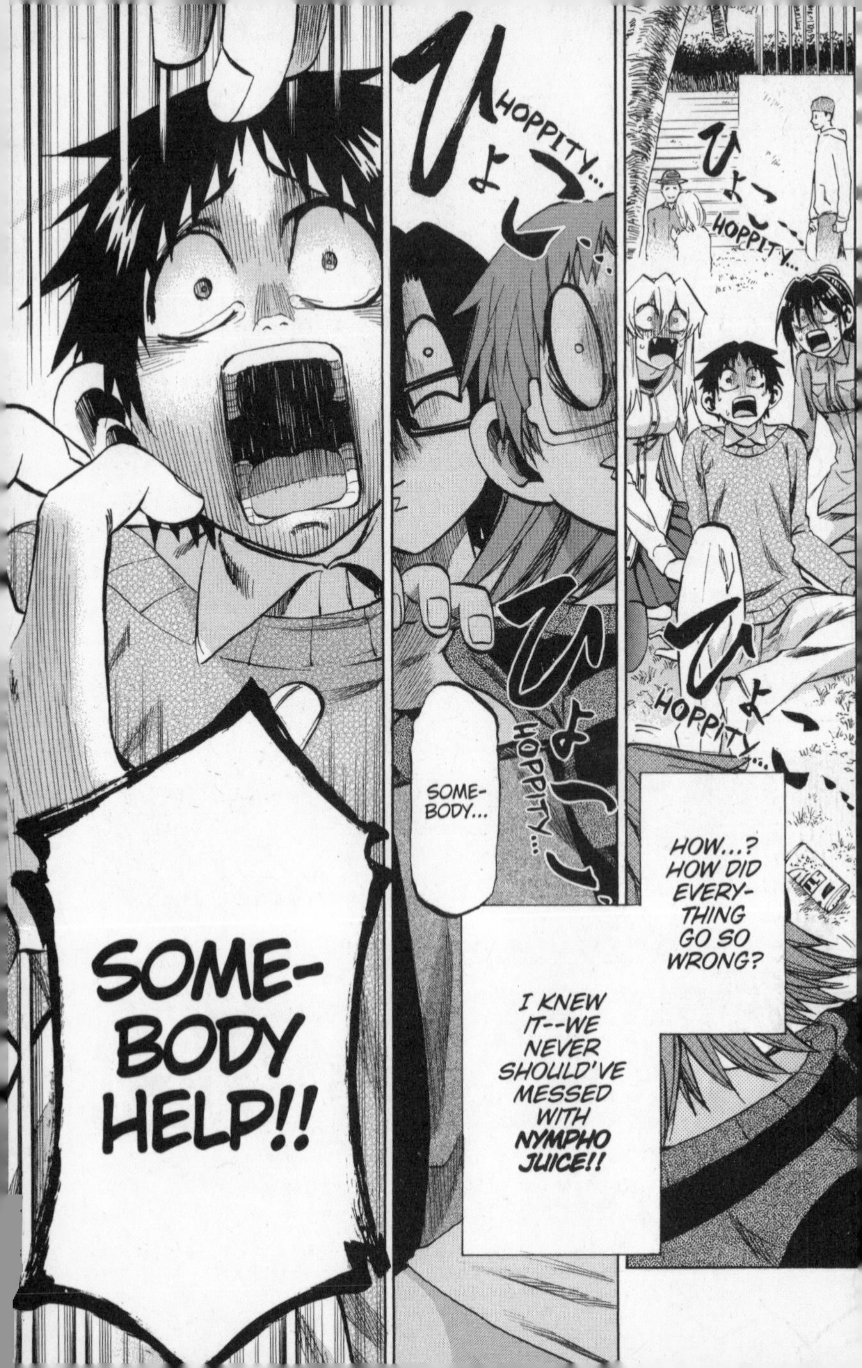
ひょこ
HOPPITY...
ひょこ
HOPPITY...
HOW...? HOW DID EVERYTHING GO SO WRONG?
I KNEW IT--WE NEVER SHOULD'VE MESSED WITH NYMPHO JUICE!!
ひょこ
HOPPITY...
ひょこ
HOPPITY...
SOME-BODY...
SOME-BODY HELP!!

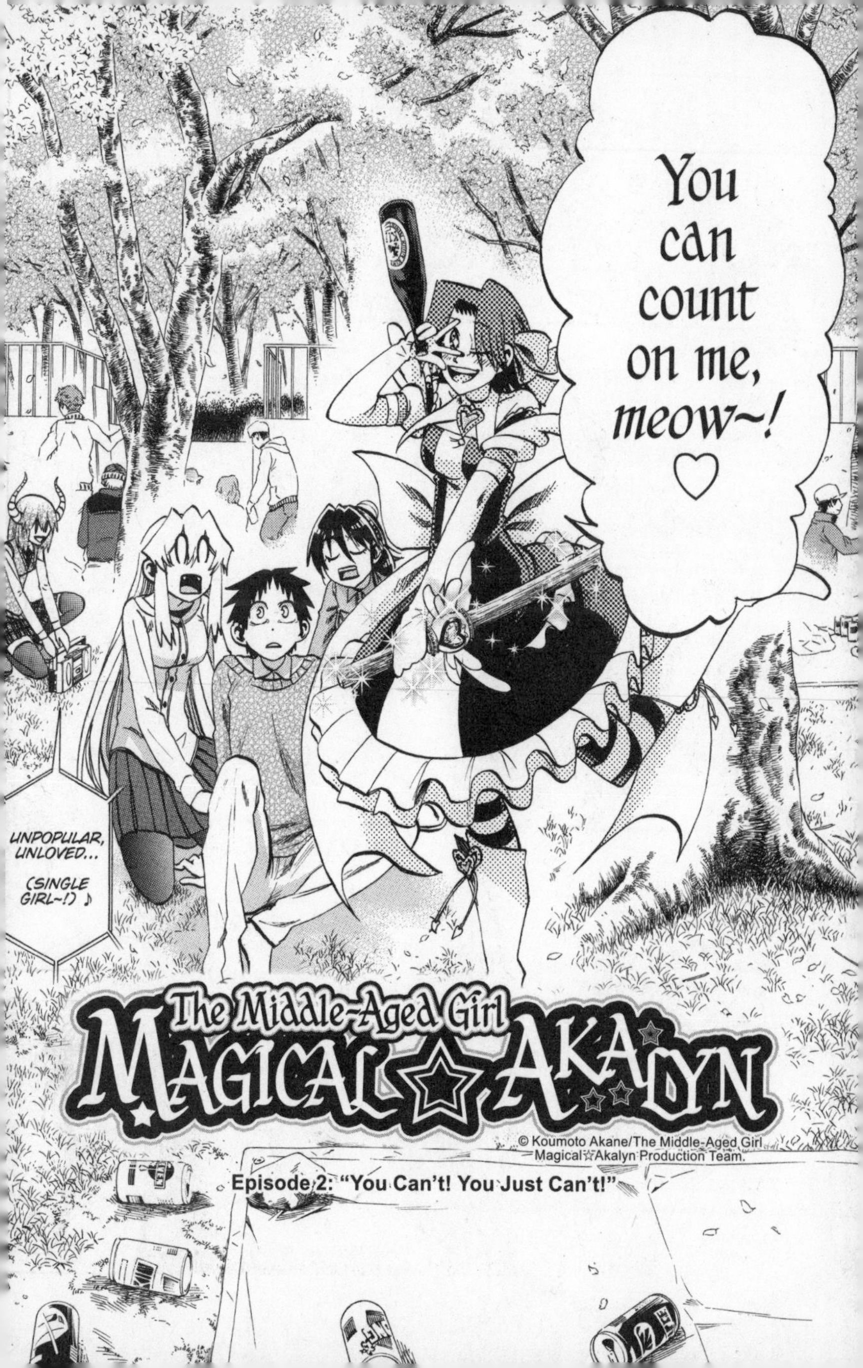
You can count on me, meow~! ♡
UNPOPULAR, UNLOVED... (SINGLE GIRL~!) ♪
The Middle-Aged Girl
MAGICAL☆AKALYN
© Koumoto Akane/The Middle-Aged Girl Magical☆Akalyn Production Team.
Episode 2: "You Can't! You Just Can't!"

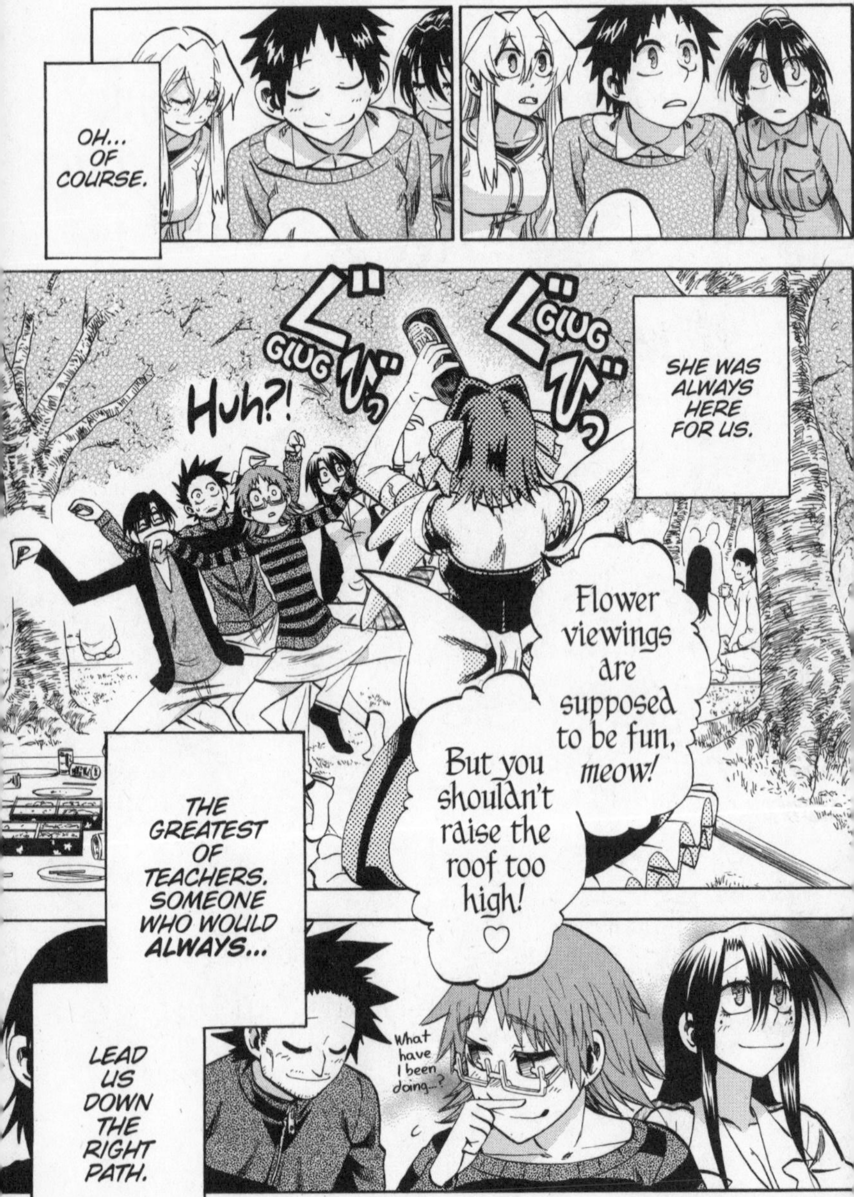
OH... OF COURSE.
SHE WAS ALWAYS HERE FOR US.
ぐびっ
GLUG
ぐびっ
GLUG
Huh?!
Flower viewings are supposed to be fun, meow!
But you shouldn't raise the roof too high! ♡
THE GREATEST OF TEACHERS. SOMEONE WHO WOULD ALWAYS...
What have I been doing...?
LEAD US DOWN THE RIGHT PATH.

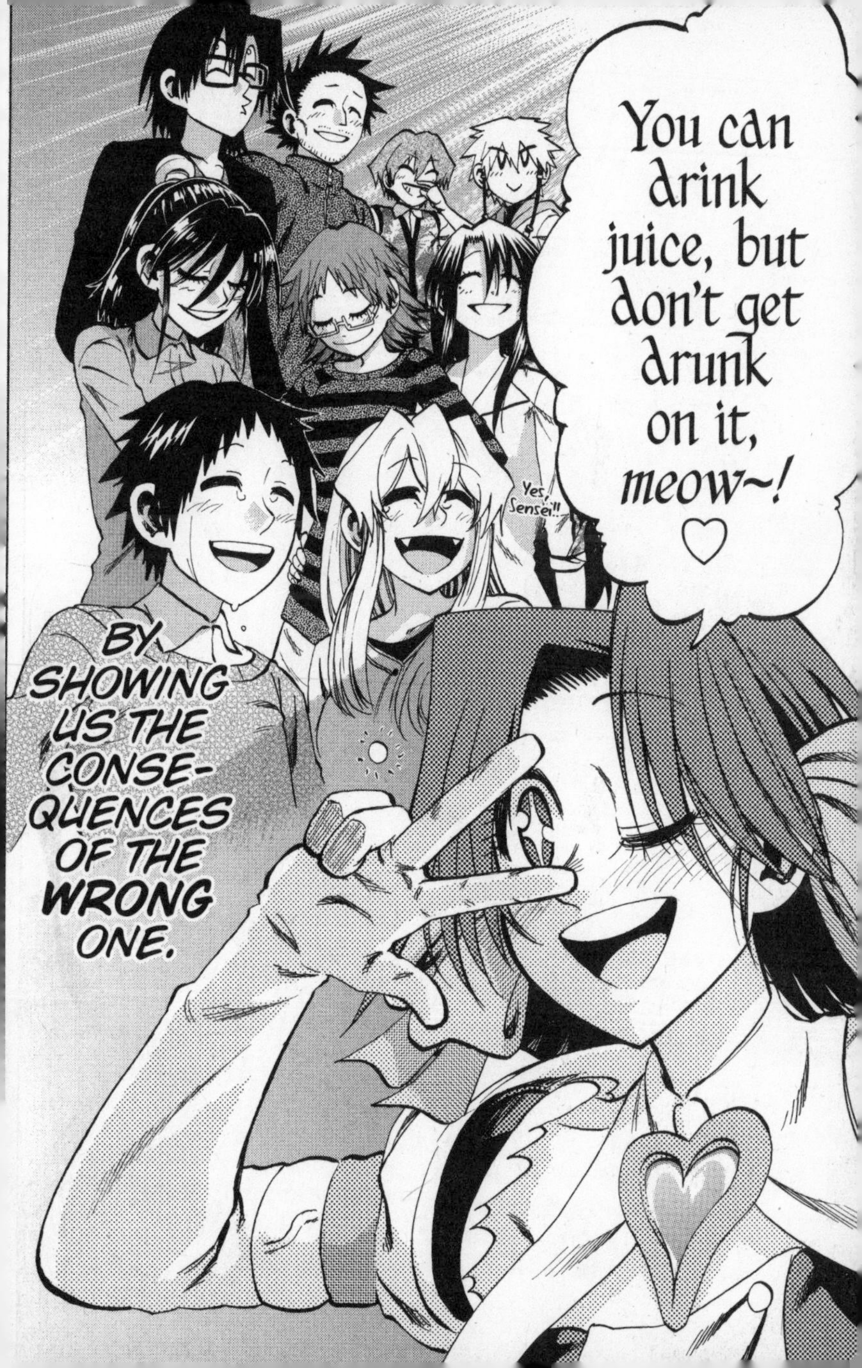
You can drink juice, but don't get drunk on it, *meow~!* ♡
Yes, Sensei!!
BY SHOWING US THE CONSE-QUENCES OF THE WRONG ONE.

Chapter 92: "Let's Become Third-Years!"

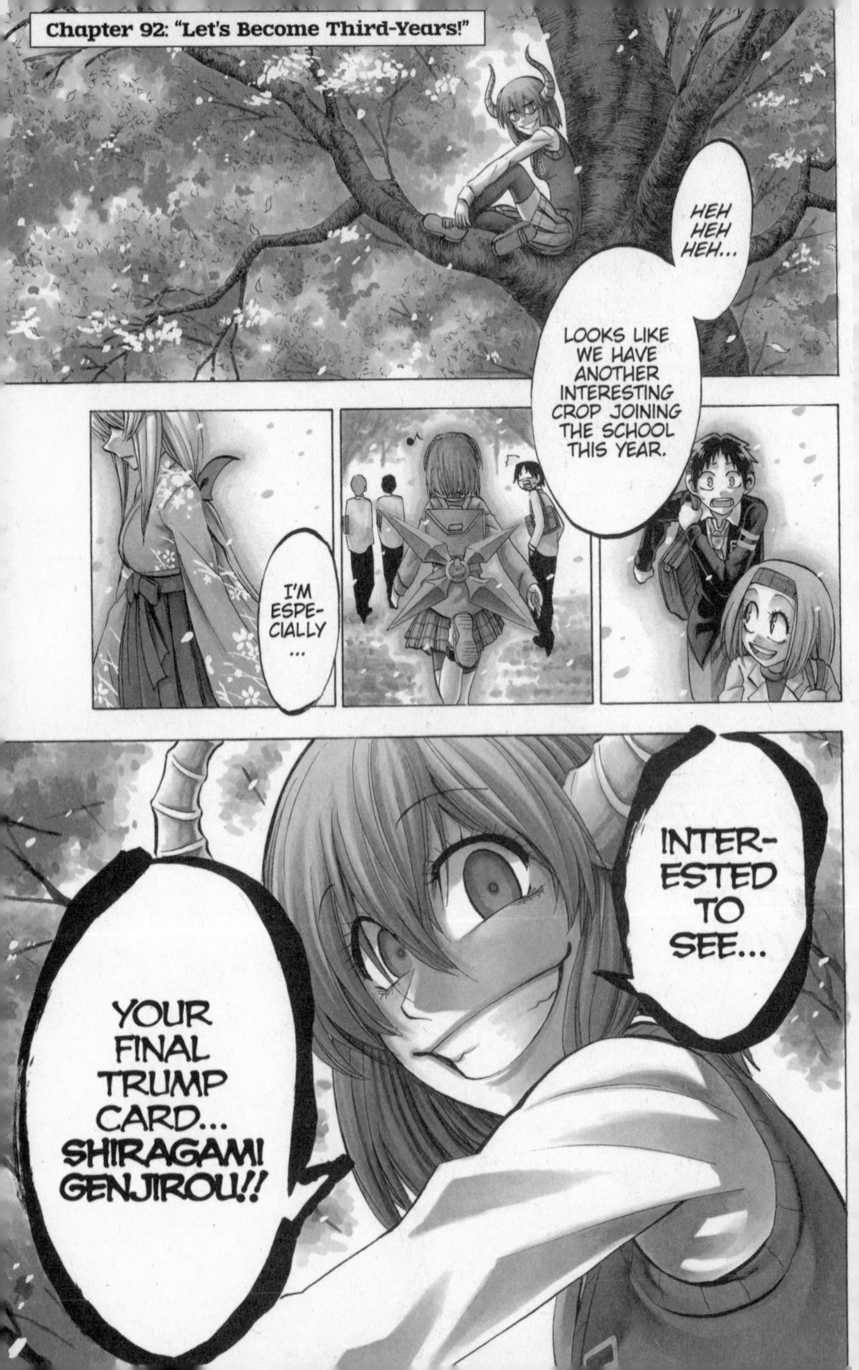
HEH HEH HEH...
LOOKS LIKE WE HAVE ANOTHER INTERESTING CROP JOINING THE SCHOOL THIS YEAR.
I'M ESPE-CIALLY...
INTER-ESTED TO SEE...
YOUR FINAL TRUMP CARD... SHIRAGAMI GENJIROU!!

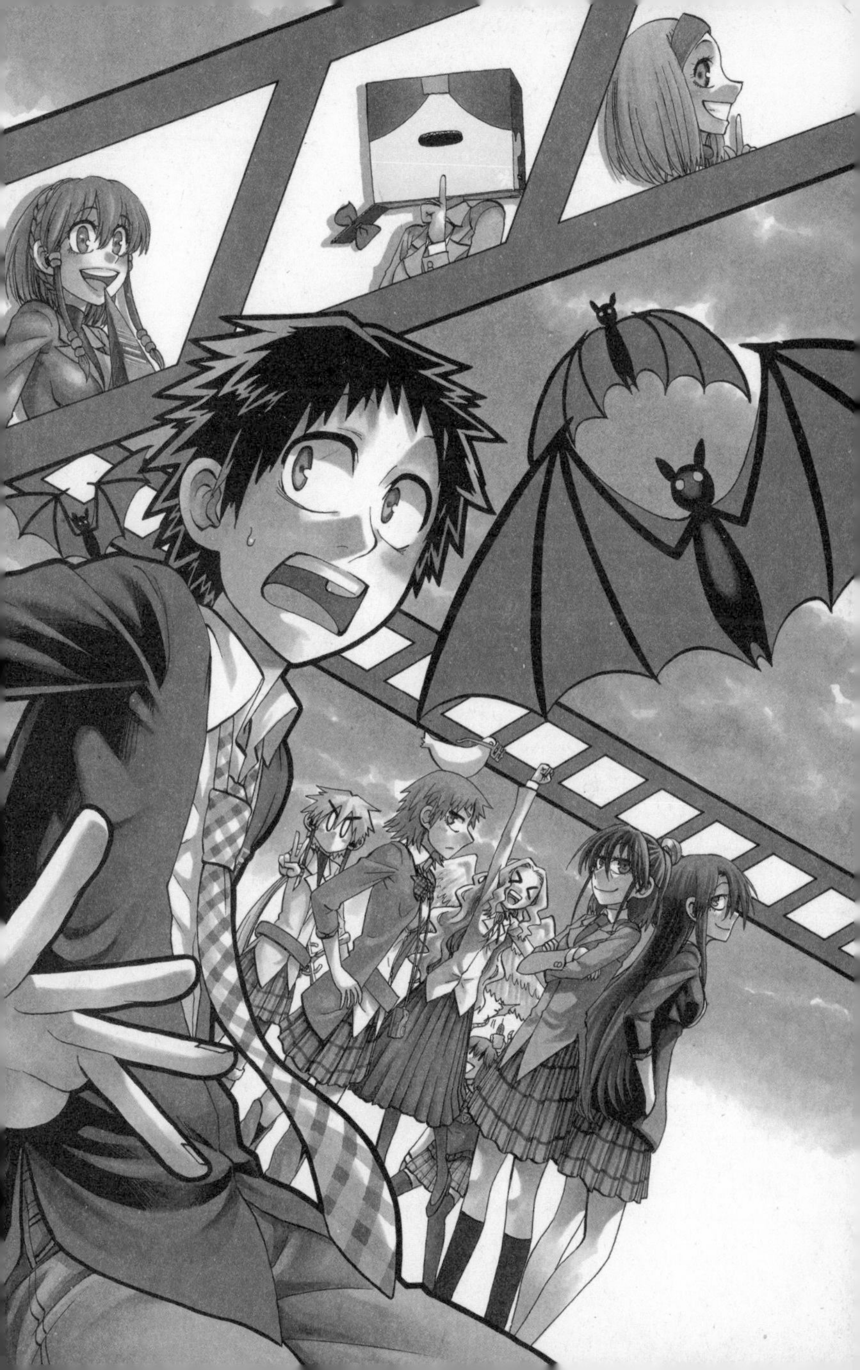

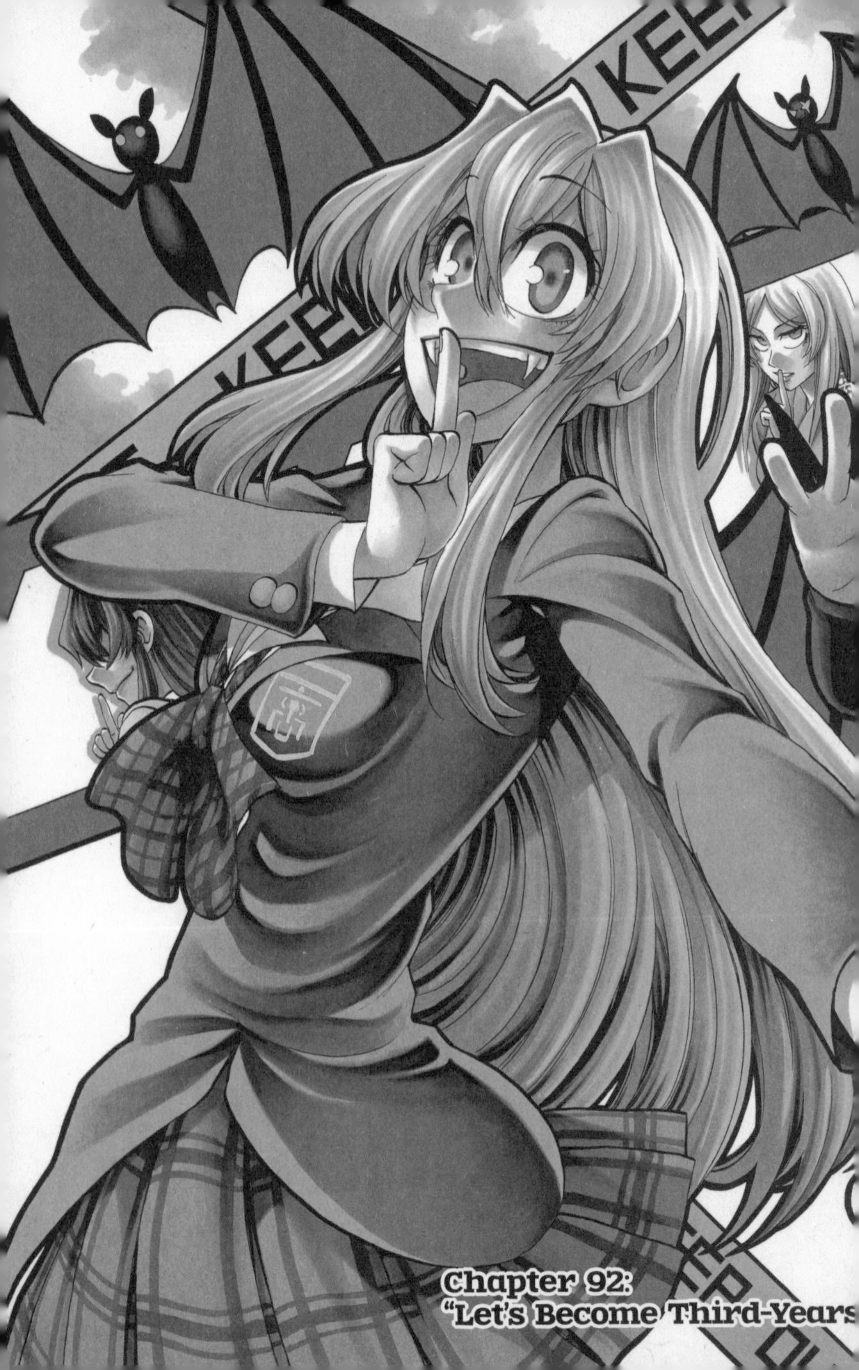

Chapter 92: “Let’s Become Third-Years

TOP SECRET

My Monster Secret 11

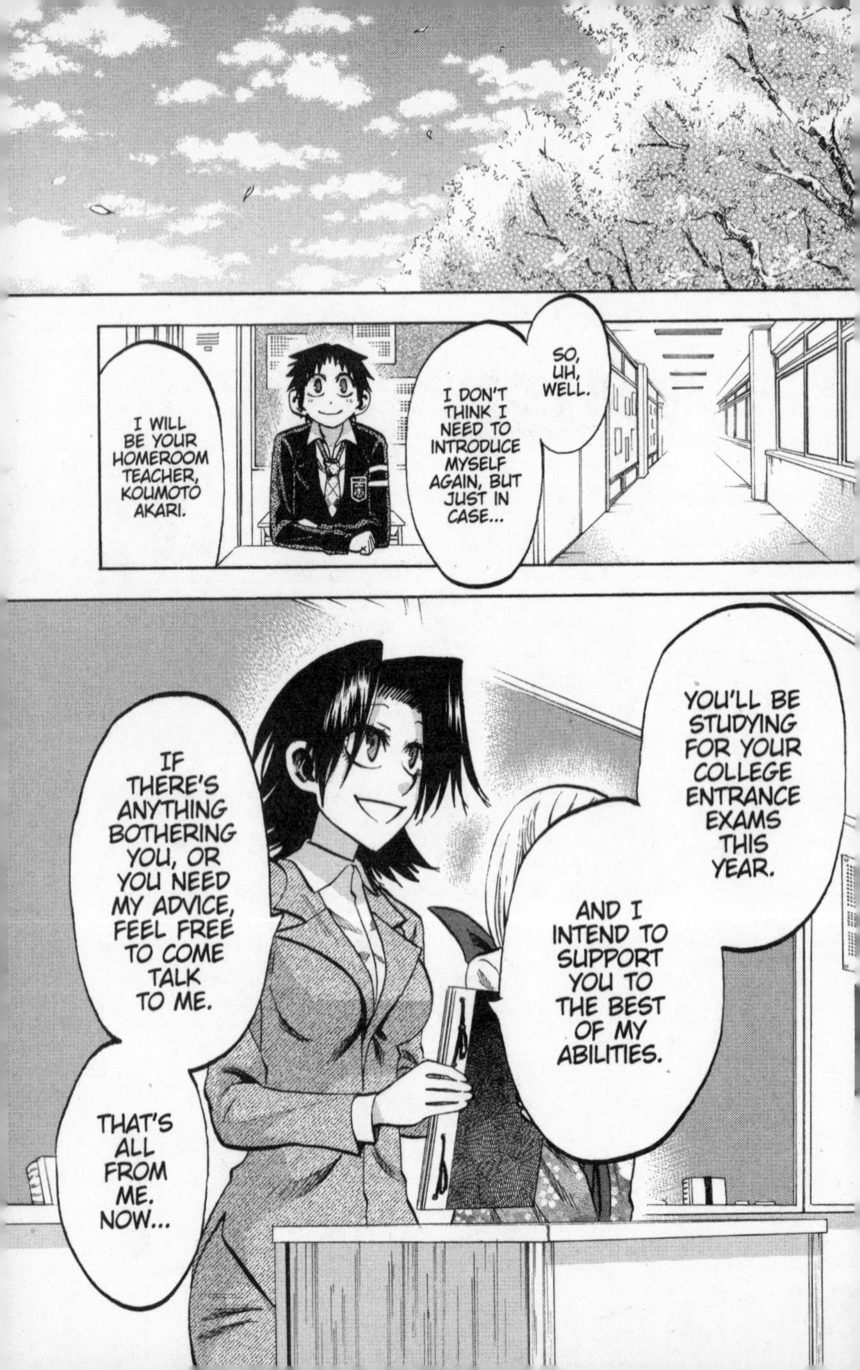
SO, UH, WELL.
I DON'T THINK I NEED TO INTRODUCE MYSELF AGAIN, BUT JUST IN CASE...
I WILL BE YOUR HOMEROOM TEACHER, KOUMOTO AKARI.
YOU'LL BE STUDYING FOR YOUR COLLEGE ENTRANCE EXAMS THIS YEAR.
AND I INTEND TO SUPPORT YOU TO THE BEST OF MY ABILITIES.
IF THERE'S ANYTHING BOTHERING YOU, OR YOU NEED MY ADVICE, FEEL FREE TO COME TALK TO ME.
THAT'S ALL FROM ME. NOW...

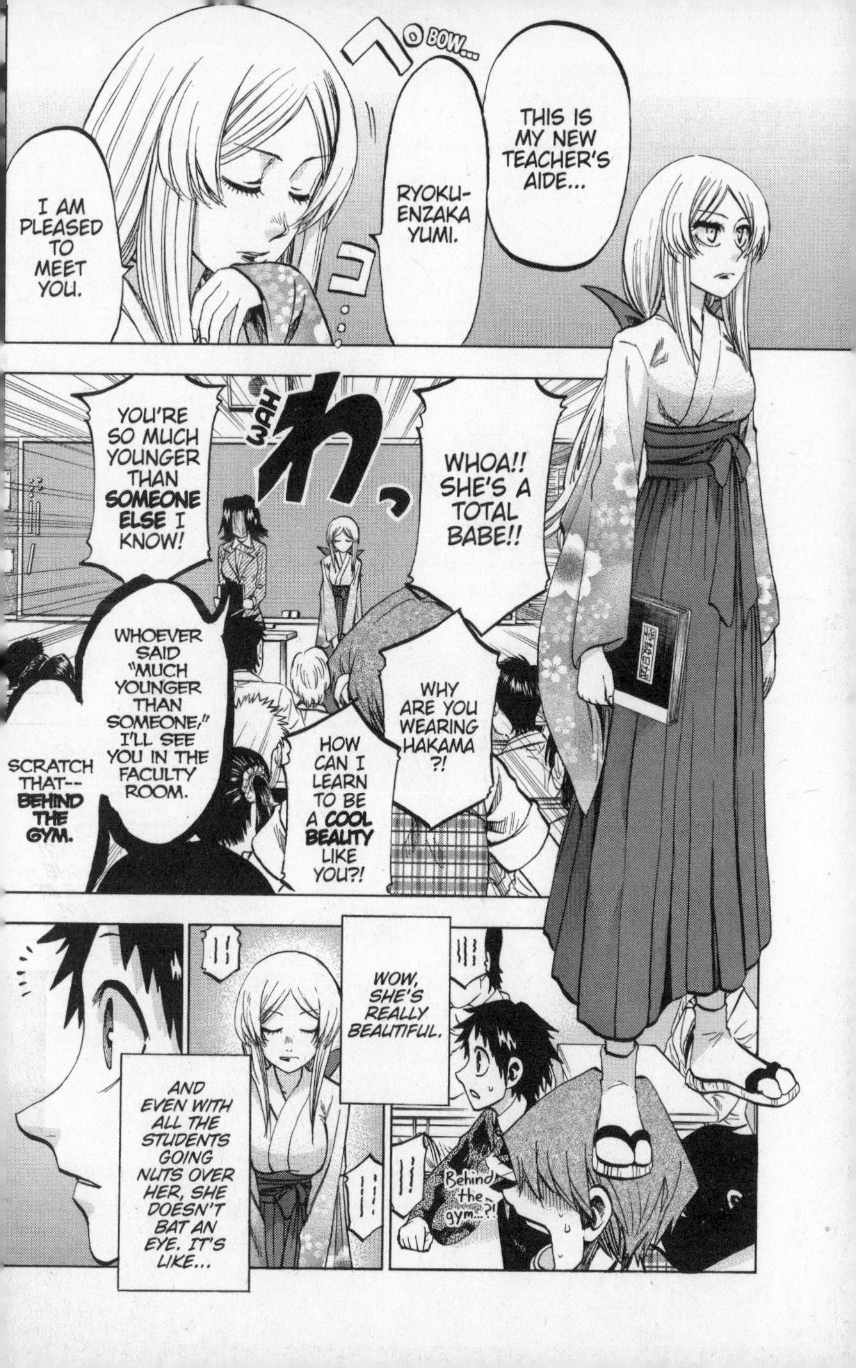
THIS IS MY NEW TEACHER'S AIDE...
RYOKU-ENZAKA YUMI.
BOW...
I AM PLEASED TO MEET YOU.
WHOA!! SHE'S A TOTAL BABE!!
WAH
YOU'RE SO MUCH YOUNGER THAN SOMEONE ELSE I KNOW!
WHY ARE YOU WEARING HAKAMA?!
HOW CAN I LEARN TO BE A COOL BEAUTY LIKE YOU?!
WHOEVER SAID "MUCH YOUNGER THAN SOMEONE," I'LL SEE YOU IN THE FACULTY ROOM.
SCRATCH THAT-- BEHIND THE GYM.
WOW, SHE'S REALLY BEAUTIFUL.
Behind the gym...?!
AND EVEN WITH ALL THE STUDENTS GOING NUTS OVER HER, SHE DOESN'T BAT AN EYE. IT'S LIKE...

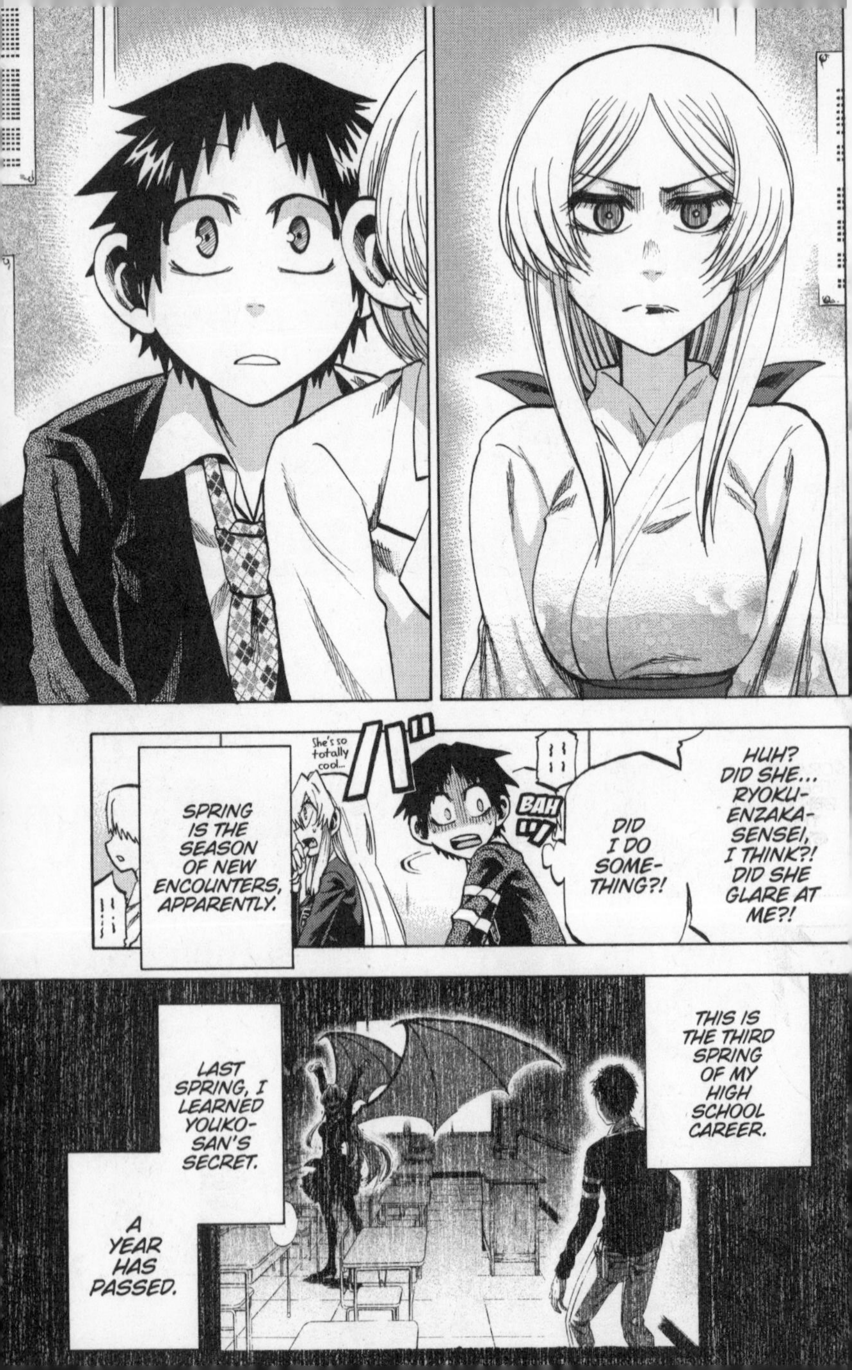
HUH? DID SHE... RYOKU-ENZAKA-SENSEI, I THINK?! DID SHE GLARE AT ME?!
DID I DO SOMETHING?!
BAH
She's so totally cool...
SPRING IS THE SEASON OF NEW ENCOUNTERS, APPARENTLY.
THIS IS THE THIRD SPRING OF MY HIGH SCHOOL CAREER.
LAST SPRING, I LEARNED YOUKO-SAN'S SECRET.
A YEAR HAS PASSED.

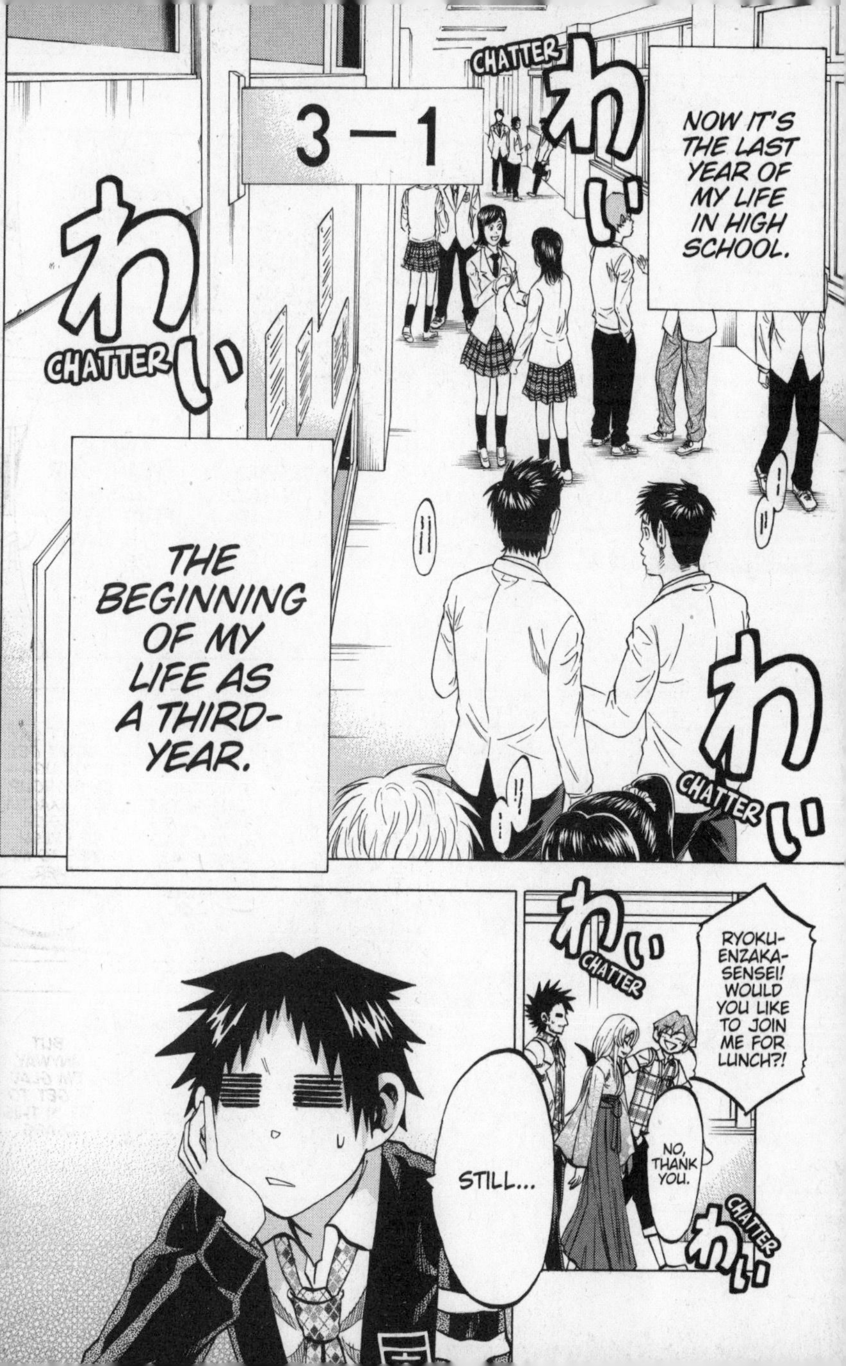
3－1
CHATTER
わい
NOW IT'S THE LAST YEAR OF MY LIFE IN HIGH SCHOOL.
わい
CHATTER
THE BEGINNING OF MY LIFE AS A THIRD-YEAR.
!!
!!
!!
わい
CHATTER
わい
CHATTER
RYOKU-ENZAKA-SENSEI! WOULD YOU LIKE TO JOIN ME FOR LUNCH?!
NO, THANK YOU.
CHATTER
わい
STILL...

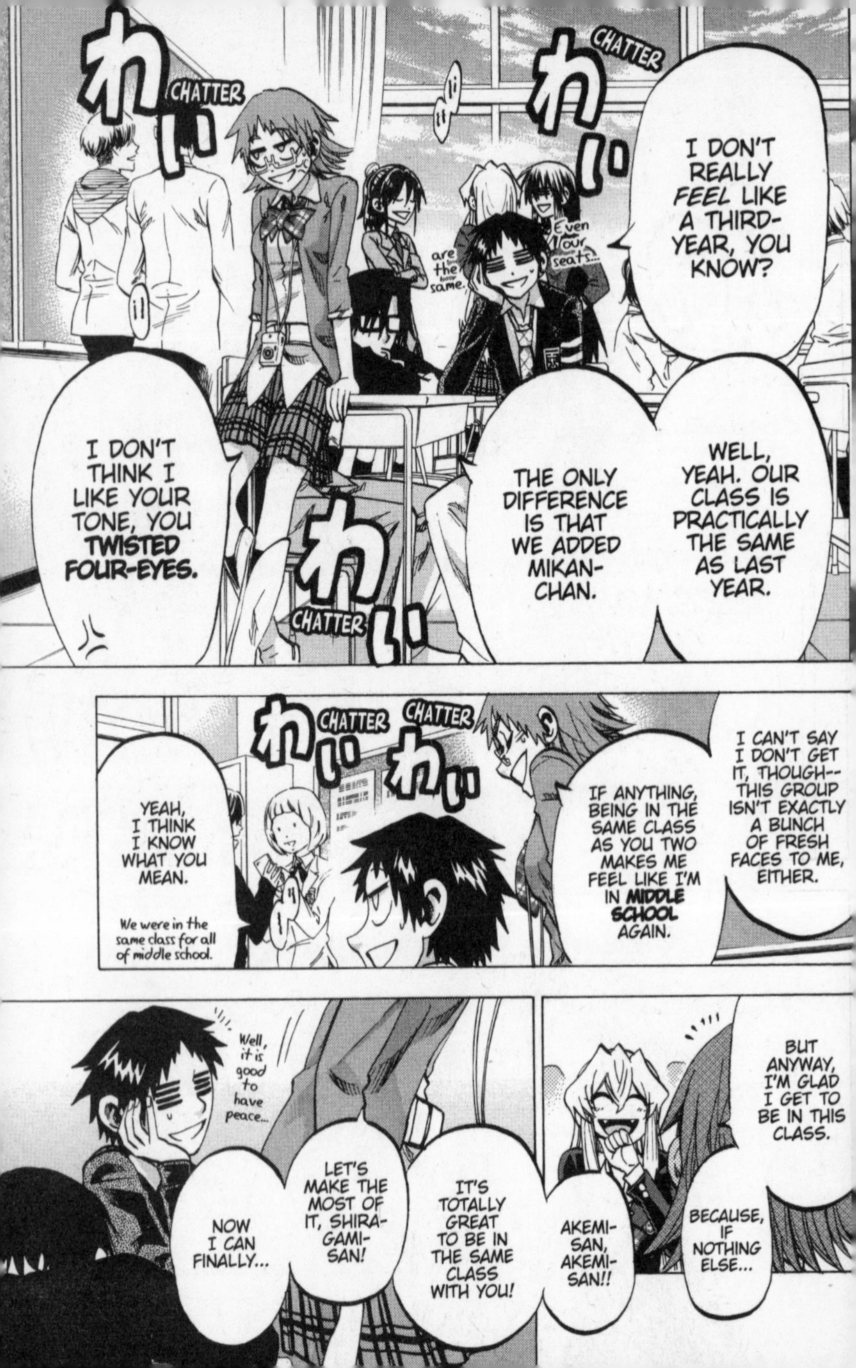
CHATTER
I DON'T REALLY FEEL LIKE A THIRD-YEAR, YOU KNOW?
WELL, YEAH. OUR CLASS IS PRACTICALLY THE SAME AS LAST YEAR.
THE ONLY DIFFERENCE IS THAT WE ADDED MIKAN-CHAN.
Even our seats...
are the same.
CHATTER
I DON'T THINK I LIKE YOUR TONE, YOU **TWISTED FOUR-EYES.**
CHATTER
I CAN'T SAY I DON'T GET IT, THOUGH-- THIS GROUP ISN'T EXACTLY A BUNCH OF FRESH FACES TO ME, EITHER.
IF ANYTHING, BEING IN THE SAME CLASS AS YOU TWO MAKES ME FEEL LIKE I'M IN **MIDDLE SCHOOL** AGAIN.
CHATTER CHATTER
YEAH, I THINK I KNOW WHAT YOU MEAN.
We were in the same class for all of middle school.
BUT ANYWAY, I'M GLAD I GET TO BE IN THIS CLASS.
BECAUSE, IF NOTHING ELSE...
AKEMI-SAN, AKEMI-SAN!!
IT'S TOTALLY GREAT TO BE IN THE SAME CLASS WITH YOU!
LET'S MAKE THE MOST OF IT, SHIRA-GAMI-SAN!
Well, it is good to have peace...
NOW I CAN FINALLY...

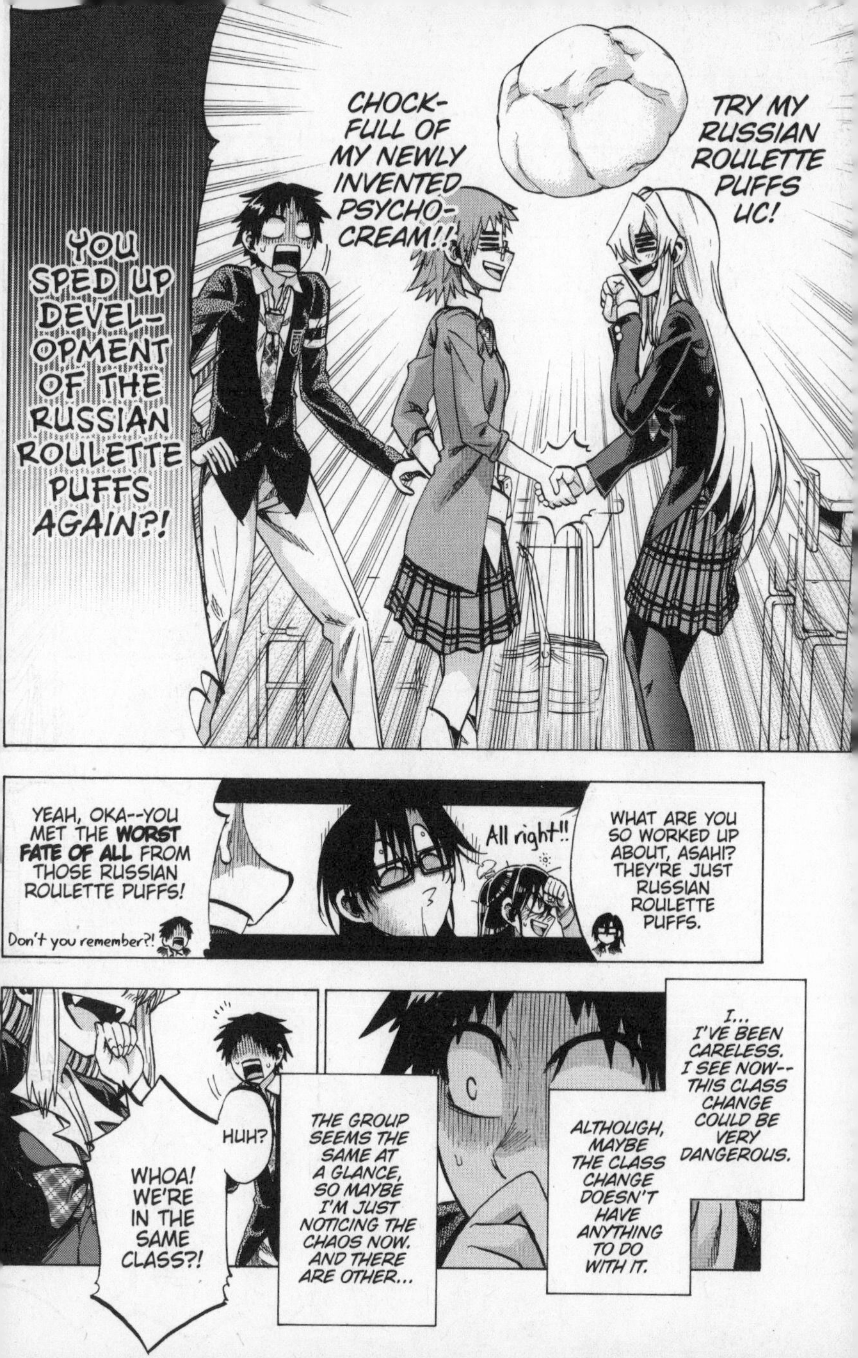
TRY MY RUSSIAN ROULETTE PUFFS UC!
CHOCK-FULL OF MY NEWLY INVENTED PSYCHO-CREAM!!
YOU SPED UP DEVEL-OPMENT OF THE RUSSIAN ROULETTE PUFFS AGAIN?!
WHAT ARE YOU SO WORKED UP ABOUT, ASAHI? THEY'RE JUST RUSSIAN ROULETTE PUFFS.
All right!!
YEAH, OKA--YOU MET THE **WORST FATE OF ALL** FROM THOSE RUSSIAN ROULETTE PUFFS!
Don't you remember?!
I... I'VE BEEN CARELESS. I SEE NOW--THIS CLASS CHANGE COULD BE VERY DANGEROUS.
ALTHOUGH, MAYBE THE CLASS CHANGE DOESN'T HAVE ANYTHING TO DO WITH IT.
THE GROUP SEEMS THE SAME AT A GLANCE, SO MAYBE I'M JUST NOTICING THE CHAOS NOW. AND THERE ARE OTHER...
HUH?
WHOA! WE'RE IN THE SAME CLASS?!

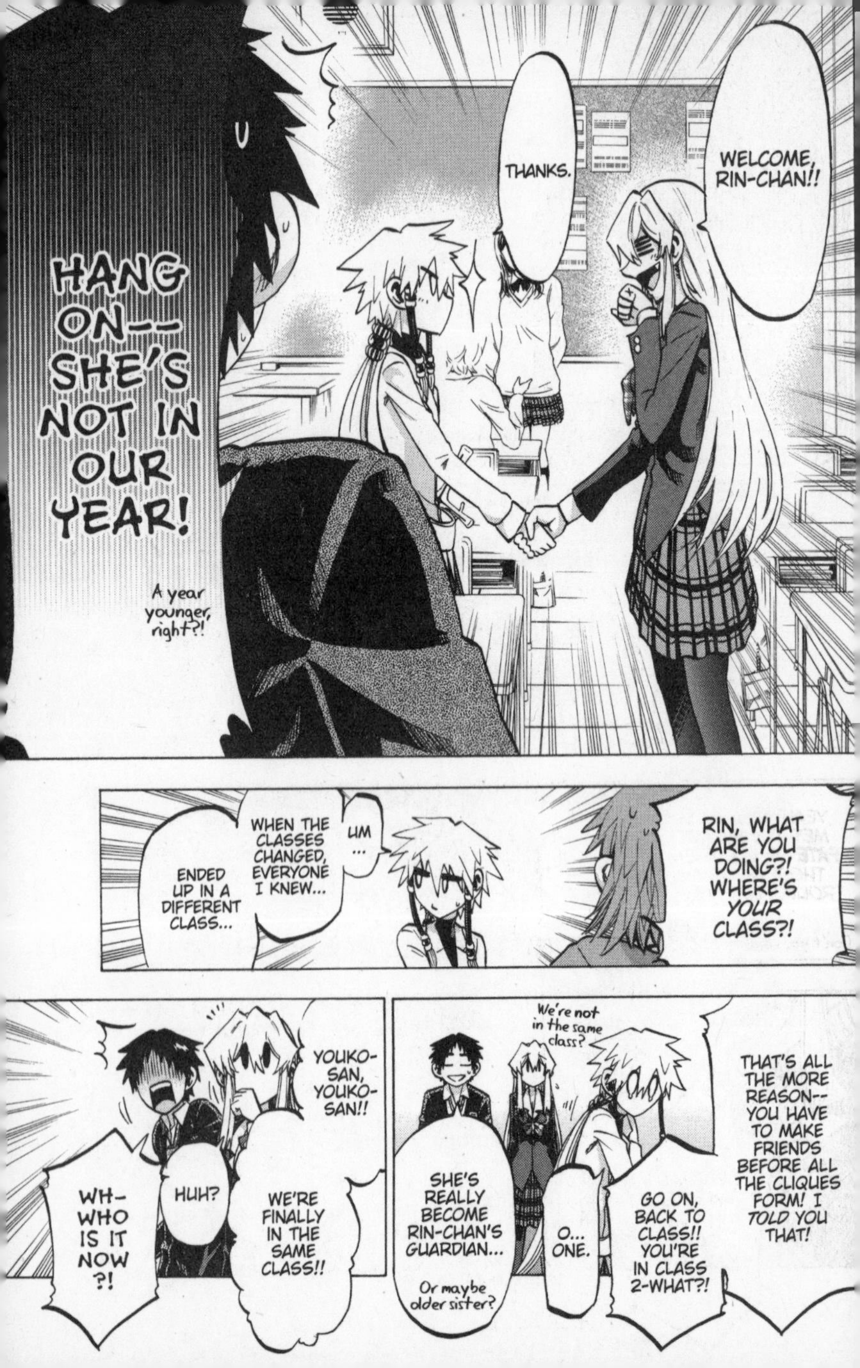
WELCOME, RIN-CHAN!!
THANKS.
HANG ON-- SHE'S NOT IN OUR YEAR!
A year younger, right?!
RIN, WHAT ARE YOU DOING?! WHERE'S *YOUR* CLASS?!
UM ...
WHEN THE CLASSES CHANGED, EVERYONE I KNEW...
ENDED UP IN A DIFFERENT CLASS...
THAT'S ALL THE MORE REASON-- YOU HAVE TO MAKE FRIENDS BEFORE ALL THE CLIQUES FORM! I *TOLD* YOU THAT!
We're not in the same class?
GO ON, BACK TO CLASS!! YOU'RE IN CLASS 2-WHAT?!
O... ONE.
SHE'S REALLY BECOME RIN-CHAN'S GUARDIAN...
Or maybe older sister?
YOUKO-SAN, YOUKO-SAN!!
WE'RE FINALLY IN THE SAME CLASS!!
HUH?
WH-WHO IS IT NOW?!

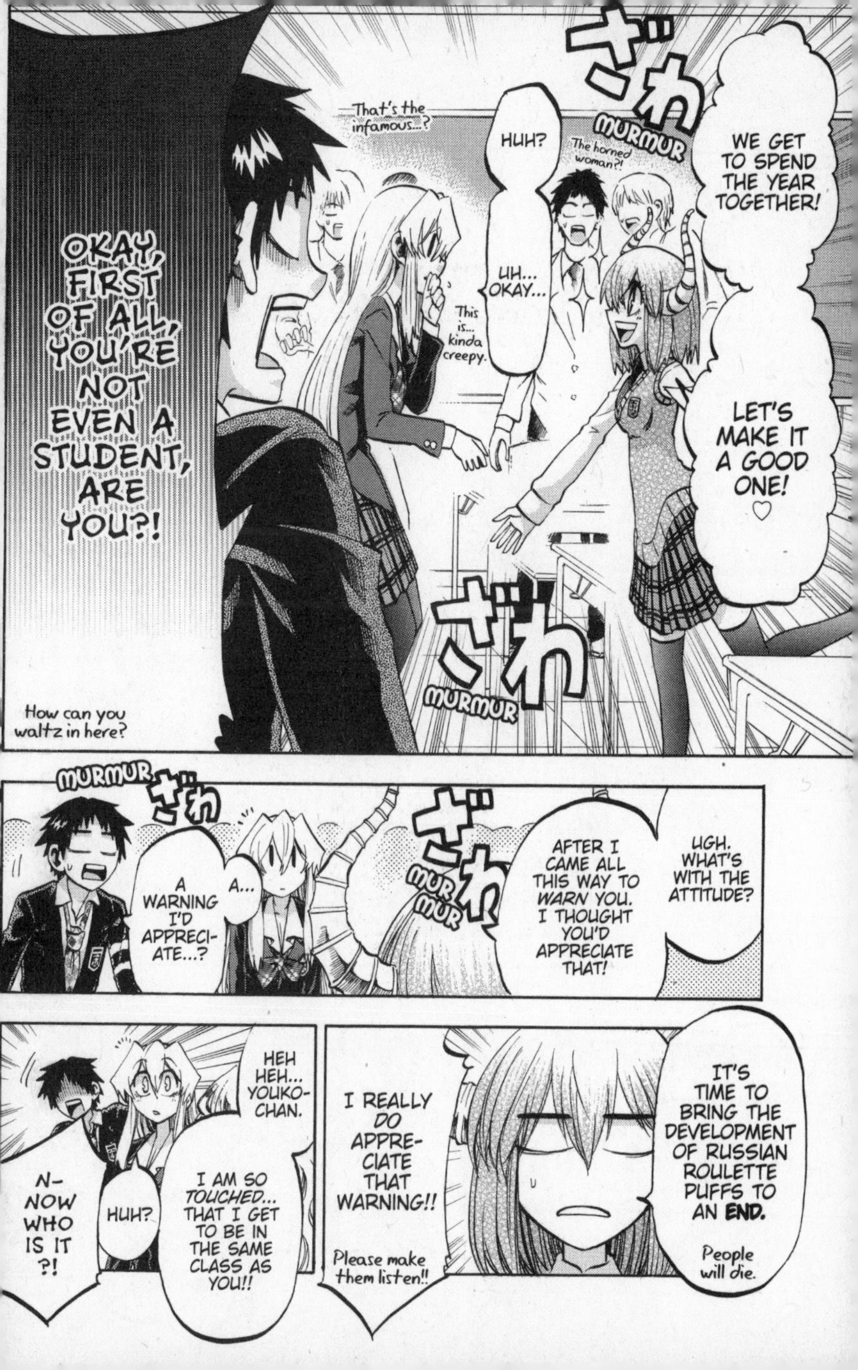
ざわ MURMUR
WE GET TO SPEND THE YEAR TOGETHER!
LET'S MAKE IT A GOOD ONE! ♡
HUH?
The horned woman?!
That's the infamous...?
UH... OKAY...
This is... kinda creepy.
OKAY, FIRST OF ALL, YOU'RE NOT EVEN A STUDENT, ARE YOU?!
ざわ MURMUR
How can you waltz in here?
UGH. WHAT'S WITH THE ATTITUDE?
AFTER I CAME ALL THIS WAY TO *WARN YOU.* I THOUGHT YOU'D APPRECIATE THAT!
ざわ MURMUR
A...
A WARNING I'D APPRECIATE...?
MURMUR ざわ
IT'S TIME TO BRING THE DEVELOPMENT OF RUSSIAN ROULETTE PUFFS TO AN **END.**
People will die.
I REALLY *DO* APPRECIATE THAT WARNING!!
Please make them listen!!
HEH HEH... YOUKO-CHAN.
I AM SO *TOUCHED*... THAT I GET TO BE IN THE SAME CLASS AS YOU!!
HUH?
N-NOW WHO IS IT?!

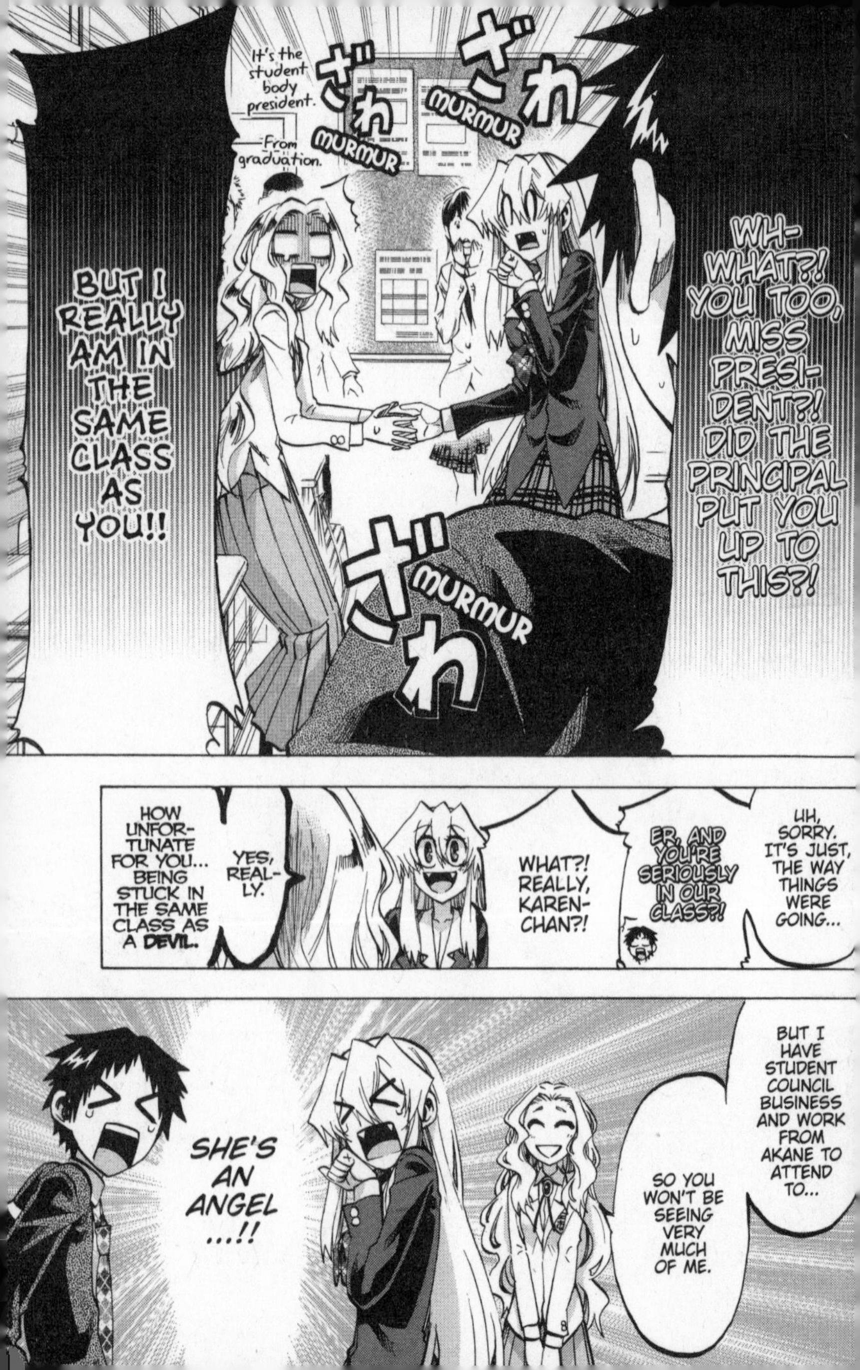
ざわ
MURMUR
ざわ
MURMUR
It's the student body president.
—From graduation.
WH-WHAT?! YOU TOO, MISS PRESIDENT?! DID THE PRINCIPAL PUT YOU UP TO THIS?!
BUT I REALLY AM IN THE SAME CLASS AS YOU!!
ざわ
MURMUR
UH, SORRY. IT'S JUST, THE WAY THINGS WERE GOING...
ER, AND YOU'RE SERIOUSLY IN OUR CLASS?!
WHAT?! REALLY, KAREN-CHAN?!
YES, REALLY.
HOW UNFORTUNATE FOR YOU... BEING STUCK IN THE SAME CLASS AS A **DEVIL.**
BUT I HAVE STUDENT COUNCIL BUSINESS AND WORK FROM AKANE TO ATTEND TO...
SO YOU WON'T BE SEEING VERY MUCH OF ME.
SHE'S AN ANGEL ...!!

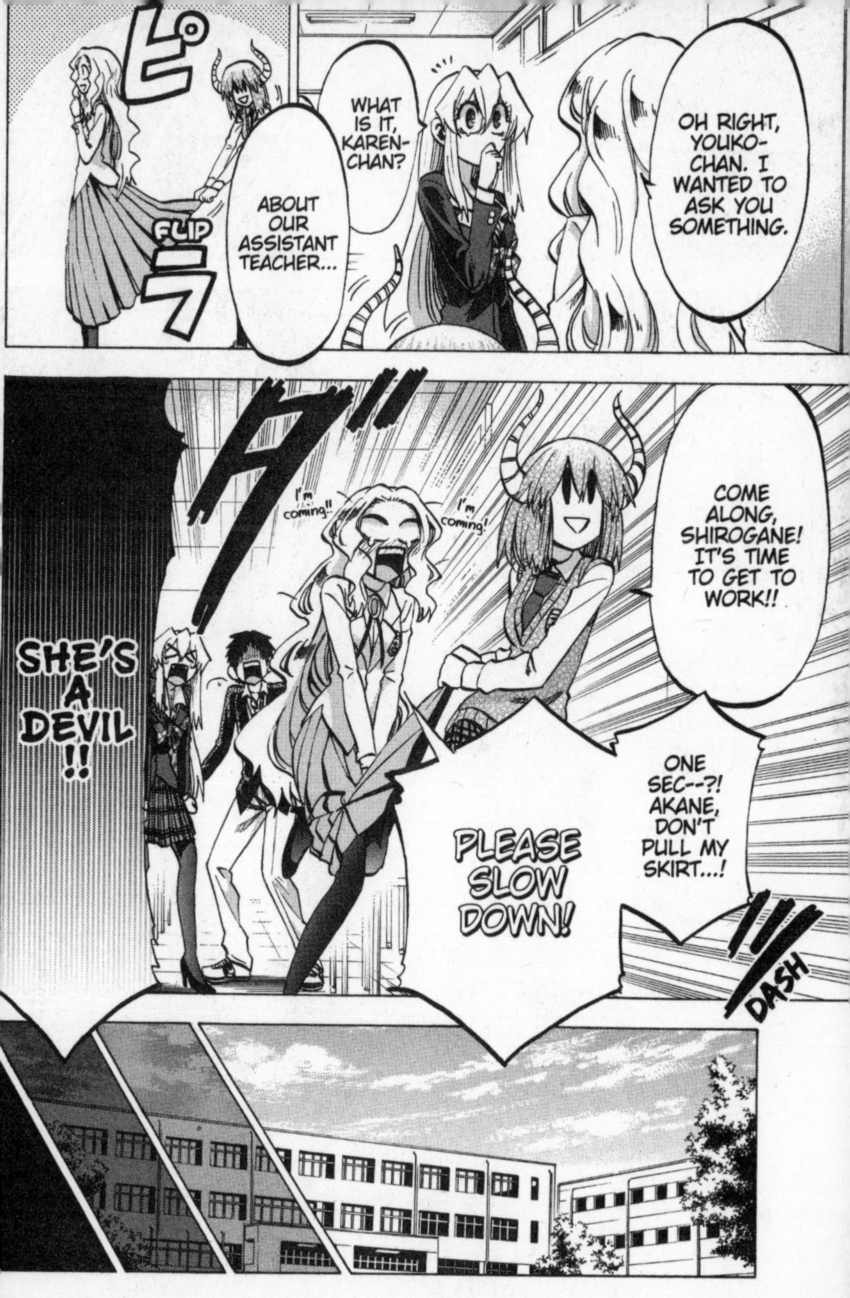
OH RIGHT, YOUKO-CHAN. I WANTED TO ASK YOU SOMETHING.
WHAT IS IT, KAREN-CHAN?
ABOUT OUR ASSISTANT TEACHER...
FLIP
COME ALONG, SHIROGANE! IT'S TIME TO GET TO WORK!!
I'm coming!
I'm coming!!
ONE SEC--?! AKANE, DON'T PULL MY SKIRT...!
DASH
PLEASE SLOW DOWN!
SHE'S A DEVIL!!

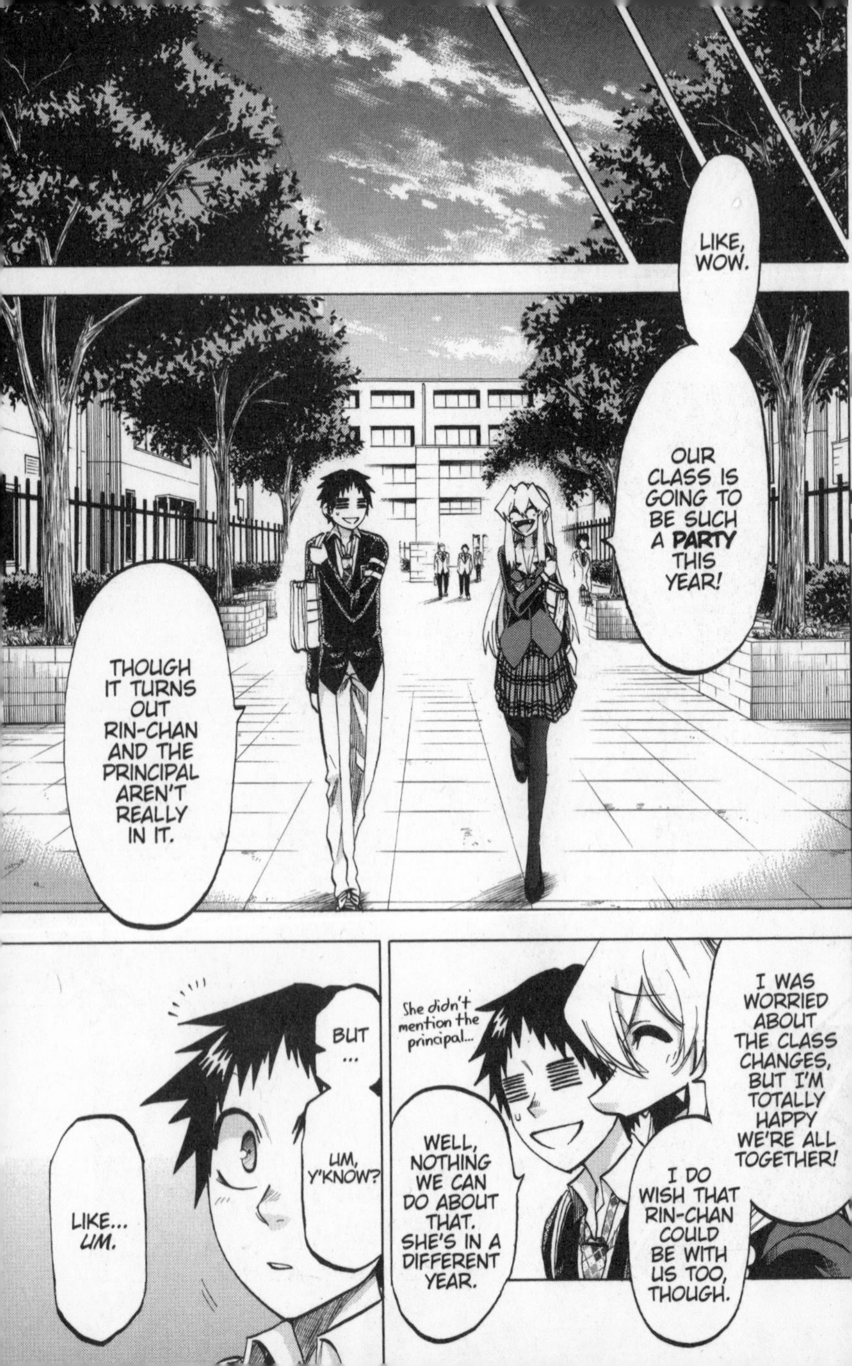
LIKE, WOW.
OUR CLASS IS GOING TO BE SUCH A **PARTY** THIS YEAR!
THOUGH IT TURNS OUT RIN-CHAN AND THE PRINCIPAL AREN'T REALLY IN IT.
I WAS WORRIED ABOUT THE CLASS CHANGES, BUT I'M TOTALLY HAPPY WE'RE ALL TOGETHER!
I DO WISH THAT RIN-CHAN COULD BE WITH US TOO, THOUGH.
She didn't mention the principal...
WELL, NOTHING WE CAN DO ABOUT THAT. SHE'S IN A DIFFERENT YEAR.
BUT ...
UM, Y'KNOW?
LIKE... UM.

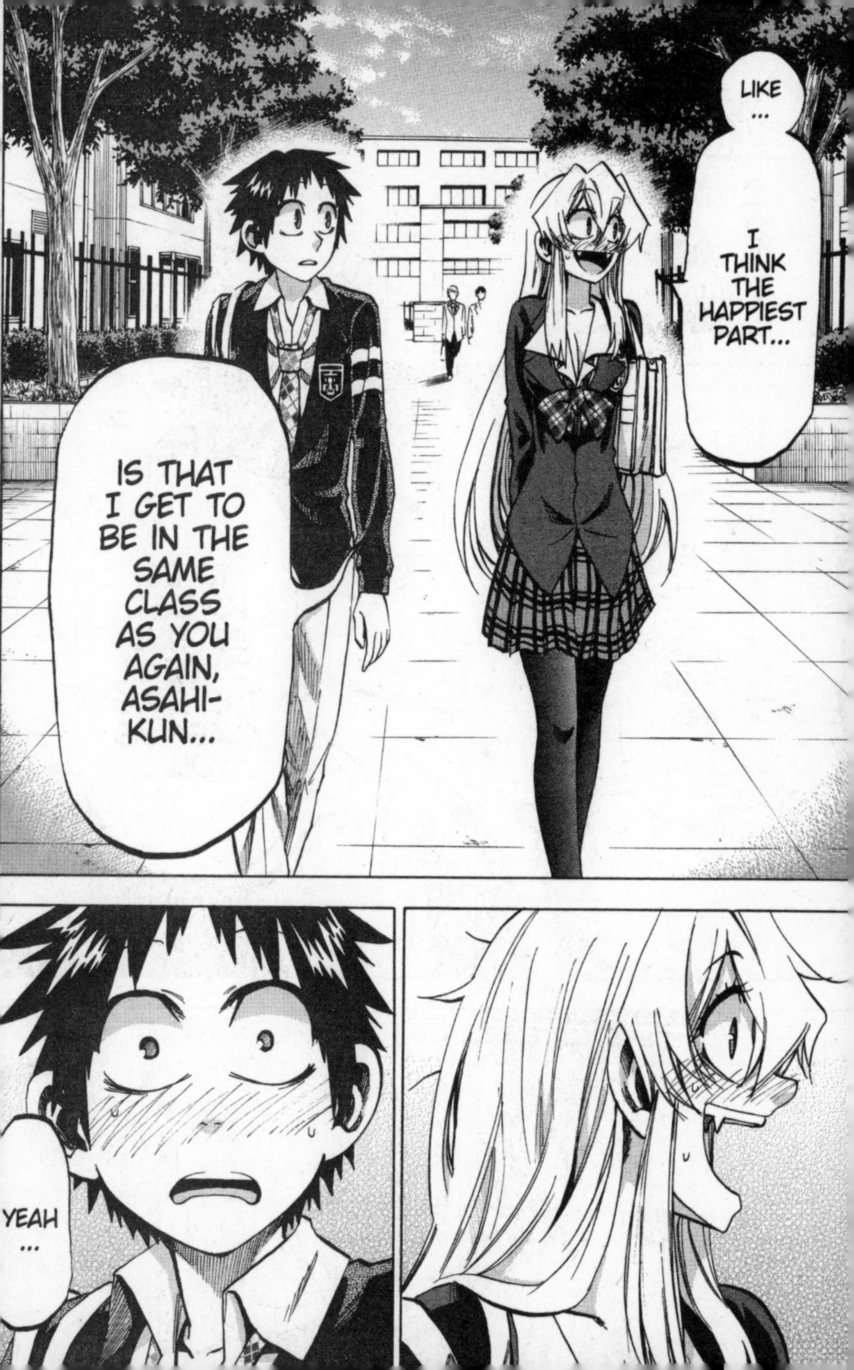
LIKE ...
I THINK THE HAPPIEST PART...
IS THAT I GET TO BE IN THE SAME CLASS AS YOU AGAIN, ASAHI-KUN...
YEAH ...

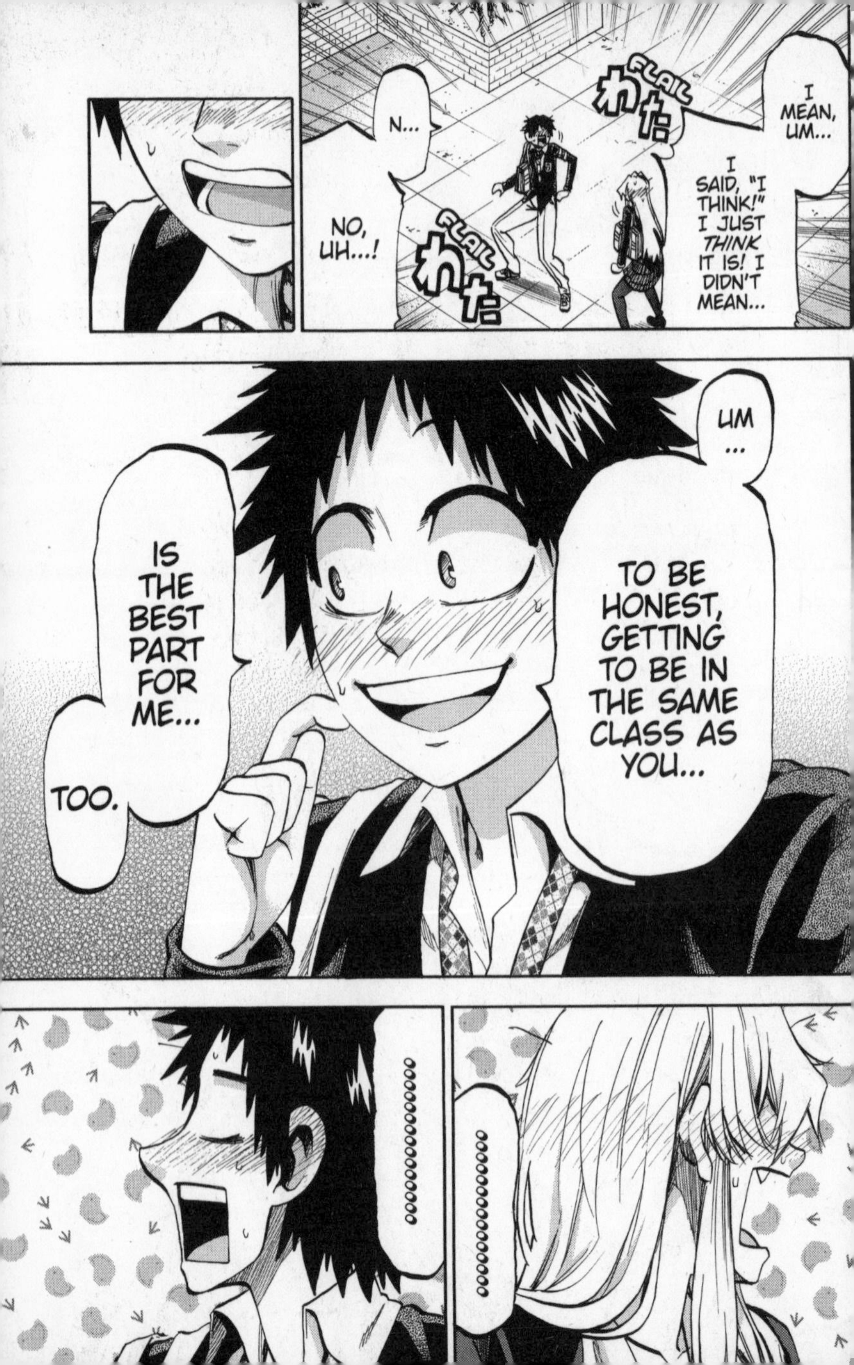
I MEAN, UM...
FLAIL
わた
I SAID, "I THINK!" I JUST *THINK* IT IS! I DIDN'T MEAN...
N...
NO, UH...!
FLAIL
わた
UM ...
TO BE HONEST, GETTING TO BE IN THE SAME CLASS AS YOU...
IS THE BEST PART FOR ME...
TOO.
....
....

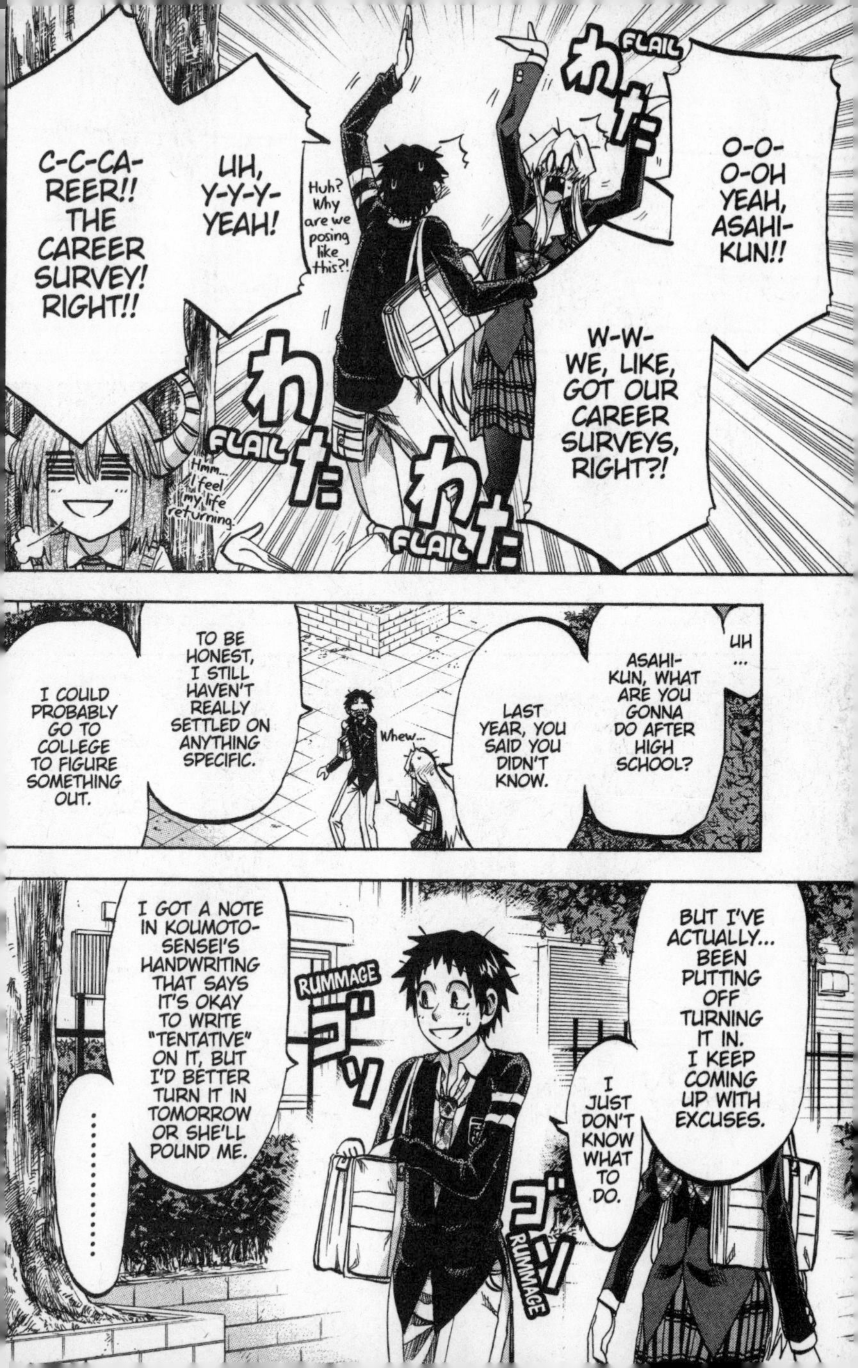
FLAIL
O-O-O-OH YEAH, ASAHI-KUN!!
W-W-WE, LIKE, GOT OUR CAREER SURVEYS, RIGHT?!
Huh? Why are we posing like this?!
UH, Y-Y-Y-YEAH!
C-C-CA-REER!! THE CAREER SURVEY! RIGHT!!
FLAIL
FLAIL
Hmm... I feel my life returning.
UH ...
ASAHI-KUN, WHAT ARE YOU GONNA DO AFTER HIGH SCHOOL?
LAST YEAR, YOU SAID YOU DIDN'T KNOW.
Whew...
TO BE HONEST, I STILL HAVEN'T REALLY SETTLED ON ANYTHING SPECIFIC.
I COULD PROBABLY GO TO COLLEGE TO FIGURE SOMETHING OUT.
BUT I'VE ACTUALLY... BEEN PUTTING OFF TURNING IT IN. I KEEP COMING UP WITH EXCUSES.
I JUST DON'T KNOW WHAT TO DO.
RUMMAGE
RUMMAGE
I GOT A NOTE IN KOUMOTO-SENSEI'S HANDWRITING THAT SAYS IT'S OKAY TO WRITE "TENTATIVE" ON IT, BUT I'D BETTER TURN IT IN TOMORROW OR SHE'LL POUND ME.
......

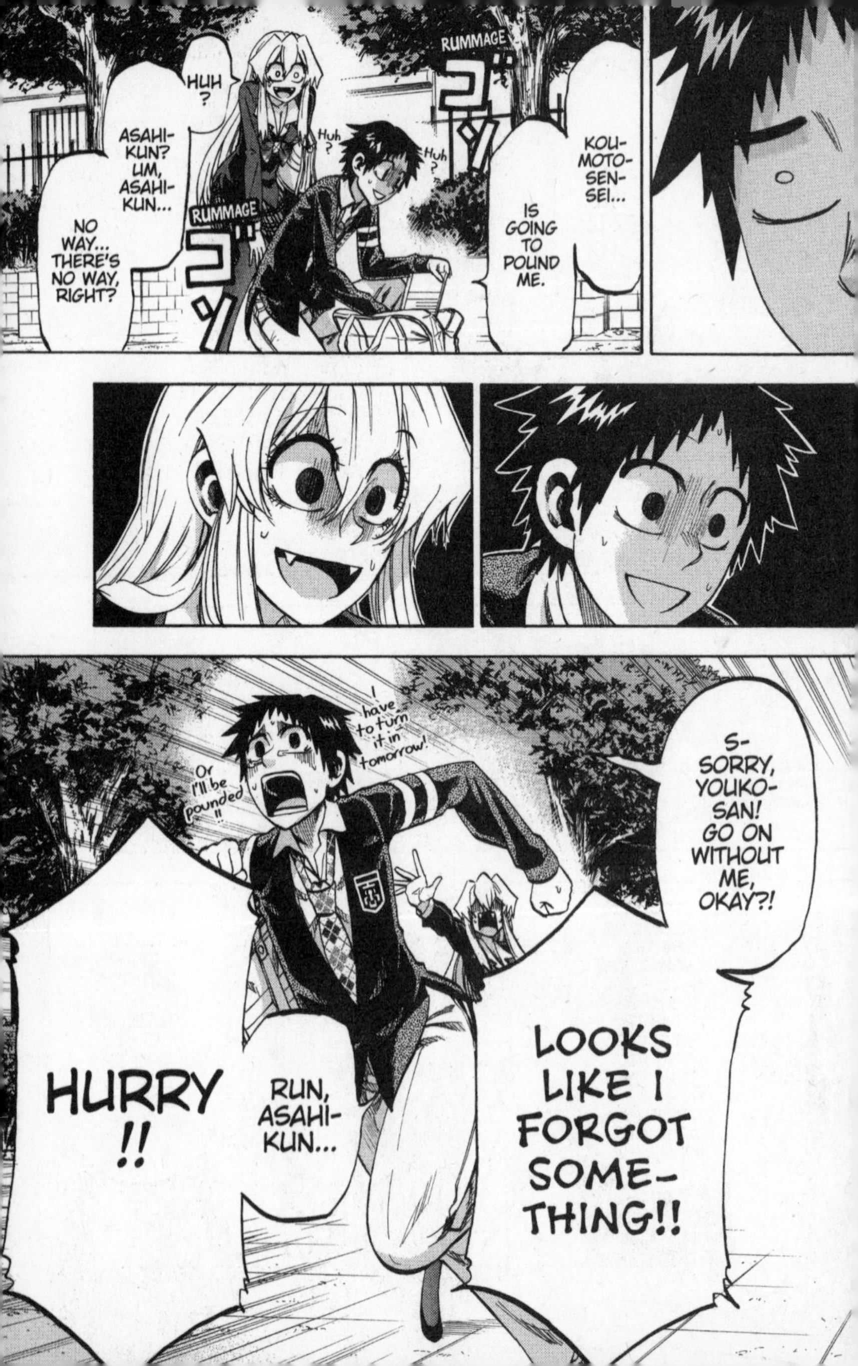
KOU-MOTO-SEN-SEI...
IS GOING TO POUND ME.
RUMMAGE
Huh?
Huh?
HUH?
ASAHI-KUN? UM, ASAHI-KUN...
RUMMAGE
NO WAY... THERE'S NO WAY, RIGHT?
S-SORRY, YOUKO-SAN! GO ON WITHOUT ME, OKAY?!
I have to turn it in tomorrow!
Or I'll be pounded!!
LOOKS LIKE I FORGOT SOME-THING!!
RUN, ASAHI-KUN...
HURRY!!

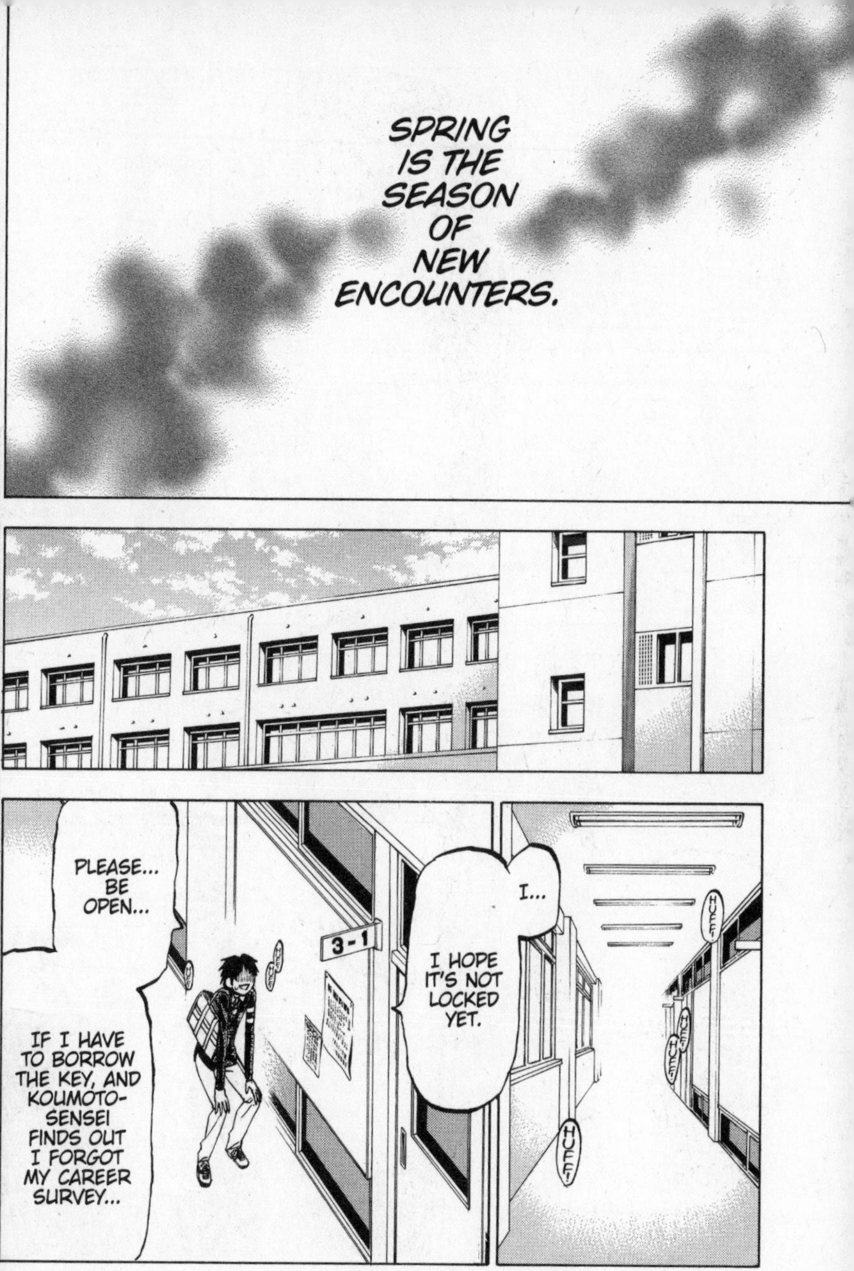
SPRING IS THE SEASON OF NEW ENCOUNTERS.
HUFF!
HUFF!
HUFF!
HUFF!
I...
I HOPE IT'S NOT LOCKED YET.
PLEASE... BE OPEN...
IF I HAVE TO BORROW THE KEY, AND KOUMOTO-SENSEI FINDS OUT I FORGOT MY CAREER SURVEY...
3-1

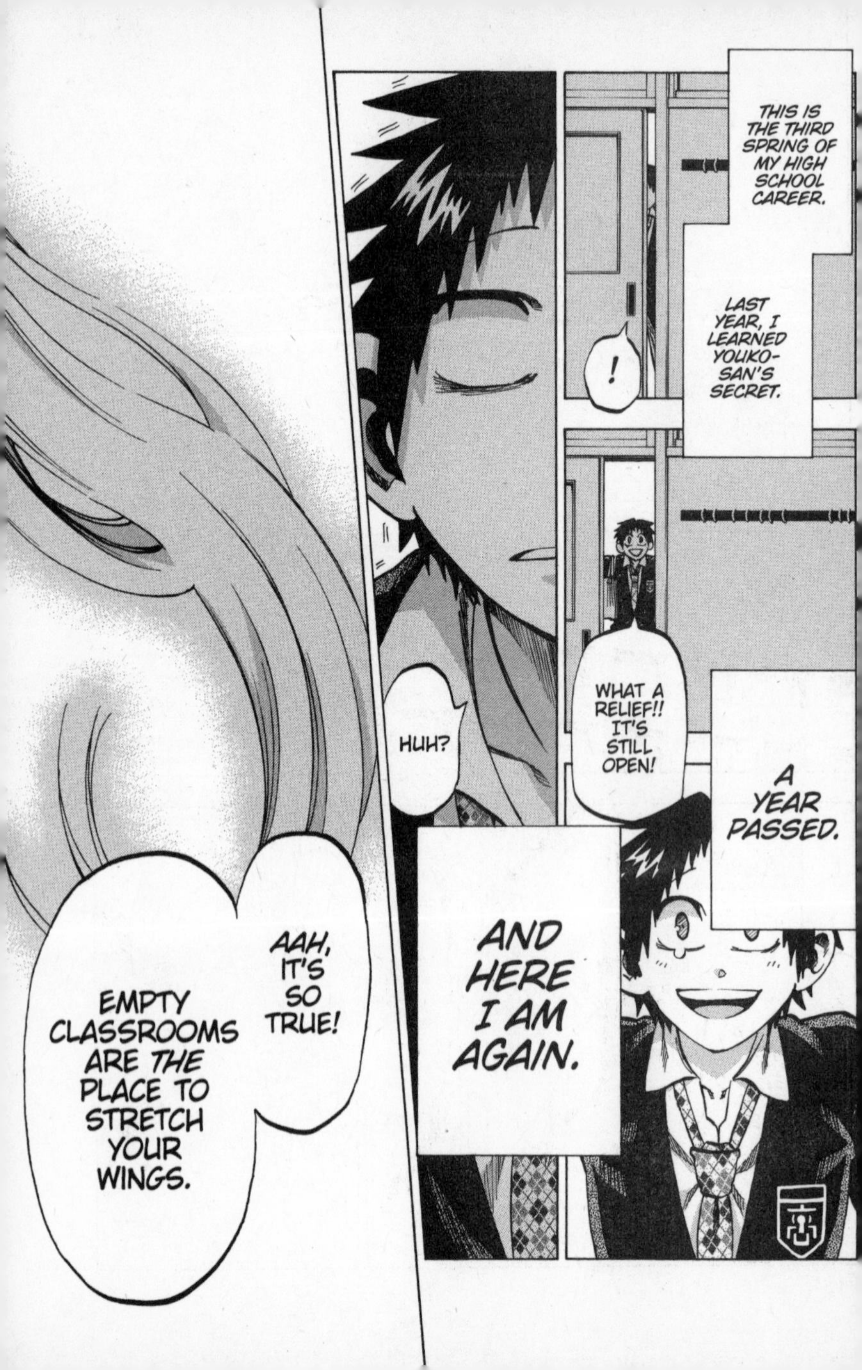
THIS IS THE THIRD SPRING OF MY HIGH SCHOOL CAREER.
LAST YEAR, I LEARNED YOUKO-SAN'S SECRET.
!
A YEAR PASSED.
WHAT A RELIEF!! IT'S STILL OPEN!
AND HERE I AM AGAIN.
HUH?
AAH, IT'S SO TRUE!
EMPTY CLASSROOMS ARE *THE* PLACE TO STRETCH YOUR WINGS.

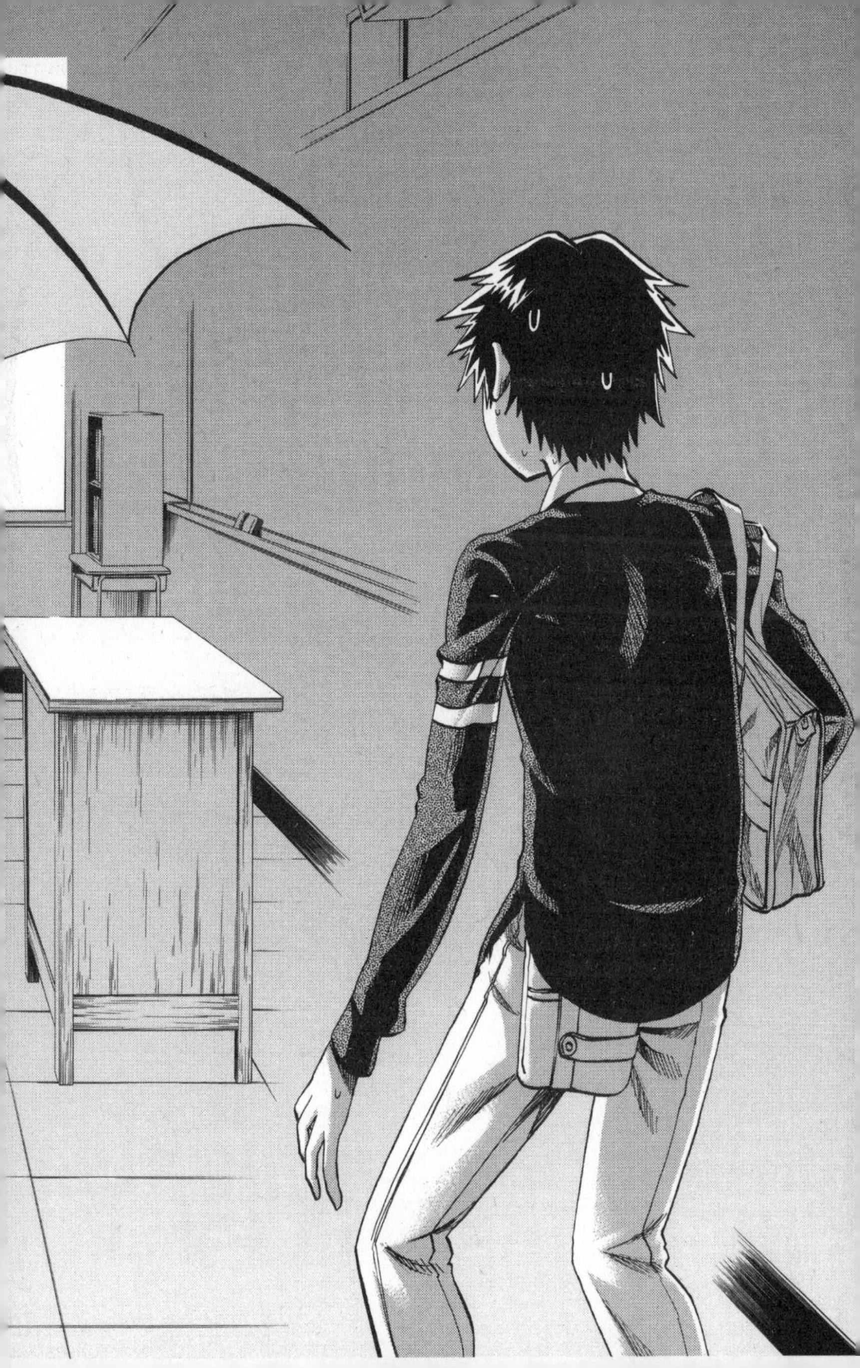

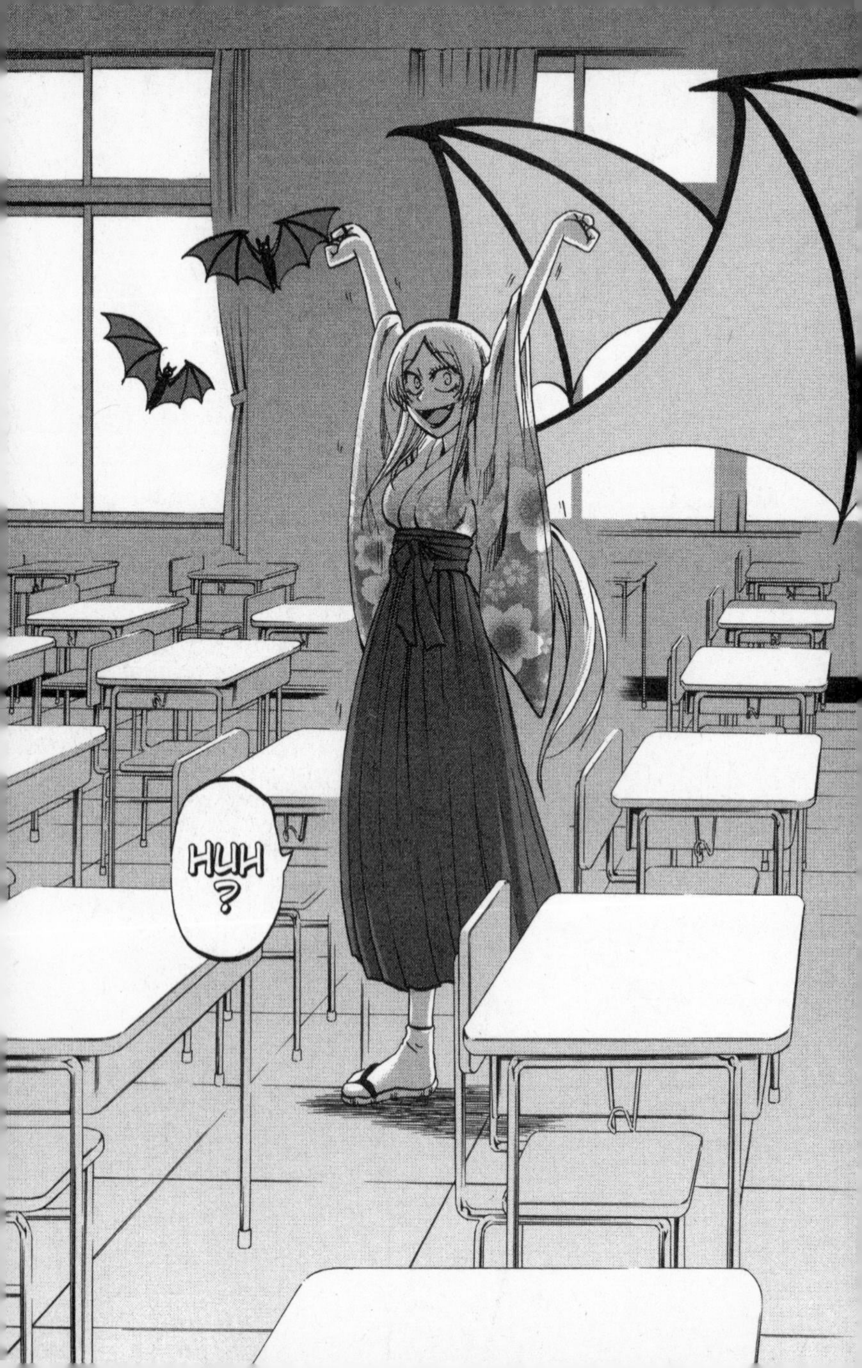
HUH?

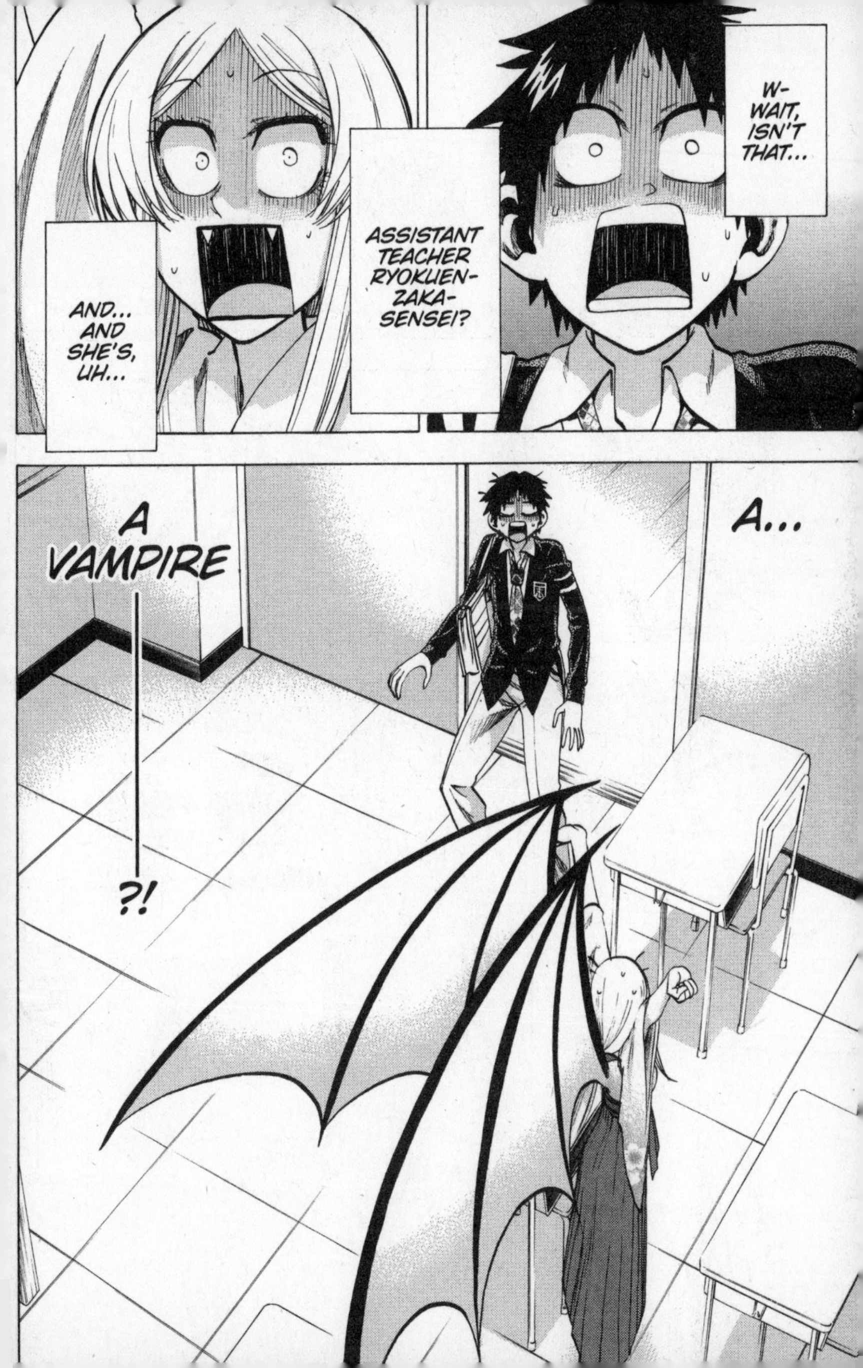
W-WAIT, ISN'T THAT...
ASSISTANT TEACHER RYOKUEN-ZAKA-SENSEI?
AND... AND SHE'S, UH...
A...
A VAMPIRE ?!

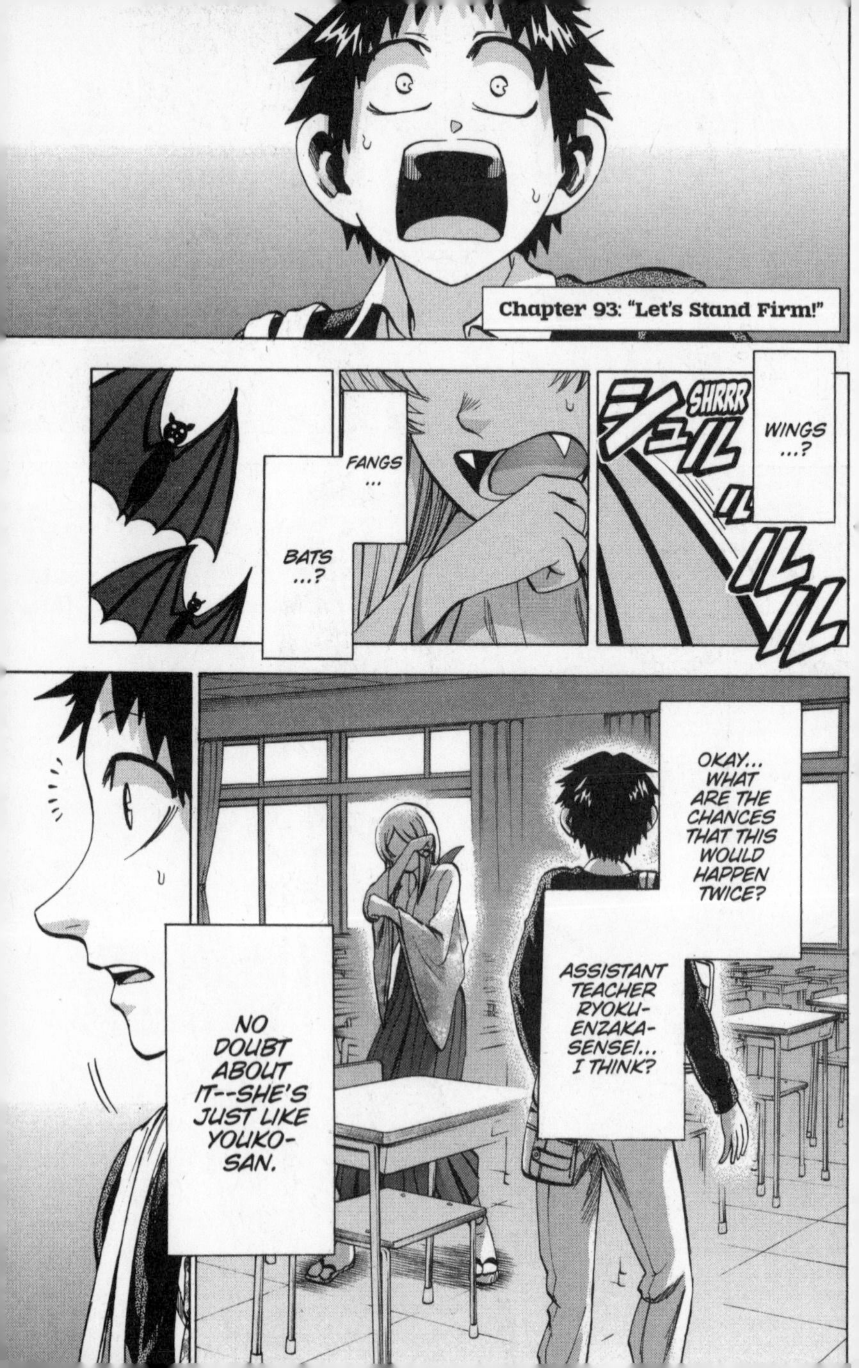
Chapter 93: "Let's Stand Firm!"
SHRRR
WINGS ...?
FANGS ...
BATS ...?
OKAY... WHAT ARE THE CHANCES THAT THIS WOULD HAPPEN TWICE?
ASSISTANT TEACHER RYOKU-ENZAKA-SENSEI... I THINK?
NO DOUBT ABOUT IT--SHE'S JUST LIKE YOUKO-SAN.

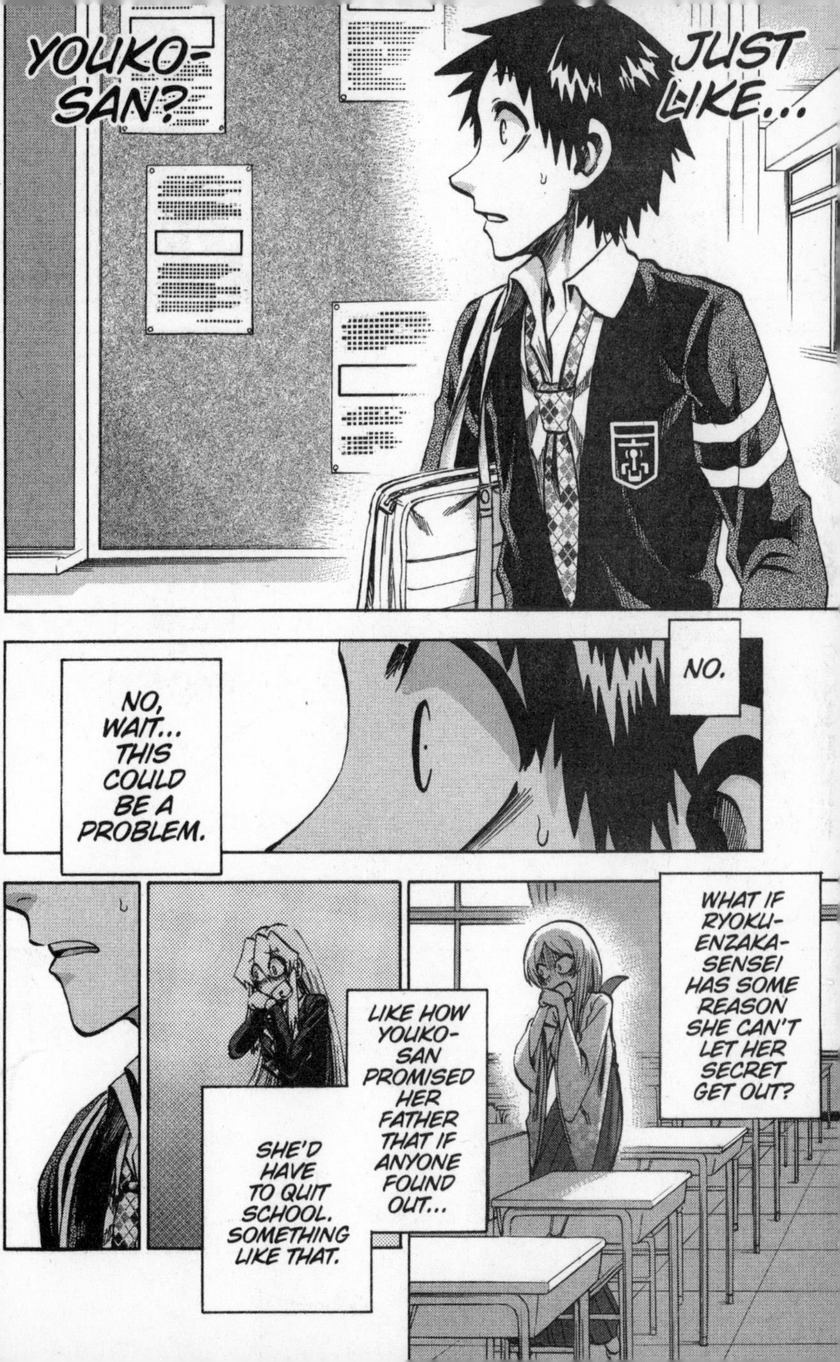
JUST LIKE...
YOUKO-SAN?
NO.
NO, WAIT... THIS COULD BE A PROBLEM.
WHAT IF RYOKU-ENZAKA-SENSEI HAS SOME REASON SHE CAN'T LET HER SECRET GET OUT?
LIKE HOW YOUKO-SAN PROMISED HER FATHER THAT IF ANYONE FOUND OUT...
SHE'D HAVE TO QUIT SCHOOL. SOMETHING LIKE THAT.

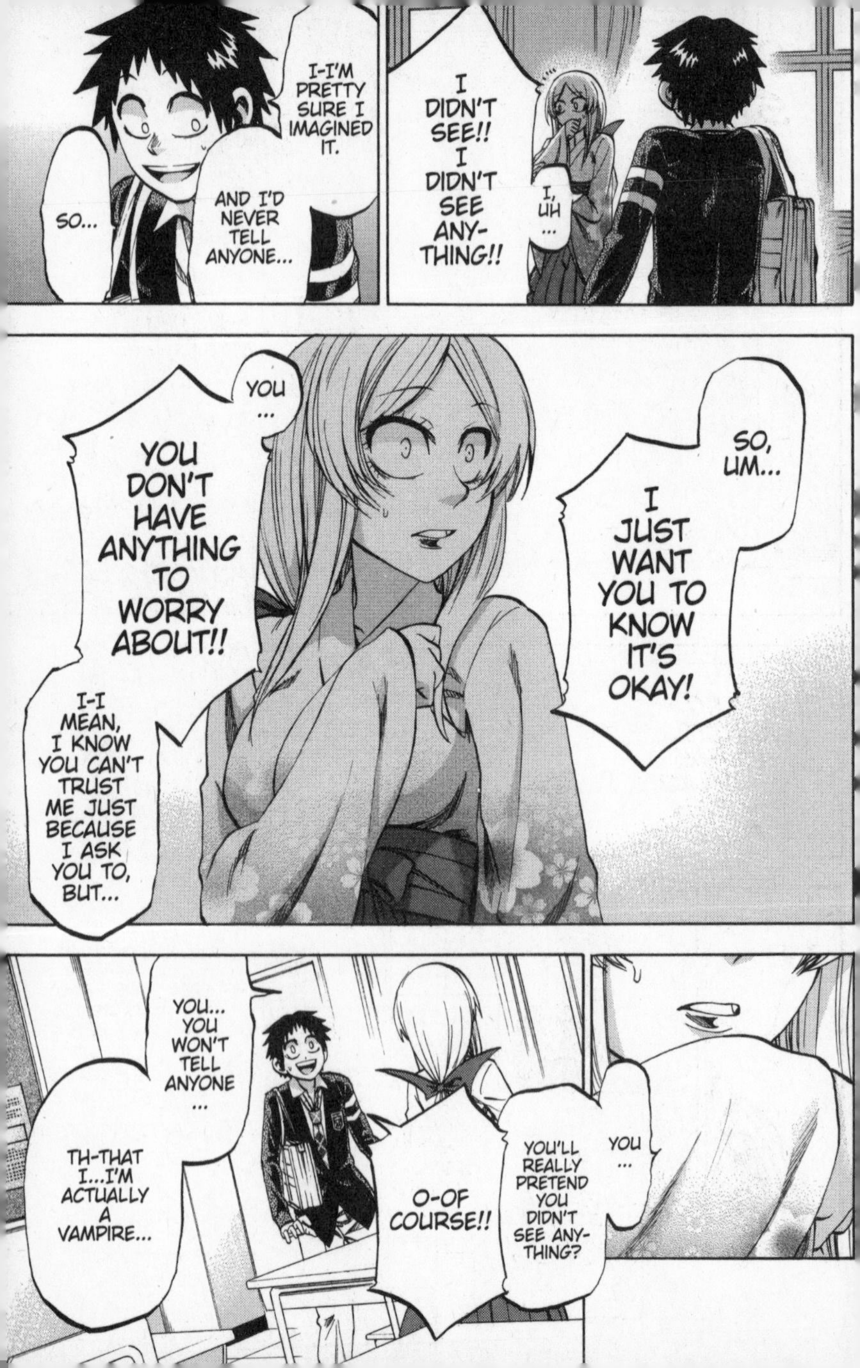
I, UH ...
I DIDN'T SEE!! I DIDN'T SEE ANY-THING!!
I-I'M PRETTY SURE I IMAGINED IT.
AND I'D NEVER TELL ANYONE...
SO...
SO, UM...
I JUST WANT YOU TO KNOW IT'S OKAY!
YOU ...
YOU DON'T HAVE ANYTHING TO WORRY ABOUT!!
I-I MEAN, I KNOW YOU CAN'T TRUST ME JUST BECAUSE I ASK YOU TO, BUT...
YOU ...
YOU'LL REALLY PRETEND YOU DIDN'T SEE ANY-THING?
YOU... YOU WON'T TELL ANYONE ...
TH-THAT I...I'M ACTUALLY A VAMPIRE...
O-OF COURSE!!

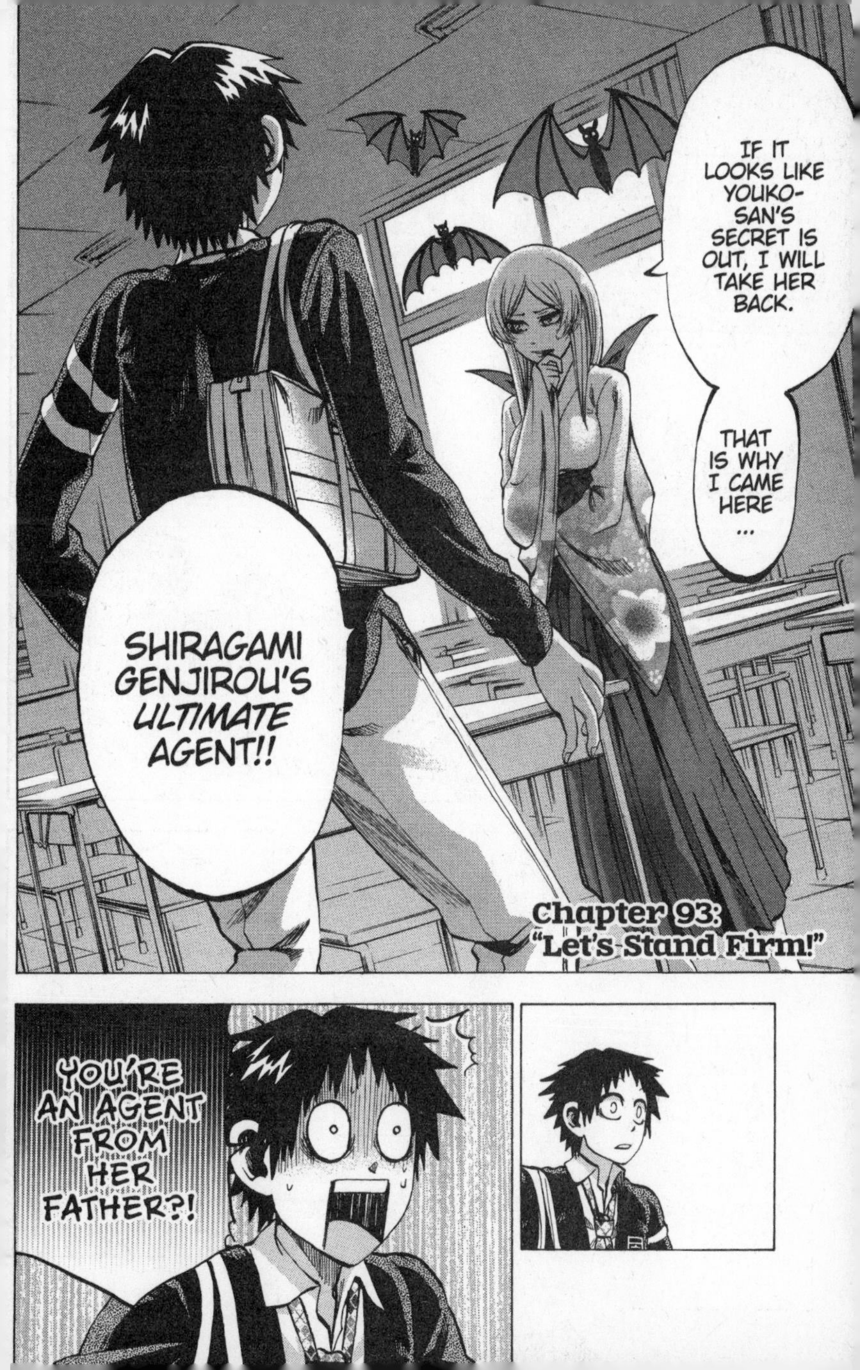
IF IT LOOKS LIKE YOUKO-SAN'S SECRET IS OUT, I WILL TAKE HER BACK.
THAT IS WHY I CAME HERE ...
SHIRAGAMI GENJIROU'S *ULTIMATE* AGENT!!
Chapter 93: "Let's Stand Firm!"
YOU'RE AN AGENT FROM HER FATHER?!

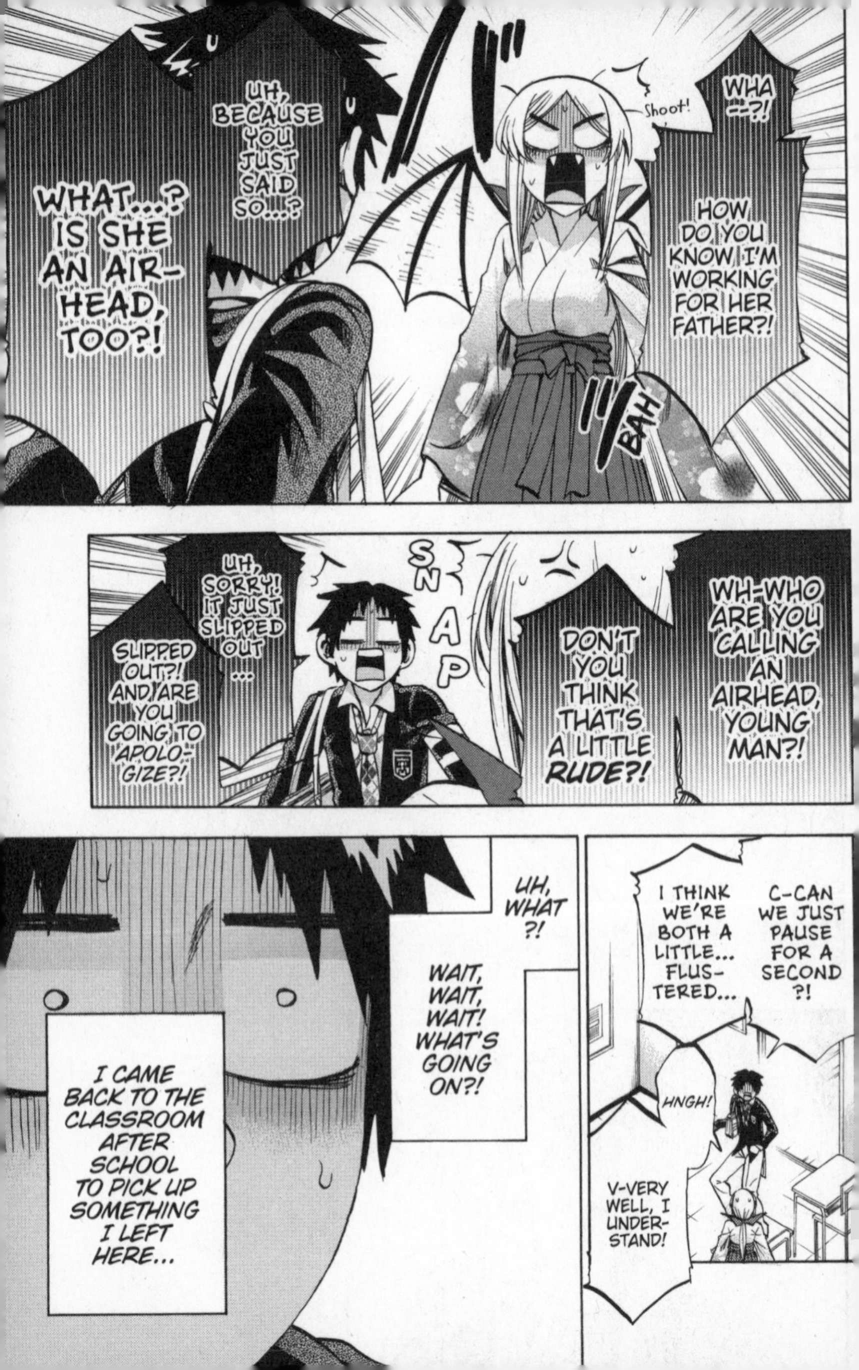
WHA--?!
Shoot!
HOW DO YOU KNOW I'M WORKING FOR HER FATHER?!
BAH
UH, BECAUSE YOU JUST SAID SO...?
WHAT...? IS SHE AN AIR-HEAD, TOO?!
WH-WHO ARE YOU CALLING AN AIRHEAD, YOUNG MAN?!
DON'T YOU THINK THAT'S A LITTLE RUDE?!
SNAP
UH, SORRY! IT JUST SLIPPED OUT...
SLIPPED OUT?! AND ARE YOU GOING TO APOLO-GIZE?!
C-CAN WE JUST PAUSE FOR A SECOND?!
I THINK WE'RE BOTH A LITTLE... FLUS-TERED...
HNGH!
V-VERY WELL, I UNDER-STAND!
UH, WHAT?!
WAIT, WAIT, WAIT! WHAT'S GOING ON?!
I CAME BACK TO THE CLASSROOM AFTER SCHOOL TO PICK UP SOMETHING I LEFT HERE...

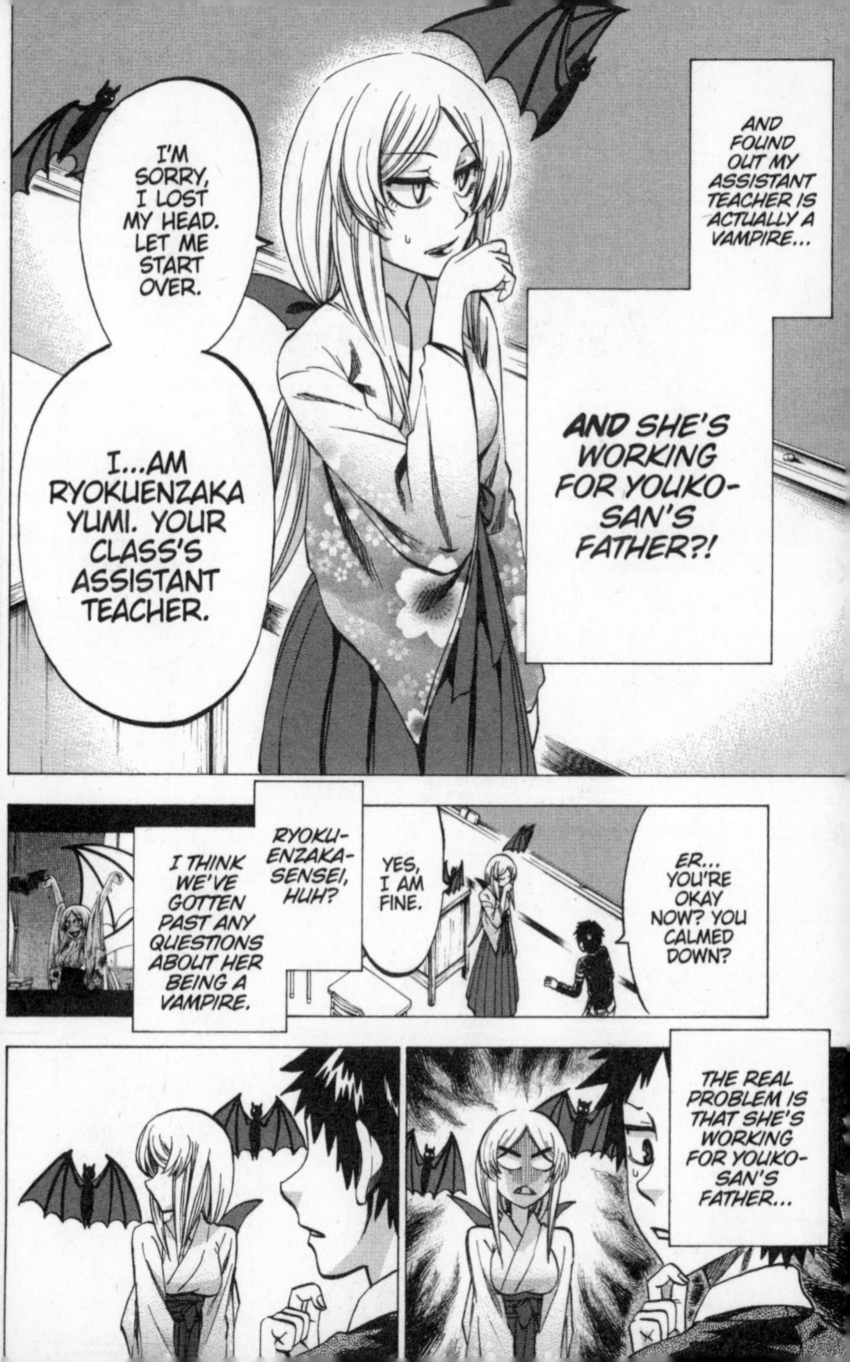
AND FOUND OUT MY ASSISTANT TEACHER IS ACTUALLY A VAMPIRE...
AND SHE'S WORKING FOR YOUKO-SAN'S FATHER?!
I'M SORRY, I LOST MY HEAD. LET ME START OVER.
I...AM RYOKUENZAKA YUMI. YOUR CLASS'S ASSISTANT TEACHER.
ER... YOU'RE OKAY NOW? YOU CALMED DOWN?
YES, I AM FINE.
RYOKU-ENZAKA-SENSEI, HUH?
I THINK WE'VE GOTTEN PAST ANY QUESTIONS ABOUT HER BEING A VAMPIRE.
THE REAL PROBLEM IS THAT SHE'S WORKING FOR YOUKO-SAN'S FATHER...

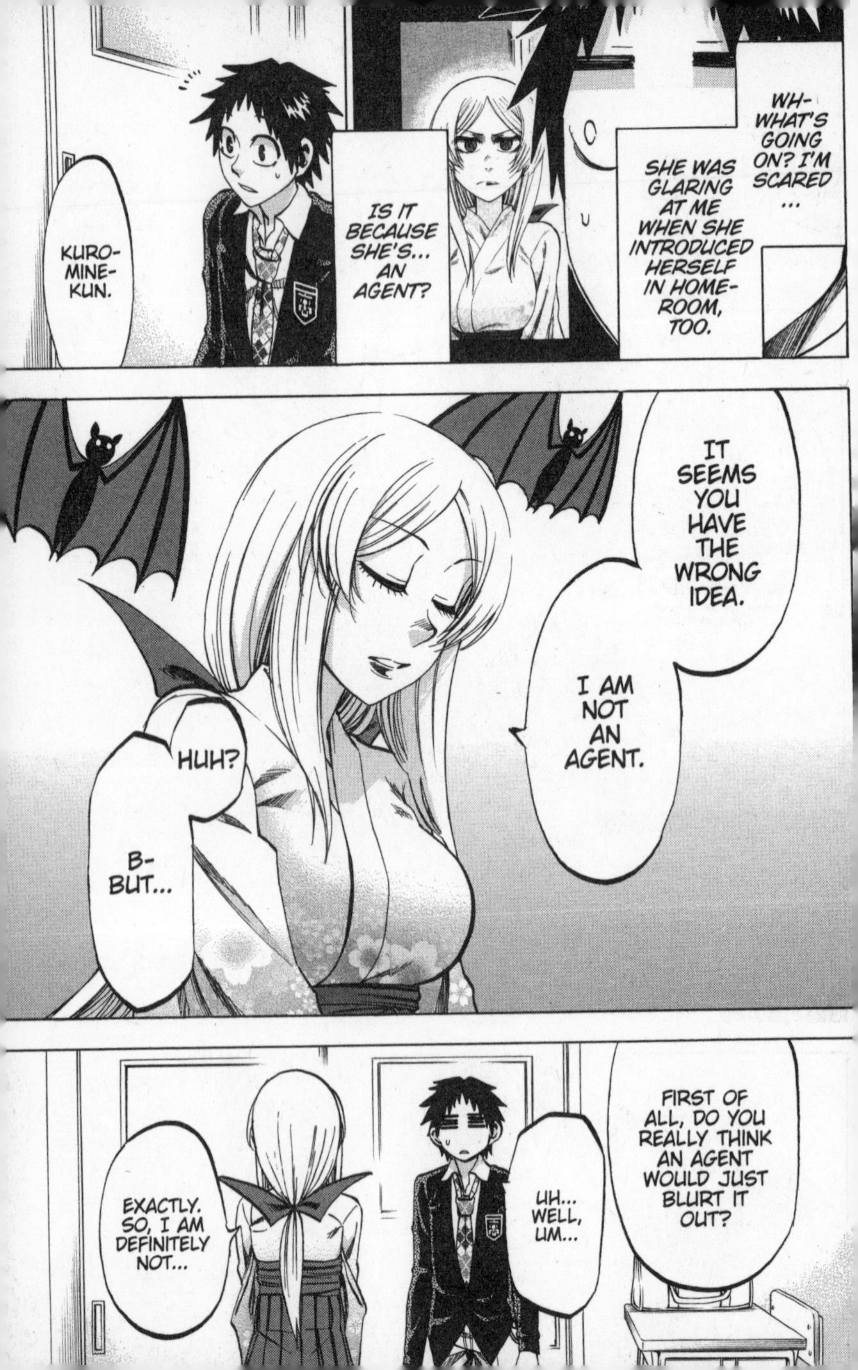
WH-WHAT'S GOING ON? I'M SCARED...
SHE WAS GLARING AT ME WHEN SHE INTRODUCED HERSELF IN HOMEROOM, TOO.
IS IT BECAUSE SHE'S... AN AGENT?
KURO-MINE-KUN.
IT SEEMS YOU HAVE THE WRONG IDEA.
I AM NOT AN AGENT.
HUH?
B-BUT...
FIRST OF ALL, DO YOU REALLY THINK AN AGENT WOULD JUST BLURT IT OUT?
UH... WELL, UM...
EXACTLY. SO, I AM DEFINITELY NOT...

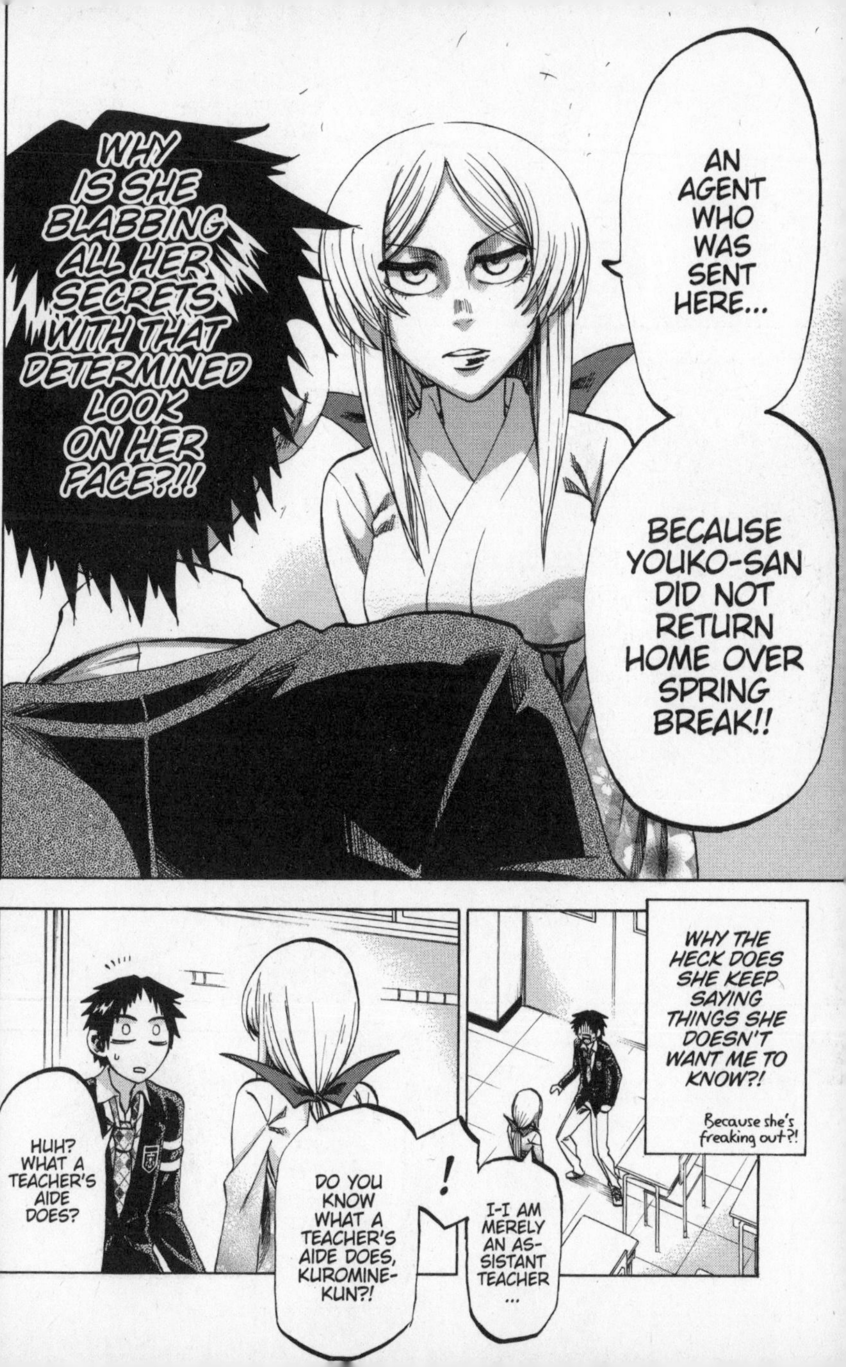
AN AGENT WHO WAS SENT HERE...
BECAUSE YOUKO-SAN DID NOT RETURN HOME OVER SPRING BREAK!!
WHY IS SHE BLABBING ALL HER SECRETS WITH THAT DETERMINED LOOK ON HER FACE?!!
WHY THE HECK DOES SHE KEEP SAYING THINGS SHE DOESN'T WANT ME TO KNOW?!
Because she's freaking out?!
I-I AM MERELY AN AS-SISTANT TEACHER ...
!
DO YOU KNOW WHAT A TEACHER'S AIDE DOES, KUROMINE-KUN?!
HUH? WHAT A TEACHER'S AIDE DOES?

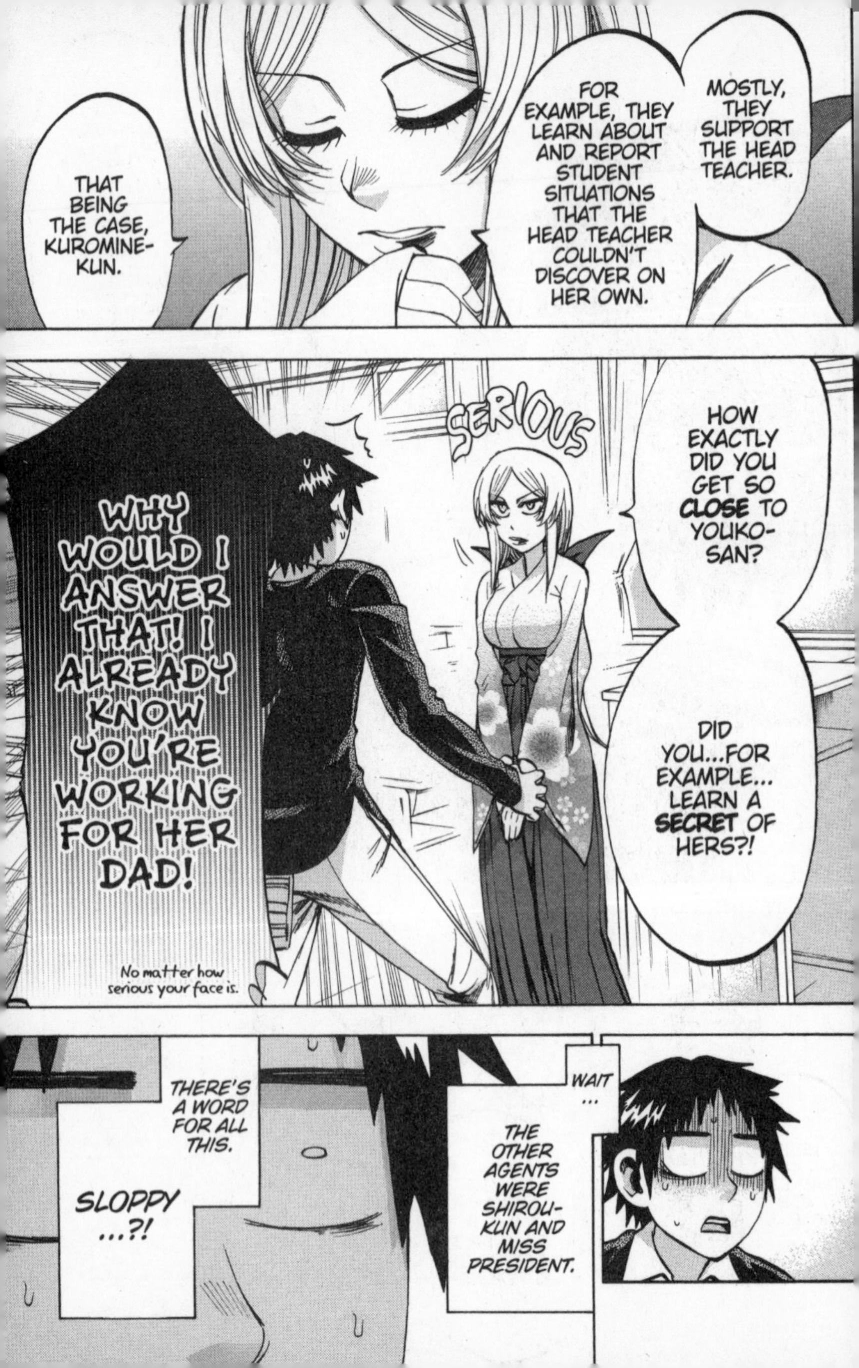
MOSTLY, THEY SUPPORT THE HEAD TEACHER.
FOR EXAMPLE, THEY LEARN ABOUT AND REPORT STUDENT SITUATIONS THAT THE HEAD TEACHER COULDN'T DISCOVER ON HER OWN.
THAT BEING THE CASE, KUROMINE-KUN.
HOW EXACTLY DID YOU GET SO **CLOSE** TO YOUKO-SAN?
DID YOU...FOR EXAMPLE... LEARN A **SECRET** OF HERS?!
SERIOUS
WHY WOULD I ANSWER THAT! I ALREADY KNOW YOU'RE WORKING FOR HER DAD!
No matter how serious your face is.
WAIT...
THE OTHER AGENTS WERE SHIROU-KUN AND MISS PRESIDENT.
THERE'S A WORD FOR ALL THIS.
SLOPPY...?!

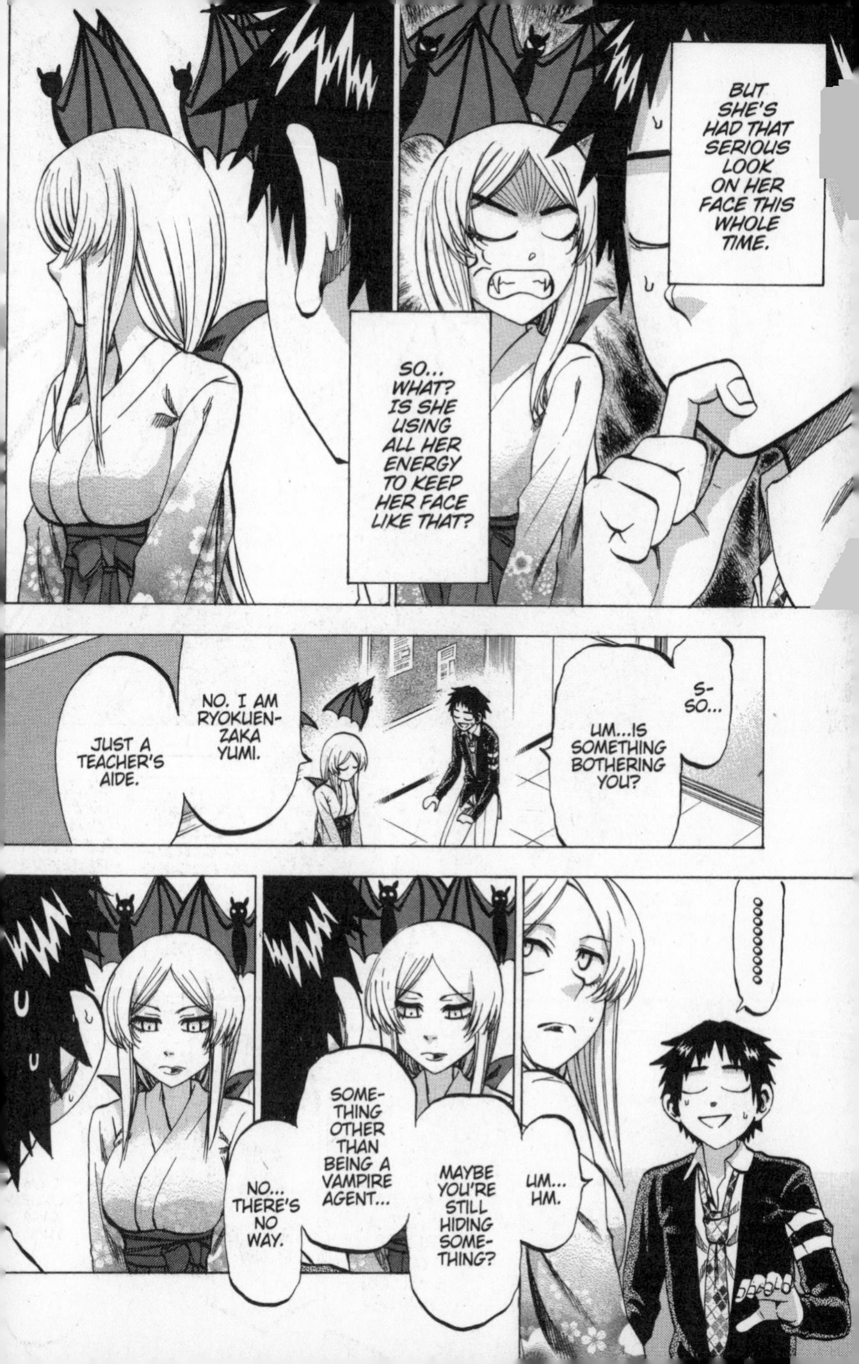
BUT SHE'S HAD THAT SERIOUS LOOK ON HER FACE THIS WHOLE TIME.
SO... WHAT? IS SHE USING ALL HER ENERGY TO KEEP HER FACE LIKE THAT?
S-SO...
UM...IS SOMETHING BOTHERING YOU?
NO. I AM RYOKUEN-ZAKA YUMI.
JUST A TEACHER'S AIDE.
UM... HM.
MAYBE YOU'RE STILL HIDING SOME-THING?
SOME-THING OTHER THAN BEING A VAMPIRE AGENT...
NO... THERE'S NO WAY.

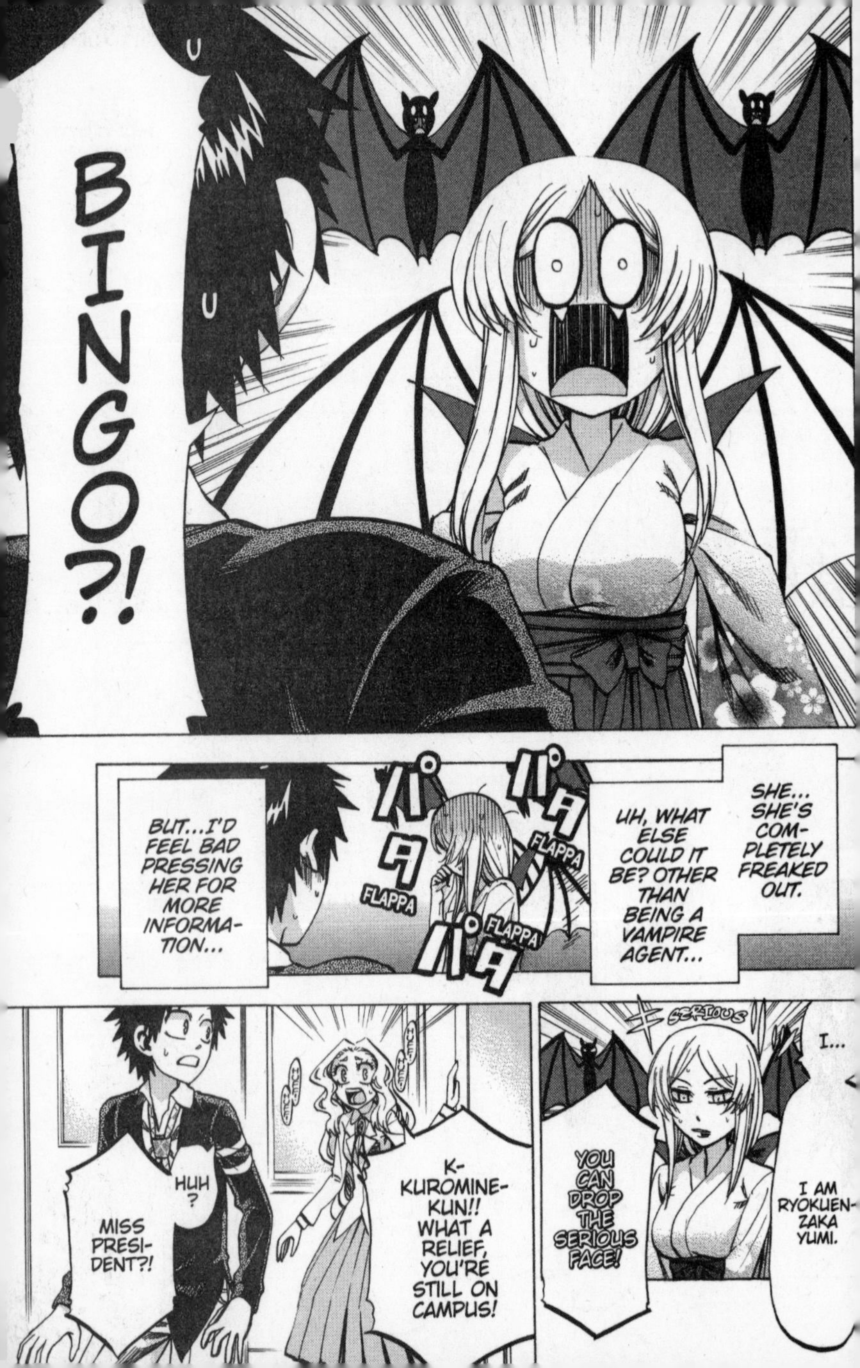
BINGO?!
SHE... SHE'S COMPLETELY FREAKED OUT.
UH, WHAT ELSE COULD IT BE? OTHER THAN BEING A VAMPIRE AGENT...
FLAPPA
FLAPPA
FLAPPA
BUT...I'D FEEL BAD PRESSING HER FOR MORE INFORMATION...
SERIOUS
I...
I AM RYOKUENZAKA YUMI.
YOU CAN DROP THE SERIOUS FACE!
K-KUROMINE-KUN!! WHAT A RELIEF, YOU'RE STILL ON CAMPUS!
HUH?
MISS PRESIDENT?!

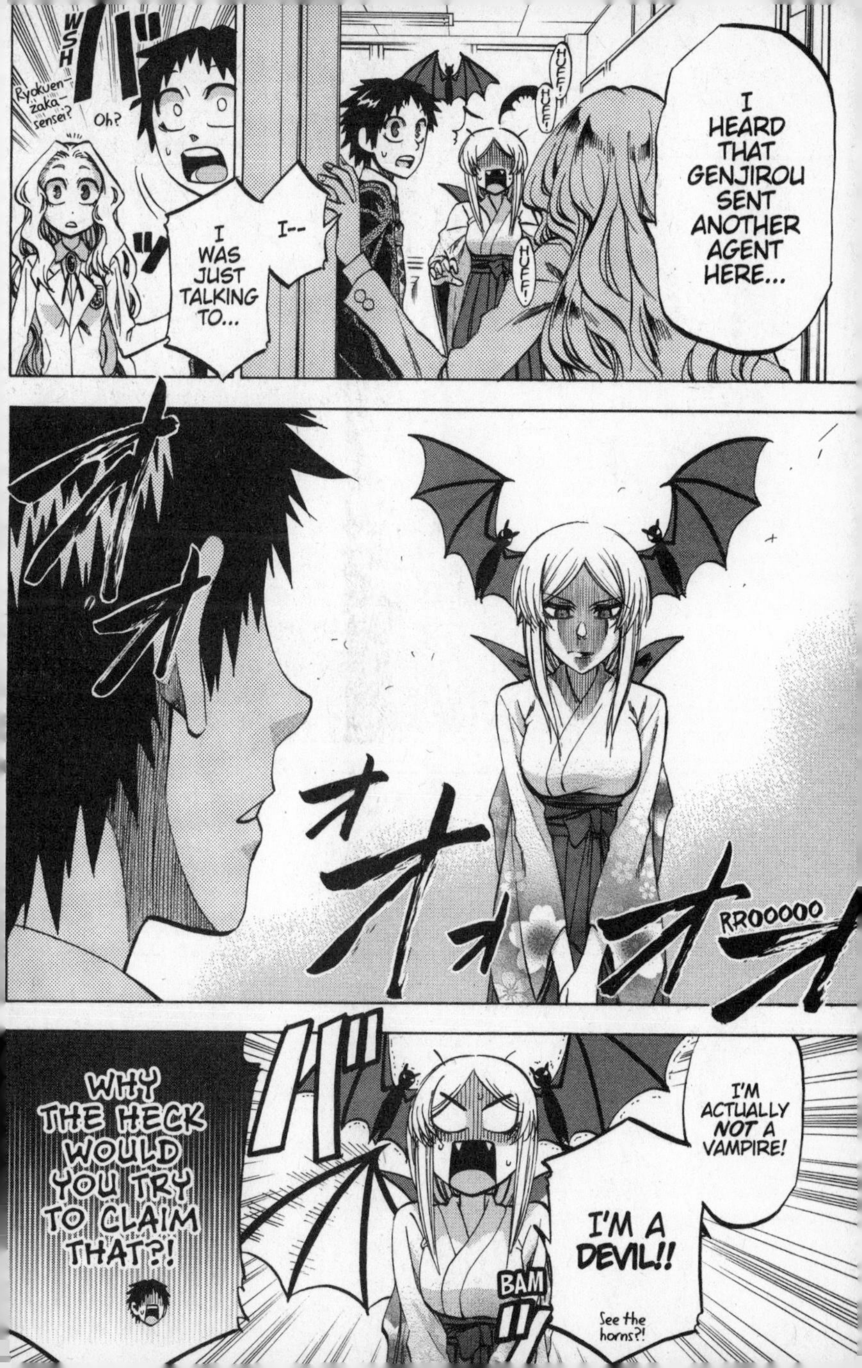
I HEARD THAT GENJIROU SENT ANOTHER AGENT HERE...
HUFF! HUFF!
HUFF!
I--
I WAS JUST TALKING TO...
WSH
Oh?
Ryokuen-zaka-sensei?
RROOOOO
I'M ACTUALLY NOT A VAMPIRE!
I'M A DEVIL!!
BAM
See the horns?!
WHY THE HECK WOULD YOU TRY TO CLAIM THAT?!

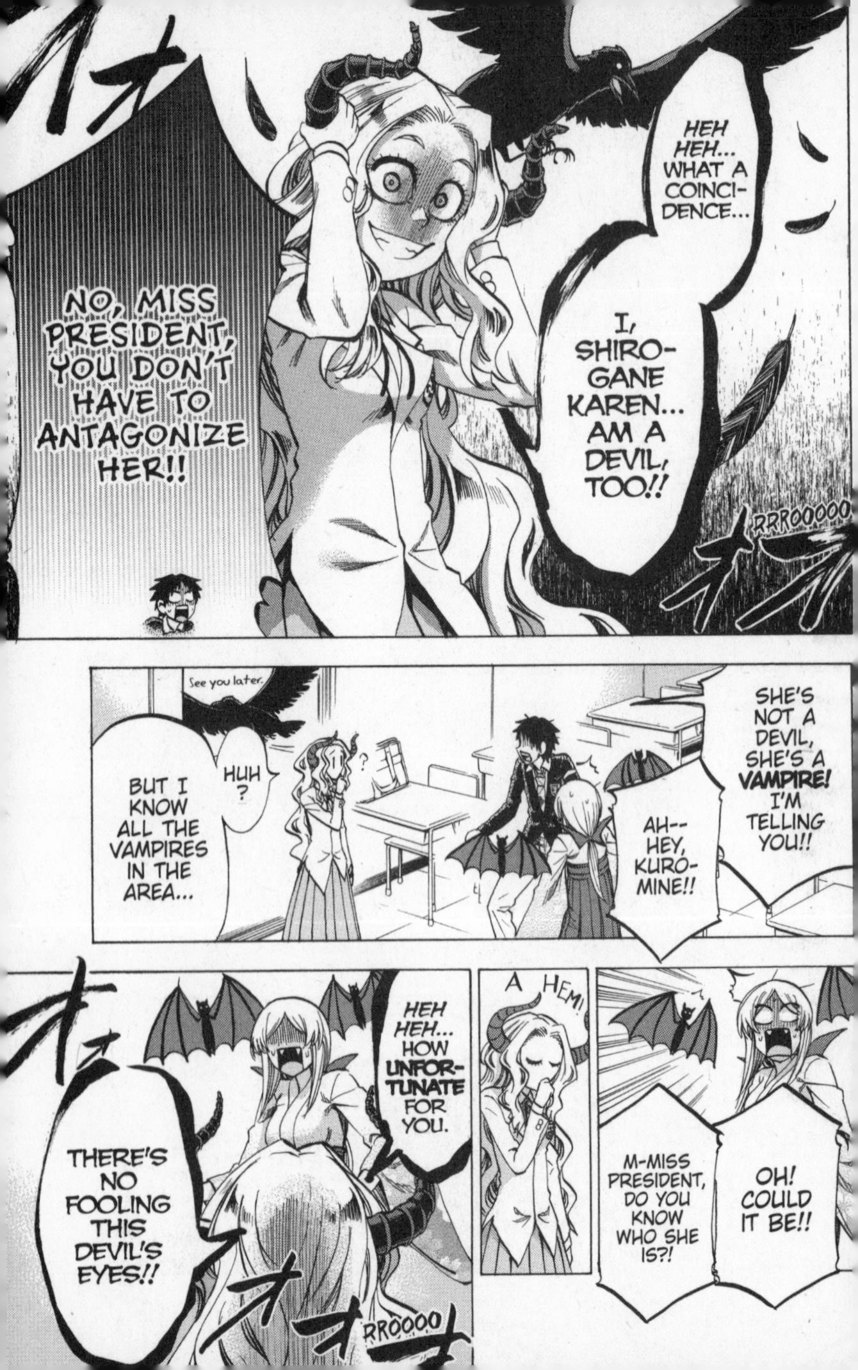
HEH HEH... WHAT A COINCIDENCE...
I, SHIROGANE KAREN... AM A DEVIL, TOO!!
RRROOOOO
NO, MISS PRESIDENT, YOU DON'T HAVE TO ANTAGONIZE HER!!
SHE'S NOT A DEVIL, SHE'S A **VAMPIRE!** I'M TELLING YOU!!
AH-- HEY, KUROMINE!!
HUH?
BUT I KNOW ALL THE VAMPIRES IN THE AREA...
See you later.
OH! COULD IT BE!!
M-MISS PRESIDENT, DO YOU KNOW WHO SHE IS?!
A HEM!
HEH HEH... HOW **UNFORTUNATE** FOR YOU.
THERE'S NO FOOLING THIS DEVIL'S EYES!!
RROOOO

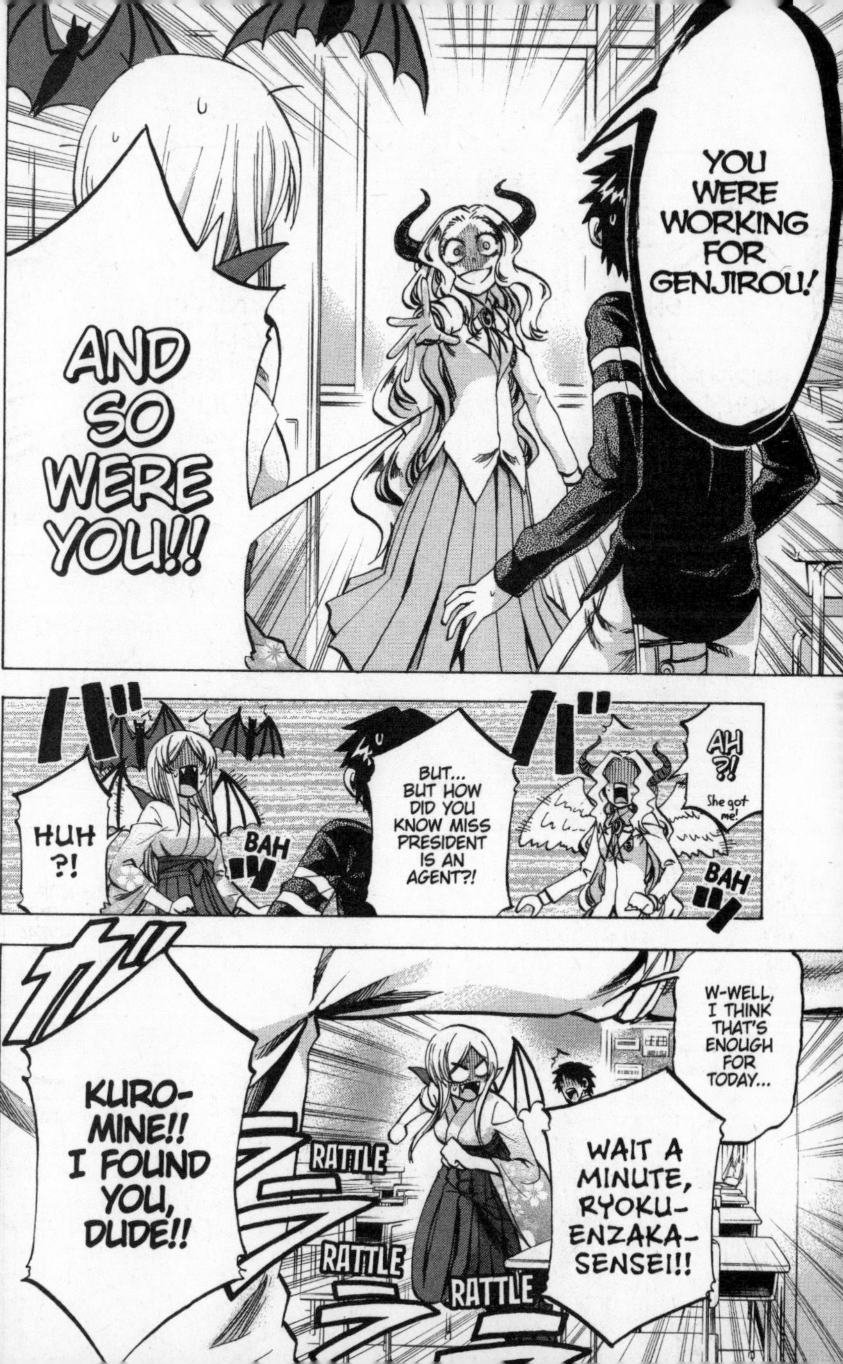
YOU WERE WORKING FOR GENJIROU!
AND SO WERE YOU!!
AH ?!
She got me!
BAH
BUT... BUT HOW DID YOU KNOW MISS PRESIDENT IS AN AGENT?!
BAH
HUH ?!
W-WELL, I THINK THAT'S ENOUGH FOR TODAY...
WAIT A MINUTE, RYOKU-ENZAKA-SENSEI!!!
RATTLE
RATTLE
RATTLE
KURO-MINE!! I FOUND YOU, DUDE!!

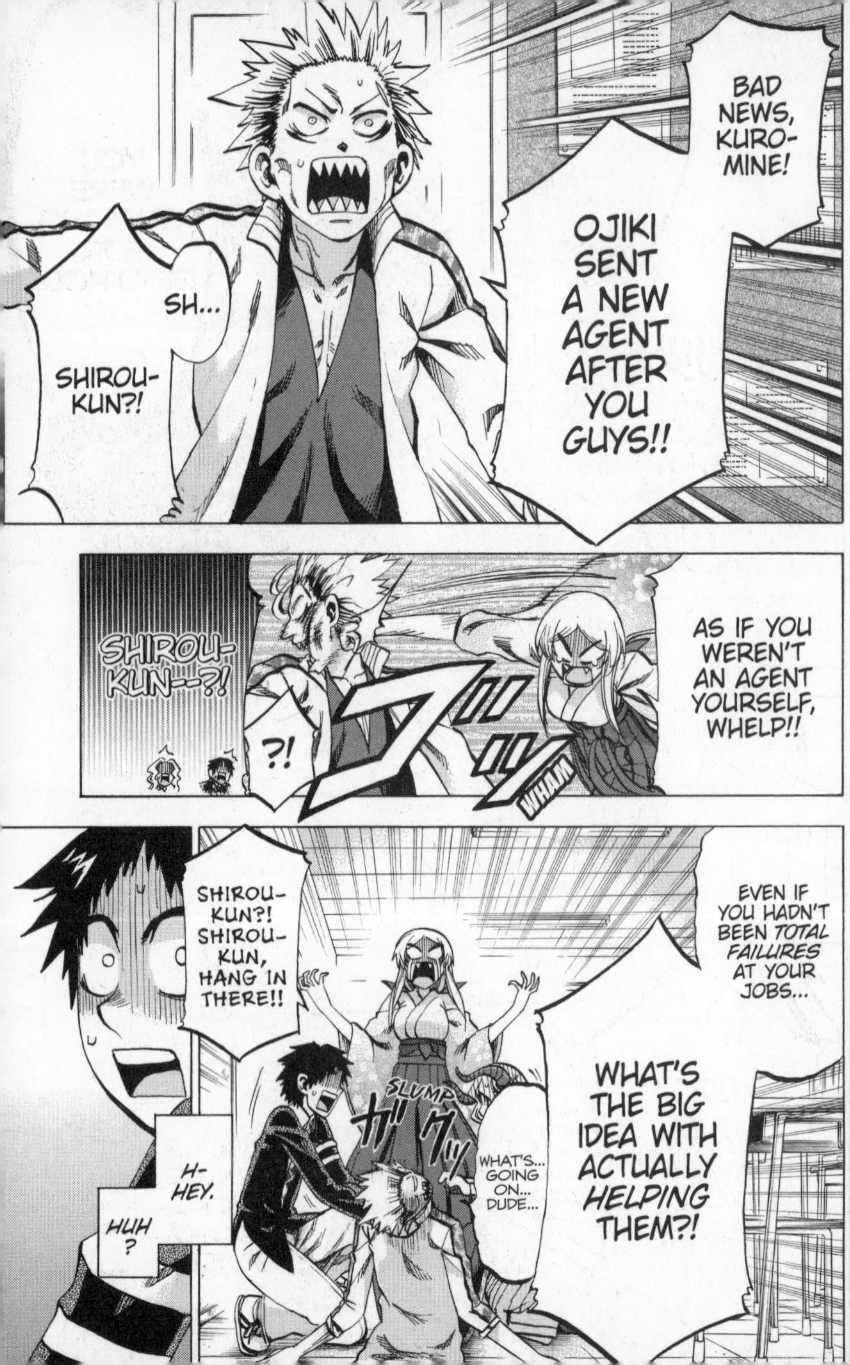
BAD NEWS, KURO-MINE!
OJIKI SENT A NEW AGENT AFTER YOU GUYS!!
SH...
SHIROU-KUN?!
AS IF YOU WEREN'T AN AGENT YOURSELF, WHELP!!
WHAM
?!
SHIROU-KUN--?!
EVEN IF YOU HADN'T BEEN *TOTAL FAILURES* AT YOUR JOBS...
WHAT'S THE BIG IDEA WITH ACTUALLY *HELPING* THEM?!
SLUMP
WHAT'S... GOING ON... DUDE...
SHIROU-KUN?! SHIROU-KUN, HANG IN THERE!!
H-HEY.
HUH?

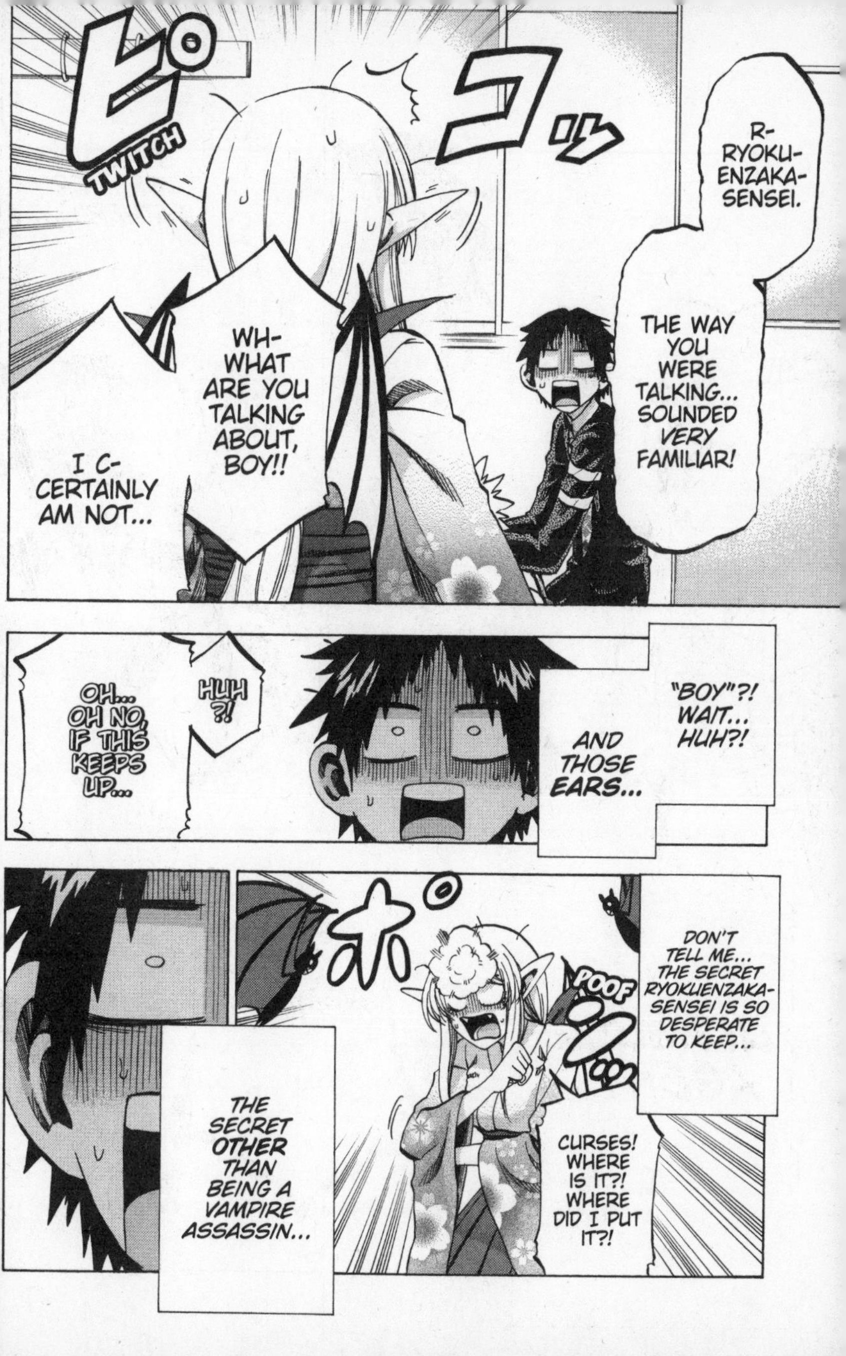

R-RYOKUENZAKA-SENSEI.
THE WAY YOU WERE TALKING... SOUNDED VERY FAMILIAR!
ピコッ
TWITCH
WH-WHAT ARE YOU TALKING ABOUT, BOY!!
I C-CERTAINLY AM NOT...
"BOY"?! WAIT... HUH?!
AND THOSE EARS...
HUH?!
OH... OH NO, IF THIS KEEPS UP...
DON'T TELL ME... THE SECRET RYOKUENZAKA-SENSEI IS SO DESPERATE TO KEEP...
ポ
POOF
CURSES! WHERE IS IT?! WHERE DID I PUT IT?!
THE SECRET OTHER THAN BEING A VAMPIRE ASSASSIN...

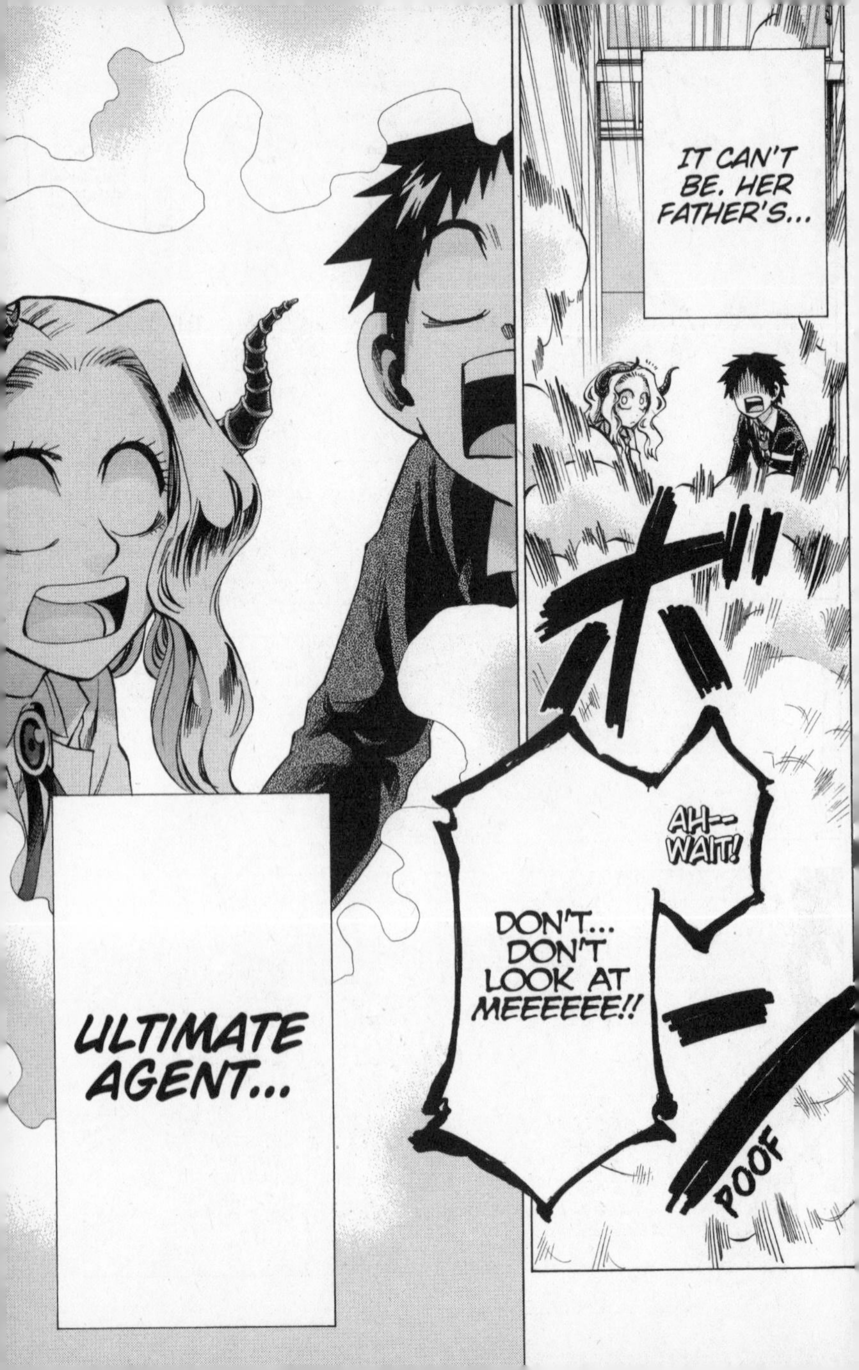
IT CAN'T BE. HER FATHER'S...
AH-- WAIT!
DON'T... DON'T LOOK AT MEEEEEEE!!
POOF
ULTIMATE AGENT...

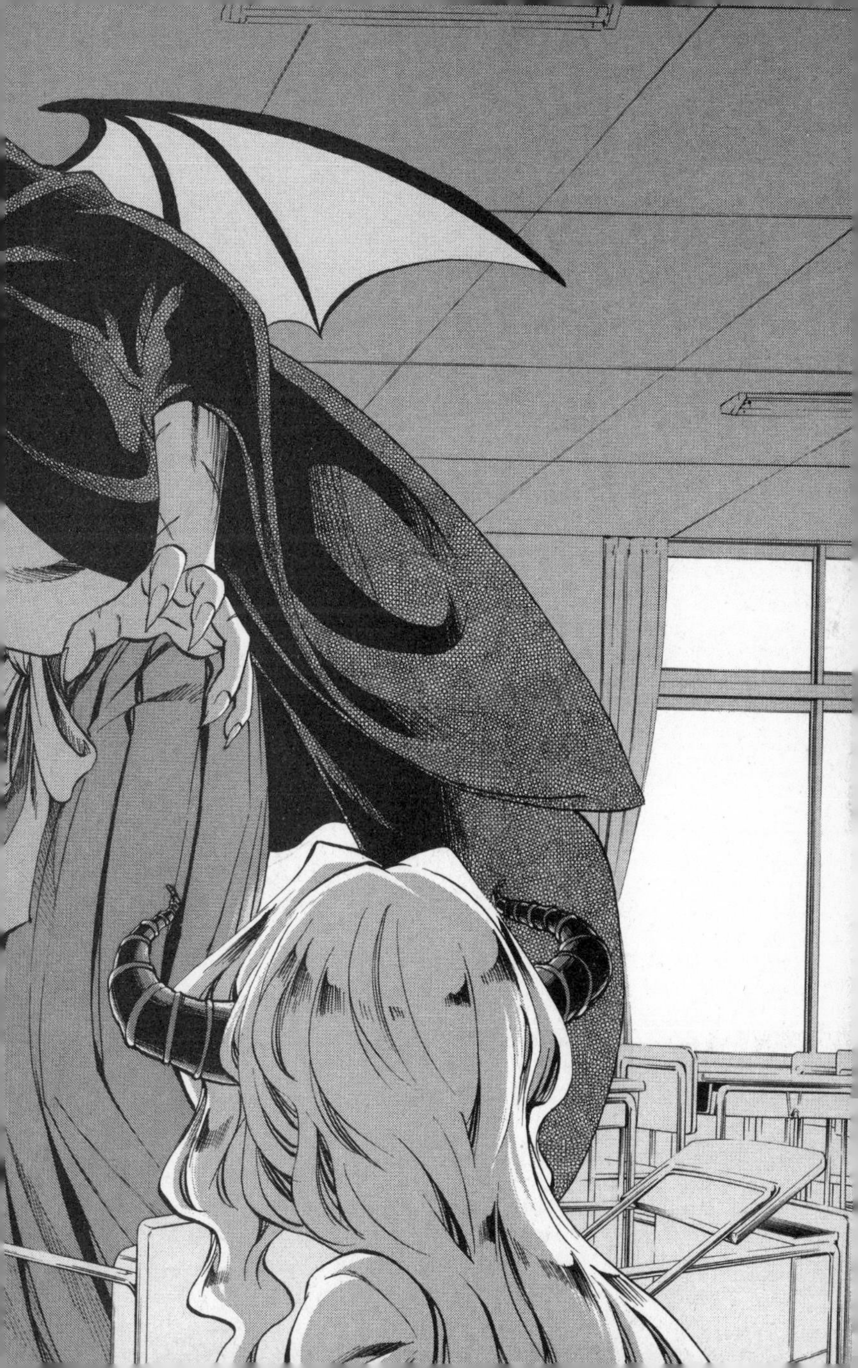

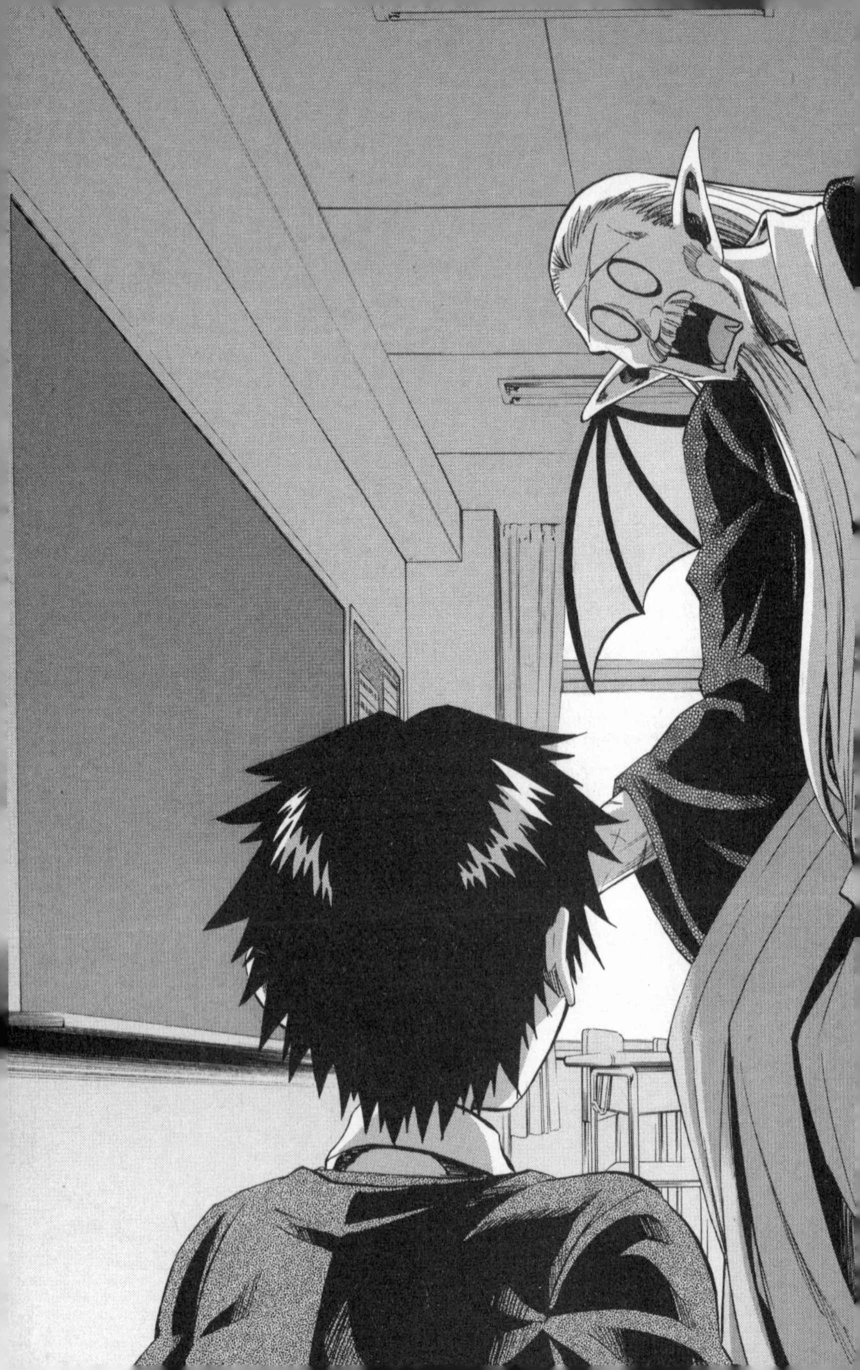

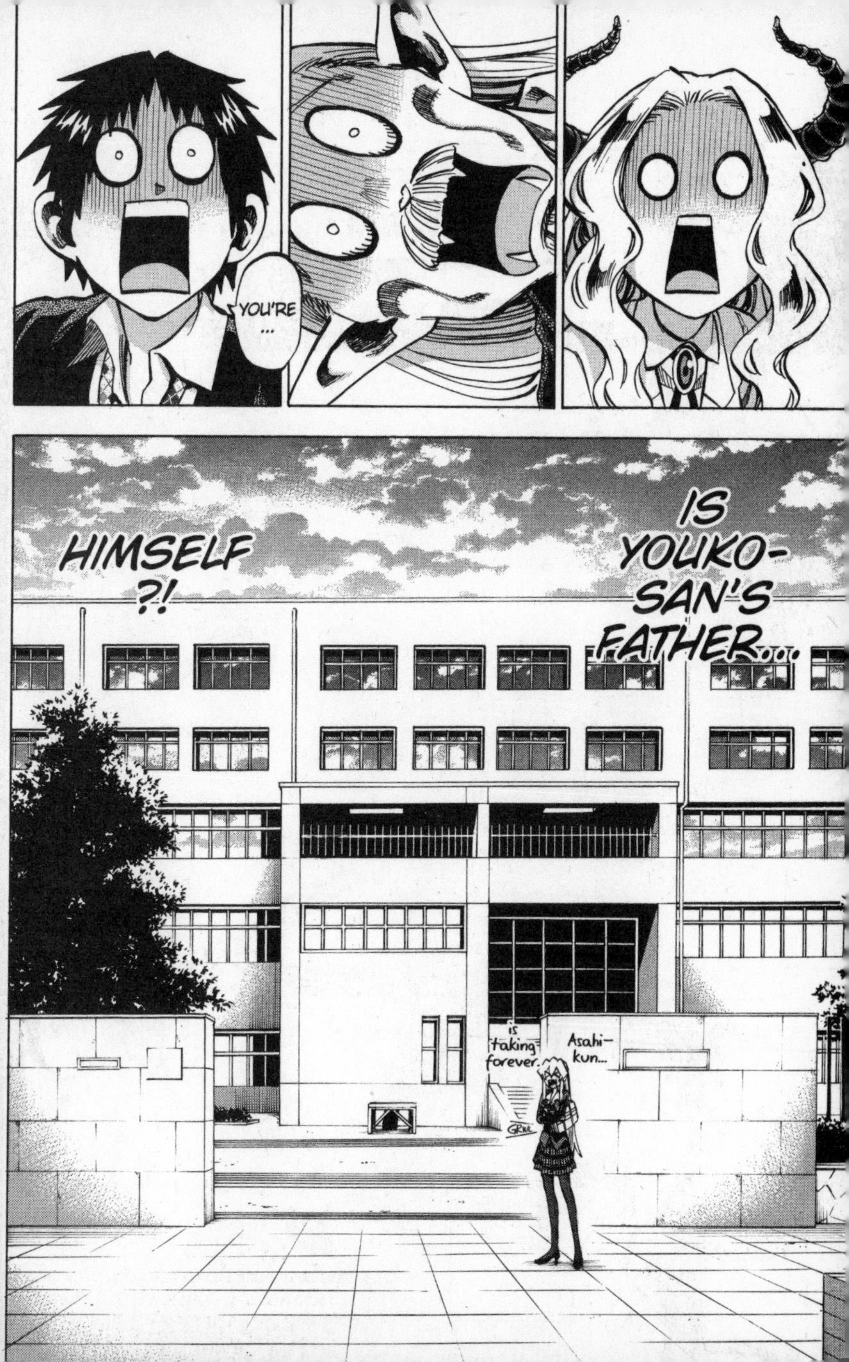
YOU'RE ...
IS YOUKO-SAN'S FATHER...
HIMSELF ?!
Asahi-kun...
is taking forever.
GRUL

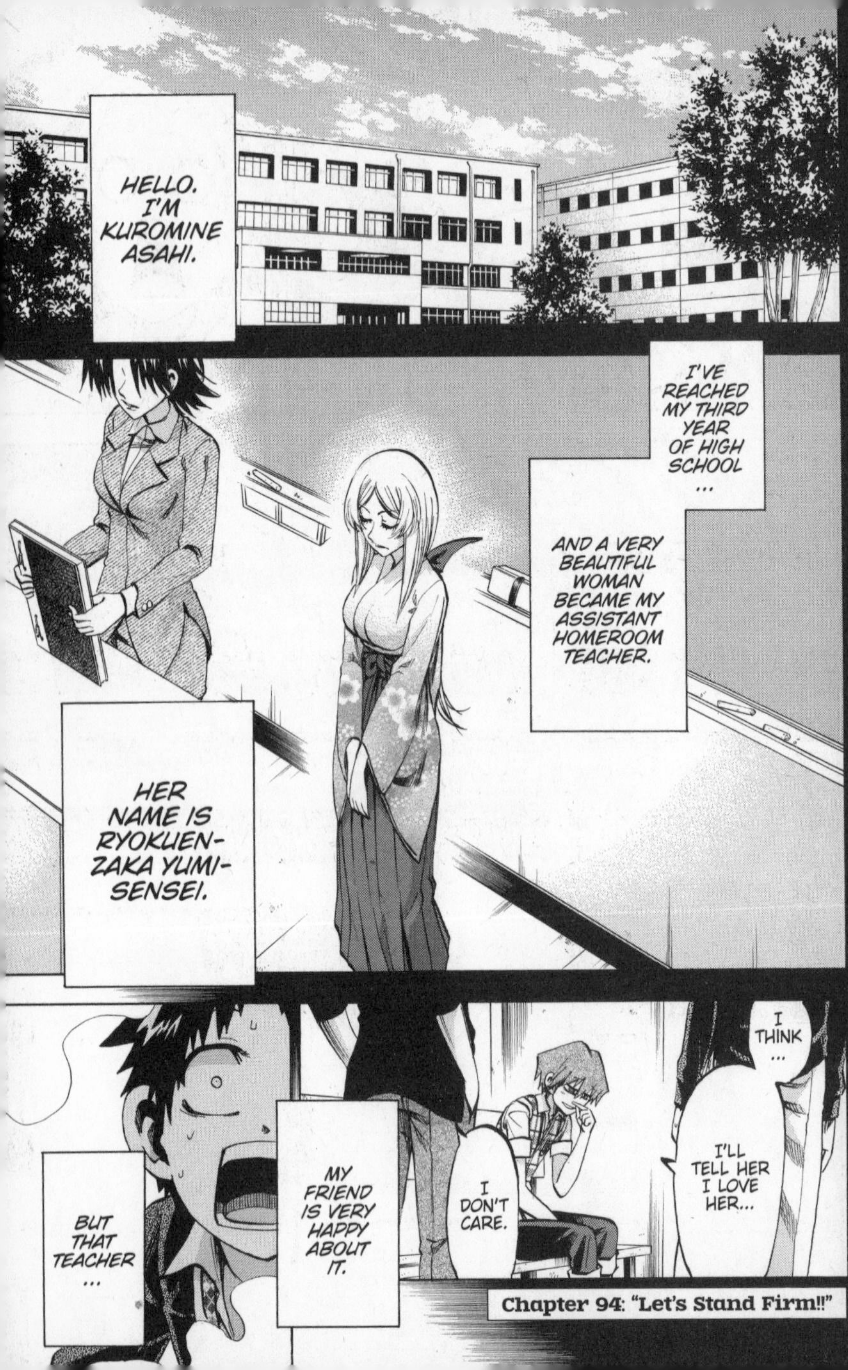
HELLO. I'M KUROMINE ASAHI.
I'VE REACHED MY THIRD YEAR OF HIGH SCHOOL...
AND A VERY BEAUTIFUL WOMAN BECAME MY ASSISTANT HOMEROOM TEACHER.
HER NAME IS RYOKUEN-ZAKA YUMI-SENSEI.
I THINK...
I'LL TELL HER I LOVE HER...
I DON'T CARE.
MY FRIEND IS VERY HAPPY ABOUT IT.
BUT THAT TEACHER...
Chapter 94: "Let's Stand Firm!!"

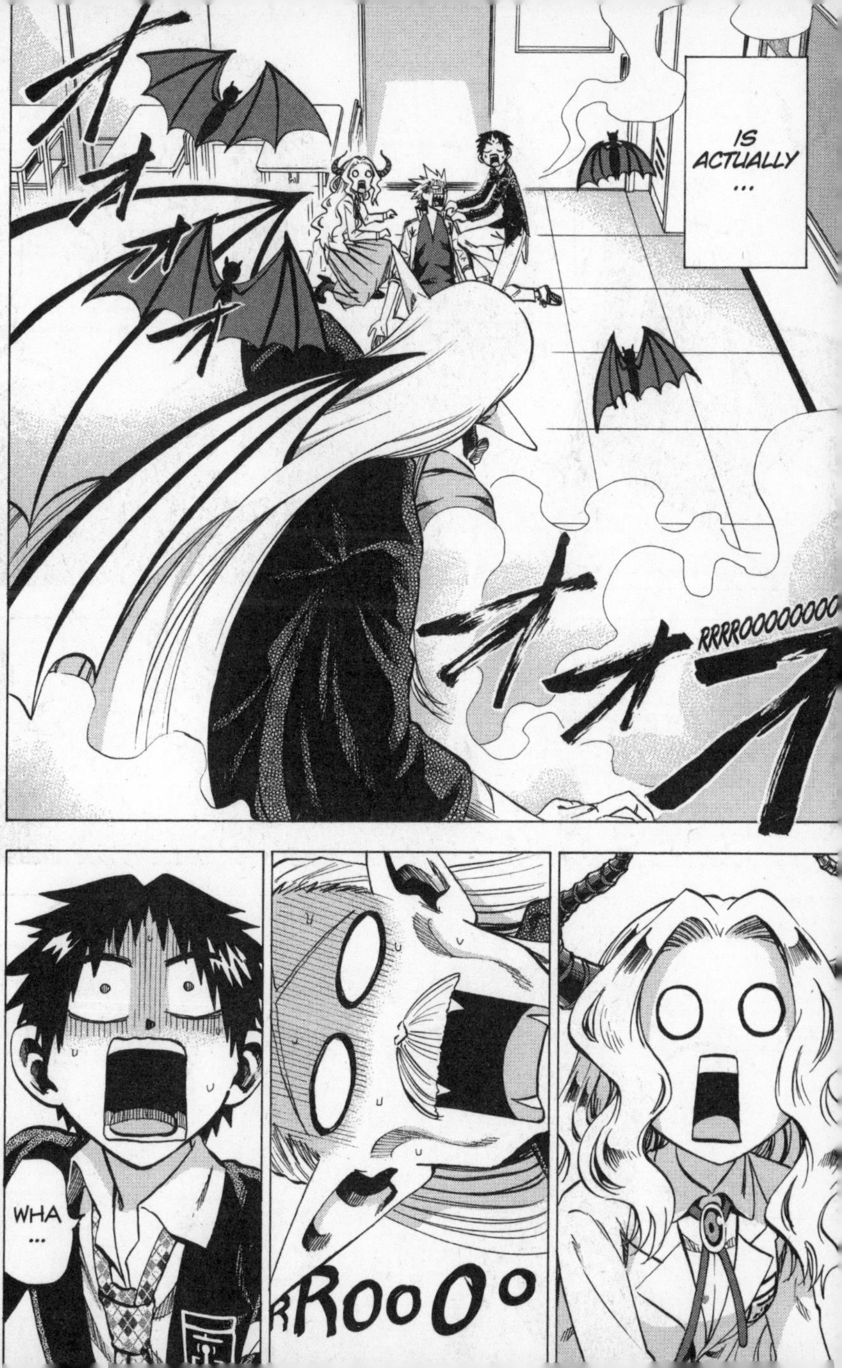
IS ACTUALLY ...
RRRROOOOOOOOO
RROOOO
WHA ...

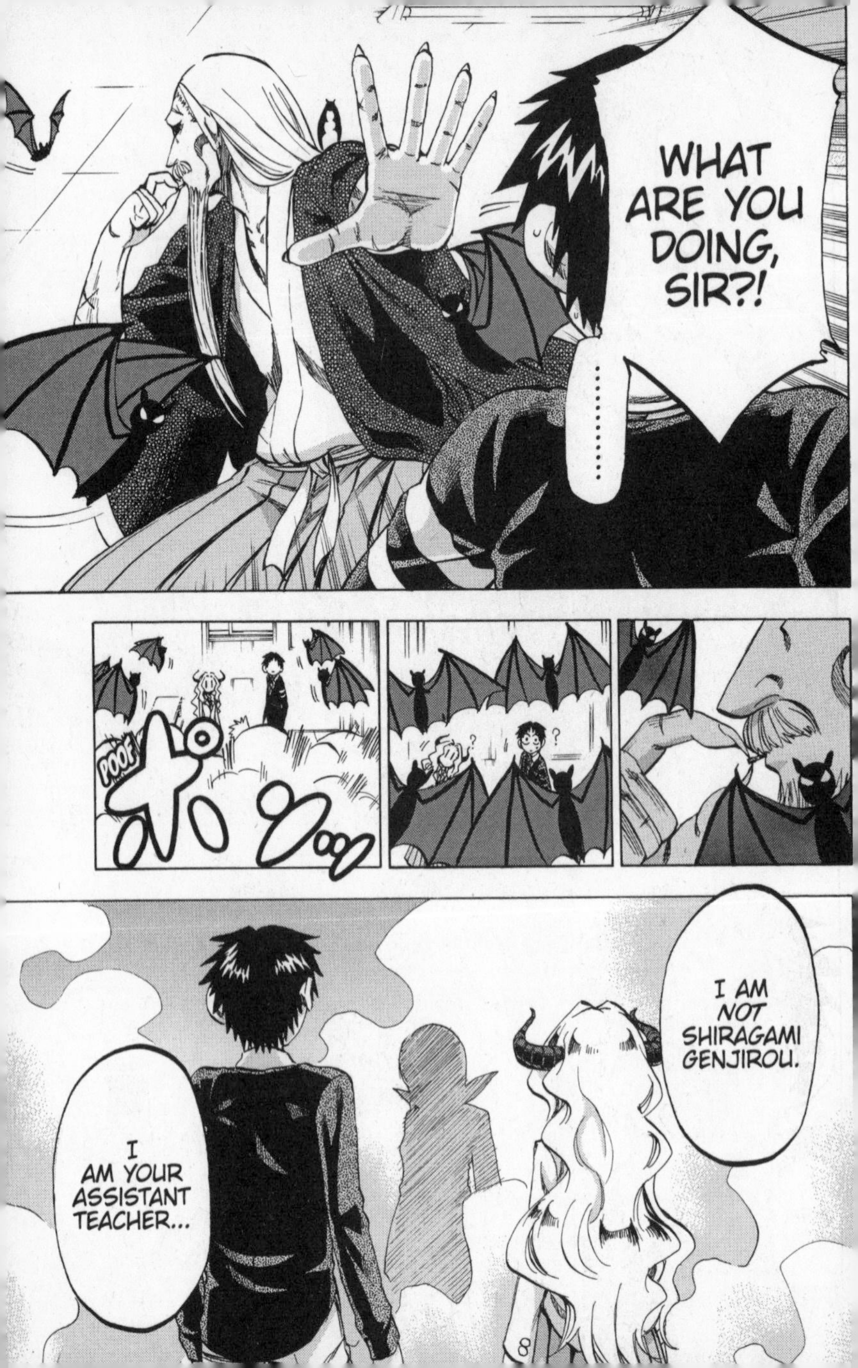
WHAT ARE YOU DOING, SIR?!
......
POOF
I AM NOT SHIRAGAMI GENJIROU.
I AM YOUR ASSISTANT TEACHER...

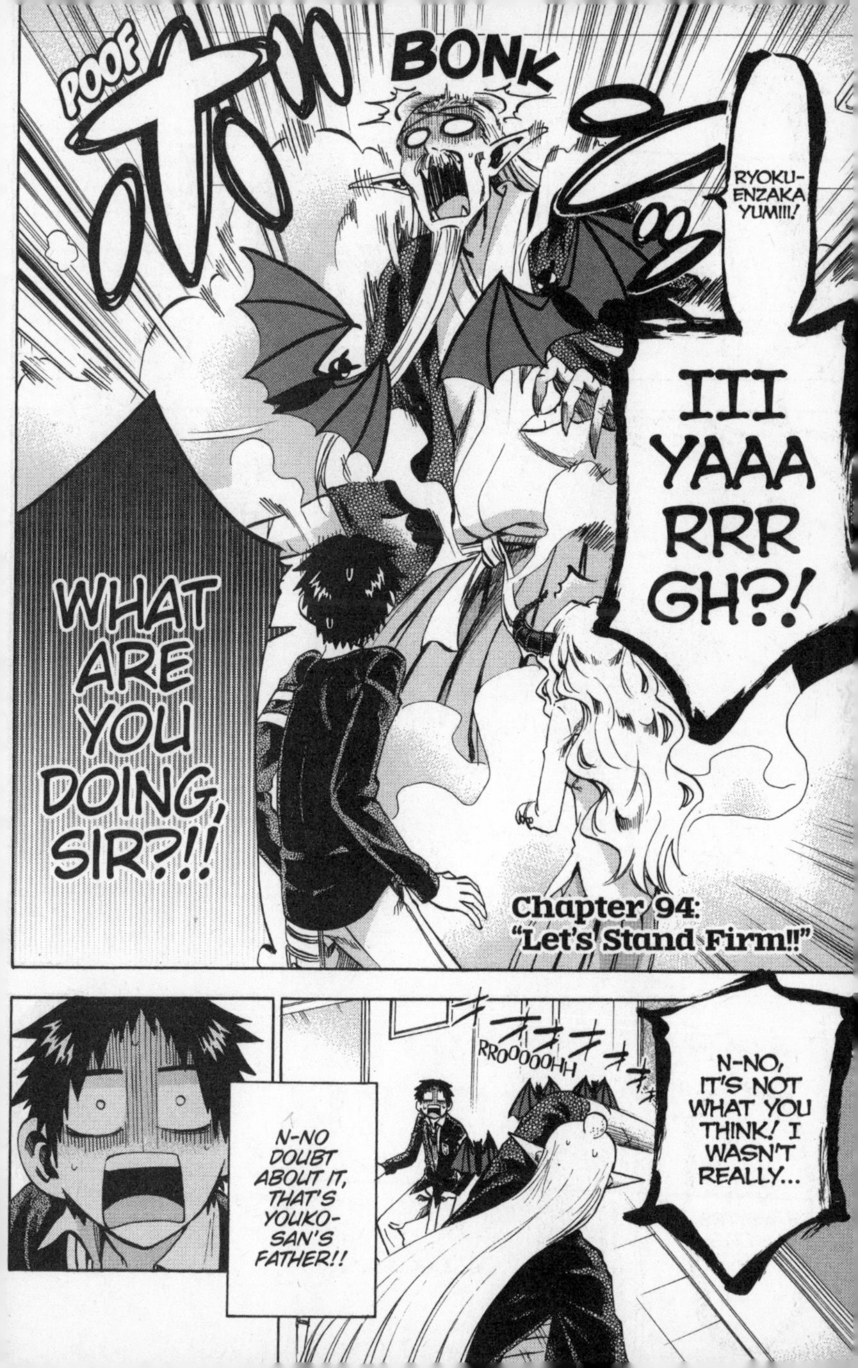
RYOKU-ENZAKA YUMI!!!
BONK
POOF
III YAAA RRR GH?!
WHAT ARE YOU DOING, SIR?!!
Chapter 94: "Let's Stand Firm!!"
N-NO, IT'S NOT WHAT YOU THINK! I WASN'T REALLY...
RROOOOOOHH
N-NO DOUBT ABOUT IT, THAT'S YOUKO-SAN'S FATHER!!

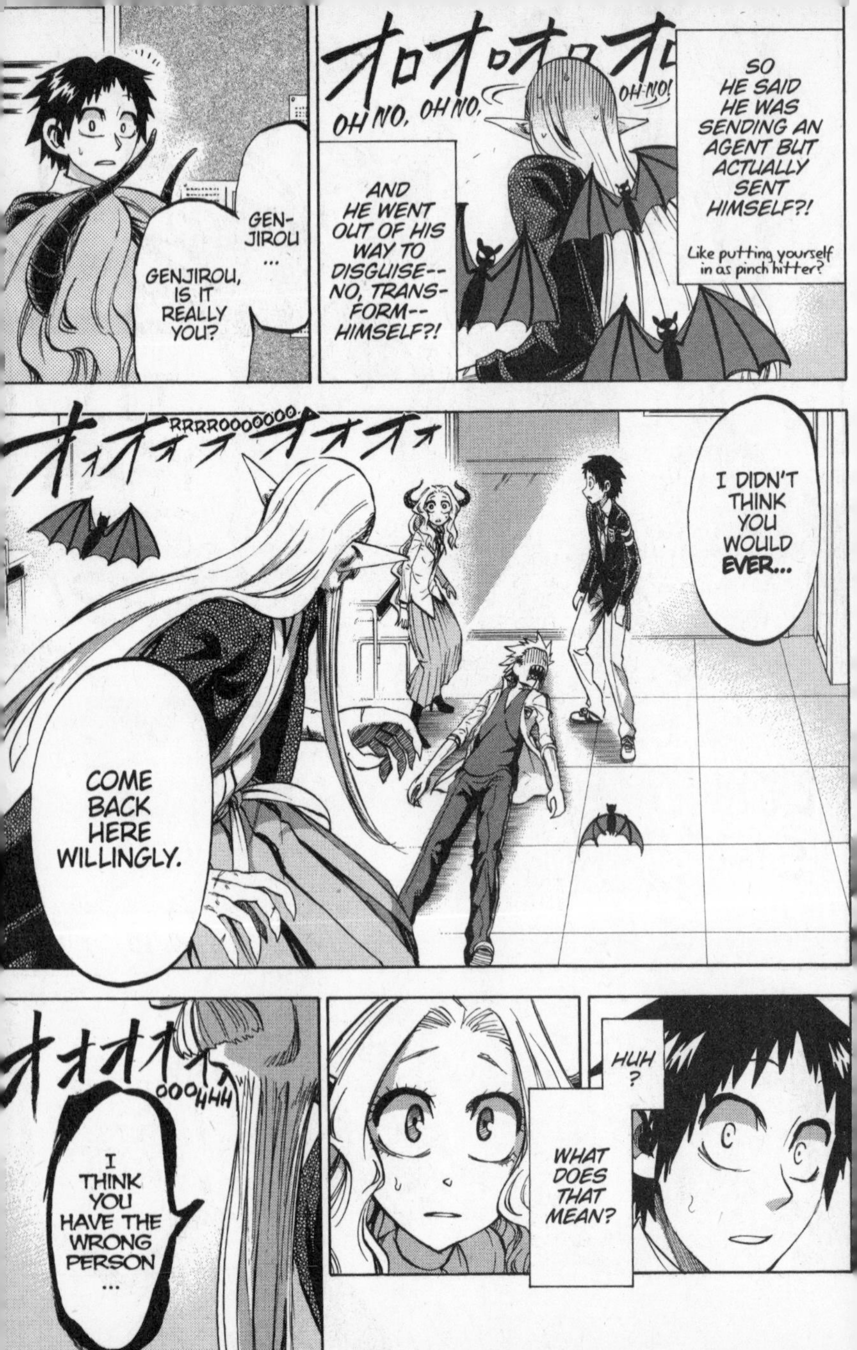
オロオロオロオロ
OH NO, OH NO, OH NO!
SO HE SAID HE WAS SENDING AN AGENT BUT ACTUALLY SENT HIMSELF?!
Like putting yourself in as pinch hitter?
AND HE WENT OUT OF HIS WAY TO DISGUISE-- NO, TRANS-FORM-- HIMSELF?!
GEN-JIROU ...
GENJIROU, IS IT REALLY YOU?
オオオオオオオオオ
RRRROOOOOOO.
I DIDN'T THINK YOU WOULD **EVER...**
COME BACK HERE WILLINGLY.
HUH?
WHAT DOES THAT MEAN?
オオオオ
OOOHHH
I THINK YOU HAVE THE WRONG PERSON ...

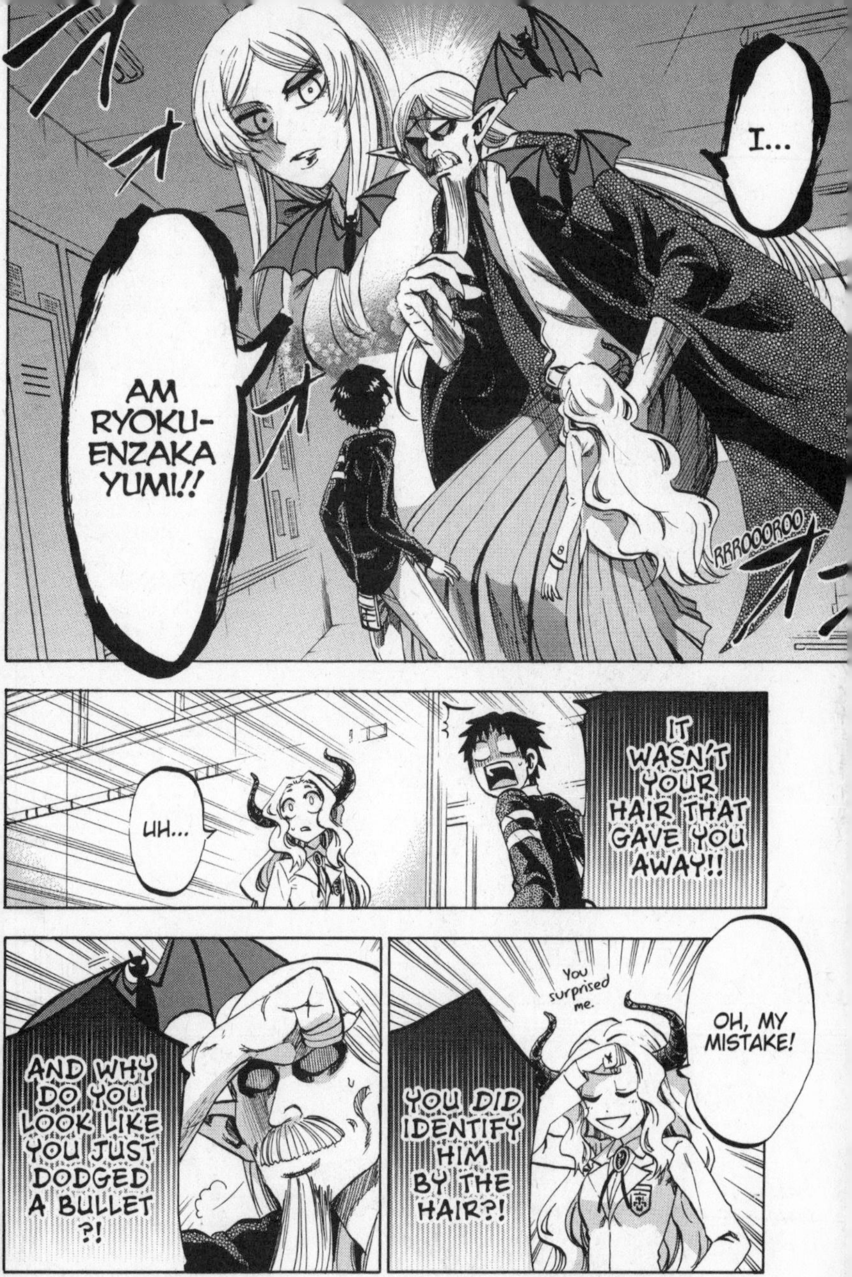
I...
AM RYOKU-ENZAKA YUMI!!
RRROOOROO
IT WASN'T YOUR HAIR THAT GAVE YOU AWAY!!
UH...
OH, MY MISTAKE!
You surprised me.
YOU DID IDENTIFY HIM BY THE HAIR?!
AND WHY DO YOU LOOK LIKE YOU JUST DODGED A BULLET?!

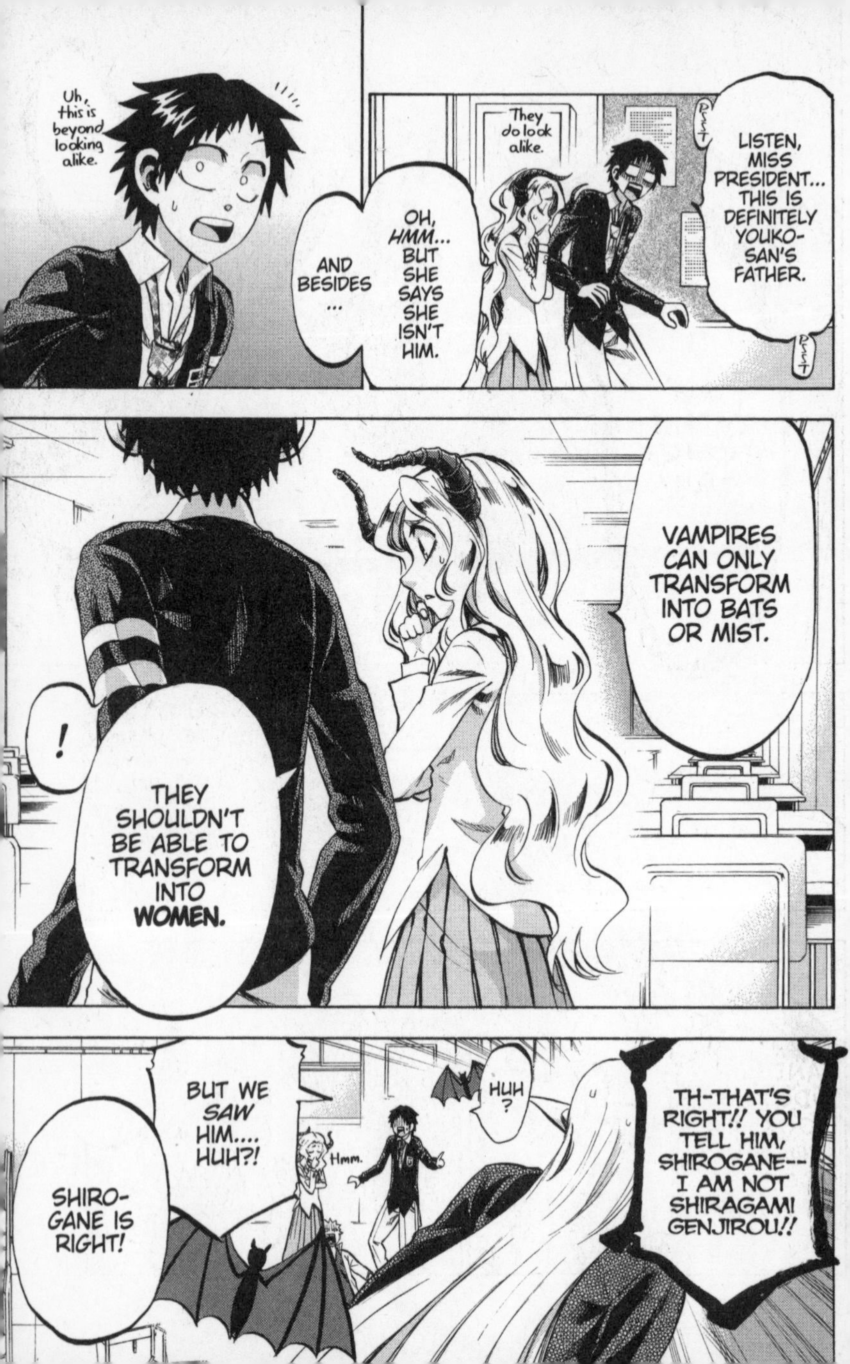
PSST
LISTEN, MISS PRESIDENT... THIS IS DEFINITELY YOUKO-SAN'S FATHER.
PSST
They do look alike.
OH, *HMM*... BUT SHE SAYS SHE ISN'T HIM.
AND BESIDES ...
Uh, this is beyond looking alike.
VAMPIRES CAN ONLY TRANSFORM INTO BATS OR MIST.
!
THEY SHOULDN'T BE ABLE TO TRANSFORM INTO **WOMEN.**
TH-THAT'S RIGHT!! YOU TELL HIM, SHIROGANE-- I AM NOT SHIRAGAMI GENJIROU!!
HUH ?
BUT WE *SAW* HIM.... HUH?!
Hmm.
SHIRO-GANE IS RIGHT!

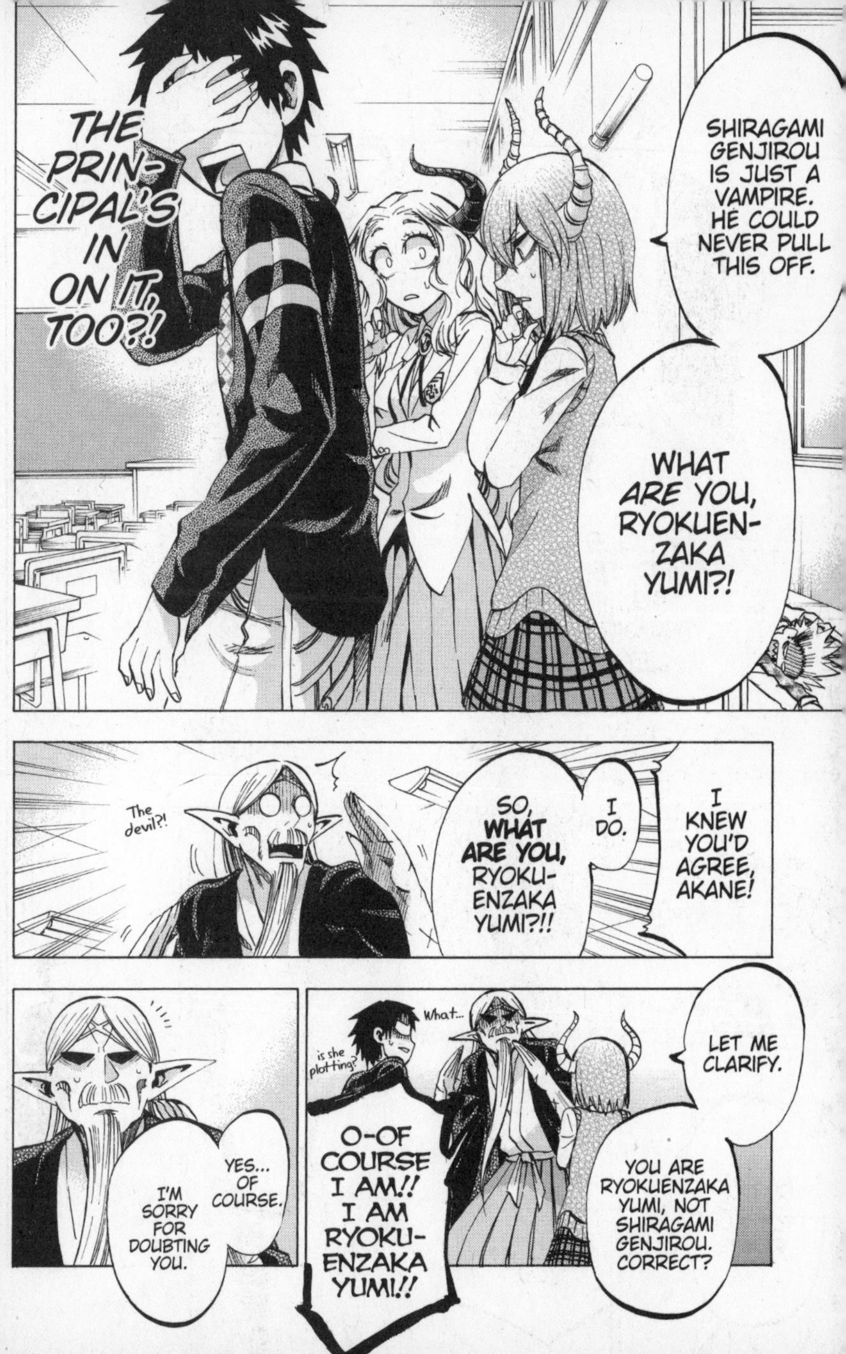
SHIRAGAMI GENJIROU IS JUST A VAMPIRE. HE COULD NEVER PULL THIS OFF.
WHAT ARE YOU, RYOKUEN-ZAKA YUMI?!
THE PRIN-CIPAL'S IN ON IT, TOO?!
I KNEW YOU'D AGREE, AKANE!
I DO.
SO, WHAT ARE YOU, RYOKU-ENZAKA YUMI?!!
The devil?!
LET ME CLARIFY.
What...
is she plotting?
YOU ARE RYOKUENZAKA YUMI, NOT SHIRAGAMI GENJIROU. CORRECT?
O-OF COURSE I AM!! I AM RYOKU-ENZAKA YUMI!!
YES... OF COURSE.
I'M SORRY FOR DOUBTING YOU.

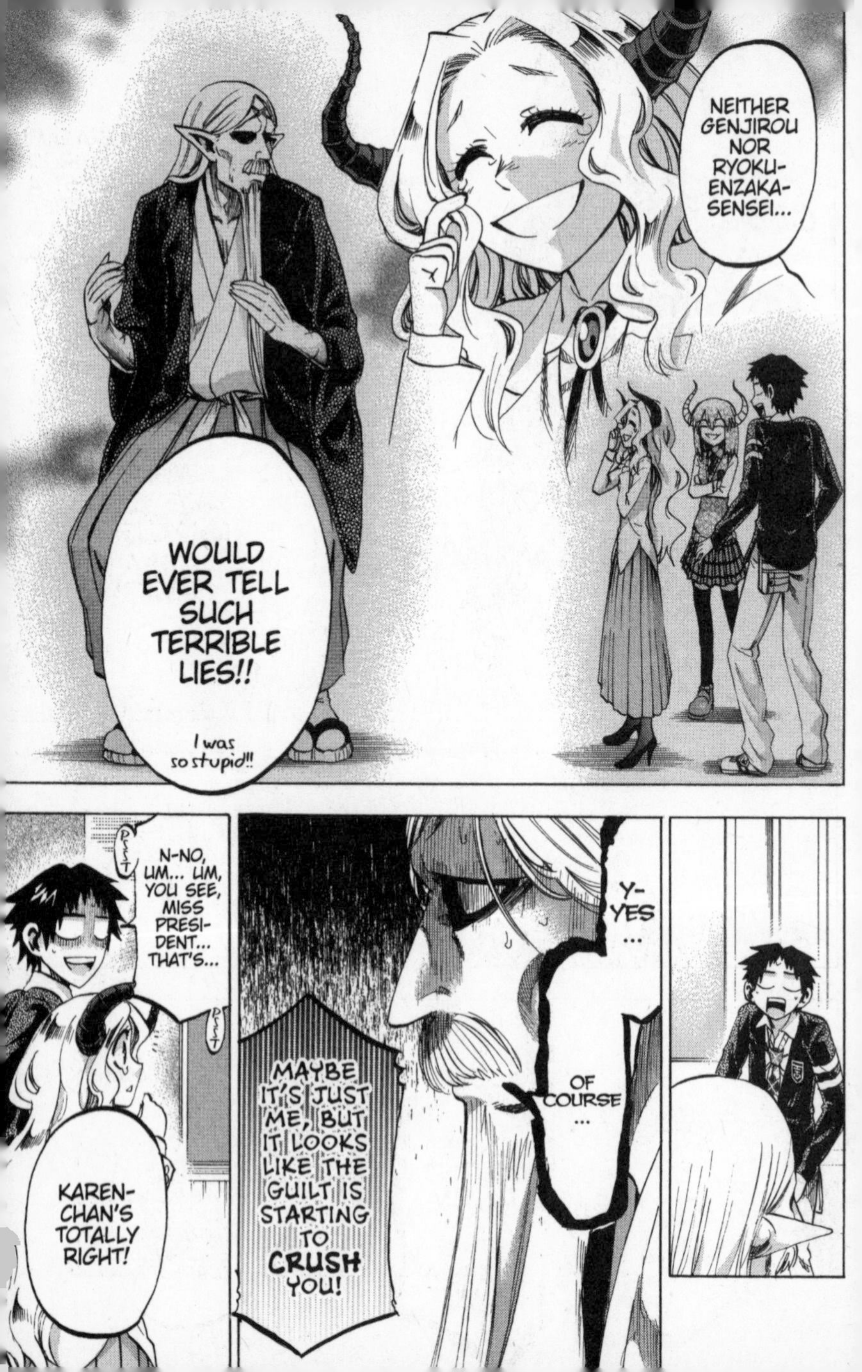
NEITHER GENJIROU NOR RYOKU-ENZAKA-SENSEI...
WOULD EVER TELL SUCH TERRIBLE LIES!!
I was so stupid!!
Y-YES...
OF COURSE...
MAYBE IT'S JUST ME, BUT IT LOOKS LIKE THE GUILT IS STARTING TO **CRUSH** YOU!
PSST
N-NO, UM... UM, YOU SEE, MISS PRESI-DENT... THAT'S...
PSST
KAREN-CHAN'S TOTALLY RIGHT!

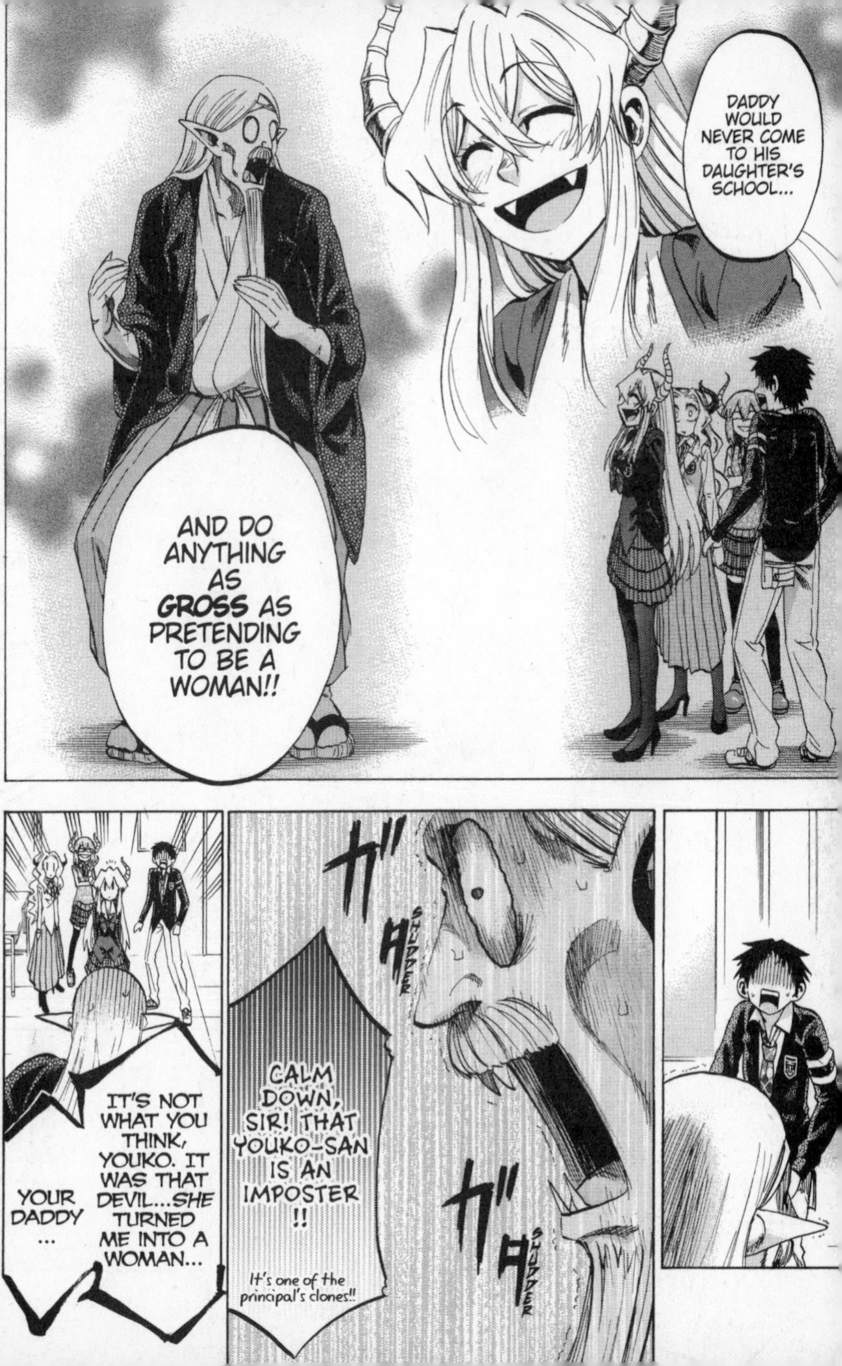
DADDY WOULD NEVER COME TO HIS DAUGHTER'S SCHOOL...
AND DO ANYTHING AS **GROSS** AS PRETENDING TO BE A WOMAN!!
SHUDDER
SHUDDER
CALM DOWN, SIR! THAT YOUKO-SAN IS AN IMPOSTER!!
It's one of the principal's clones!!
IT'S NOT WHAT YOU THINK, YOUKO. IT WAS THAT DEVIL...SHE TURNED ME INTO A WOMAN...
YOUR DADDY ...

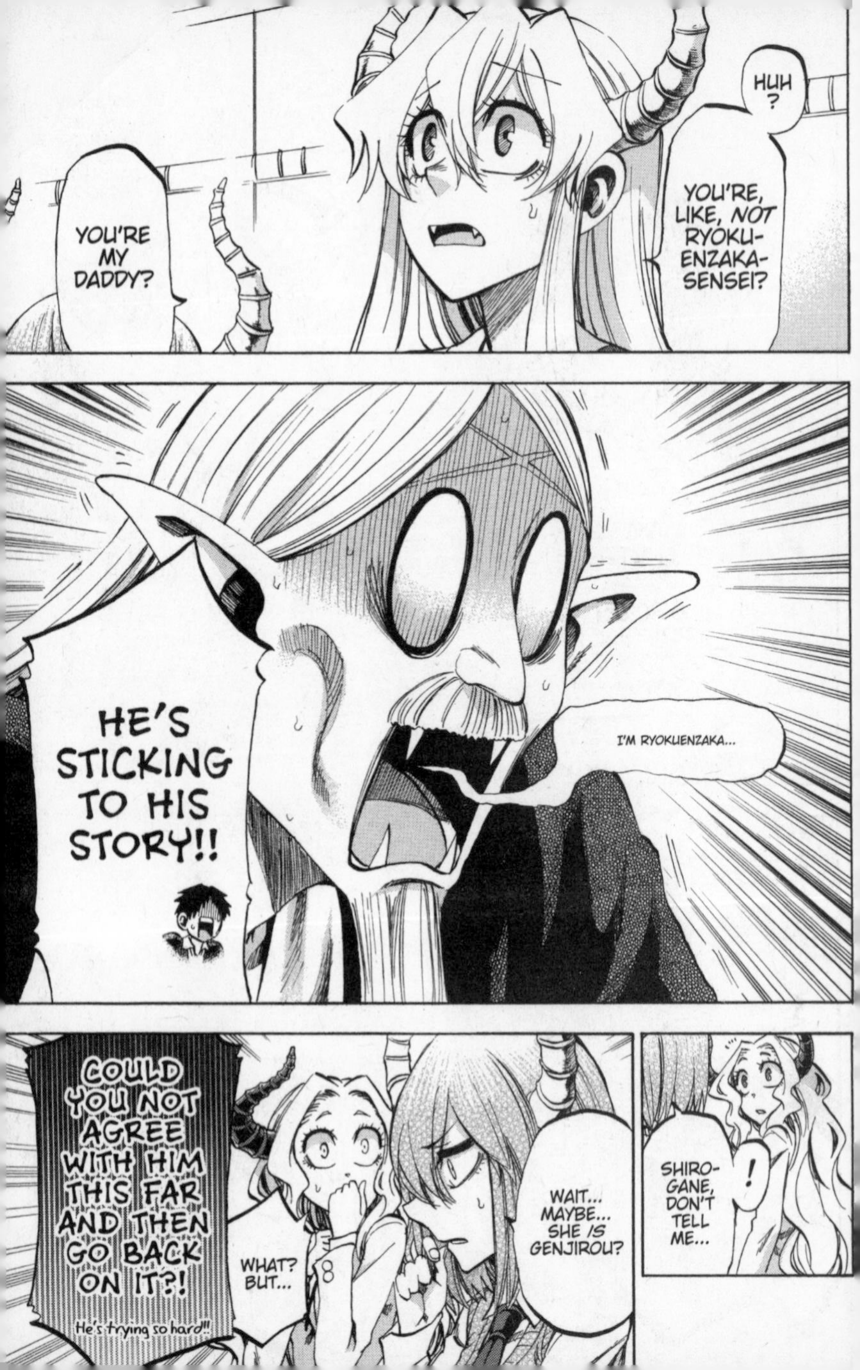
HUH ?
YOU'RE, LIKE, *NOT* RYOKU-ENZAKA-SENSEI?
YOU'RE MY DADDY?
I'M RYOKUENZAKA...
HE'S STICKING TO HIS STORY!!
!
SHIRO-GANE, DON'T TELL ME...
WAIT... MAYBE... SHE *IS* GENJIROU?
WHAT? BUT...
COULD YOU NOT AGREE WITH HIM THIS FAR AND THEN GO BACK ON IT?!
He's trying so hard!!

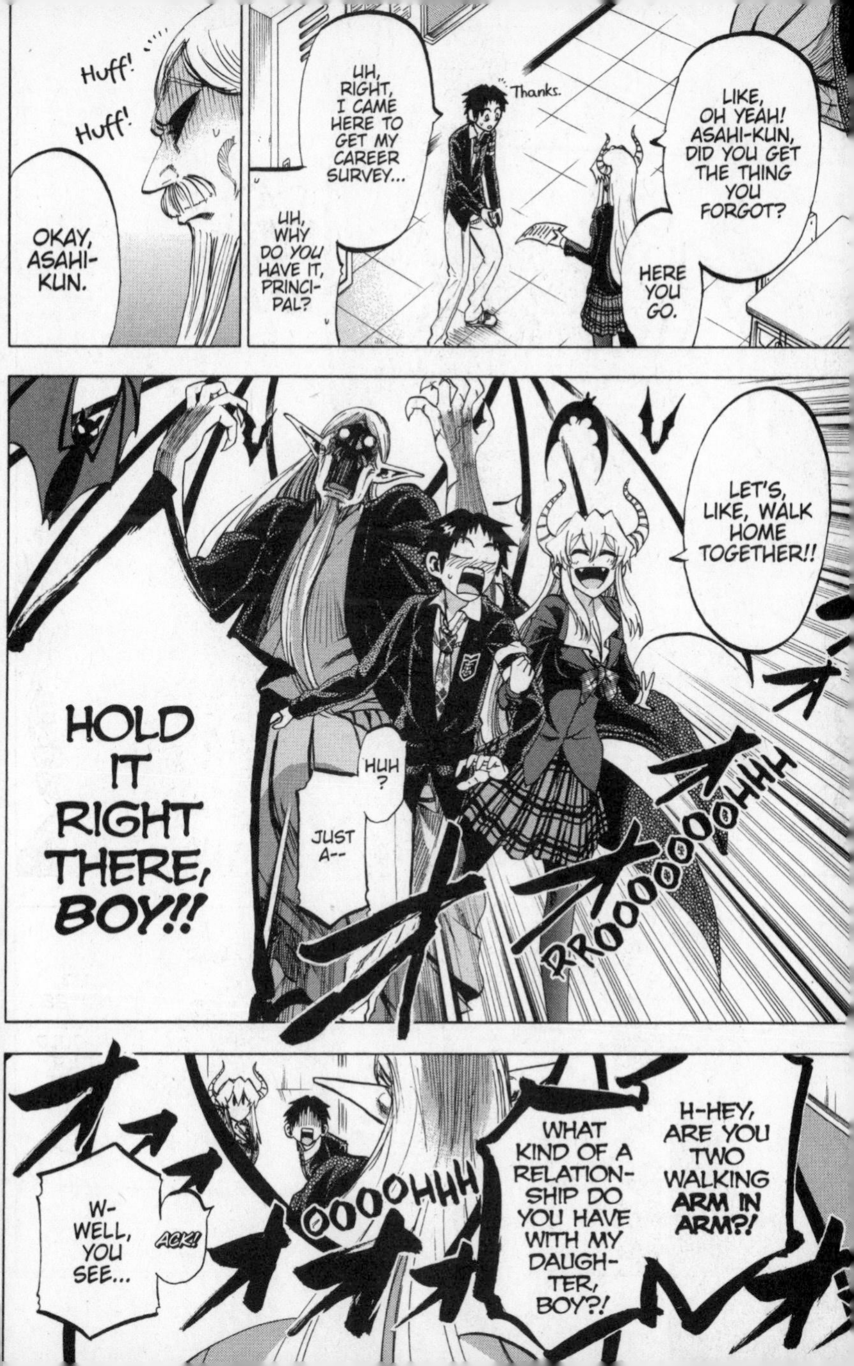
LIKE, OH YEAH! ASAHI-KUN, DID YOU GET THE THING YOU FORGOT?
HERE YOU GO.
Thanks.
UH, RIGHT, I CAME HERE TO GET MY CAREER SURVEY...
UH, WHY DO YOU HAVE IT, PRINCIPAL?
Huff!
Huff!
OKAY, ASAHI-KUN.
LET'S, LIKE, WALK HOME TOGETHER!!
RROOOOOOOOOHHH
HUH?
JUST A--
HOLD IT RIGHT THERE, BOY!!
H-HEY, ARE YOU TWO WALKING ARM IN ARM?!
WHAT KIND OF A RELATIONSHIP DO YOU HAVE WITH MY DAUGHTER, BOY?!
OOOOHHH
ACK!
W-WELL, YOU SEE...

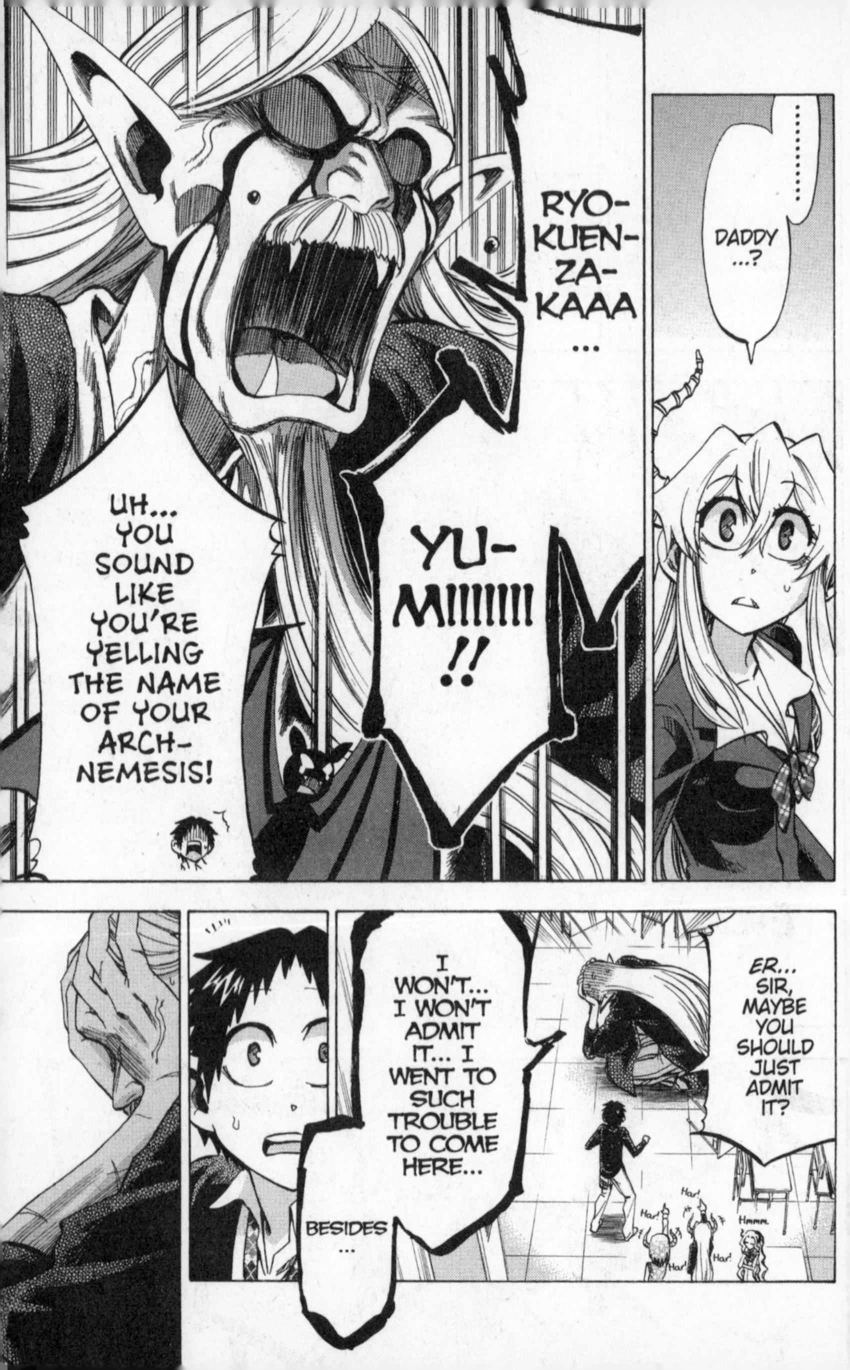
......
DADDY ...?
RYO-KUEN-ZA-KAAA ...
YU-MIIIIIII !!
UH... YOU SOUND LIKE YOU'RE YELLING THE NAME OF YOUR ARCH-NEMESIS!
ER... SIR, MAYBE YOU SHOULD JUST ADMIT IT?
Hmmm.
Har!
Har!
Har!
Har!
I WON'T... I WON'T ADMIT IT... I WENT TO SUCH TROUBLE TO COME HERE...
BESIDES ...

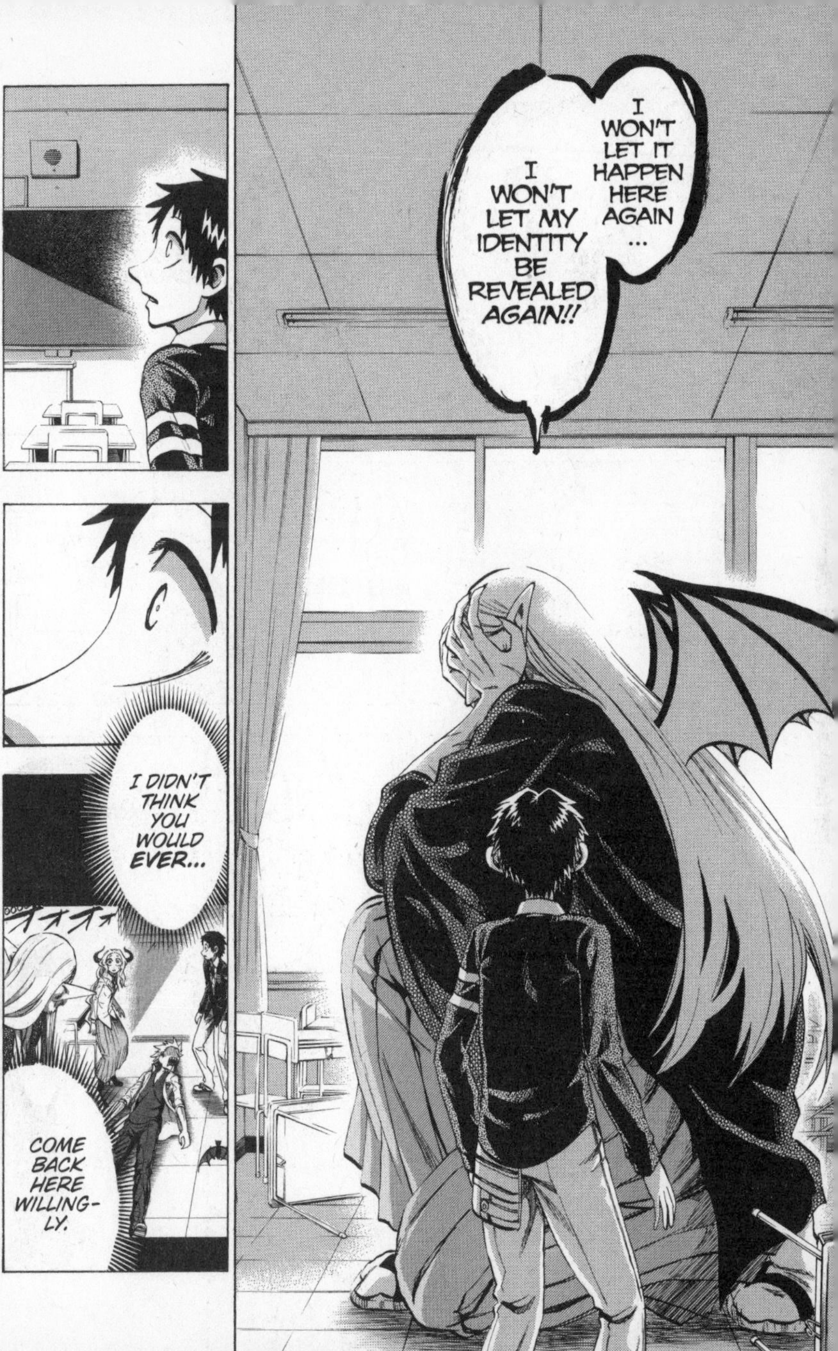
I WON'T LET IT HAPPEN HERE AGAIN ...
I WON'T LET MY IDENTITY BE REVEALED AGAIN!!
I DIDN'T THINK YOU WOULD EVER...
COME BACK HERE WILLING-LY.

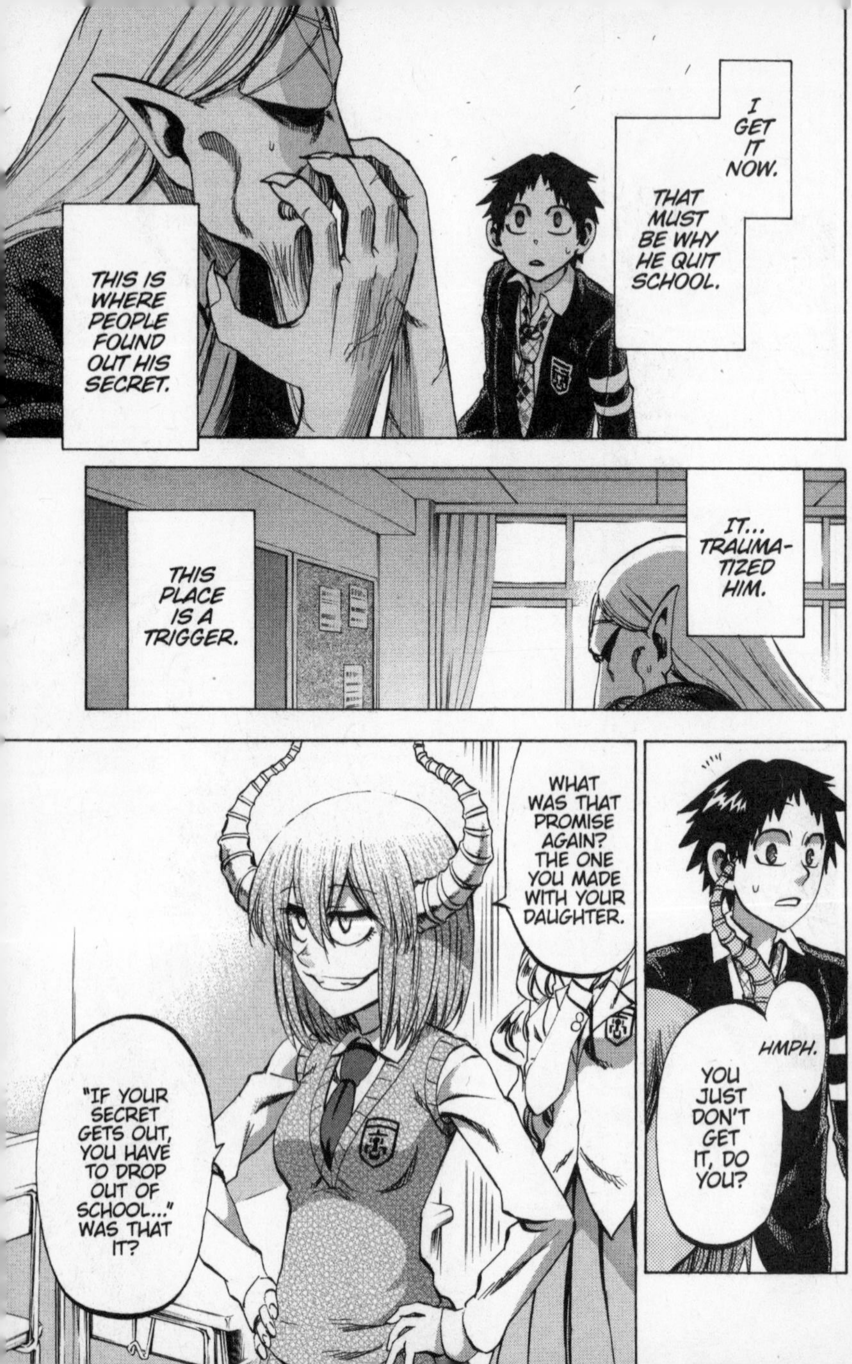
I GET IT NOW.
THAT MUST BE WHY HE QUIT SCHOOL.
THIS IS WHERE PEOPLE FOUND OUT HIS SECRET.
IT... TRAUMATIZED HIM.
THIS PLACE IS A TRIGGER.
HMPH.
YOU JUST DON'T GET IT, DO YOU?
WHAT WAS THAT PROMISE AGAIN? THE ONE YOU MADE WITH YOUR DAUGHTER.
"IF YOUR SECRET GETS OUT, YOU HAVE TO DROP OUT OF SCHOOL..." WAS THAT IT?

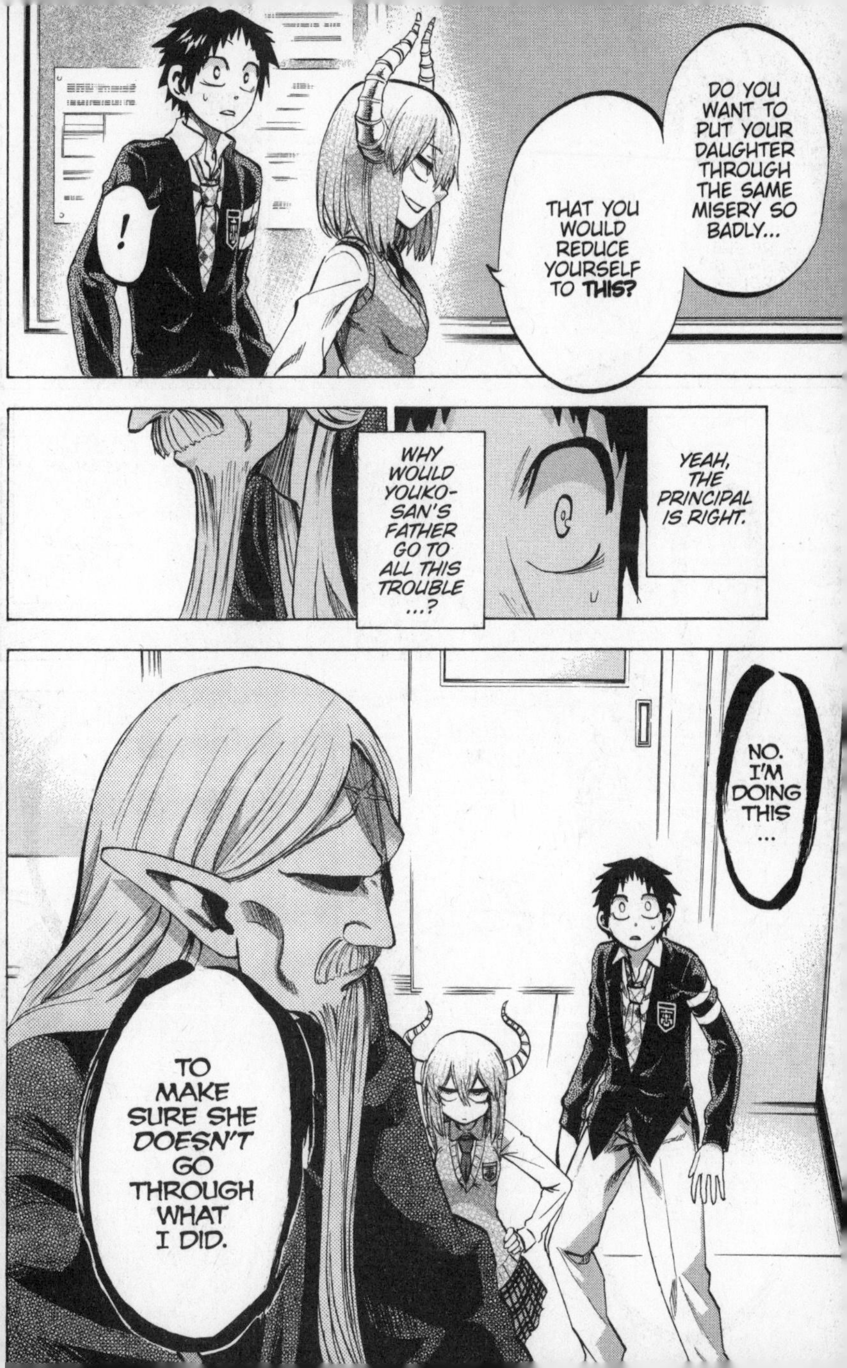
DO YOU WANT TO PUT YOUR DAUGHTER THROUGH THE SAME MISERY SO BADLY...
THAT YOU WOULD REDUCE YOURSELF TO **THIS?**
!
YEAH, THE PRINCIPAL IS RIGHT.
WHY WOULD YOUKO-SAN'S FATHER GO TO ALL THIS TROUBLE ...?
NO. I'M DOING THIS ...
TO MAKE SURE SHE *DOESN'T* GO THROUGH WHAT I DID.

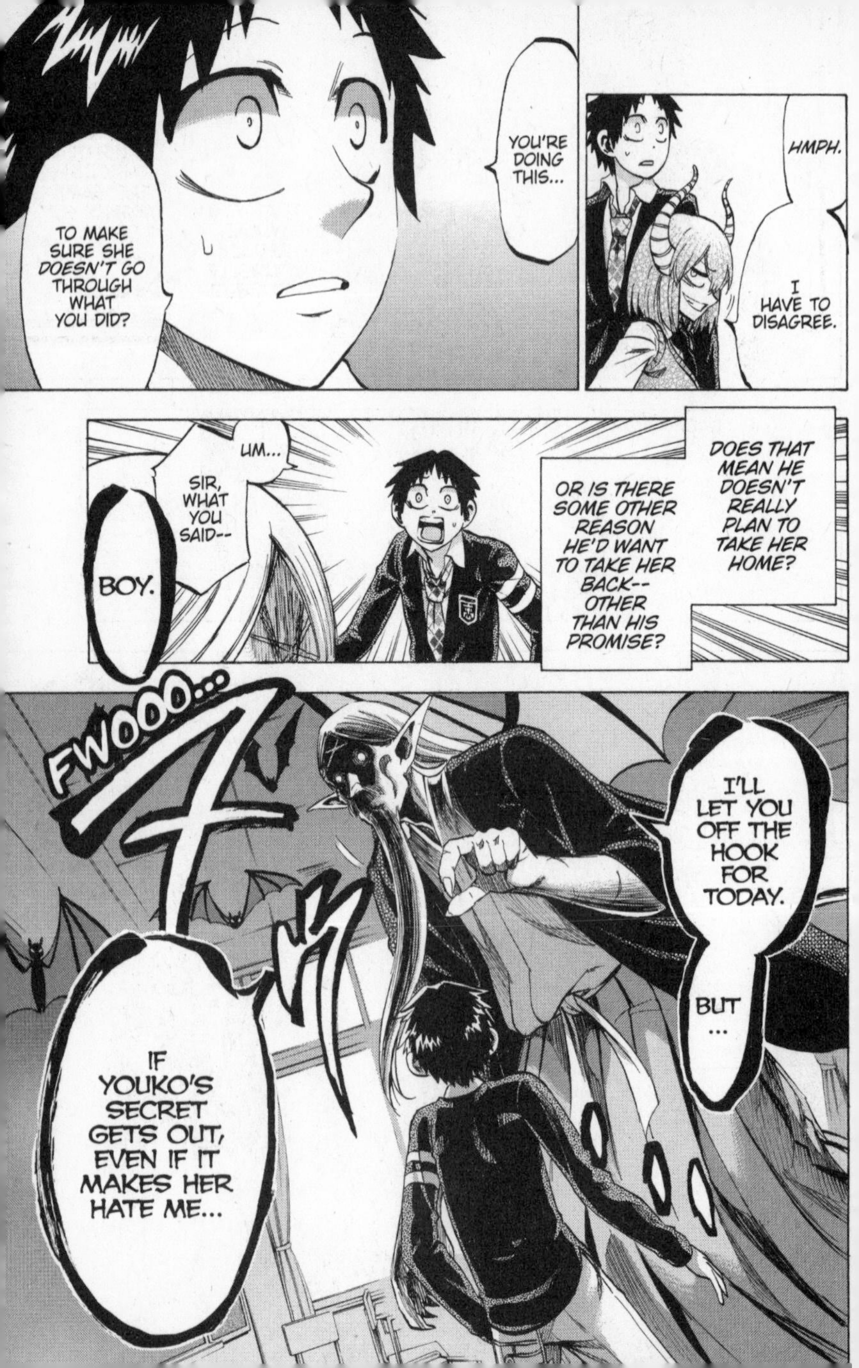
YOU'RE DOING THIS...
TO MAKE SURE SHE DOESN'T GO THROUGH WHAT YOU DID?
HMPH.
I HAVE TO DISAGREE.
DOES THAT MEAN HE DOESN'T REALLY PLAN TO TAKE HER HOME?
OR IS THERE SOME OTHER REASON HE'D WANT TO TAKE HER BACK-- OTHER THAN HIS PROMISE?
UM...
SIR, WHAT YOU SAID--
BOY.
I'LL LET YOU OFF THE HOOK FOR TODAY.
FWOOO...
BUT ...
IF YOUKO'S SECRET GETS OUT, EVEN IF IT MAKES HER HATE ME...

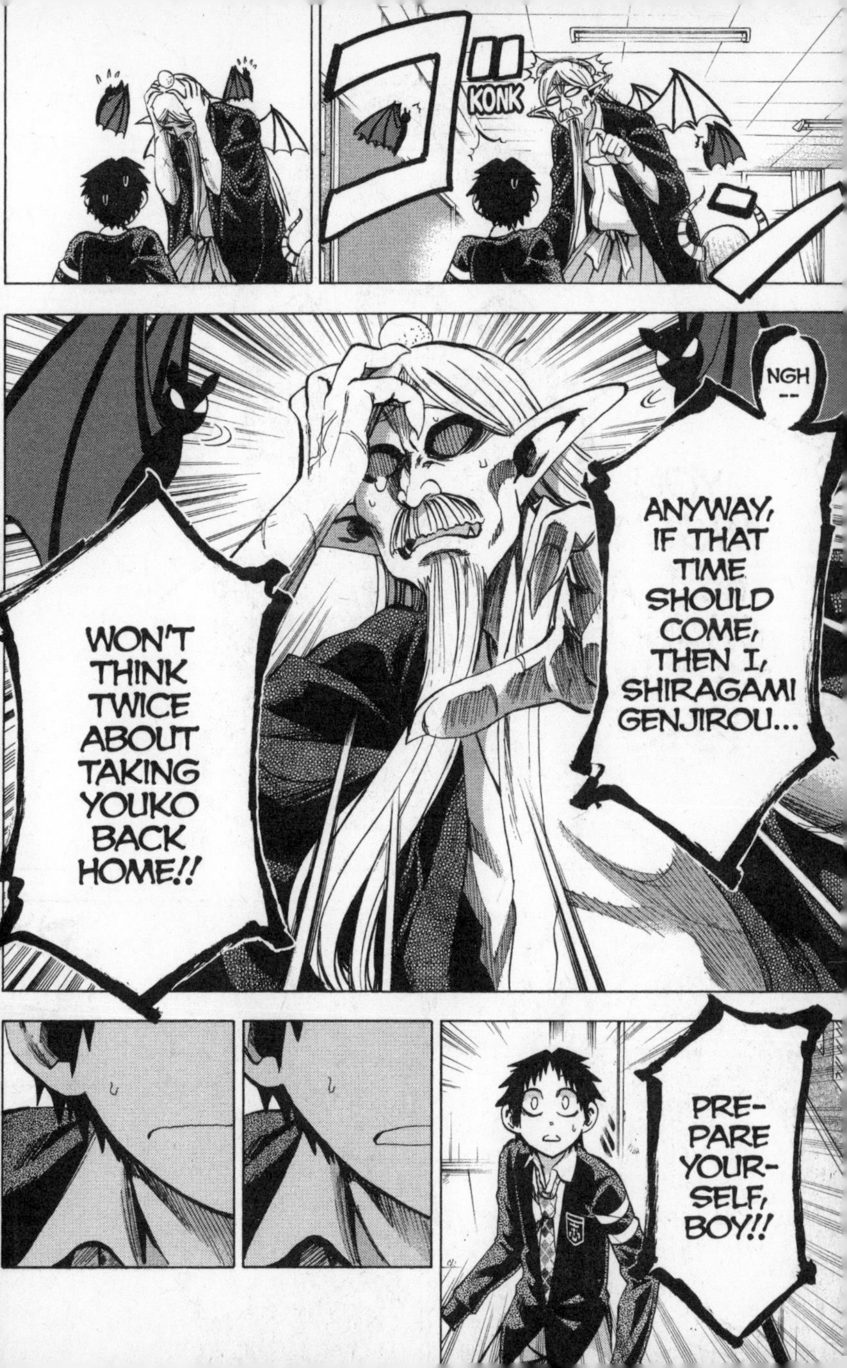
KONK
NGH --
ANYWAY, IF THAT TIME SHOULD COME, THEN I, SHIRAGAMI GENJIROU...
WON'T THINK TWICE ABOUT TAKING YOUKO BACK HOME!!
PRE-PARE YOUR-SELF, BOY!!

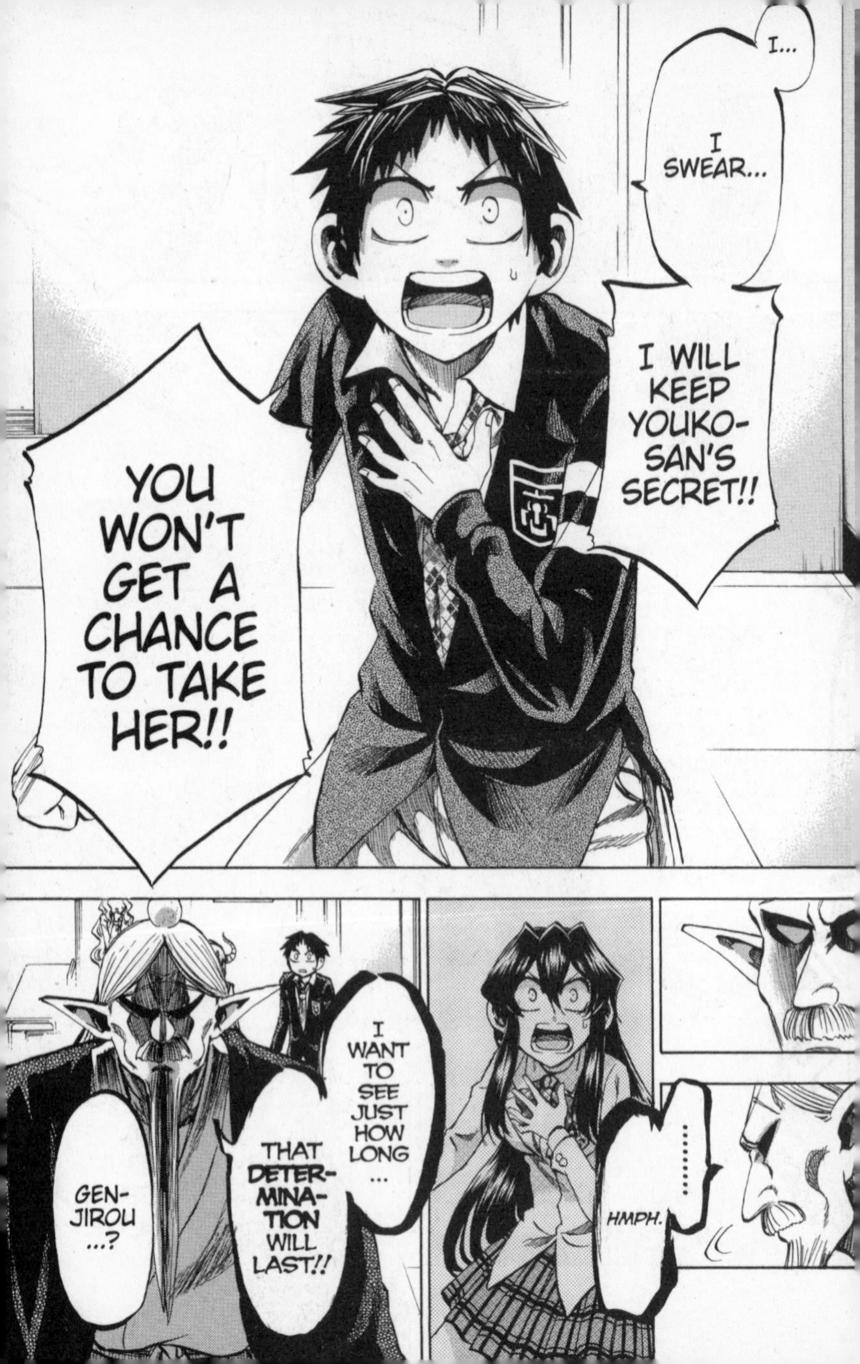
I...
I SWEAR...
I WILL KEEP YOUKO-SAN'S SECRET!!
YOU WON'T GET A CHANCE TO TAKE HER!!
HMPH.
......
I WANT TO SEE JUST HOW LONG...
THAT DETERMINATION WILL LAST!!
GEN-JIROU...?

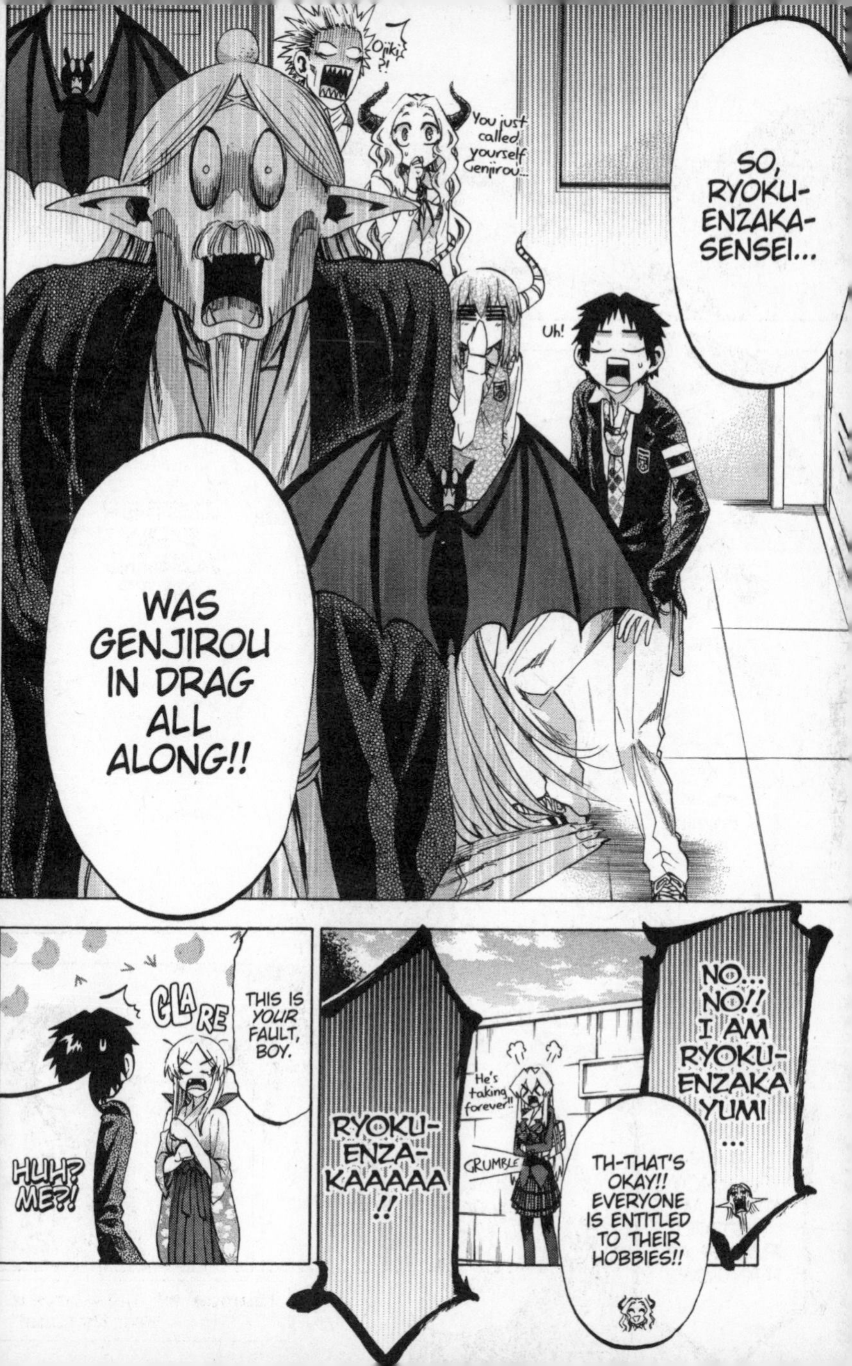
SO, RYOKU-ENZAKA-SENSEI...
Ojiki?!
You just called yourself Genjirou...
Uh!
WAS GENJIROU IN DRAG ALL ALONG!!
NO... NO!! I AM RYOKU-ENZAKA YUMI! ...
TH-THAT'S OKAY!! EVERYONE IS ENTITLED TO THEIR HOBBIES!!
He's taking forever!!
GRUMBLE
RYOKU-ENZA-KAAAAAA!!
THIS IS YOUR FAULT, BOY.
GLARE
HUH? ME?!

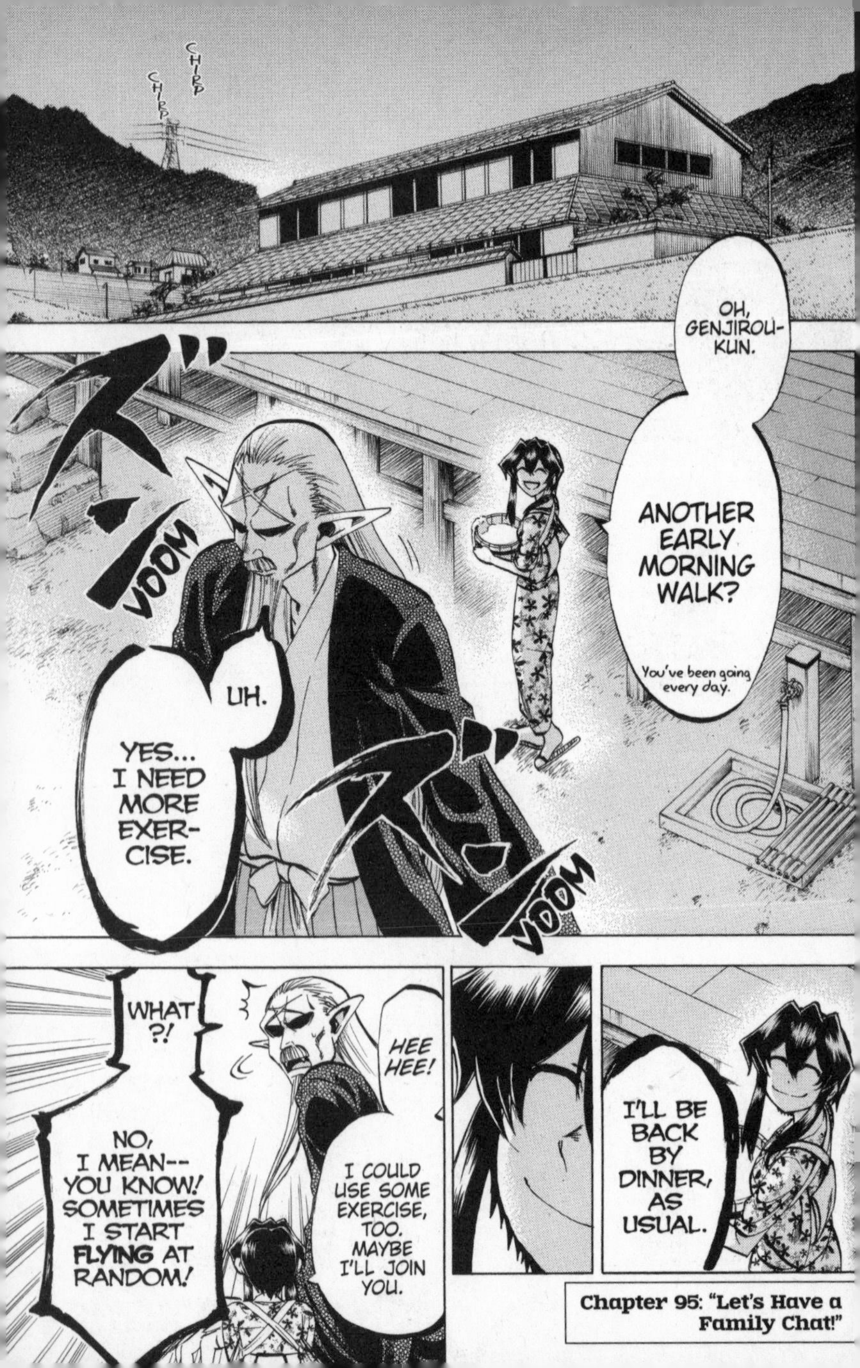
CHIRP
CHIRP
OH, GENJIROU-KUN.
ANOTHER EARLY MORNING WALK?
You've been going every day.
VOOM
UH.
YES... I NEED MORE EXERCISE.
VOOM
I'LL BE BACK BY DINNER, AS USUAL.
HEE HEE!
WHAT?!
I COULD USE SOME EXERCISE, TOO. MAYBE I'LL JOIN YOU.
NO, I MEAN-- YOU KNOW! SOMETIMES I START **FLYING** AT RANDOM!

Chapter 95: "Let's Have a Family Chat!"

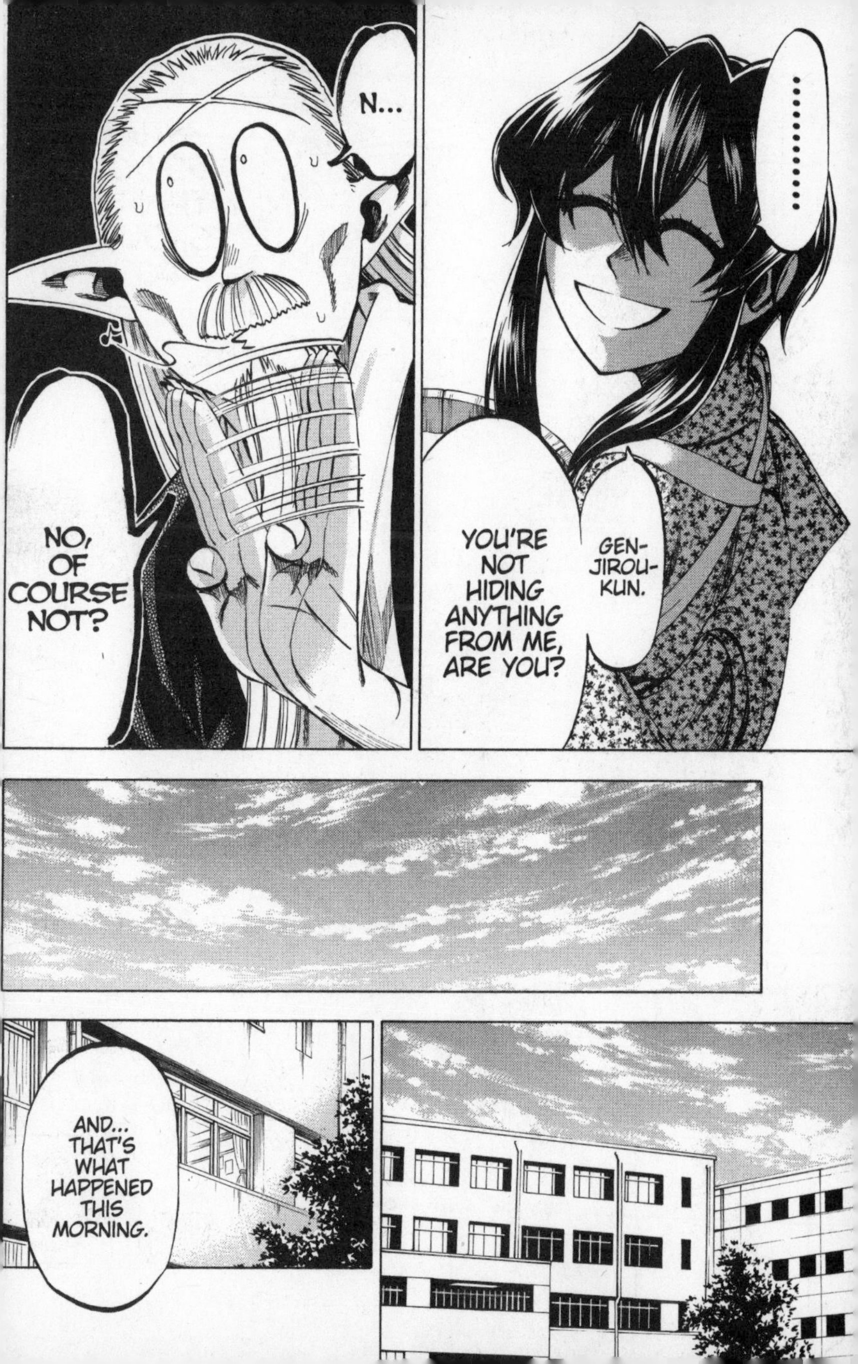
......
GEN-JIROU-KUN.
YOU'RE NOT HIDING ANYTHING FROM ME, ARE YOU?
N...
NO, OF COURSE NOT?
AND... THAT'S WHAT HAPPENED THIS MORNING.

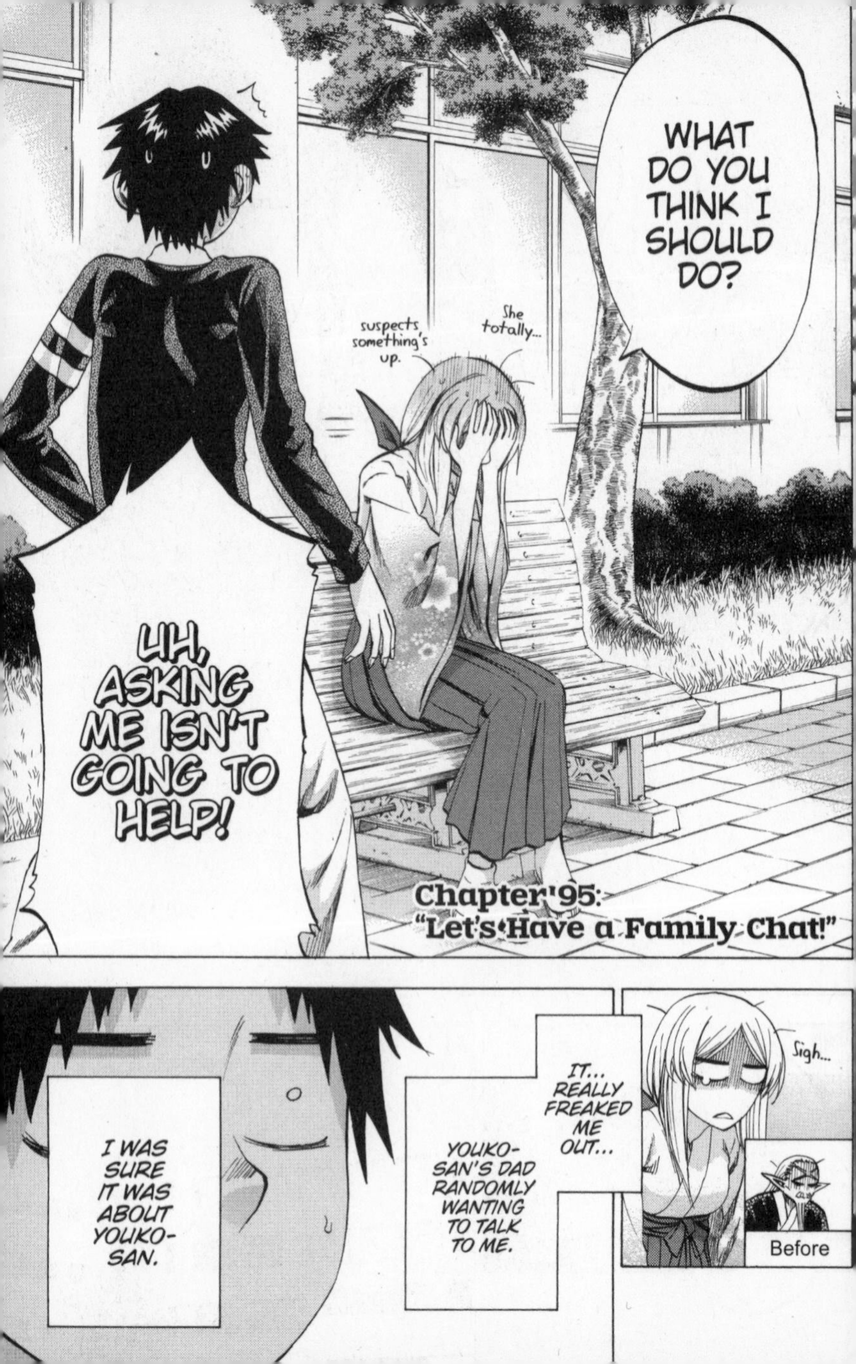
WHAT DO YOU THINK I SHOULD DO?
She totally... suspects something's up.
UH, ASKING ME ISN'T GOING TO HELP!
Chapter 95: "Let's Have a Family Chat!"
Sigh...
Before
IT... REALLY FREAKED ME OUT...
YOUKO-SAN'S DAD RANDOMLY WANTING TO TALK TO ME.
I WAS SURE IT WAS ABOUT YOUKO-SAN.

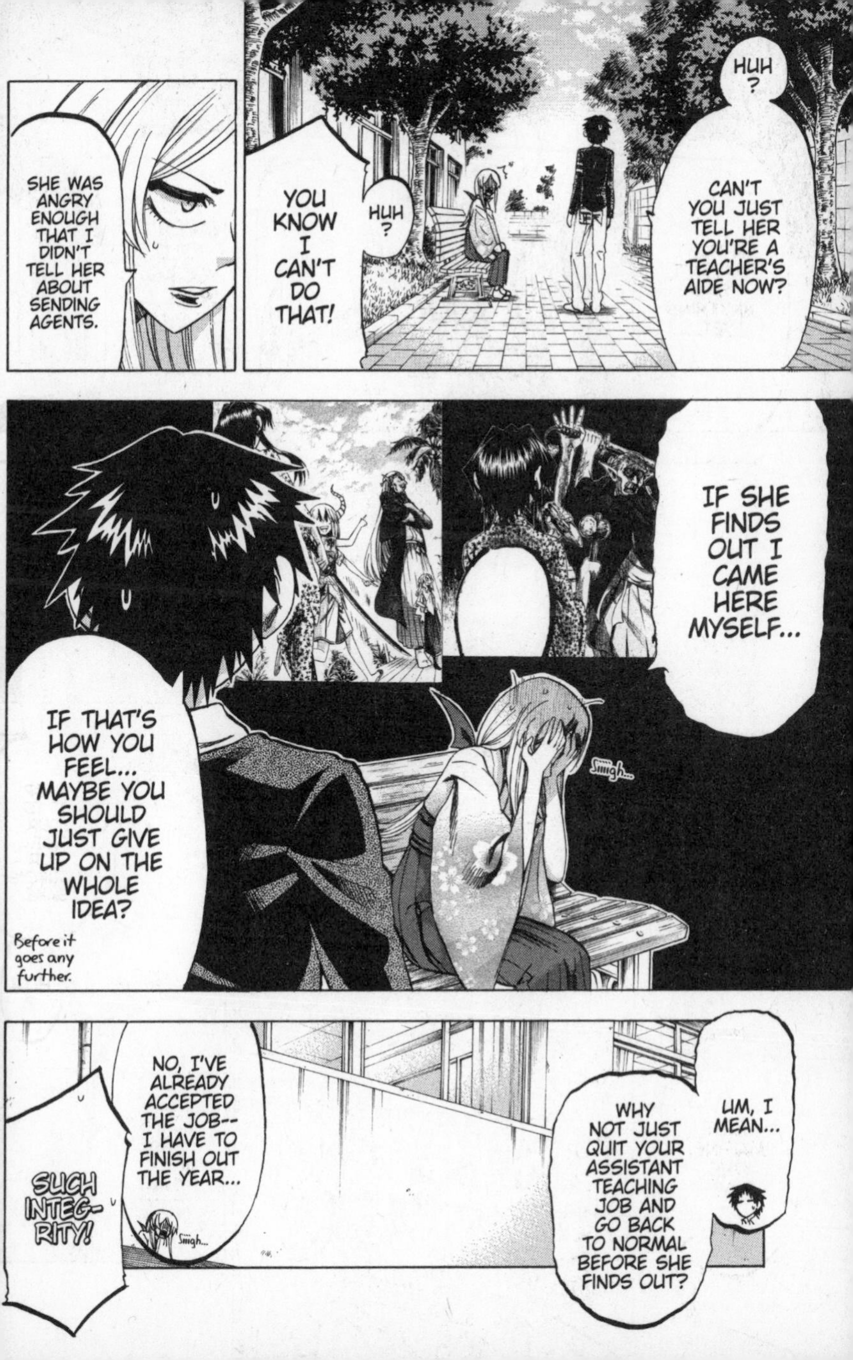
HUH ?
CAN'T YOU JUST TELL HER YOU'RE A TEACHER'S AIDE NOW?
HUH ?
YOU KNOW I CAN'T DO THAT!
SHE WAS ANGRY ENOUGH THAT I DIDN'T TELL HER ABOUT SENDING AGENTS.
IF SHE FINDS OUT I CAME HERE MYSELF...
Siiigh...
IF THAT'S HOW YOU FEEL... MAYBE YOU SHOULD JUST GIVE UP ON THE WHOLE IDEA?
Before it goes any further.
UM, I MEAN...
WHY NOT JUST QUIT YOUR ASSISTANT TEACHING JOB AND GO BACK TO NORMAL BEFORE SHE FINDS OUT?
NO, I'VE ALREADY ACCEPTED THE JOB-- I HAVE TO FINISH OUT THE YEAR...
Siiigh...
SUCH INTEGRITY!

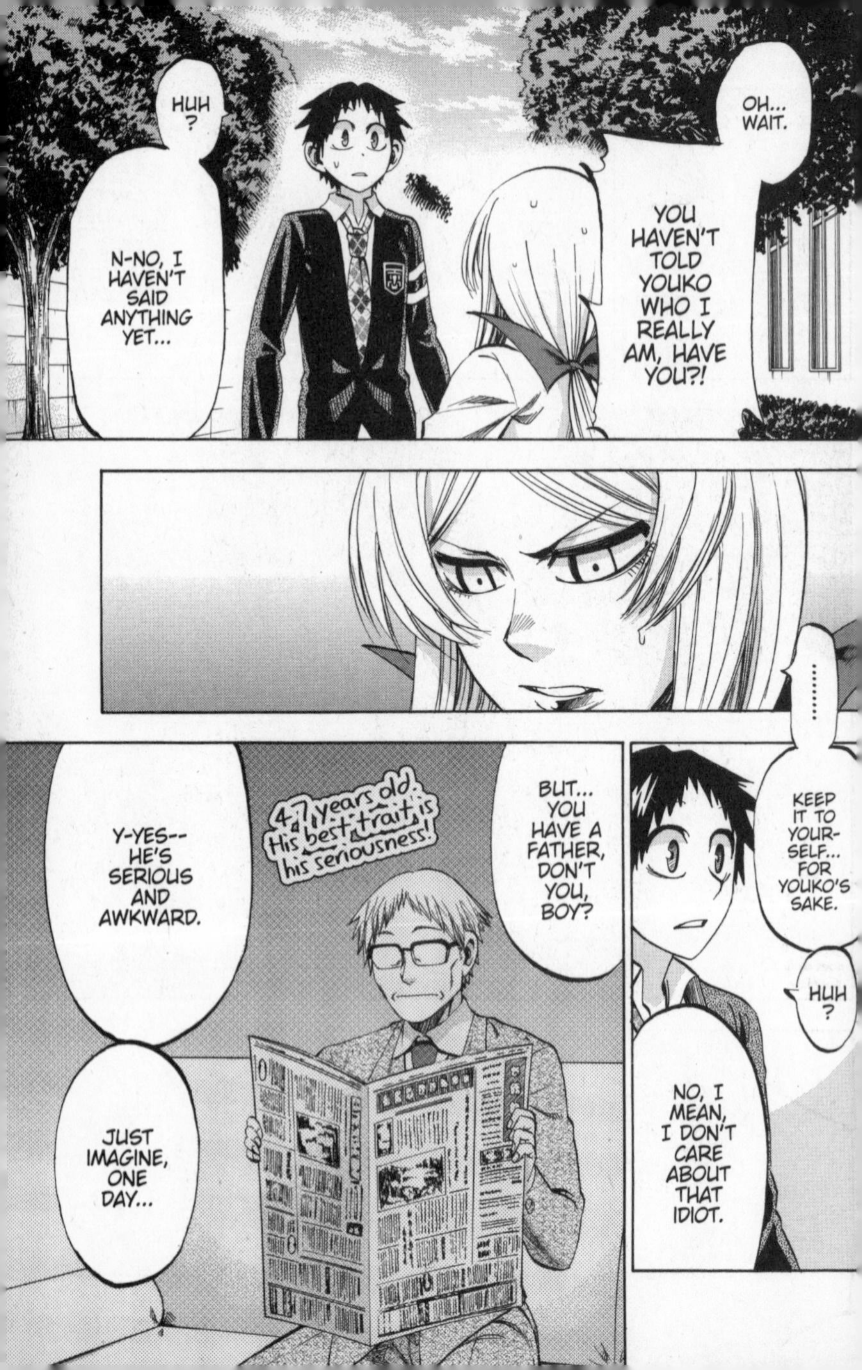
OH... WAIT.
YOU HAVEN'T TOLD YOUKO WHO I REALLY AM, HAVE YOU?!
HUH?
N-NO, I HAVEN'T SAID ANYTHING YET...
......
KEEP IT TO YOURSELF... FOR YOUKO'S SAKE.
HUH?
NO, I MEAN, I DON'T CARE ABOUT THAT IDIOT.
BUT... YOU HAVE A FATHER, DON'T YOU, BOY?
47 years old. His best trait is his seriousness!
Y-YES-- HE'S SERIOUS AND AWKWARD.
JUST IMAGINE, ONE DAY...

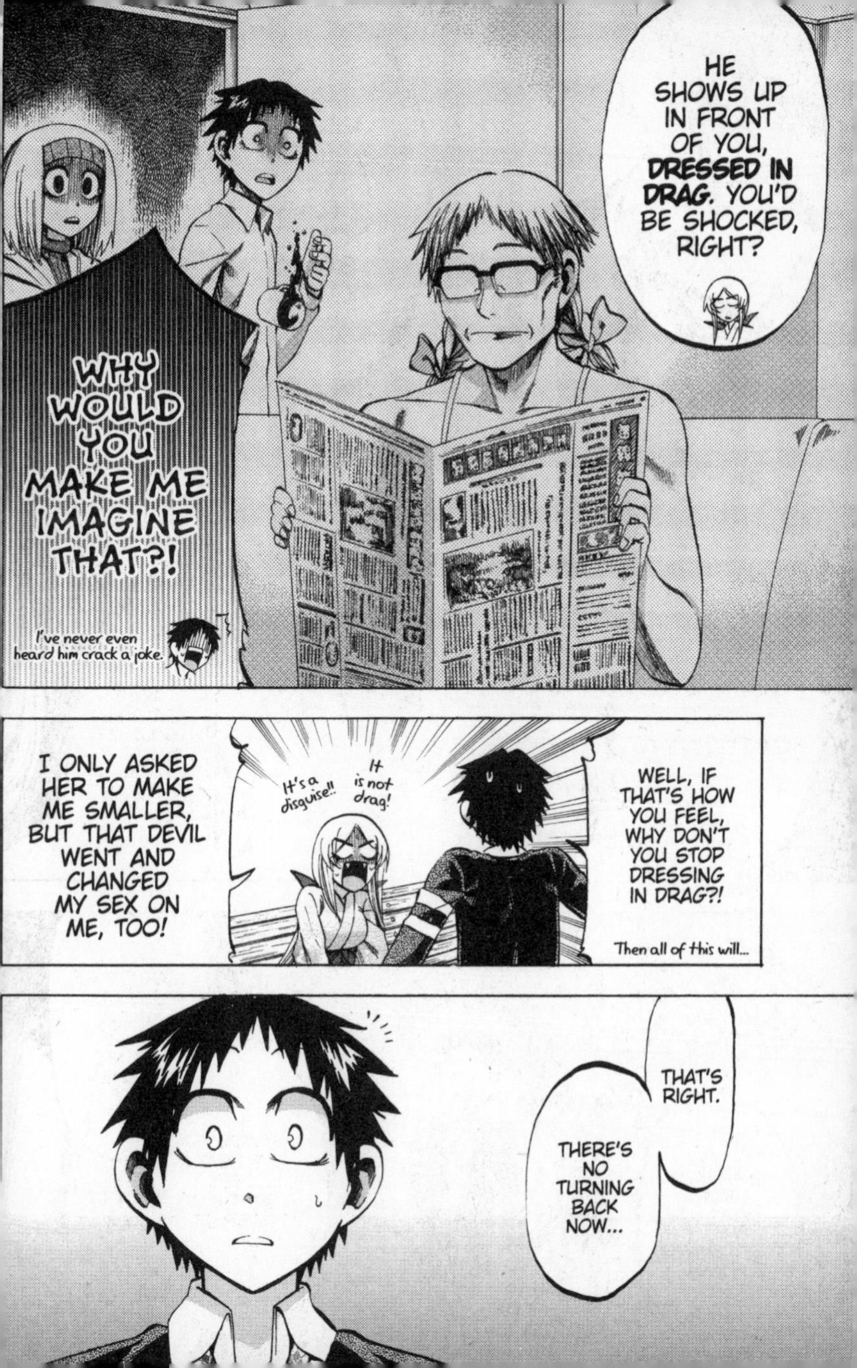
HE SHOWS UP IN FRONT OF YOU, **DRESSED IN DRAG**. YOU'D BE SHOCKED, RIGHT?
WHY WOULD YOU MAKE ME IMAGINE THAT?!
I've never even heard him crack a joke.
WELL, IF THAT'S HOW YOU FEEL, WHY DON'T YOU STOP DRESSING IN DRAG?!
Then all of this will...
It is not drag!
It's a disguise!!
I ONLY ASKED HER TO MAKE ME SMALLER, BUT THAT DEVIL WENT AND CHANGED MY SEX ON ME, TOO!
THAT'S RIGHT.
THERE'S NO TURNING BACK NOW...

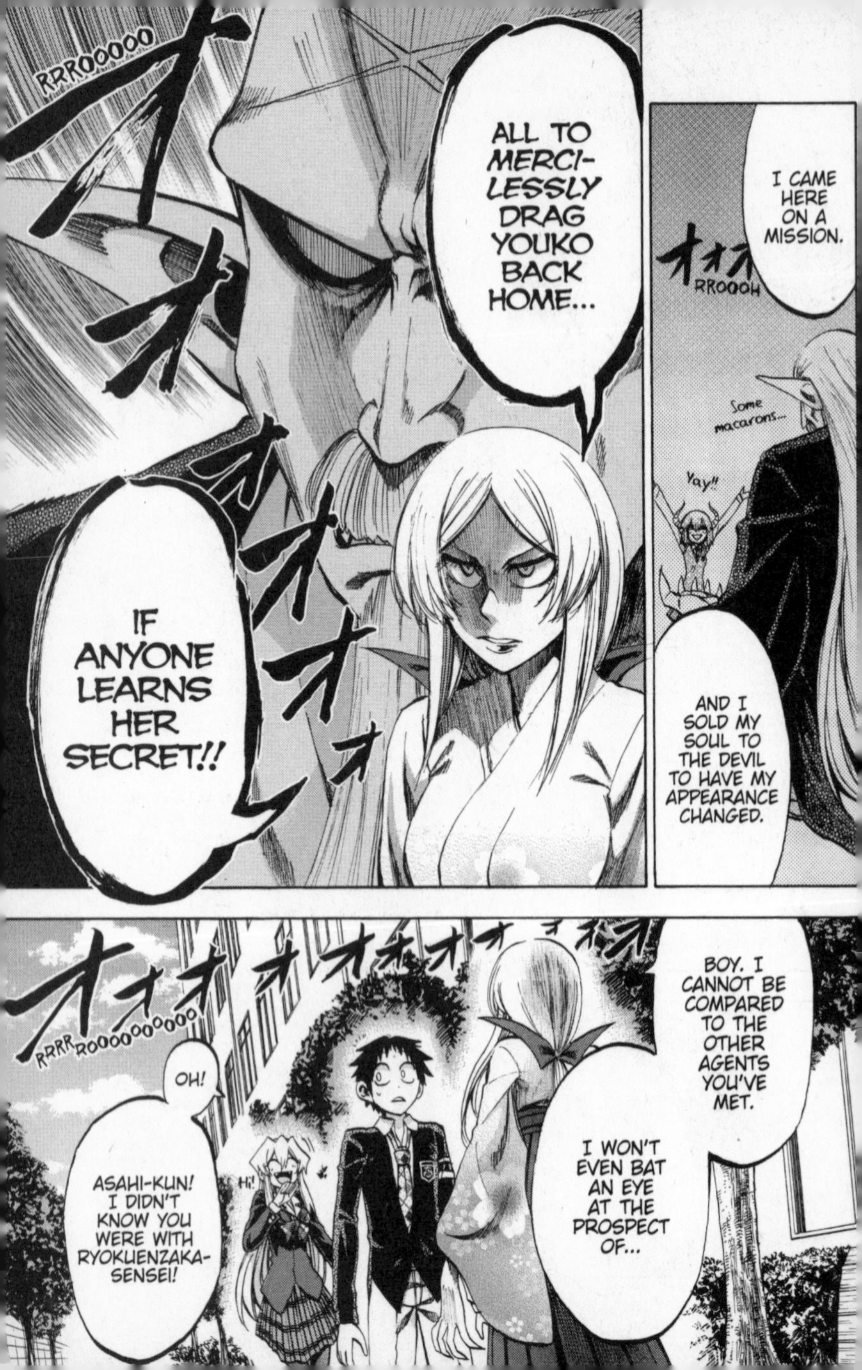
I CAME HERE ON A MISSION.
RROOOH
Some macarons...
Yay!!
AND I SOLD MY SOUL TO THE DEVIL TO HAVE MY APPEARANCE CHANGED.
RRROOOOO
ALL TO MERCI-LESSLY DRAG YOUKO BACK HOME...
IF ANYONE LEARNS HER SECRET!!
BOY. I CANNOT BE COMPARED TO THE OTHER AGENTS YOU'VE MET.
I WON'T EVEN BAT AN EYE AT THE PROSPECT OF...
RRRRROOOOOOOOOO
OH!
HI!
ASAHI-KUN! I DIDN'T KNOW YOU WERE WITH RYOKUENZAKA-SENSEI!

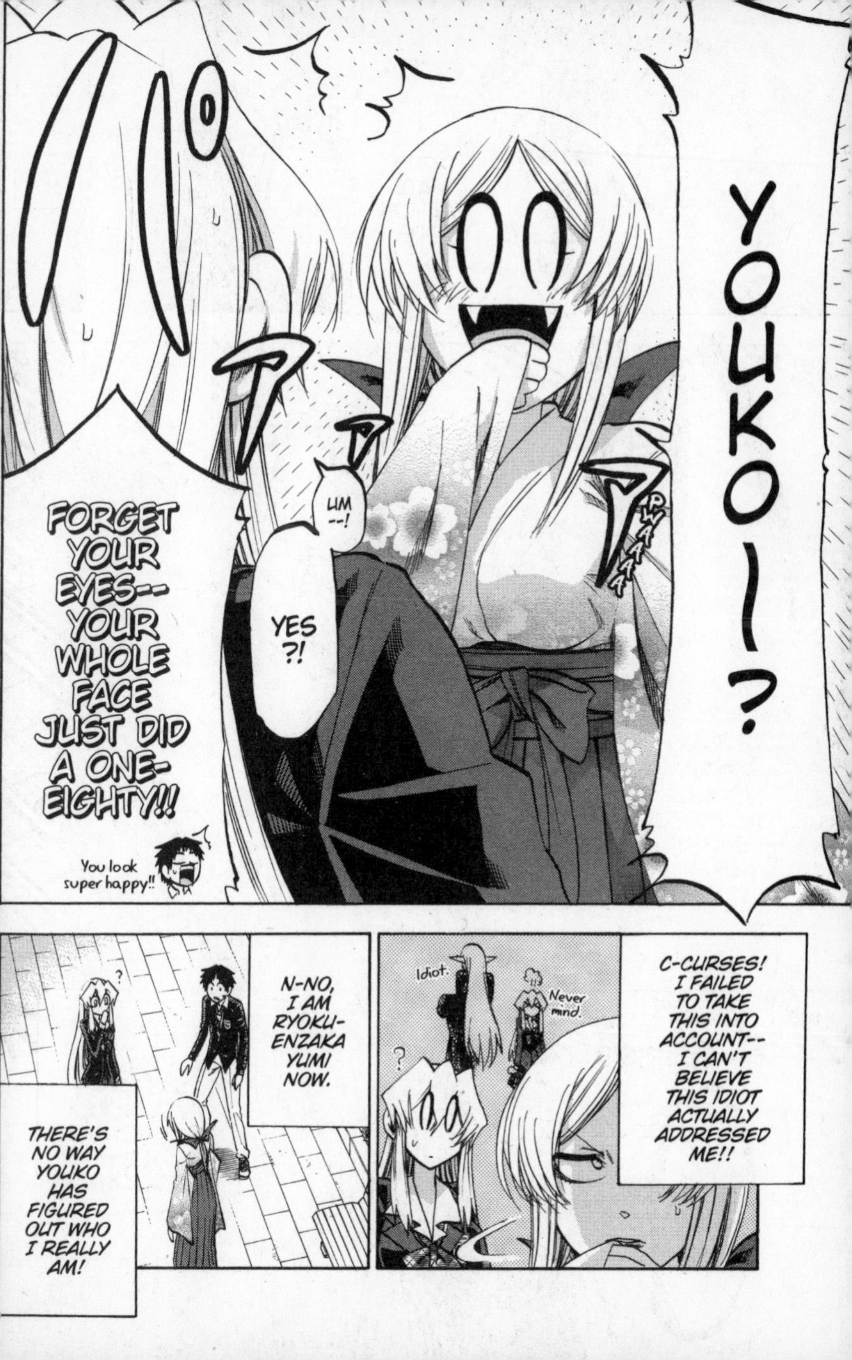
YOUKO!?
PWAAAA
UM--!
YES?!
FORGET YOUR EYES--YOUR WHOLE FACE JUST DID A ONE-EIGHTY!!
You look super happy!!
C-CURSES! I FAILED TO TAKE THIS INTO ACCOUNT--I CAN'T BELIEVE THIS IDIOT ACTUALLY ADDRESSED ME!!
Never mind.
Idiot.
N-NO, I AM RYOKU-ENZAKA YUMI NOW.
THERE'S NO WAY YOUKO HAS FIGURED OUT WHO I REALLY AM!

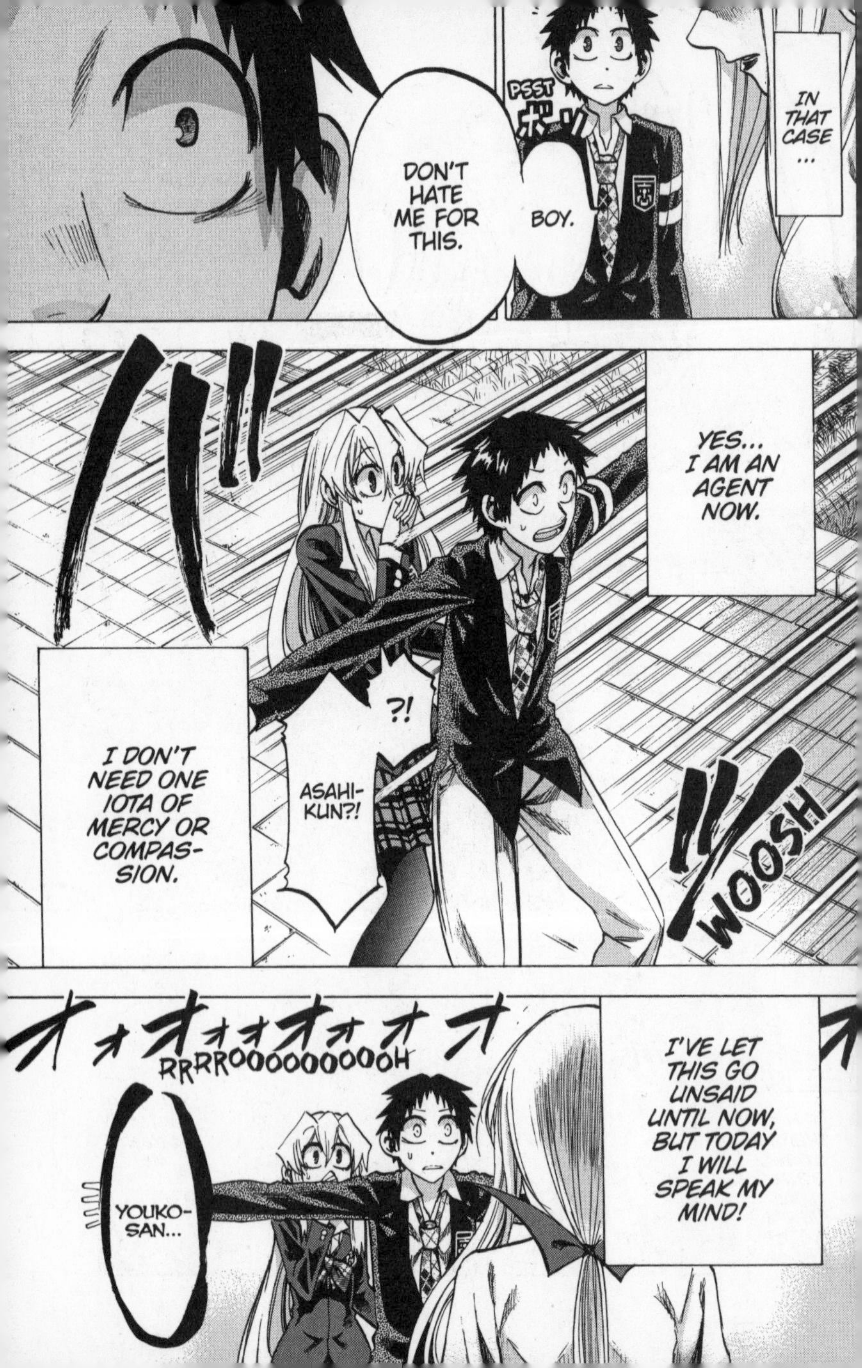
IN THAT CASE...
PSST
BOY.
DON'T HATE ME FOR THIS.
YES... I AM AN AGENT NOW.
WOOSH
?!
ASAHI-KUN?!
I DON'T NEED ONE IOTA OF MERCY OR COMPAS-SION.
I'VE LET THIS GO UNSAID UNTIL NOW, BUT TODAY I WILL SPEAK MY MIND!
RRRROOOOOOOOOOH
YOUKO-SAN...

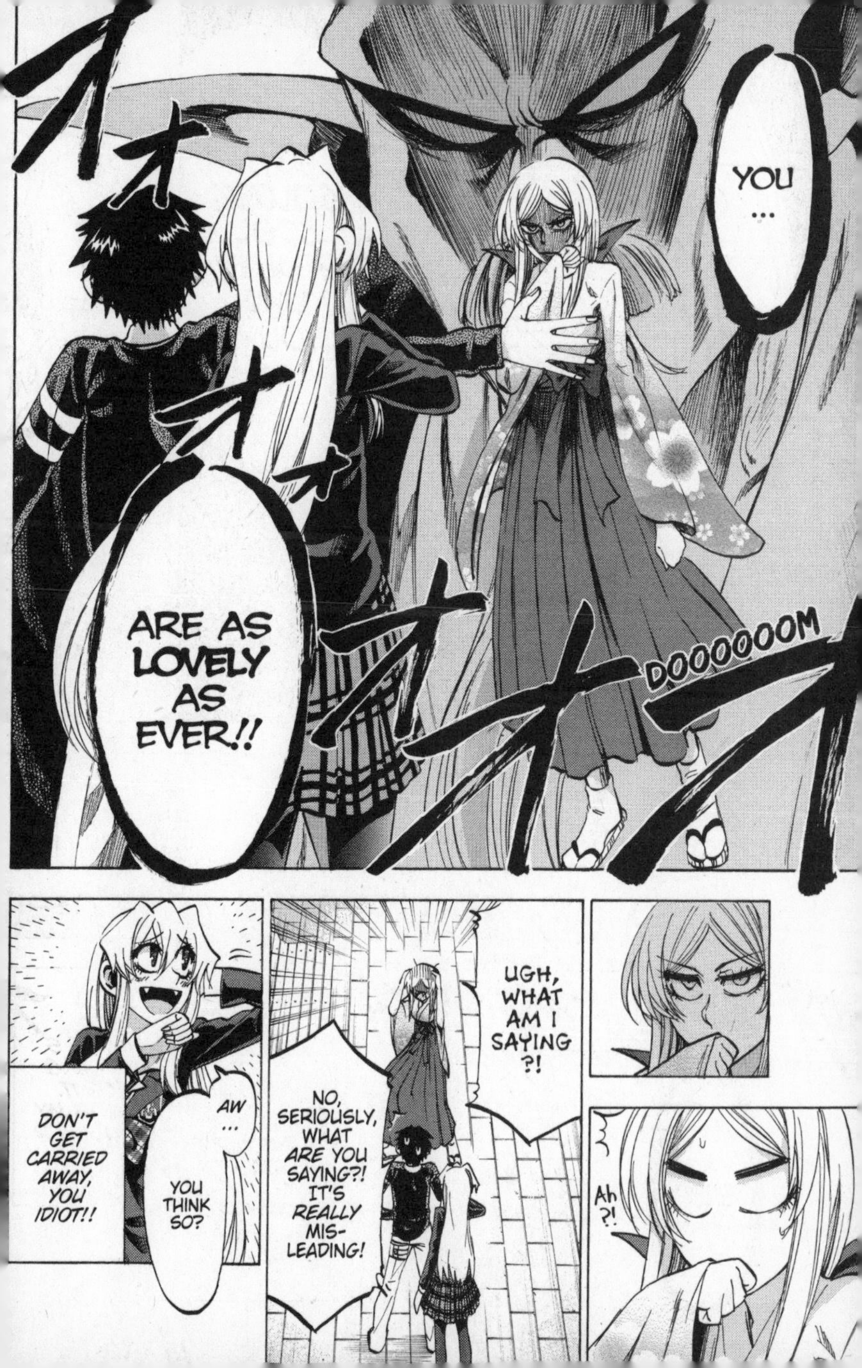
YOU ...
ARE AS LOVELY AS EVER!!
DOOOOOOOM
Ah ?!
UGH, WHAT AM I SAYING ?!
NO, SERIOUSLY, WHAT ARE YOU SAYING?! IT'S REALLY MIS-LEADING!
AW ... YOU THINK SO?
DON'T GET CARRIED AWAY, YOU IDIOT!!

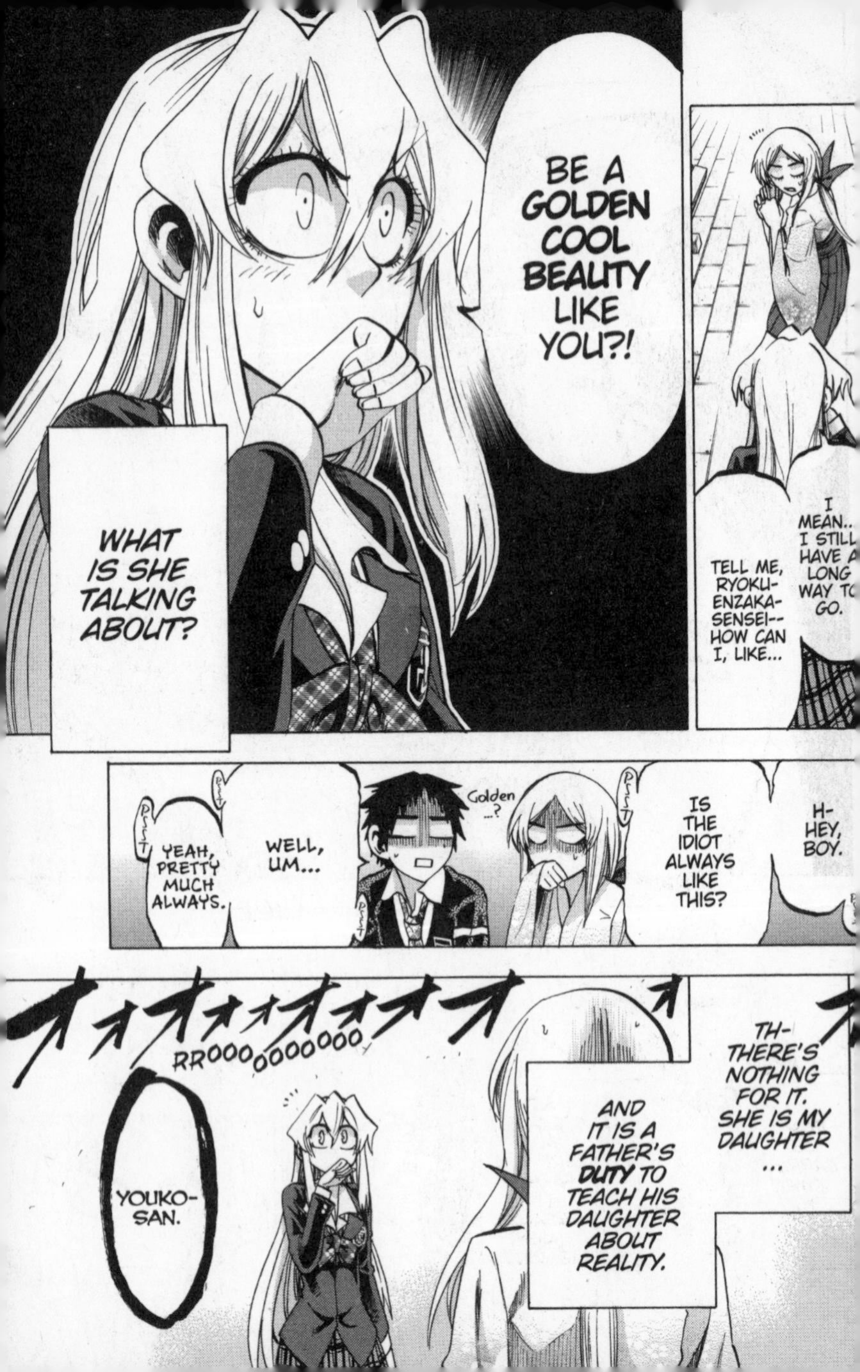
I MEAN... I STILL HAVE A LONG WAY TO GO.
TELL ME, RYOKU-ENZAKA-SENSEI-- HOW CAN I, LIKE...
BE A GOLDEN COOL BEAUTY LIKE YOU?!
WHAT IS SHE TALKING ABOUT?
H- HEY, BOY.
IS THE IDIOT ALWAYS LIKE THIS?
Golden ...?
WELL, UM...
YEAH, PRETTY MUCH ALWAYS.
TH- THERE'S NOTHING FOR IT. SHE IS MY DAUGHTER ...
AND IT IS A FATHER'S DUTY TO TEACH HIS DAUGHTER ABOUT REALITY.
RROOOOOOOOOO
YOUKO-SAN.

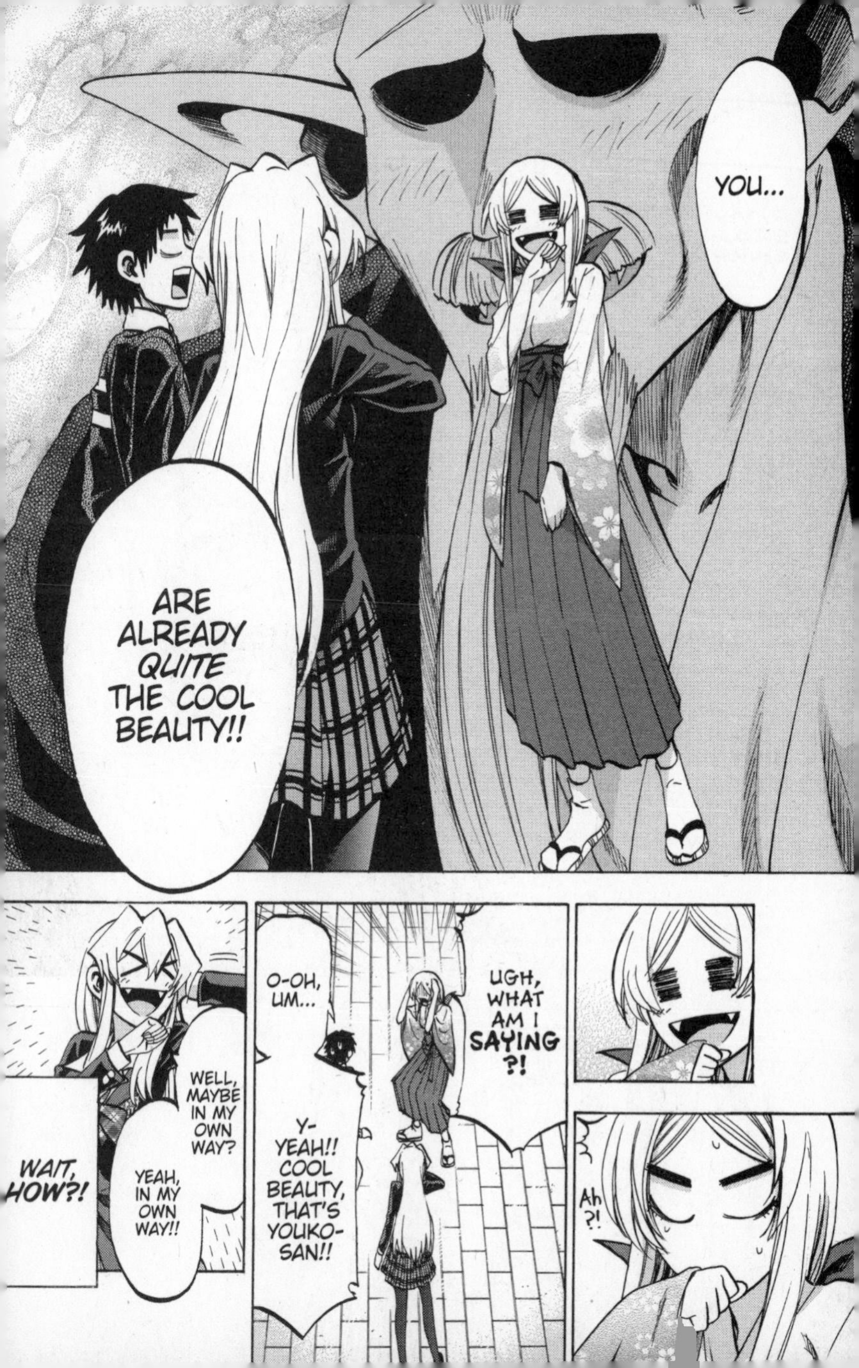
YOU...
ARE ALREADY *QUITE* THE COOL BEAUTY!!
Ah?!
UGH, WHAT AM I **SAYING**?!
O-OH, UM...
Y-YEAH!! COOL BEAUTY, THAT'S YOUKO-SAN!!
WELL, MAYBE IN MY OWN WAY?
YEAH, IN MY OWN WAY!!
WAIT, HOW?!

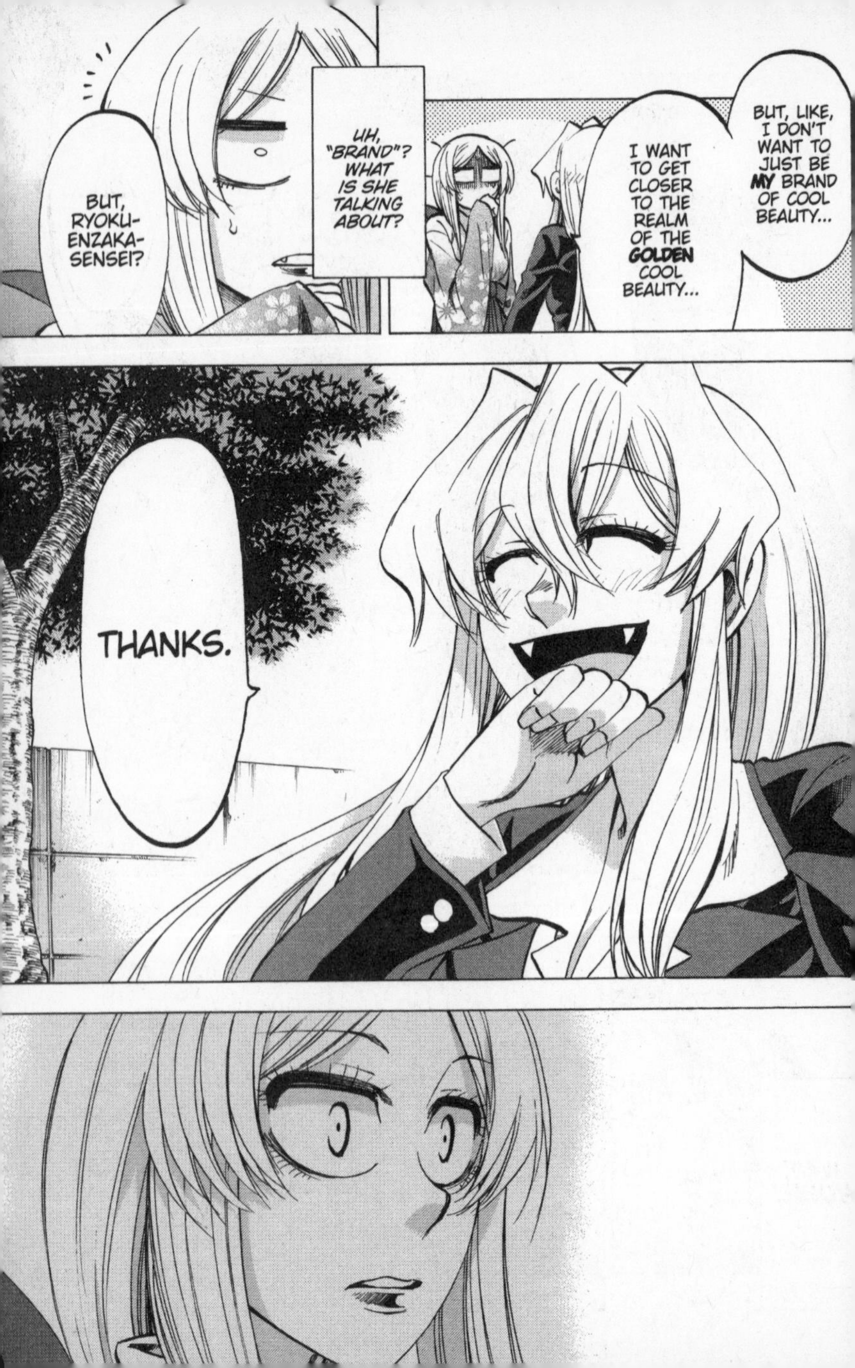
BUT, LIKE, I DON'T WANT TO JUST BE MY BRAND OF COOL BEAUTY...
I WANT TO GET CLOSER TO THE REALM OF THE GOLDEN COOL BEAUTY...
UH, "BRAND"? WHAT IS SHE TALKING ABOUT?
BUT, RYOKU-ENZAKA-SENSEI?
THANKS.

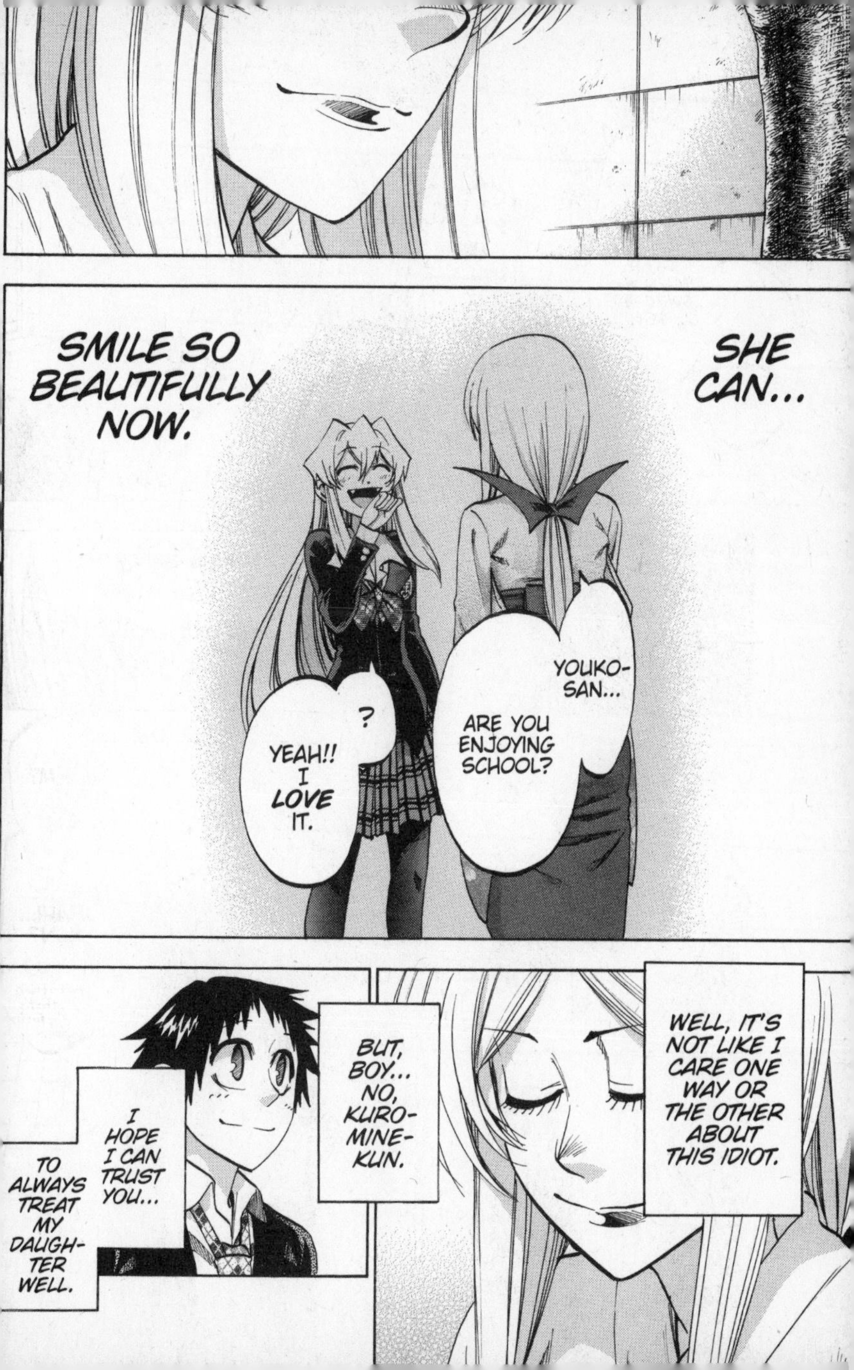
SHE CAN...
SMILE SO BEAUTIFULLY NOW.
YOUKO-SAN...
ARE YOU ENJOYING SCHOOL?
?
YEAH!! I *LOVE* IT.
WELL, IT'S NOT LIKE I CARE ONE WAY OR THE OTHER ABOUT THIS IDIOT.
BUT, BOY... NO, KUROMINE-KUN.
I HOPE I CAN TRUST YOU...
TO ALWAYS TREAT MY DAUGHTER WELL.

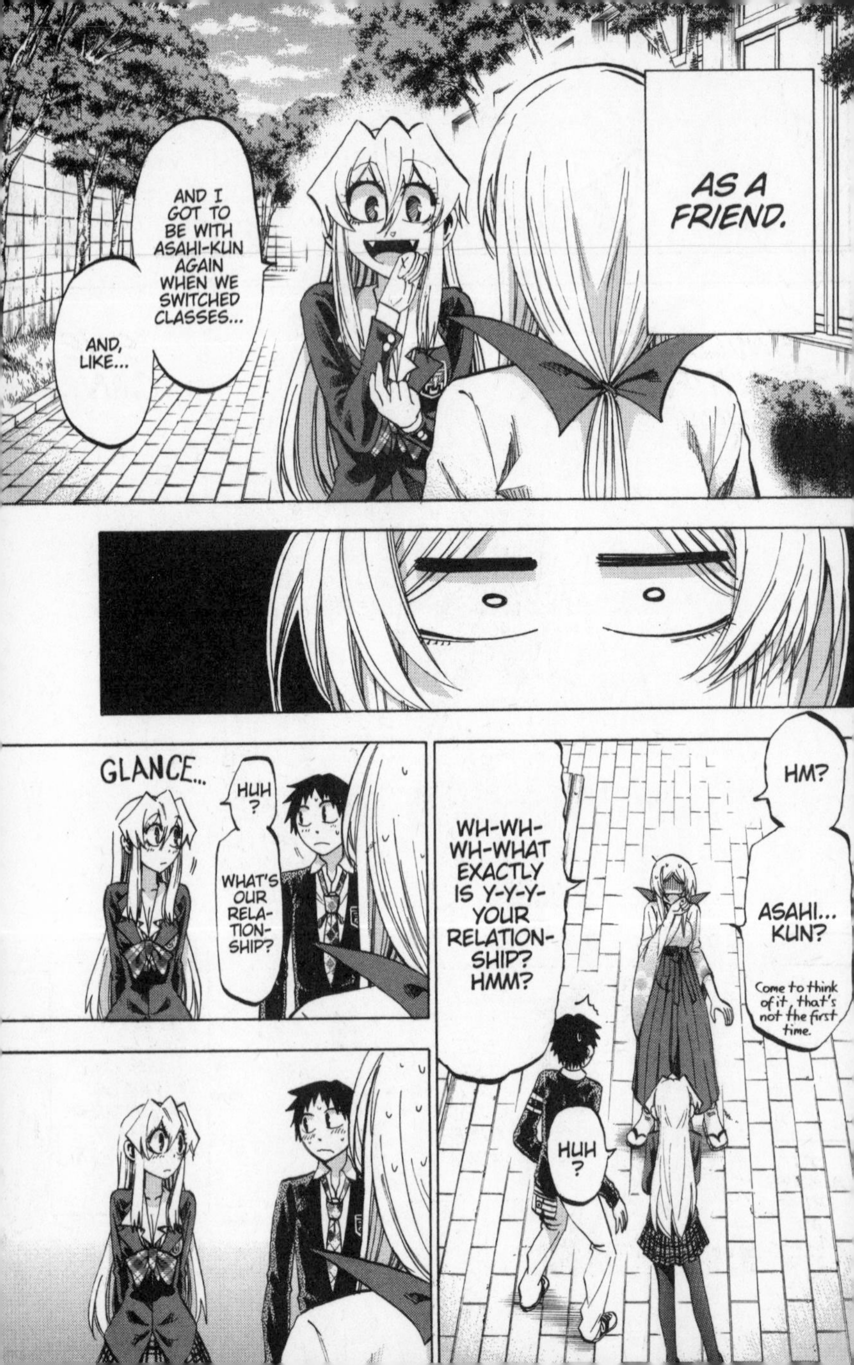
AS A FRIEND.
AND I GOT TO BE WITH ASAHI-KUN AGAIN WHEN WE SWITCHED CLASSES...
AND, LIKE...
HM?
ASAHI... KUN?
Come to think of it, that's not the first time.
WH-WH-WH-WHAT EXACTLY IS Y-Y-Y-YOUR RELATION-SHIP? HMM?
HUH?
GLANCE...
HUH?
WHAT'S OUR RELA-TION-SHIP?

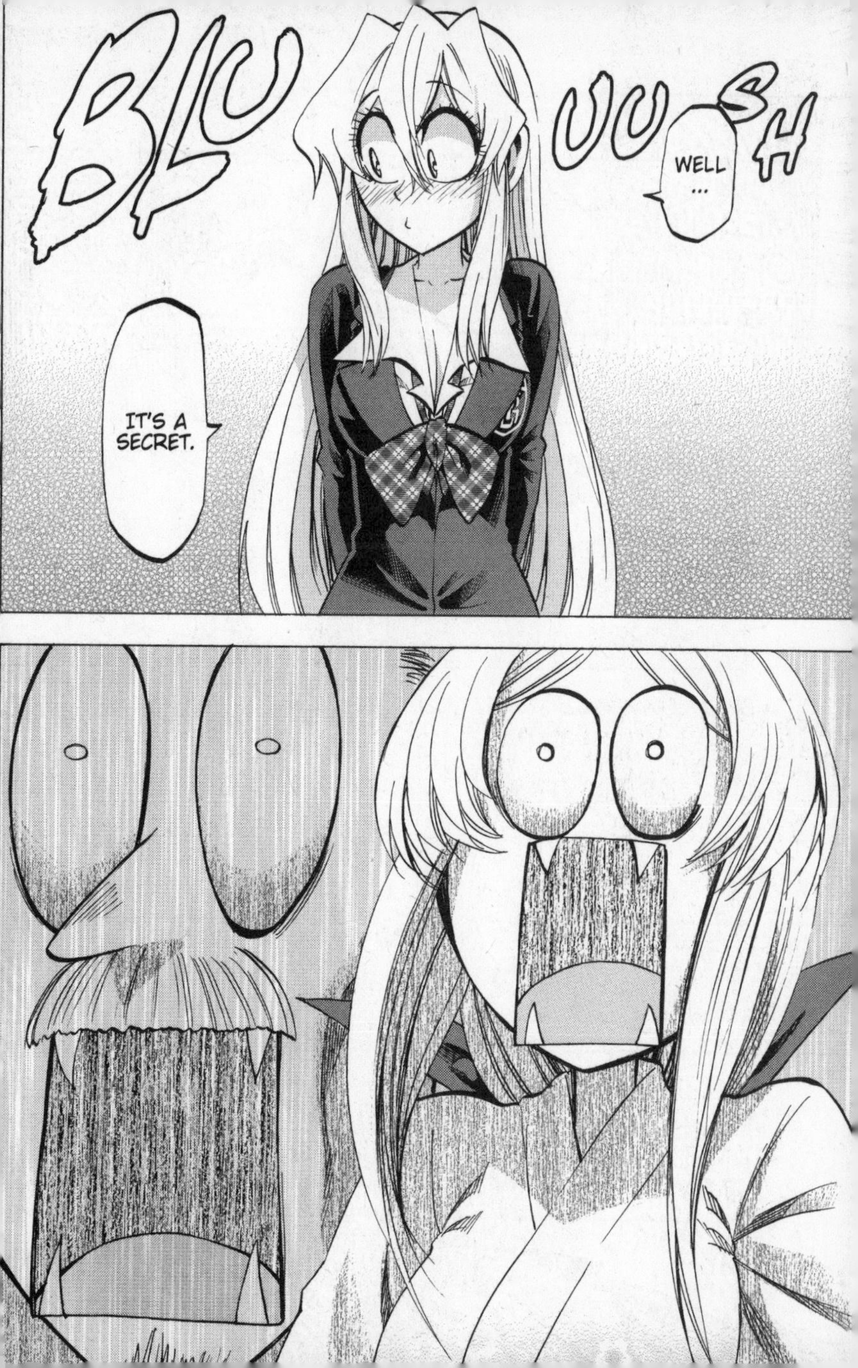
WELL ...
BLUUUSH
IT'S A SECRET.

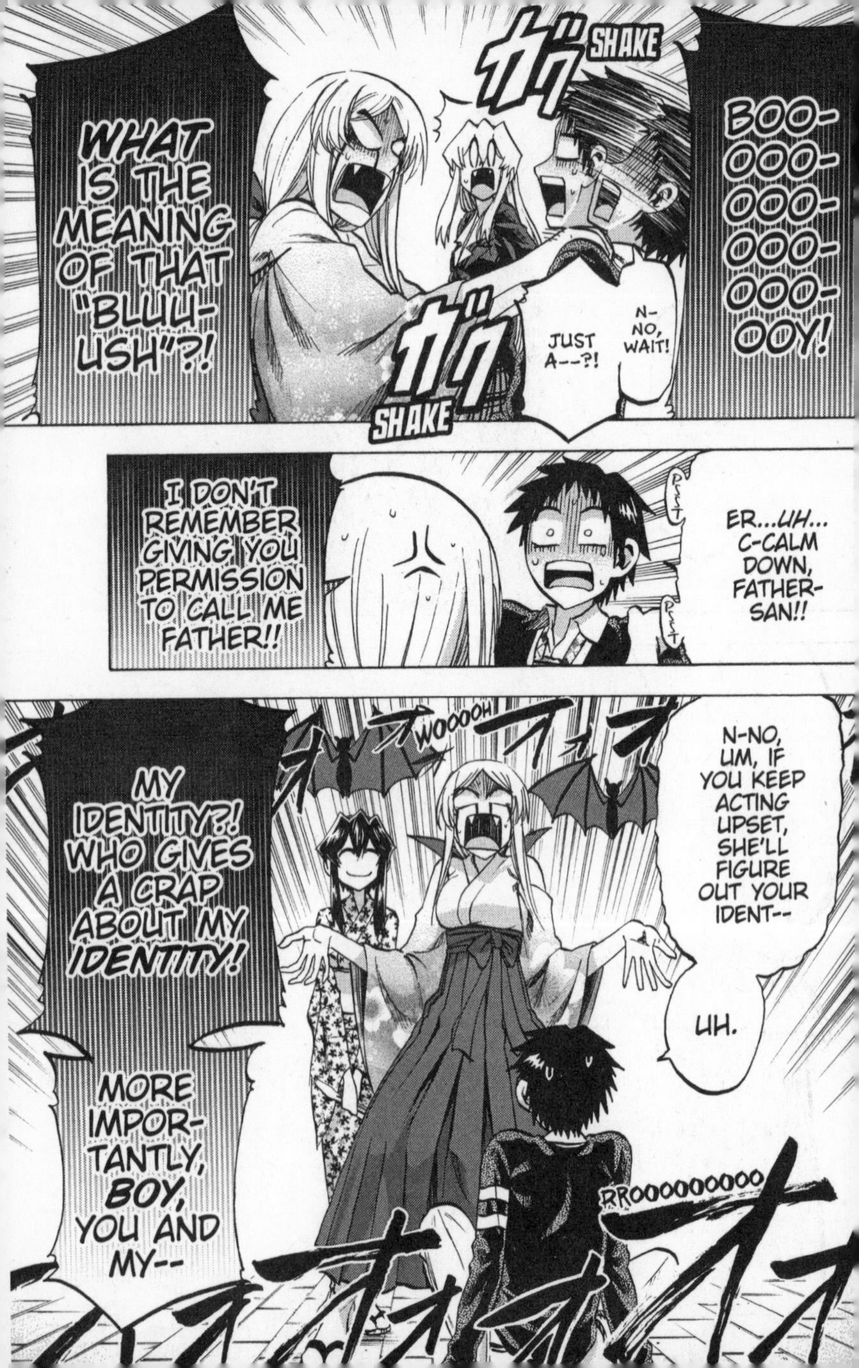
BOO-OOO-OOO-OOO-OOO-OOY!
SHAKE
N-NO, WAIT!
JUST A--?!
WHAT IS THE MEANING OF THAT "BLUU-USH"?!
SHAKE
ER...UH... C-CALM DOWN, FATHER-SAN!!
PSST
PSST
I DON'T REMEMBER GIVING YOU PERMISSION TO CALL ME FATHER!!
N-NO, UM, IF YOU KEEP ACTING UPSET, SHE'LL FIGURE OUT YOUR IDENT--
UH.
WOOOOH
MY IDENTITY?! WHO GIVES A CRAP ABOUT MY IDENTITY!
MORE IMPORTANTLY, BOY, YOU AND MY--
DROOOOOOOOO

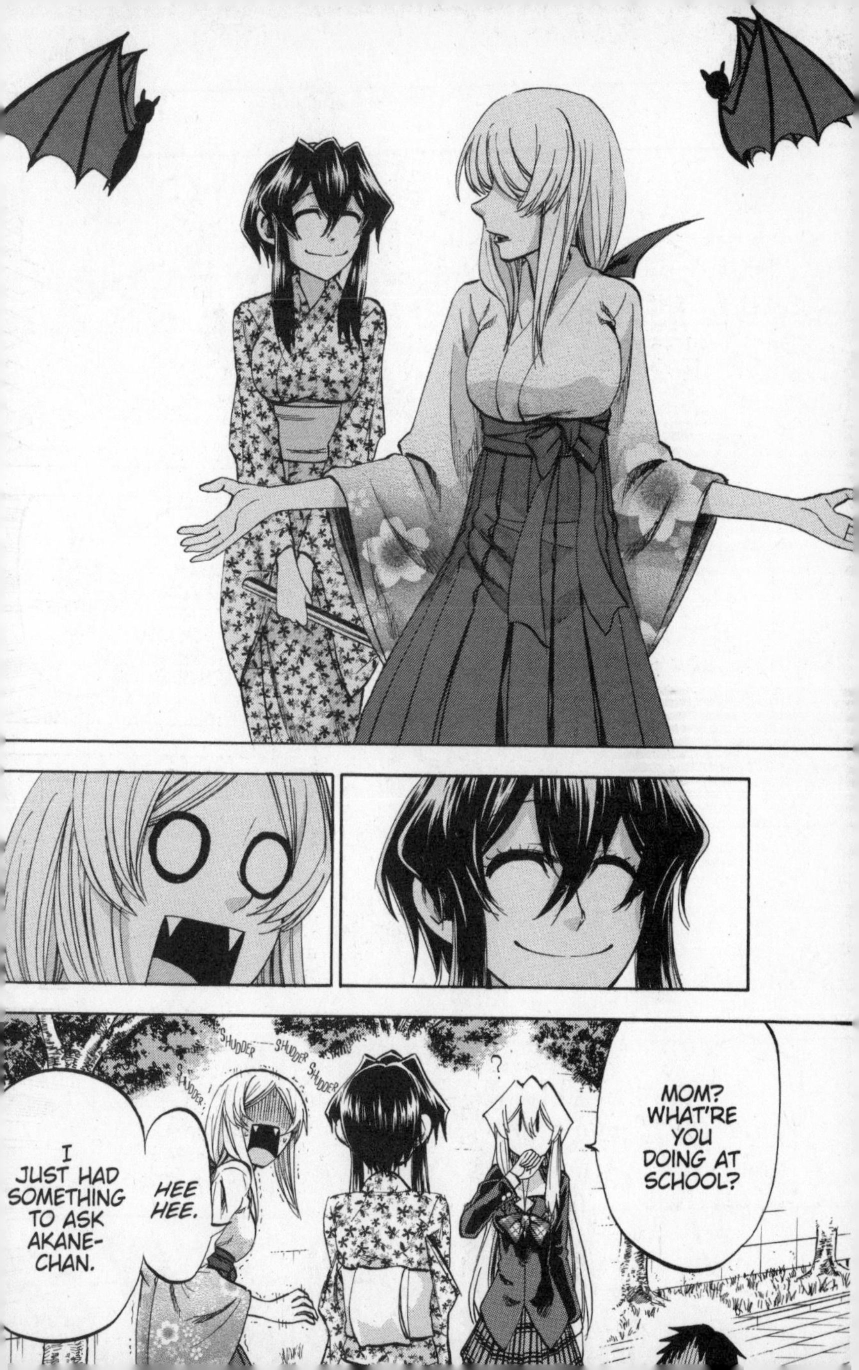
MOM? WHAT'RE YOU DOING AT SCHOOL?
SHUDDER SHUDDER SHUDDER SHUDDER
HEE HEE.
I JUST HAD SOMETHING TO ASK AKANE-CHAN.

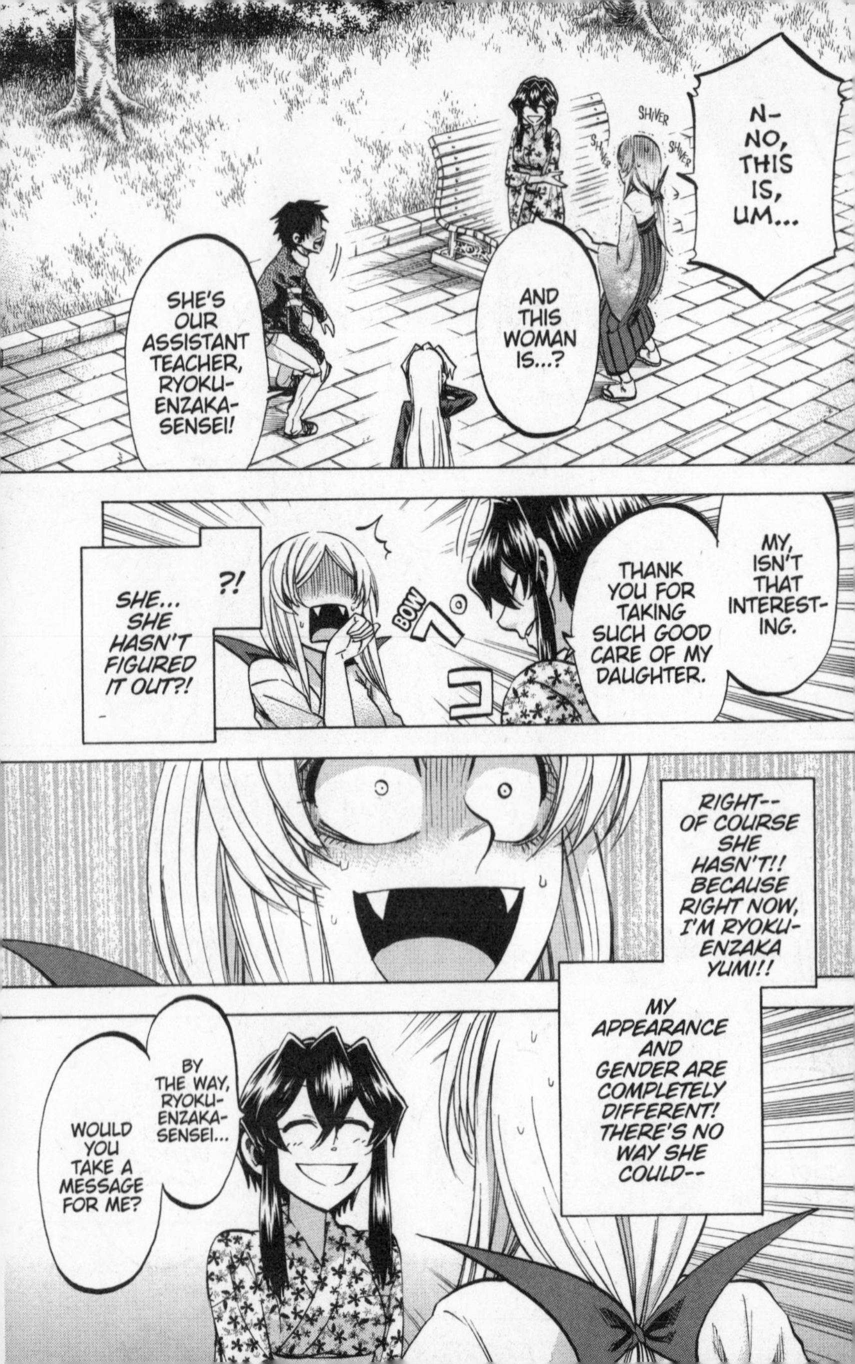
N-NO, THIS IS, UM...
SHIVER SHIVER SHIVER
AND THIS WOMAN IS...?
SHE'S OUR ASSISTANT TEACHER, RYOKU-ENZAKA-SENSEI!
MY, ISN'T THAT INTEREST-ING.
THANK YOU FOR TAKING SUCH GOOD CARE OF MY DAUGHTER.
BOW
?!
SHE... SHE HASN'T FIGURED IT OUT?!
RIGHT-- OF COURSE SHE HASN'T!! BECAUSE RIGHT NOW, I'M RYOKU-ENZAKA YUMI!!
MY APPEARANCE AND GENDER ARE COMPLETELY DIFFERENT! THERE'S NO WAY SHE COULD--
BY THE WAY, RYOKU-ENZAKA-SENSEI...
WOULD YOU TAKE A MESSAGE FOR ME?

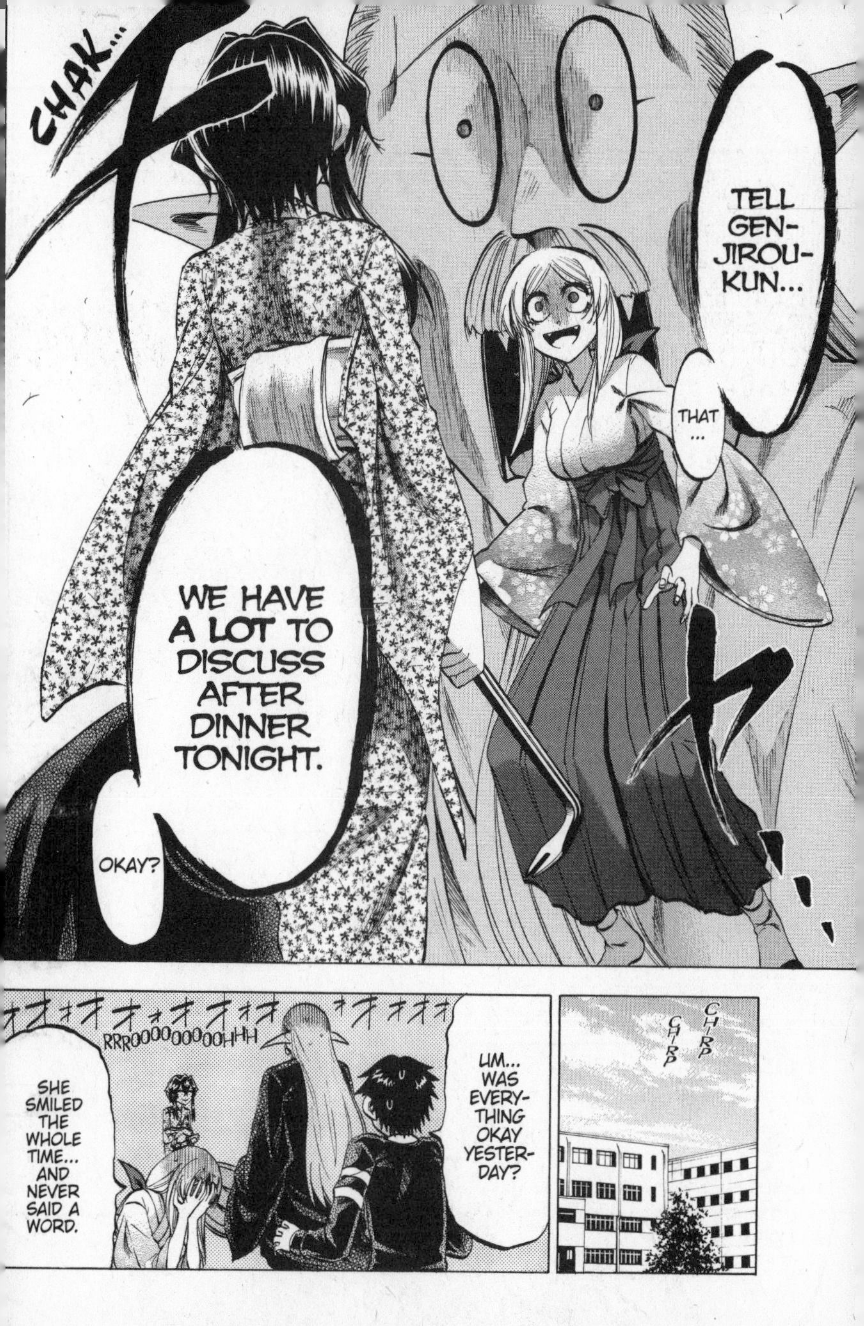
TELL GEN-JIROU-KUN...
THAT...
CHAK...
WE HAVE A LOT TO DISCUSS AFTER DINNER TONIGHT.
OKAY?
CHIRP
CHIRP
UM... WAS EVERY-THING OKAY YESTER-DAY?
RRROOOOOOOOOHHH
SHE SMILED THE WHOLE TIME... AND NEVER SAID A WORD.

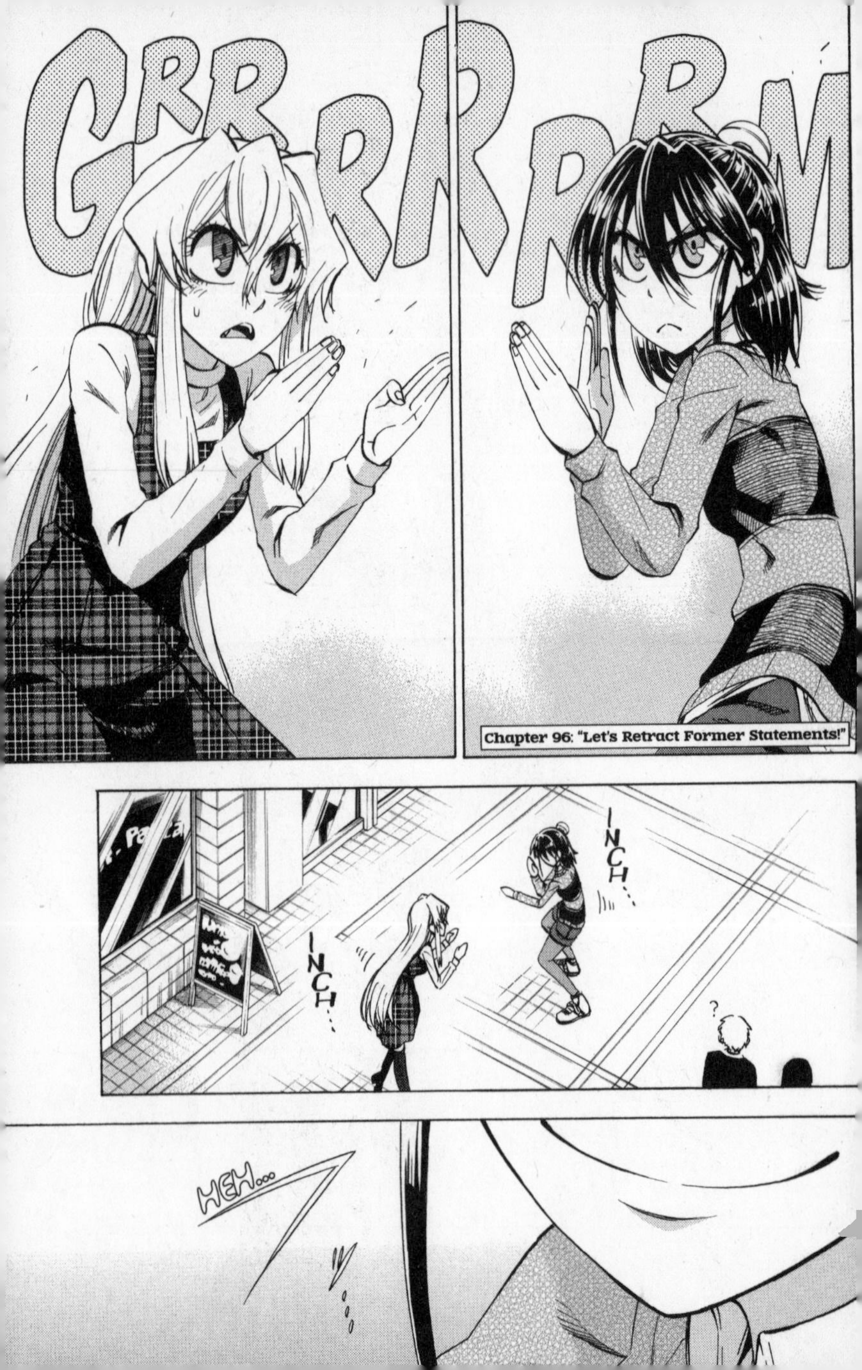
GRRRRRRM
Chapter 96: "Let's Retract Former Statements!"
INCH...
INCH...
HEH...

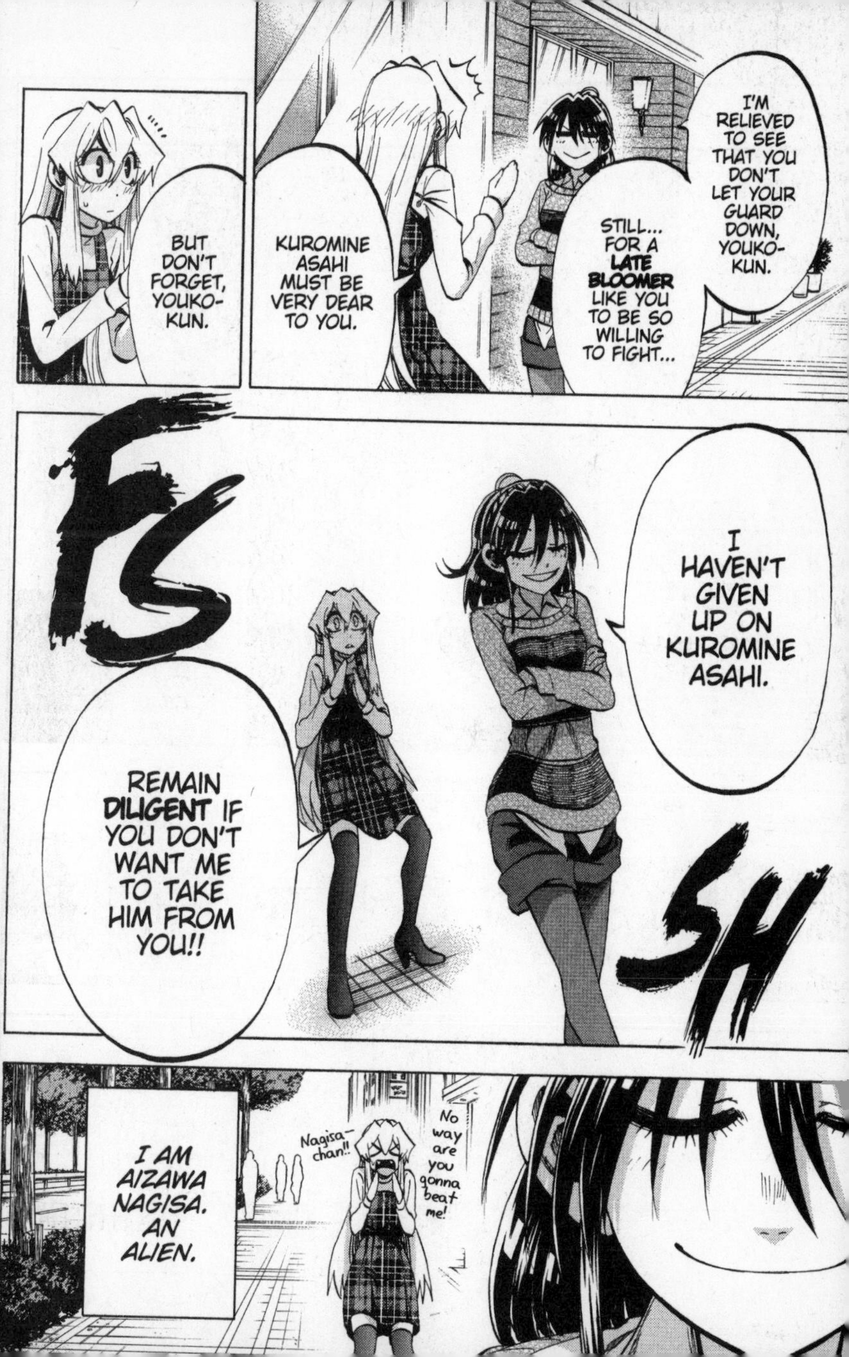

I'M RELIEVED TO SEE THAT YOU DON'T LET YOUR GUARD DOWN, YOUKO-KUN.
STILL... FOR A **LATE BLOOMER** LIKE YOU TO BE SO WILLING TO FIGHT...
KUROMINE ASAHI MUST BE VERY DEAR TO YOU.
BUT DON'T FORGET, YOUKO-KUN.
I HAVEN'T GIVEN UP ON KUROMINE ASAHI.
FS
SH
REMAIN **DILIGENT** IF YOU DON'T WANT ME TO TAKE HIM FROM YOU!!
No way are you gonna beat me!
Nagisa-chan!!
I AM AIZAWA NAGISA. AN ALIEN.

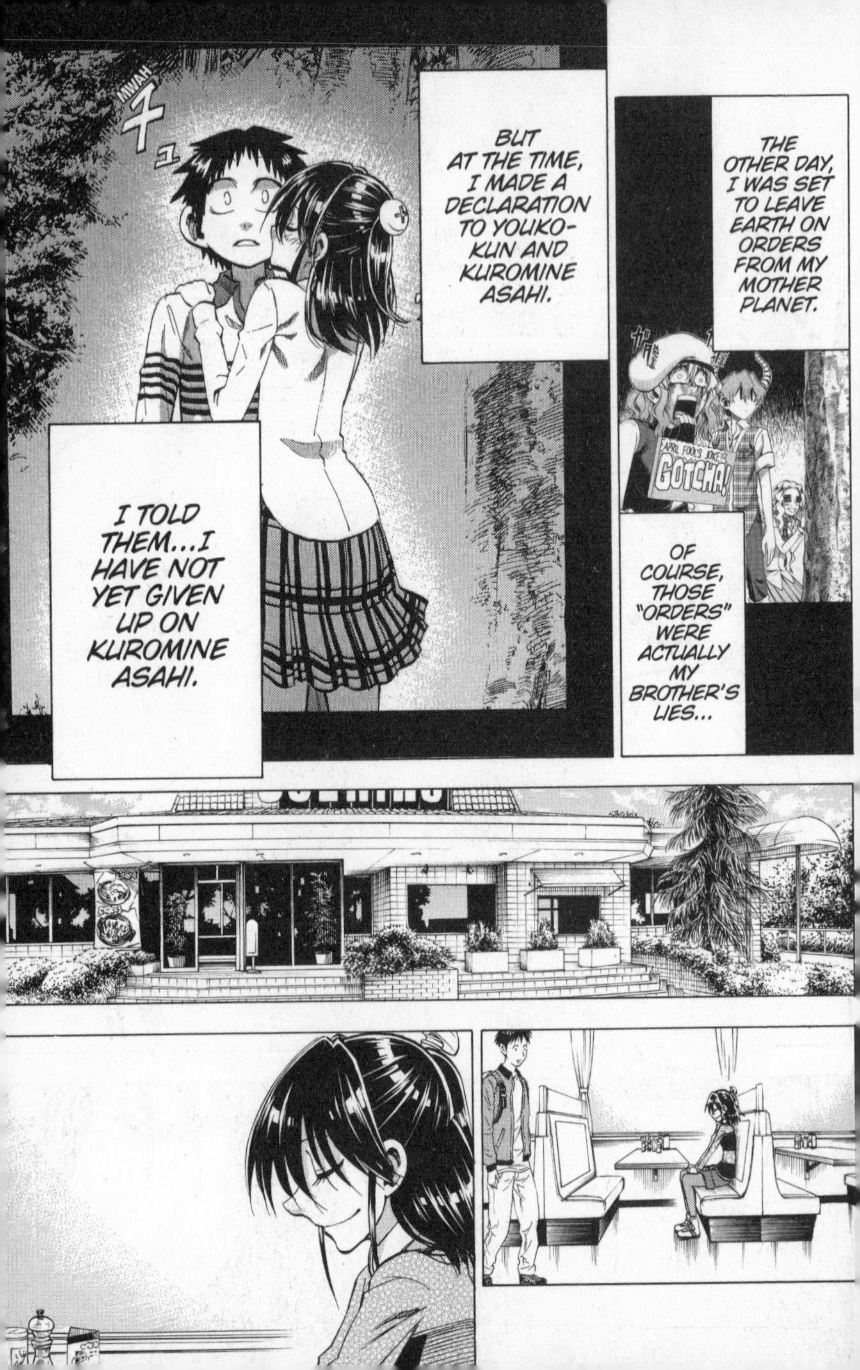
THE OTHER DAY, I WAS SET TO LEAVE EARTH ON ORDERS FROM MY MOTHER PLANET.
APRIL FOOLS JOKE
GOTCHA!
OF COURSE, THOSE "ORDERS" WERE ACTUALLY MY BROTHER'S LIES...
BUT AT THE TIME, I MADE A DECLARATION TO YOUKO-KUN AND KUROMINE ASAHI.
MWAH
I TOLD THEM...I HAVE NOT YET GIVEN UP ON KUROMINE ASAHI.

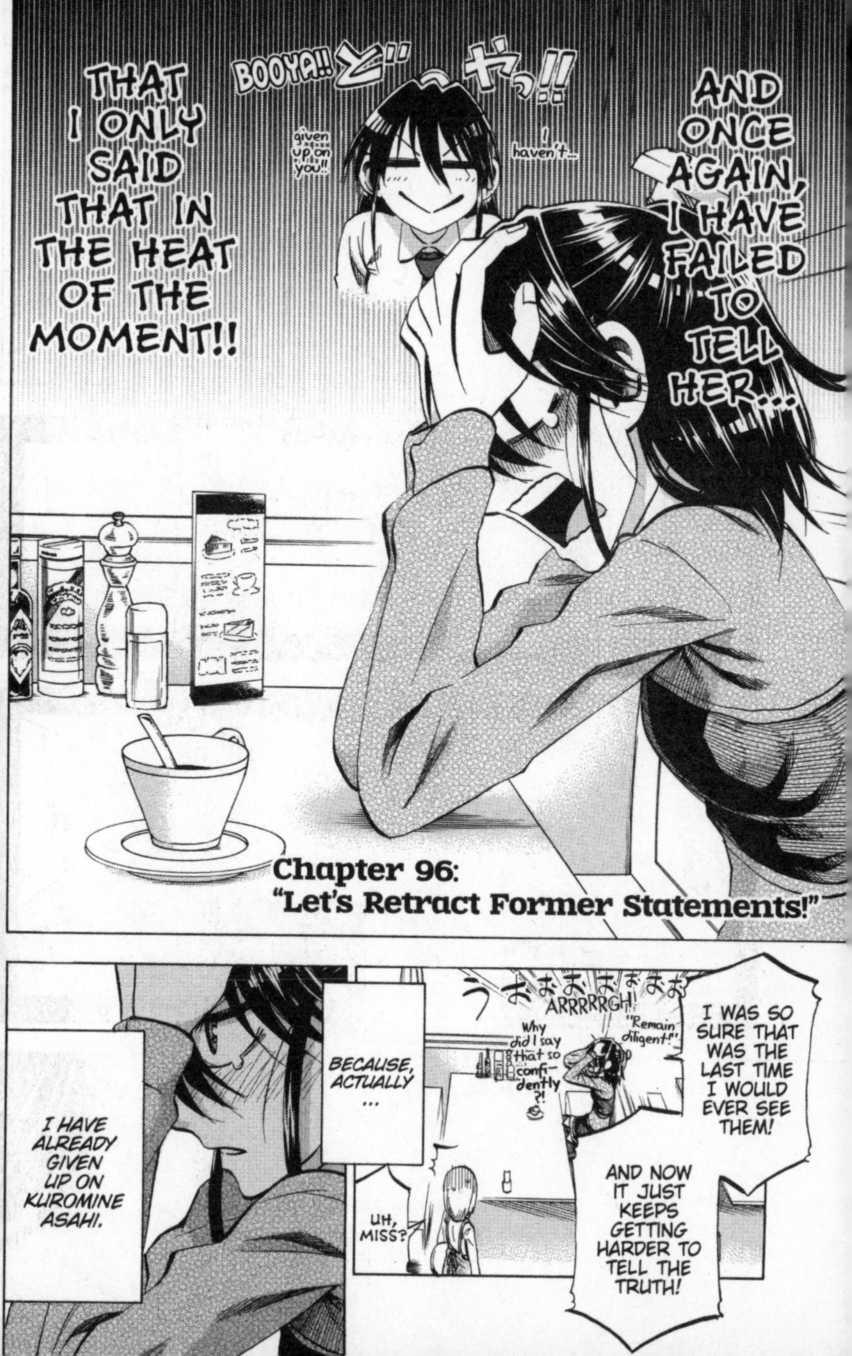
AND ONCE AGAIN, I HAVE FAILED TO TELL HER...
BOOYA!! ど~やっ!!
I haven't...
given up on you!!
THAT I ONLY SAID THAT IN THE HEAT OF THE MOMENT!!
Chapter 96:
"Let's Retract Former Statements!"
うおおおおおおお
ARRRRRGH!
I WAS SO SURE THAT WAS THE LAST TIME I WOULD EVER SEE THEM!
"Remain diligent!"
Why did I say that so confidently?!
AND NOW IT JUST KEEPS GETTING HARDER TO TELL THE TRUTH!
UH, MISS?
BECAUSE, ACTUALLY...
I HAVE ALREADY GIVEN UP ON KUROMINE ASAHI.

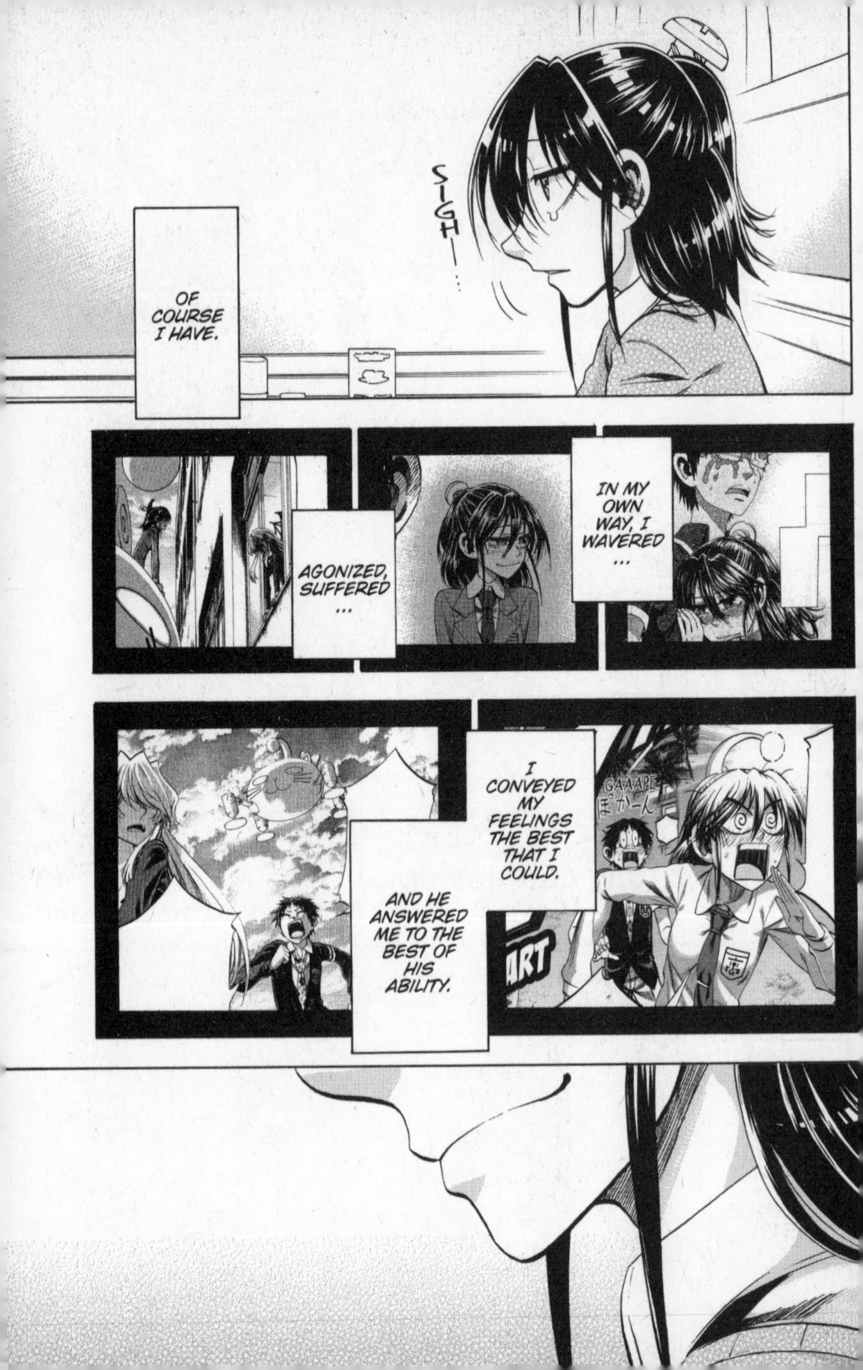
SIGH...
OF COURSE I HAVE.
IN MY OWN WAY, I WAVERED ...
AGONIZED, SUFFERED ...
GAAAPE
ぽかーん
I CONVEYED MY FEELINGS THE BEST THAT I COULD.
ART
AND HE ANSWERED ME TO THE BEST OF HIS ABILITY.

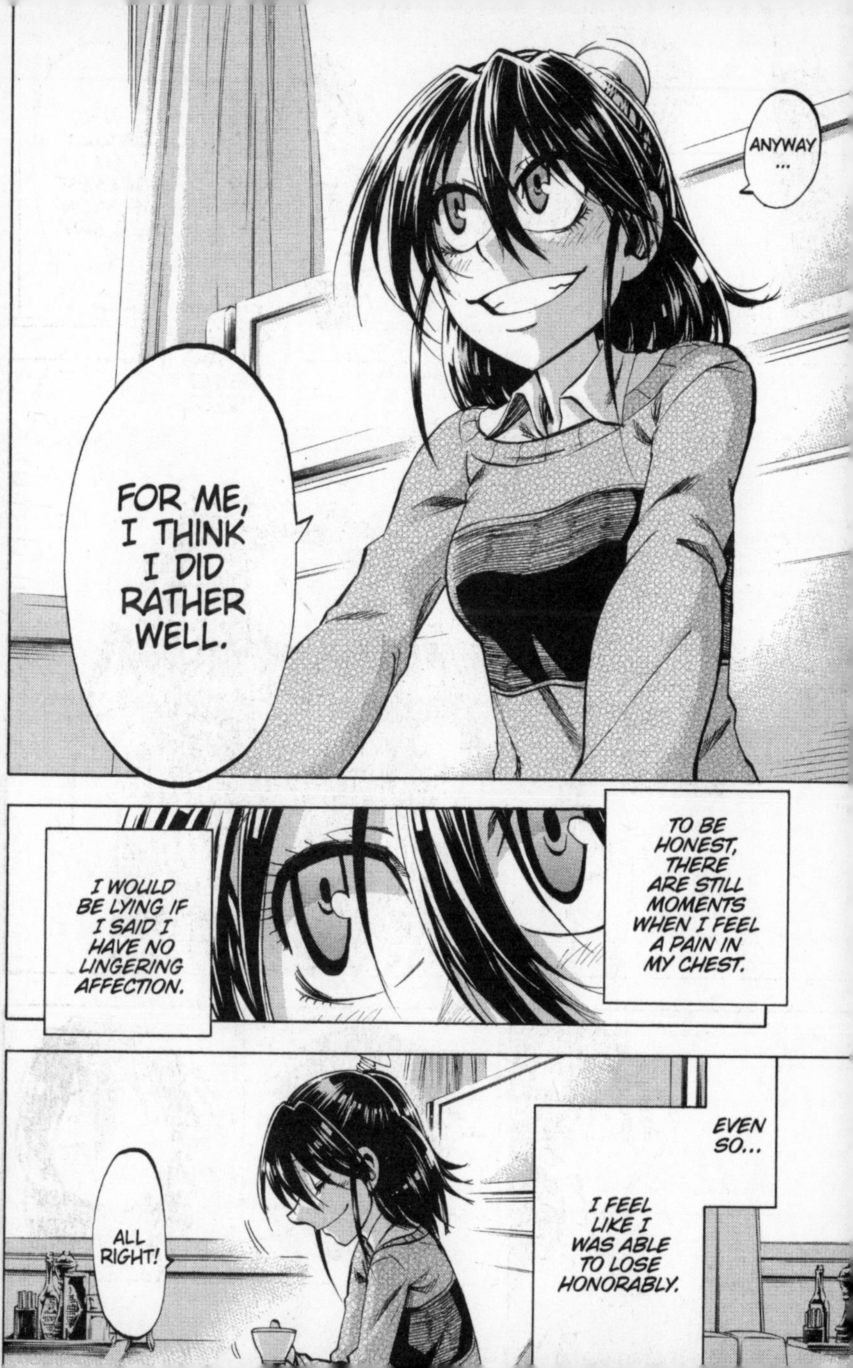
ANYWAY ...
FOR ME, I THINK I DID RATHER WELL.
TO BE HONEST, THERE ARE STILL MOMENTS WHEN I FEEL A PAIN IN MY CHEST.
I WOULD BE LYING IF I SAID I HAVE NO LINGERING AFFECTION.
EVEN SO...
I FEEL LIKE I WAS ABLE TO LOSE HONORABLY.
ALL RIGHT!

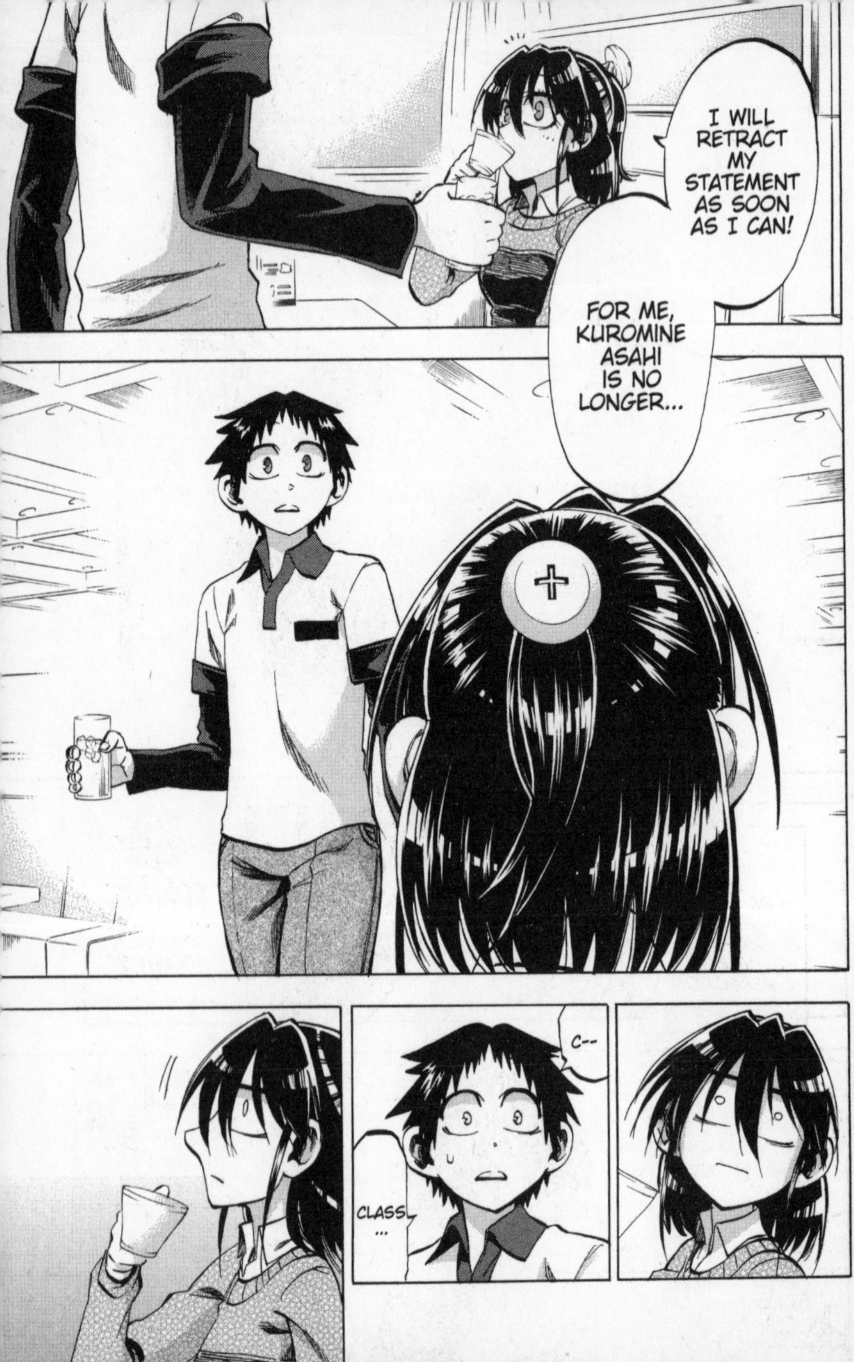
I WILL RETRACT MY STATEMENT AS SOON AS I CAN!
FOR ME, KUROMINE ASAHI IS NO LONGER...
C--
CLASS ...

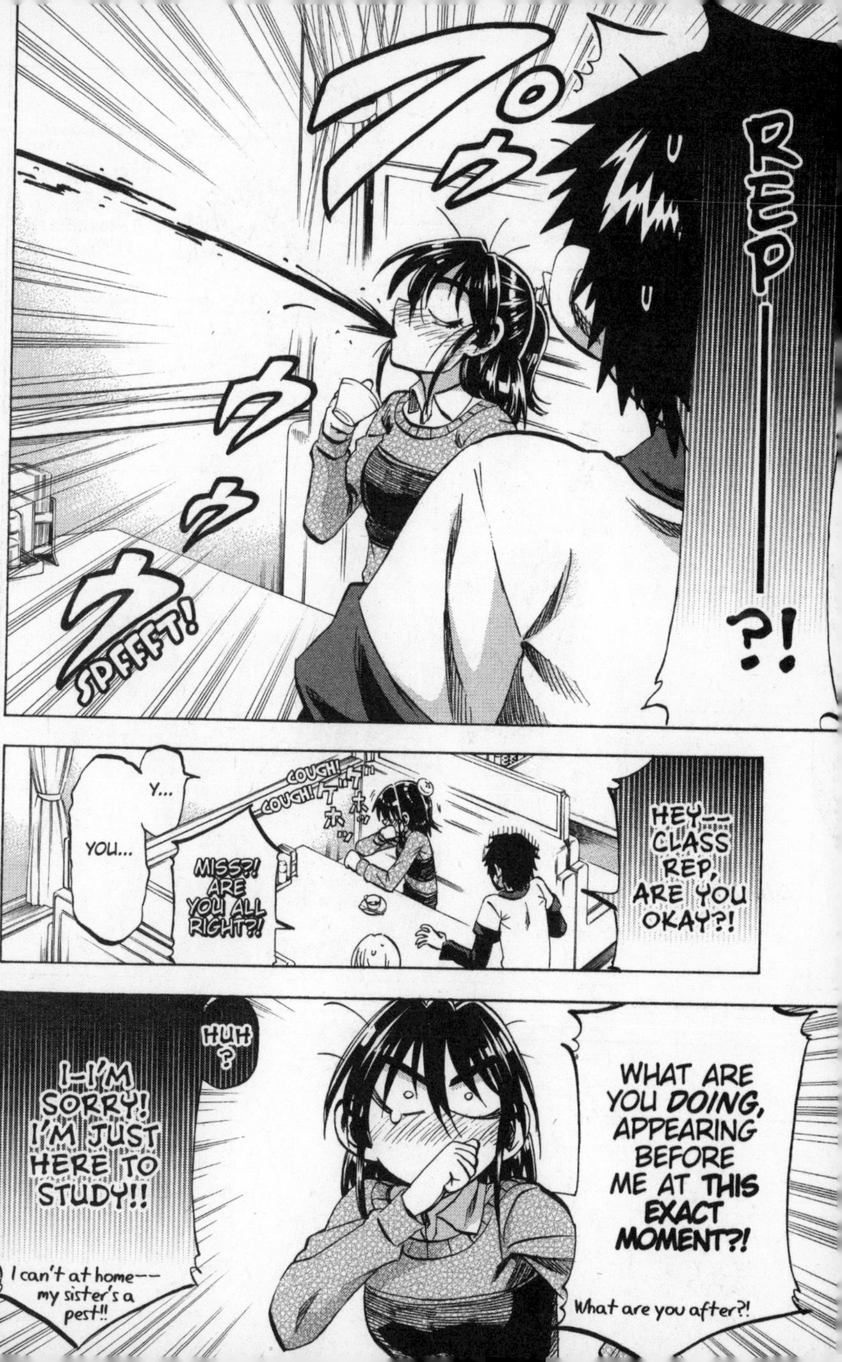
REP——?!
SPFFFT!
HEY-- CLASS REP, ARE YOU OKAY?!
COUGH! COUGH!
MISS?! ARE YOU ALL RIGHT?!
Y...
YOU...
WHAT ARE YOU DOING, APPEARING BEFORE ME AT THIS EXACT MOMENT?!
What are you after?!
HUH?
I-I'M SORRY! I'M JUST HERE TO STUDY!!
I can't at home-- my sister's a pest!!

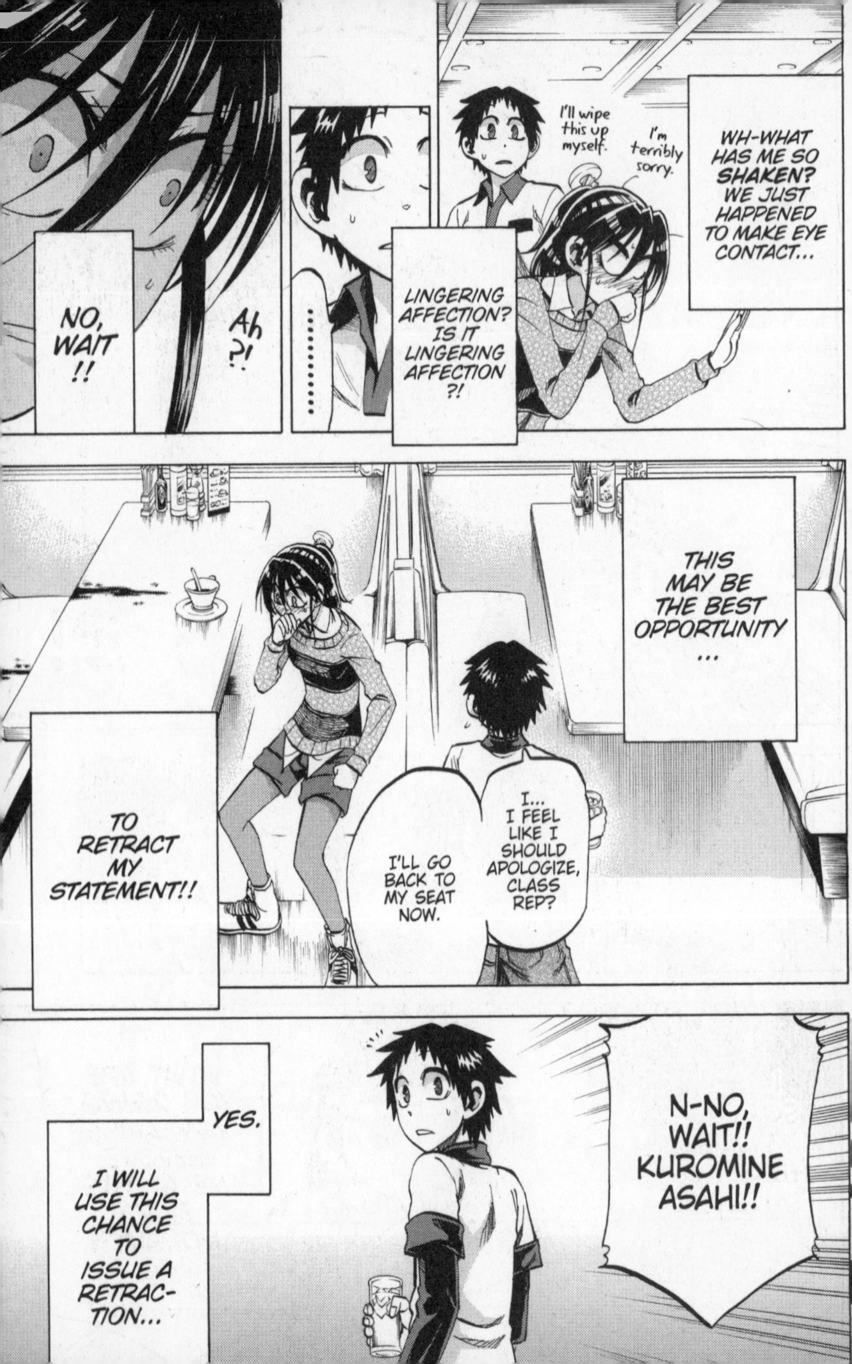
WH-WHAT HAS ME SO SHAKEN? WE JUST HAPPENED TO MAKE EYE CONTACT...
I'm terribly sorry.
I'll wipe this up myself.
LINGERING AFFECTION? IS IT LINGERING AFFECTION?!
......
Ah ?!
NO, WAIT !!
THIS MAY BE THE BEST OPPORTUNITY...
I... I FEEL LIKE I SHOULD APOLOGIZE, CLASS REP?
I'LL GO BACK TO MY SEAT NOW.
TO RETRACT MY STATEMENT!!
N-NO, WAIT!! KUROMINE ASAHI!!
YES.
I WILL USE THIS CHANCE TO ISSUE A RETRAC-TION...

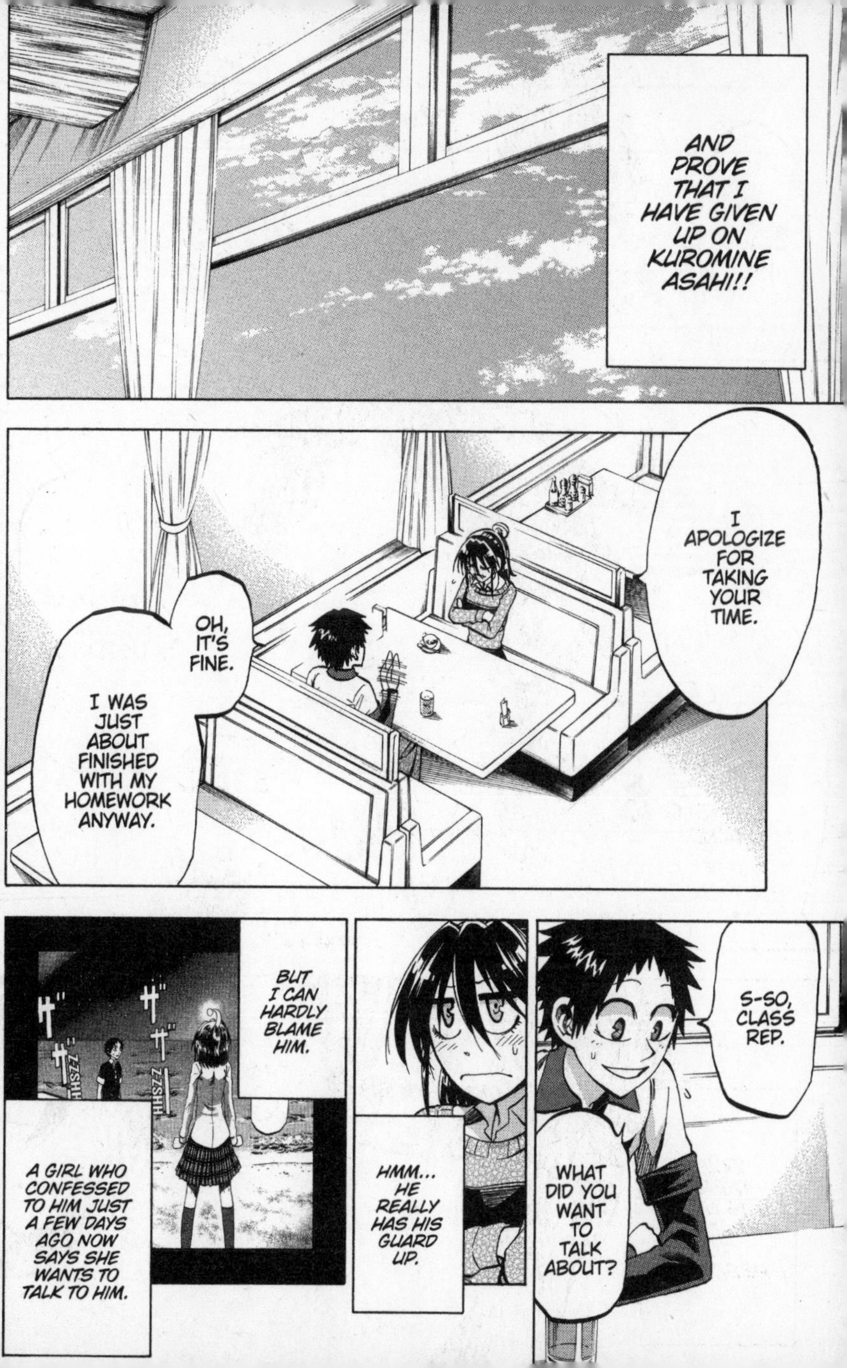
AND PROVE THAT I HAVE GIVEN UP ON KUROMINE ASAHI!!
I APOLOGIZE FOR TAKING YOUR TIME.
OH, IT'S FINE.
I WAS JUST ABOUT FINISHED WITH MY HOMEWORK ANYWAY.
S-SO, CLASS REP.
WHAT DID YOU WANT TO TALK ABOUT?
HMM... HE REALLY HAS HIS GUARD UP.
BUT I CAN HARDLY BLAME HIM.
A GIRL WHO CONFESSED TO HIM JUST A FEW DAYS AGO NOW SAYS SHE WANTS TO TALK TO HIM.

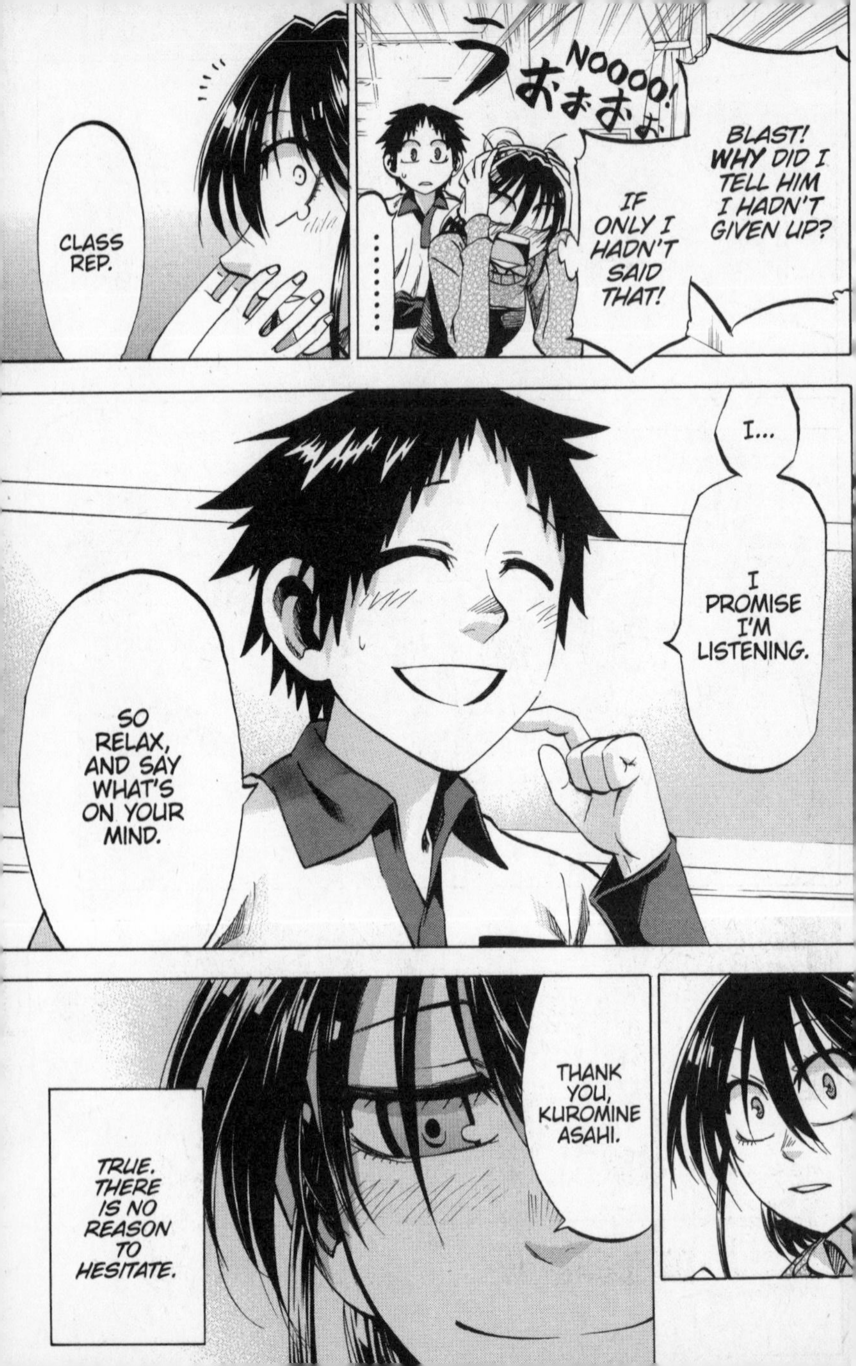
NOOOOO!
BLAST! WHY DID I TELL HIM I HADN'T GIVEN UP?
IF ONLY I HADN'T SAID THAT!
CLASS REP.
I...
I PROMISE I'M LISTENING.
SO RELAX, AND SAY WHAT'S ON YOUR MIND.
THANK YOU, KUROMINE ASAHI.
TRUE. THERE IS NO REASON TO HESITATE.

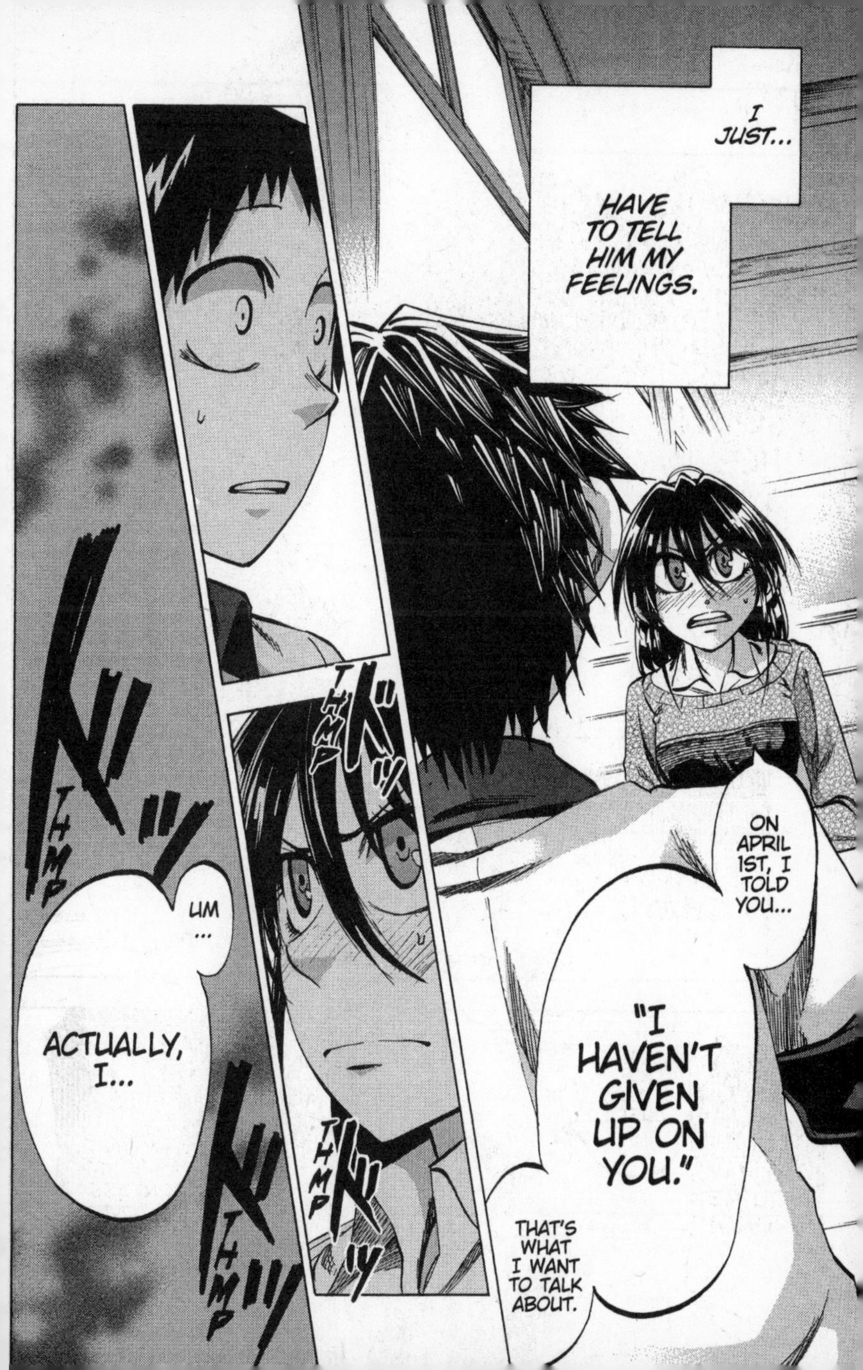
I JUST...
HAVE TO TELL HIM MY FEELINGS.
ON APRIL 1ST, I TOLD YOU...
"I HAVEN'T GIVEN UP ON YOU."
THAT'S WHAT I WANT TO TALK ABOUT.
THMP
THMP
THMP
UM...
ACTUALLY, I...
THMP

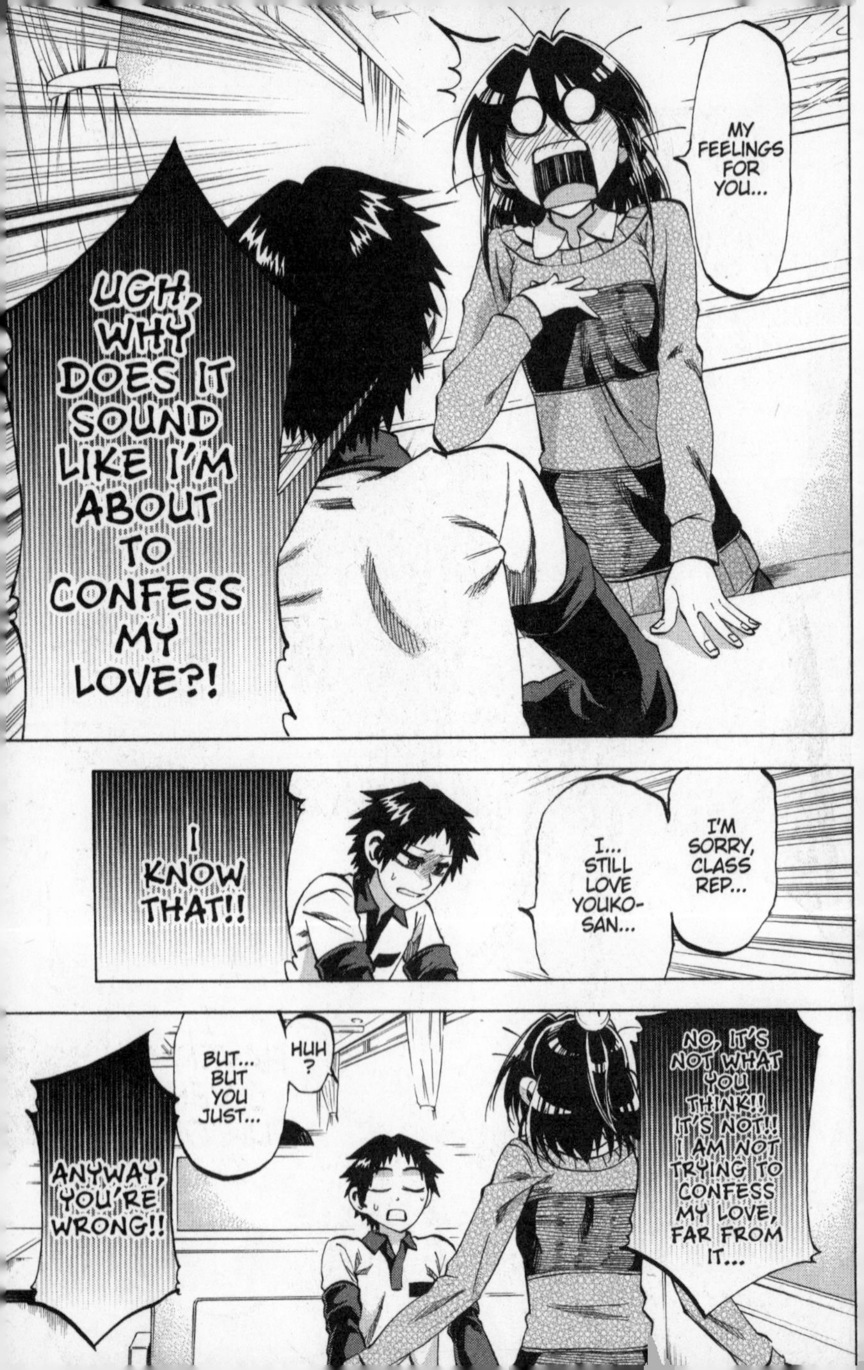
MY FEELINGS FOR YOU...
UGH, WHY DOES IT SOUND LIKE I'M ABOUT TO CONFESS MY LOVE?!
I'M SORRY, CLASS REP...
I... STILL LOVE YOUKO-SAN...
I KNOW THAT!!
NO, IT'S NOT WHAT YOU THINK!! IT'S NOT!! I AM NOT TRYING TO CONFESS MY LOVE, FAR FROM IT...
HUH?
BUT... BUT YOU JUST...
ANYWAY, YOU'RE WRONG!!

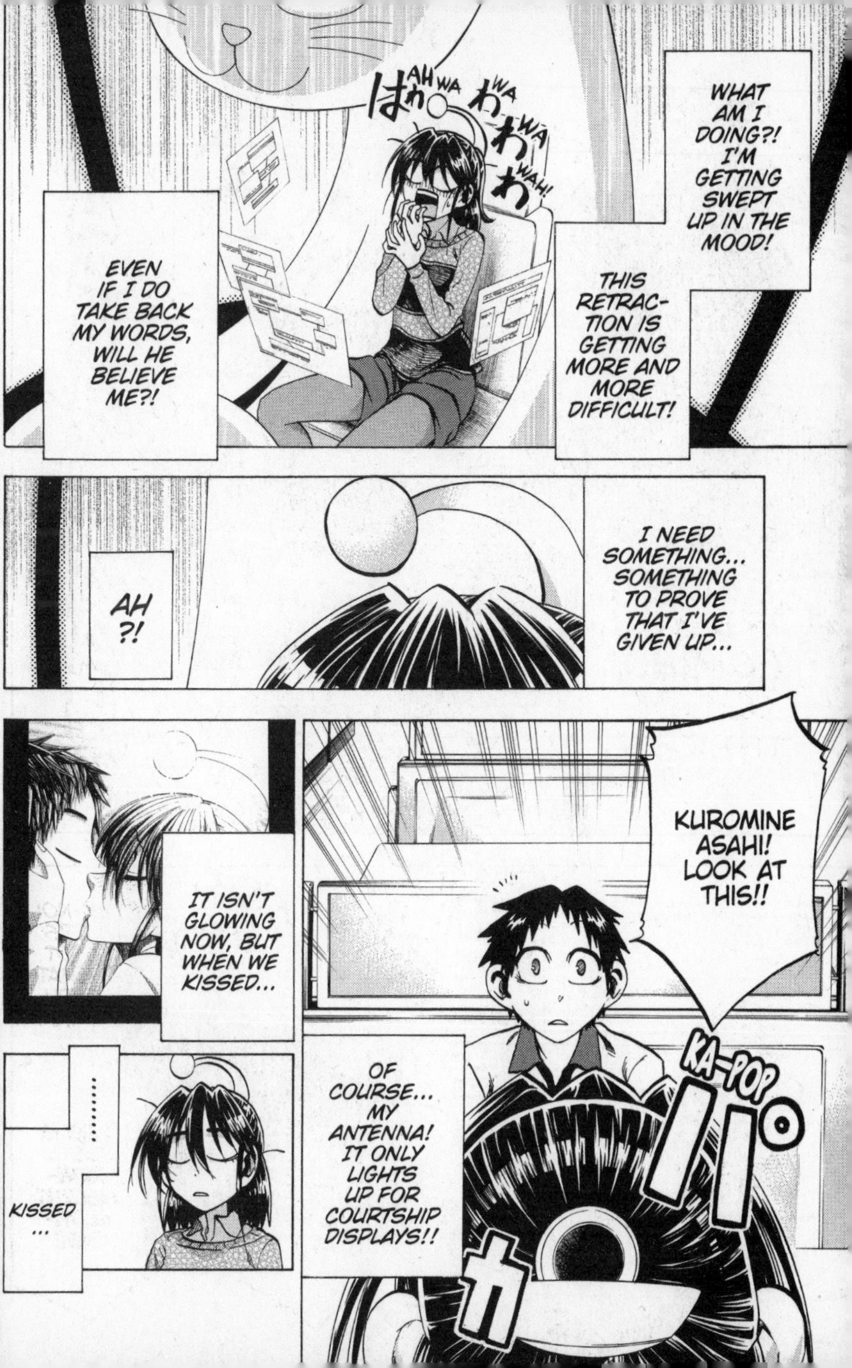
WHAT AM I DOING?! I'M GETTING SWEPT UP IN THE MOOD!
はわわわわ
AH WA WA WA WAH!
THIS RETRACTION IS GETTING MORE AND MORE DIFFICULT!
EVEN IF I DO TAKE BACK MY WORDS, WILL HE BELIEVE ME?!
I NEED SOMETHING... SOMETHING TO PROVE THAT I'VE GIVEN UP...
AH ?!
IT ISN'T GLOWING NOW, BUT WHEN WE KISSED...
......
KISSED ...
OF COURSE... MY ANTENNA! IT ONLY LIGHTS UP FOR COURTSHIP DISPLAYS!!
KUROMINE ASAHI! LOOK AT THIS!!
KA-POP
カ

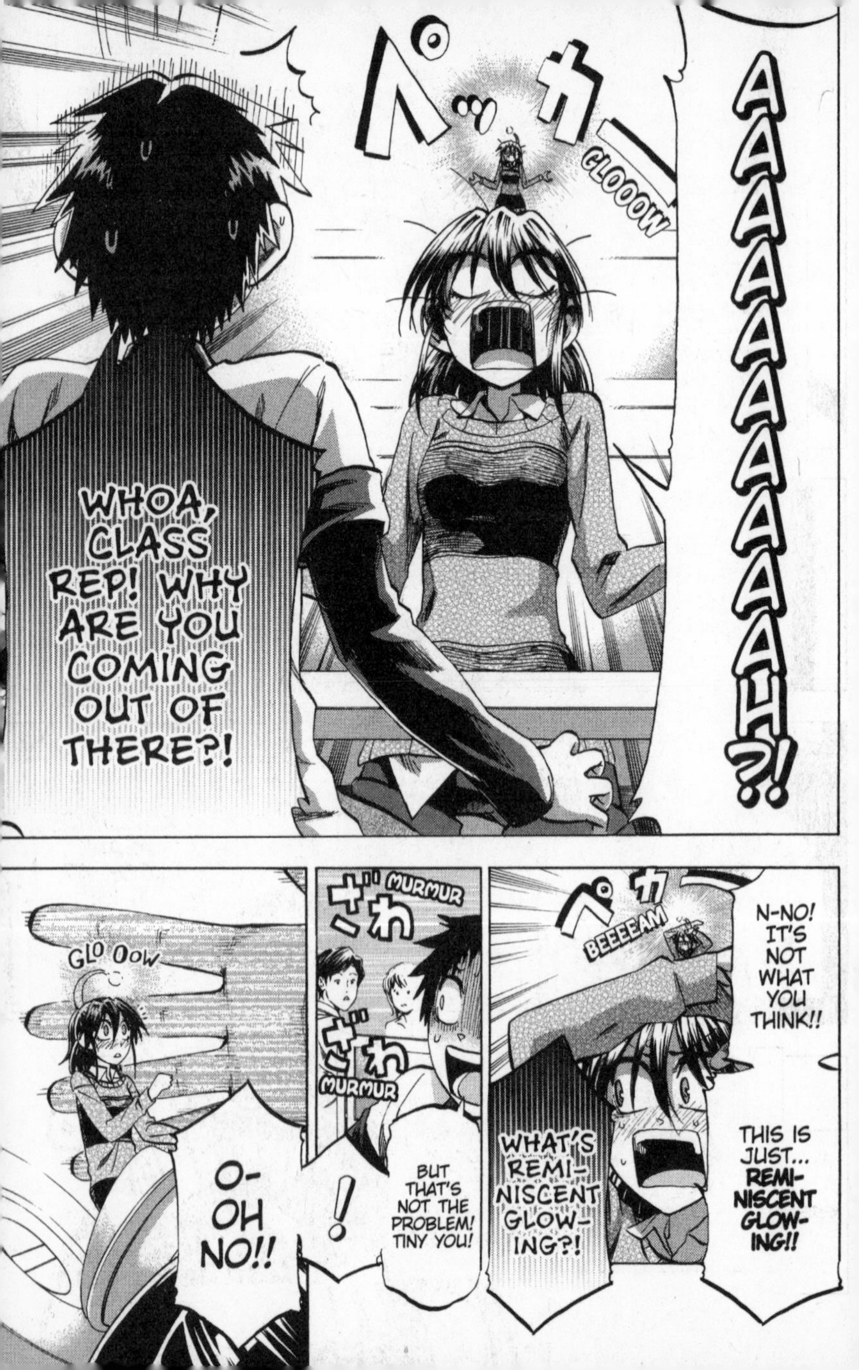
AAAAAAAAAAAAAUH?!
ペッカー
GLOOOW
WHOA, CLASS REP! WHY ARE YOU COMING OUT OF THERE?!
ペカ
BEEEEAM
N-NO! IT'S NOT WHAT YOU THINK!!
THIS IS JUST... REMINISCENT GLOWING!!
WHAT'S REMINISCENT GLOWING?!
ざわ
MURMUR
ざわ
MURMUR
BUT THAT'S NOT THE PROBLEM! TINY YOU!
GLO OOW
!
O-OH NO!!

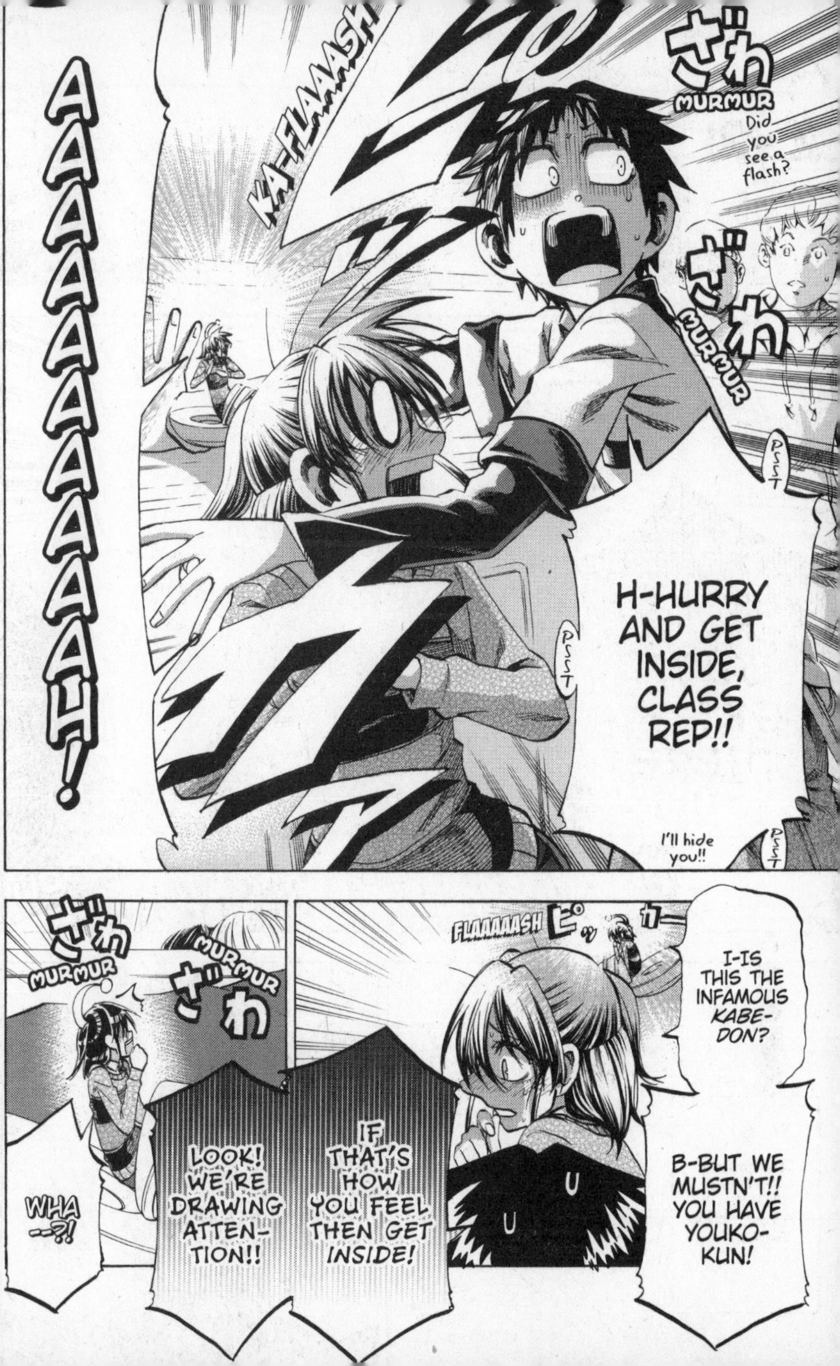
ざわ
MURMUR
Did you see a flash?
ざわ
MURMUR
PSST
H-HURRY AND GET INSIDE, CLASS REP!!
PSST
I'll hide you!!
PSST
KA-FLAAASH
AAAAAAAAAAAH!
FLAAAAASH ピッ カー
I-IS THIS THE INFAMOUS *KABEDON?*
B-BUT WE MUSTN'T!! YOU HAVE YOUKO-KUN!
ざわ
MURMUR
ざわ
MURMUR
IF THAT'S HOW YOU FEEL THEN GET *INSIDE!*
LOOK! WE'RE DRAWING ATTENTION!!
WHA--?!

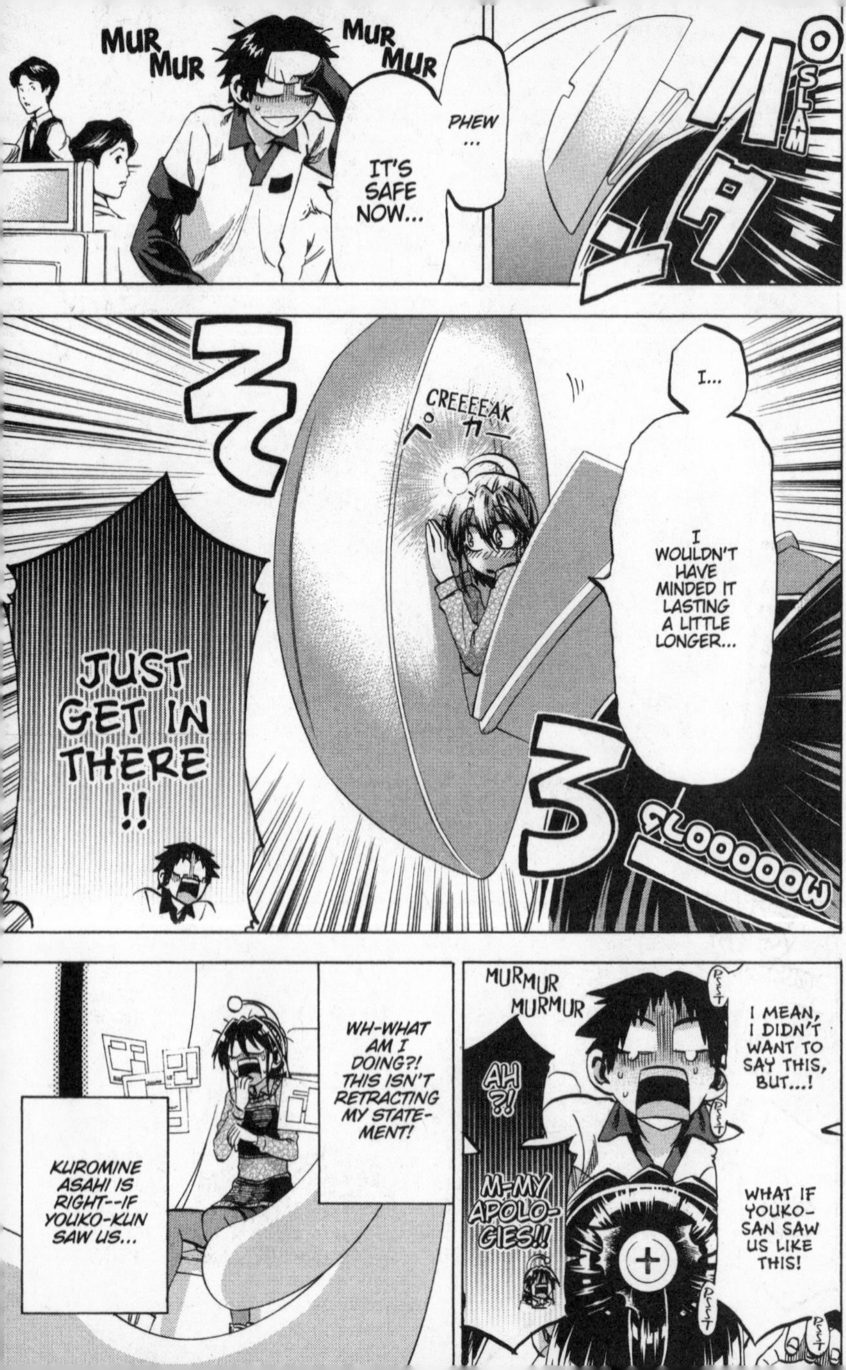
SLAM
MUR MUR
MUR MUR
PHEW...
IT'S SAFE NOW...
I...
CREEEEAK
I WOULDN'T HAVE MINDED IT LASTING A LITTLE LONGER...
GLOOOOOOW
JUST GET IN THERE!!
MURMUR MURMUR
PSST
I MEAN, I DIDN'T WANT TO SAY THIS, BUT...!
AH?!
WHAT IF YOUKO-SAN SAW US LIKE THIS!
M-MY APOLOGIES!!
WH-WHAT AM I DOING?! THIS ISN'T RETRACTING MY STATEMENT!
KUROMINE ASAHI IS RIGHT--IF YOUKO-KUN SAW US...

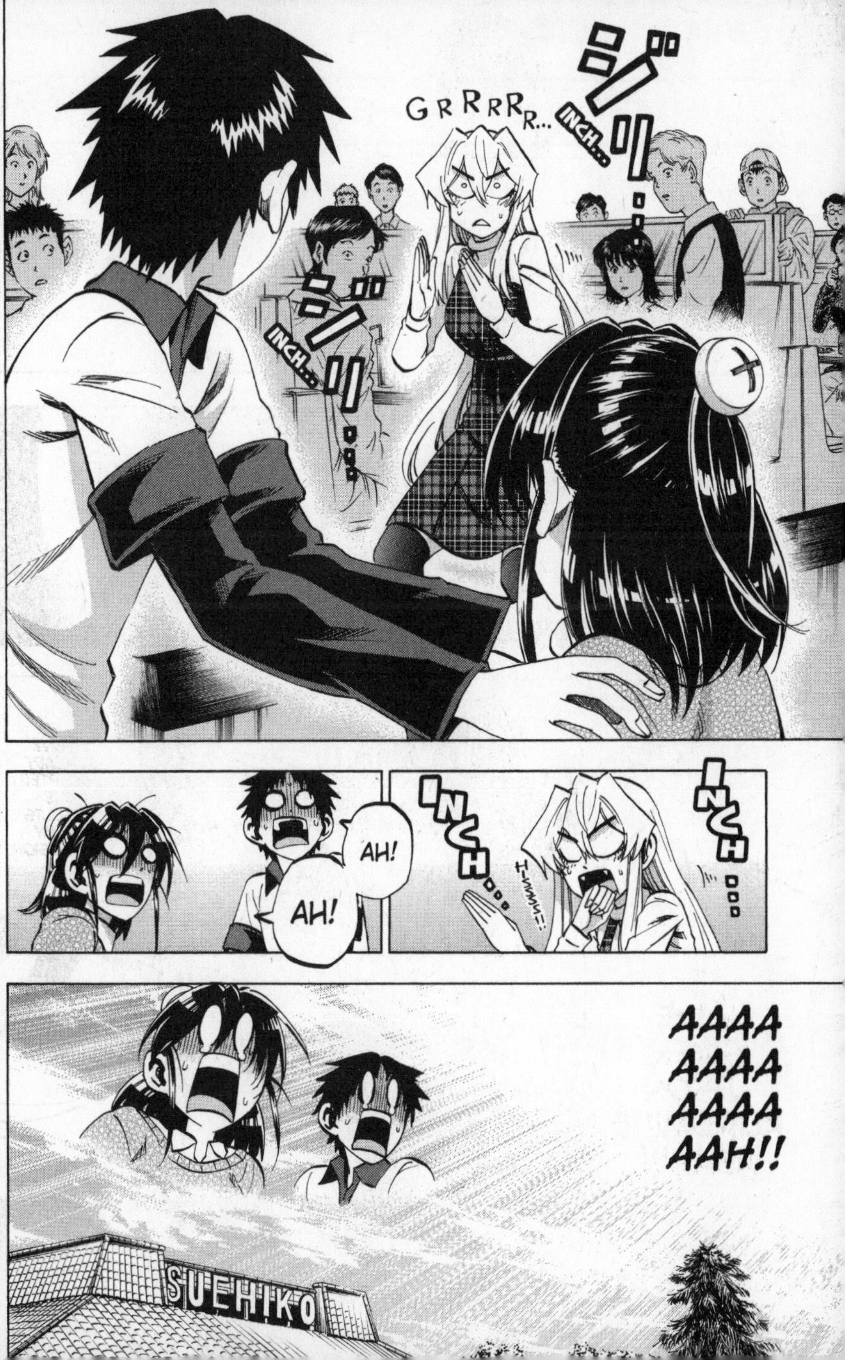
GRRRRR...
INCH...
INCH...
INCH...
INCH...
HISSSS!!
AH!
AH!
AAAA
AAAA
AAAA
AAH!!
SUEHIKO

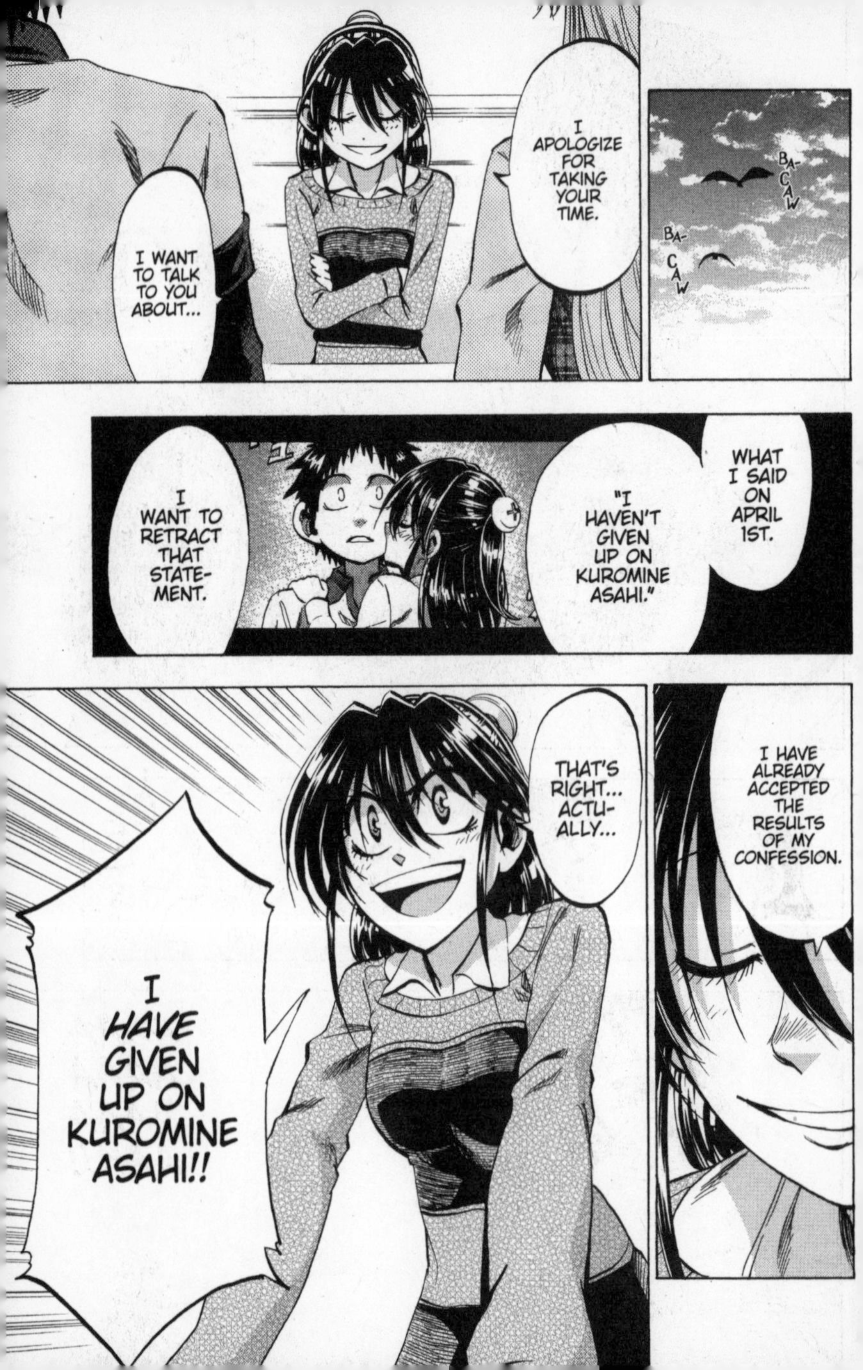
BA-CAW
BA-CAW
I APOLOGIZE FOR TAKING YOUR TIME.
I WANT TO TALK TO YOU ABOUT...
WHAT I SAID ON APRIL 1ST.
"I HAVEN'T GIVEN UP ON KUROMINE ASAHI."
I WANT TO RETRACT THAT STATEMENT.
I HAVE ALREADY ACCEPTED THE RESULTS OF MY CONFESSION.
THAT'S RIGHT... ACTU-ALLY...
I *HAVE* GIVEN UP ON KUROMINE ASAHI!!

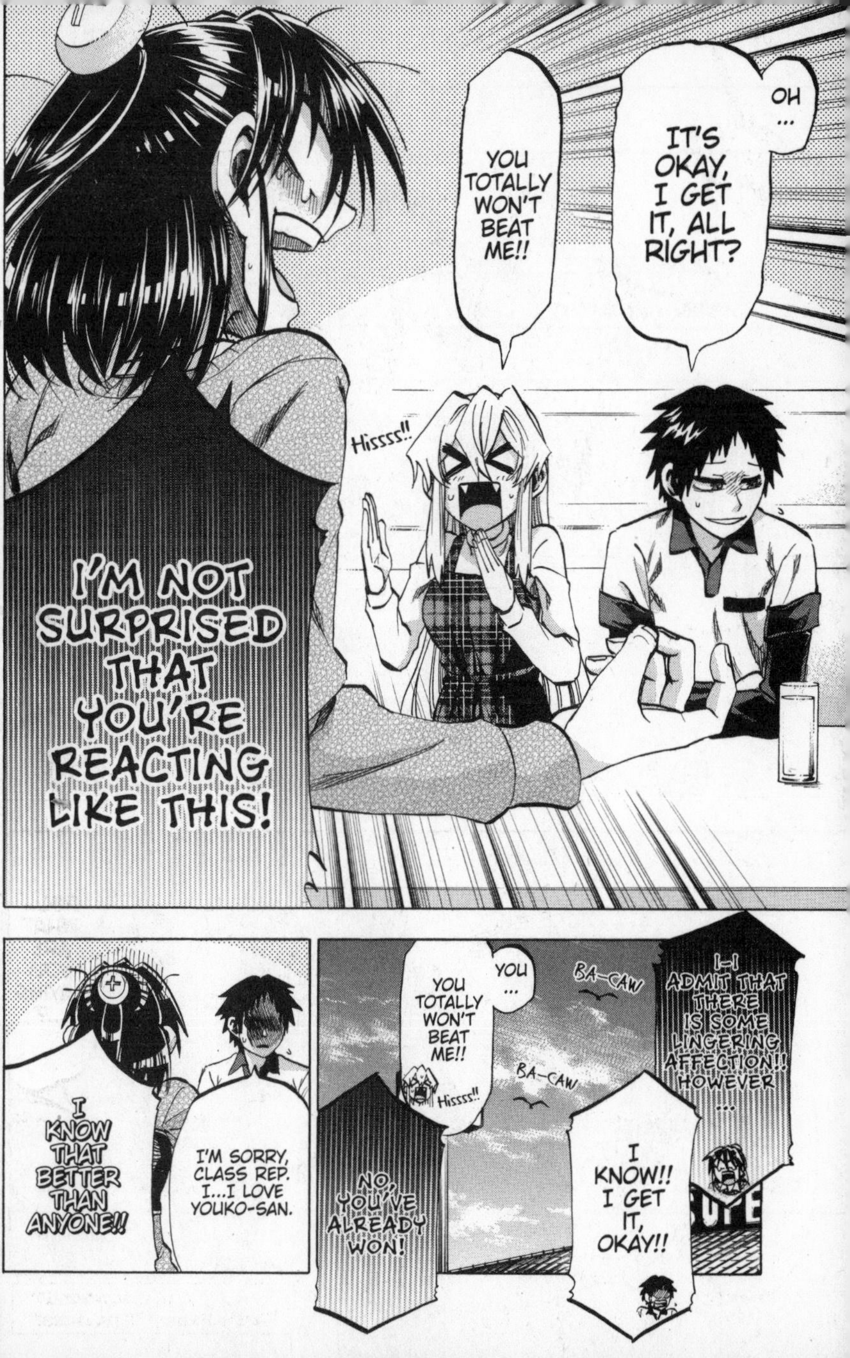
OH ...
IT'S OKAY, I GET IT, ALL RIGHT?
YOU TOTALLY WON'T BEAT ME!!
Hissss!!
I'M NOT SURPRISED THAT YOU'RE REACTING LIKE THIS!
I-I ADMIT THAT THERE IS SOME LINGERING AFFECTION!! HOWEVER ...
YOU ...
YOU TOTALLY WON'T BEAT ME!!
BA-CAW
BA-CAW
Hissss!!
I KNOW!! I GET IT, OKAY!!
NO, YOU'VE ALREADY WON!
I'M SORRY, CLASS REP. I...I LOVE YOUKO-SAN.
I KNOW THAT BETTER THAN ANYONE!!

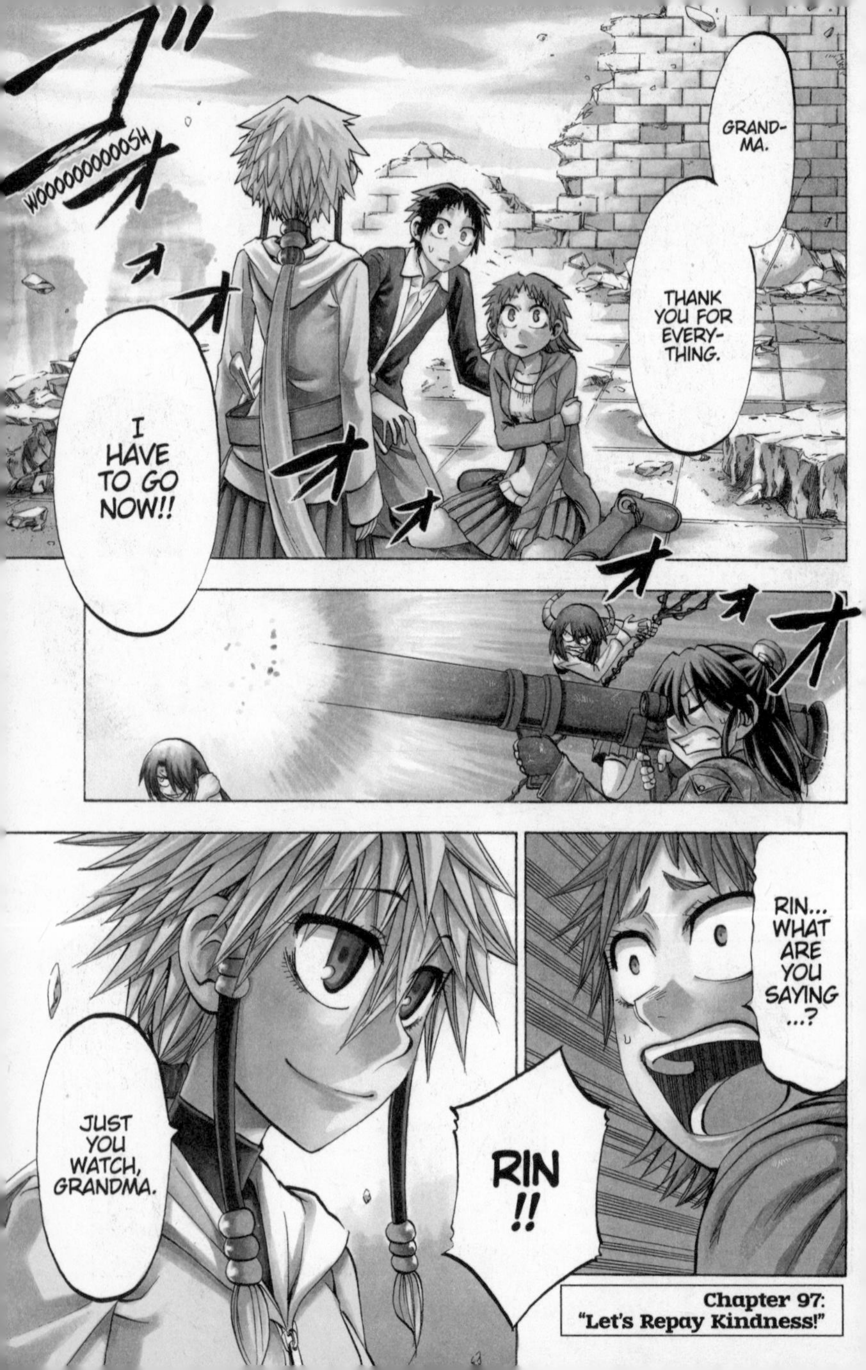
GRAND-MA.
THANK YOU FOR EVERY-THING.
I HAVE TO GO NOW!!
ゴォォォォォ
WOOOOOOOOOOSH
RIN... WHAT ARE YOU SAYING...?
RIN!!
JUST YOU WATCH, GRANDMA.
Chapter 97: "Let's Repay Kindness!"

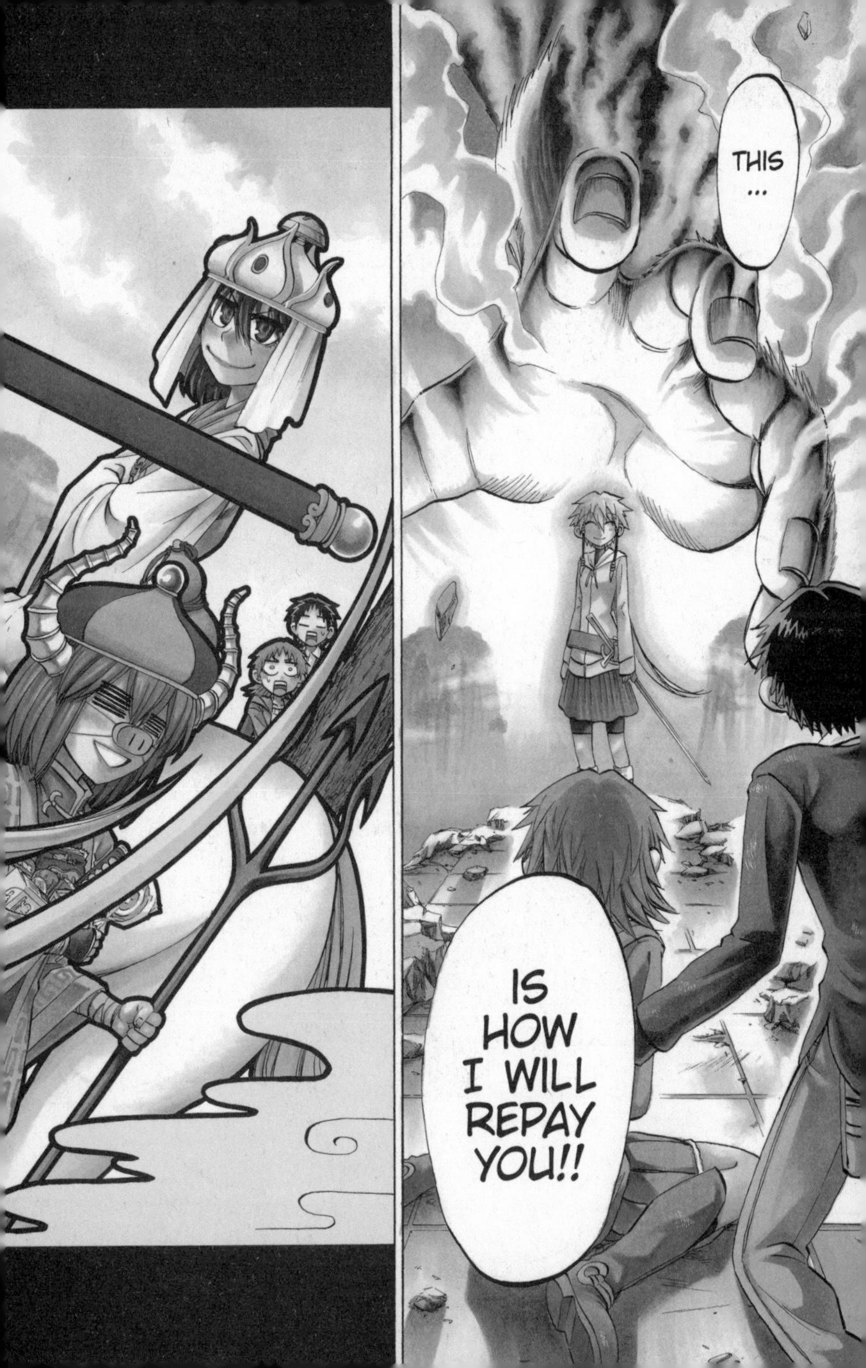
THIS ...
IS HOW I WILL REPAY YOU!!

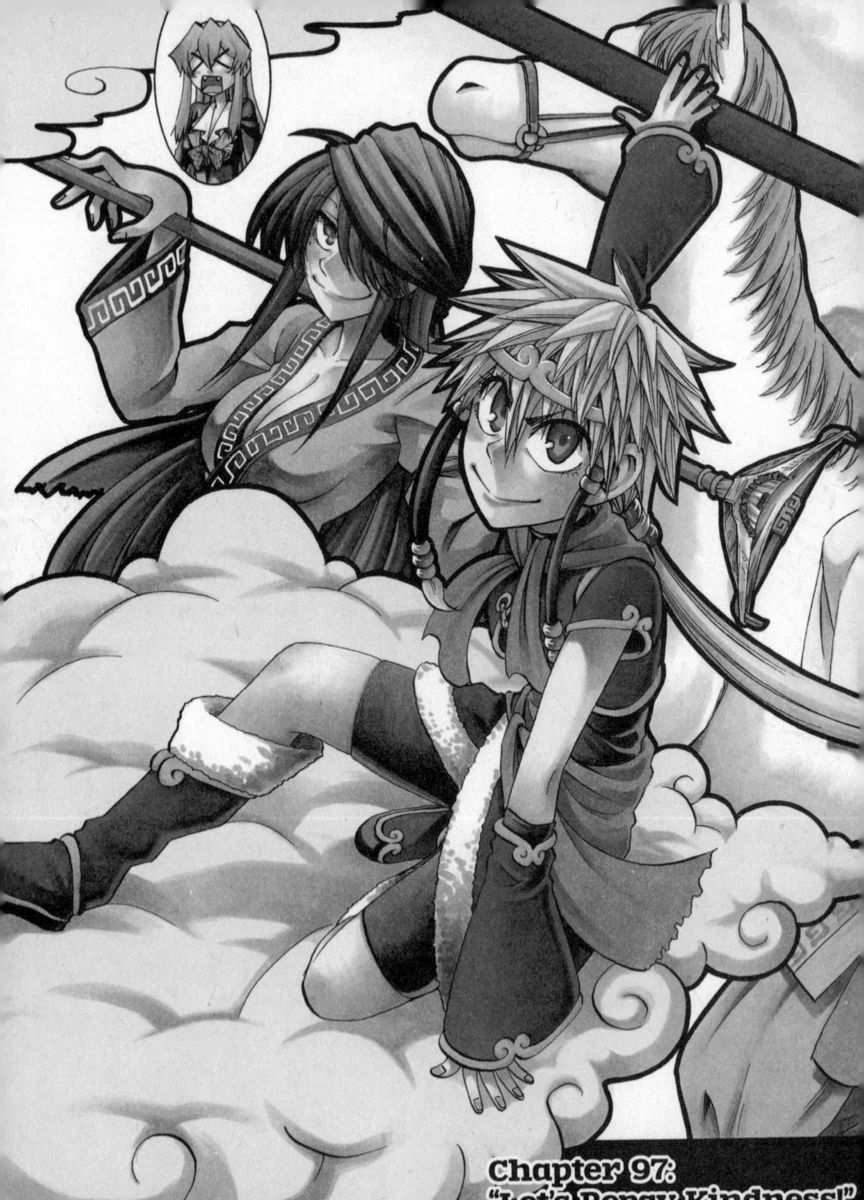

Chapter 97: "Let's Repay Kindness!"

TOP SECRET

My Monster Secret 11

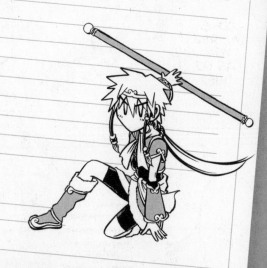

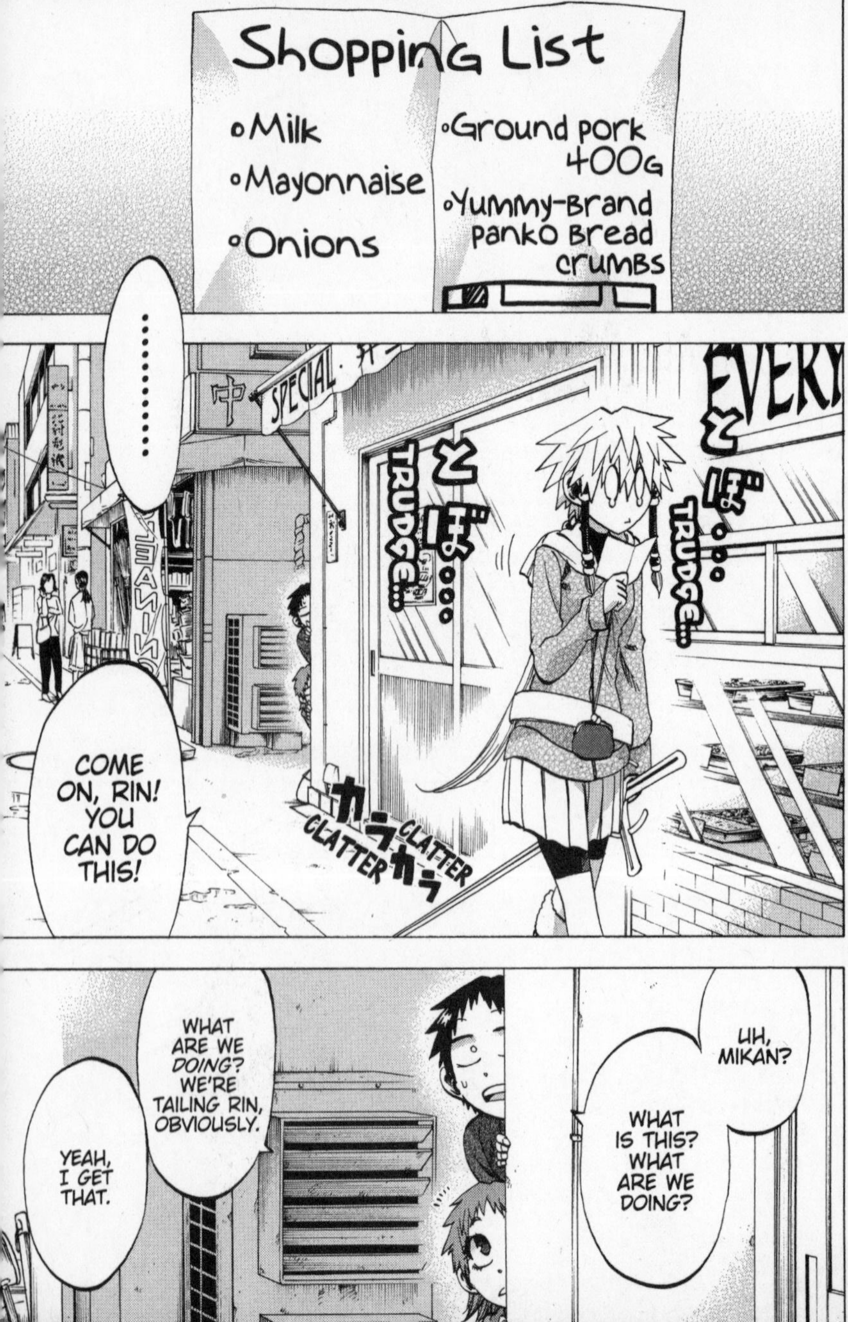
Shopping List
Milk
Mayonnaise
Onions
Ground pork 400g
Yummy-Brand panko bread crumbs
SPECIAL
EVERY
とぼ…
TRUDGE…
とぼ…
TRUDGE…
……
カラカラ
CLATTER CLATTER
COME ON, RIN! YOU CAN DO THIS!
UH, MIKAN?
WHAT IS THIS? WHAT ARE WE DOING?
WHAT ARE WE *DOING*? WE'RE TAILING RIN, OBVIOUSLY.
YEAH, I GET THAT.

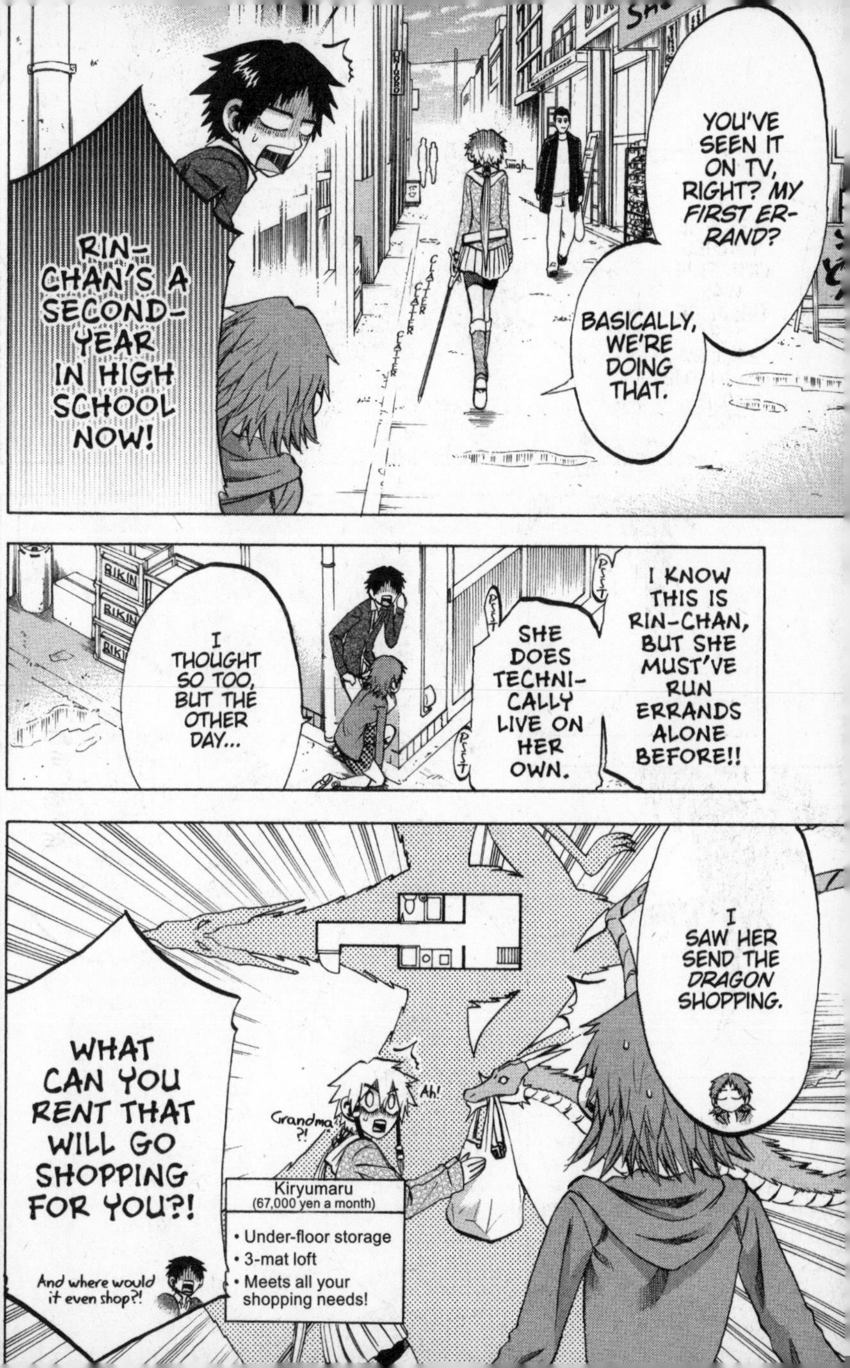
YOU'VE SEEN IT ON TV, RIGHT? MY FIRST ER-RAND?
BASICALLY, WE'RE DOING THAT.
Sigh...
CLATTER
CLATTER
CLATTER
RIN-CHAN'S A SECOND-YEAR IN HIGH SCHOOL NOW!
I KNOW THIS IS RIN-CHAN, BUT SHE MUST'VE RUN ERRANDS ALONE BEFORE!!
PSST
SHE DOES TECHNI-CALLY LIVE ON HER OWN.
PSST
PSST
I THOUGHT SO TOO, BUT THE OTHER DAY...
BIKIN
BIKIN
BIKIN
I SAW HER SEND THE DRAGON SHOPPING.
Ah!
Grandma?!
WHAT CAN YOU RENT THAT WILL GO SHOPPING FOR YOU?!
Kiryumaru
(67,000 yen a month)
• Under-floor storage
• 3-mat loft
• Meets all your shopping needs!
And where would it even shop?!

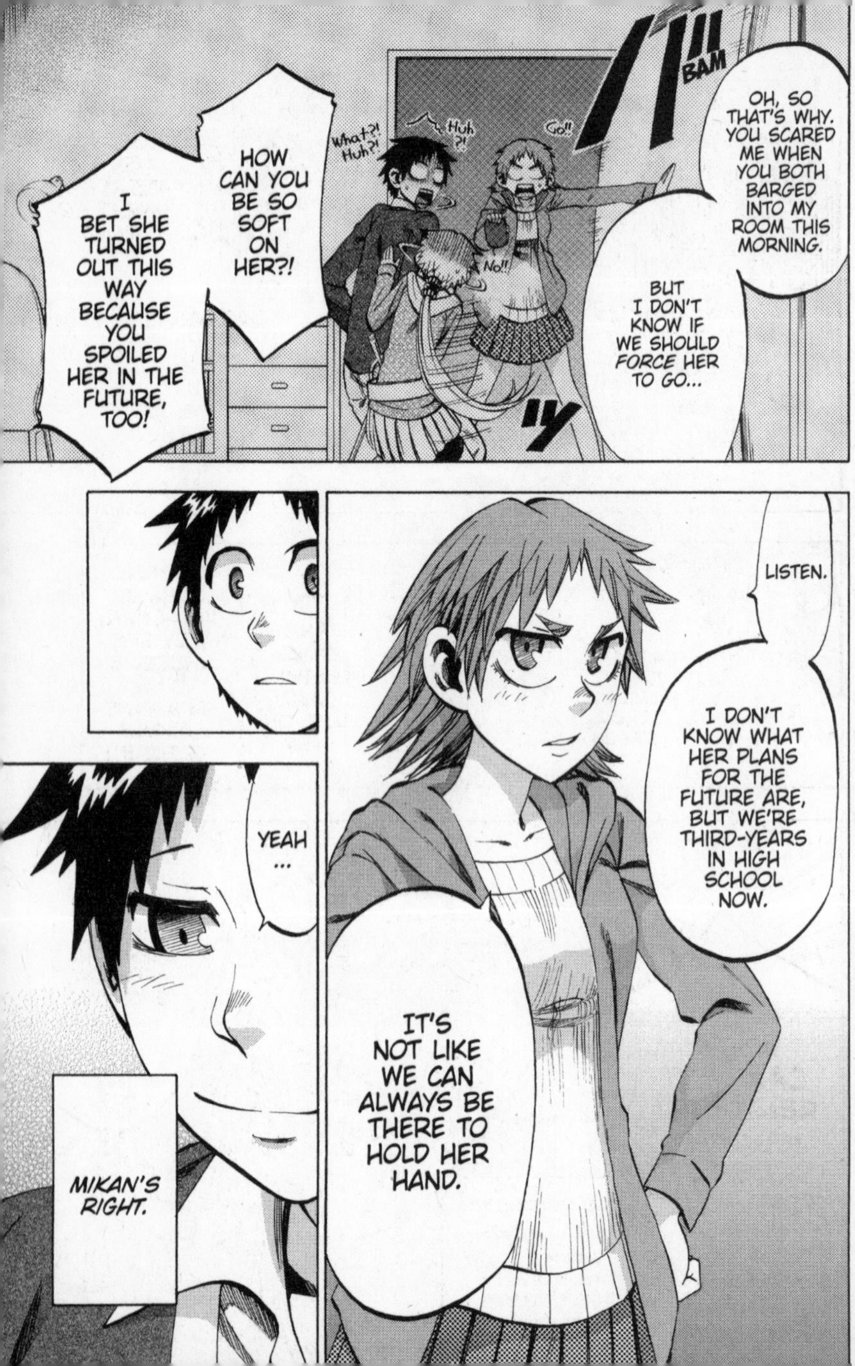
BAM
OH, SO THAT'S WHY. YOU SCARED ME WHEN YOU BOTH BARGED INTO MY ROOM THIS MORNING.
BUT I DON'T KNOW IF WE SHOULD *FORCE* HER TO GO...
Go!!
Huh ?!
What?! Huh?!
No!!
HOW CAN YOU BE SO SOFT ON HER?!
I BET SHE TURNED OUT THIS WAY BECAUSE YOU SPOILED HER IN THE FUTURE, TOO!
LISTEN.
I DON'T KNOW WHAT HER PLANS FOR THE FUTURE ARE, BUT WE'RE THIRD-YEARS IN HIGH SCHOOL NOW.
IT'S NOT LIKE WE CAN ALWAYS BE THERE TO HOLD HER HAND.
YEAH ...
MIKAN'S RIGHT.

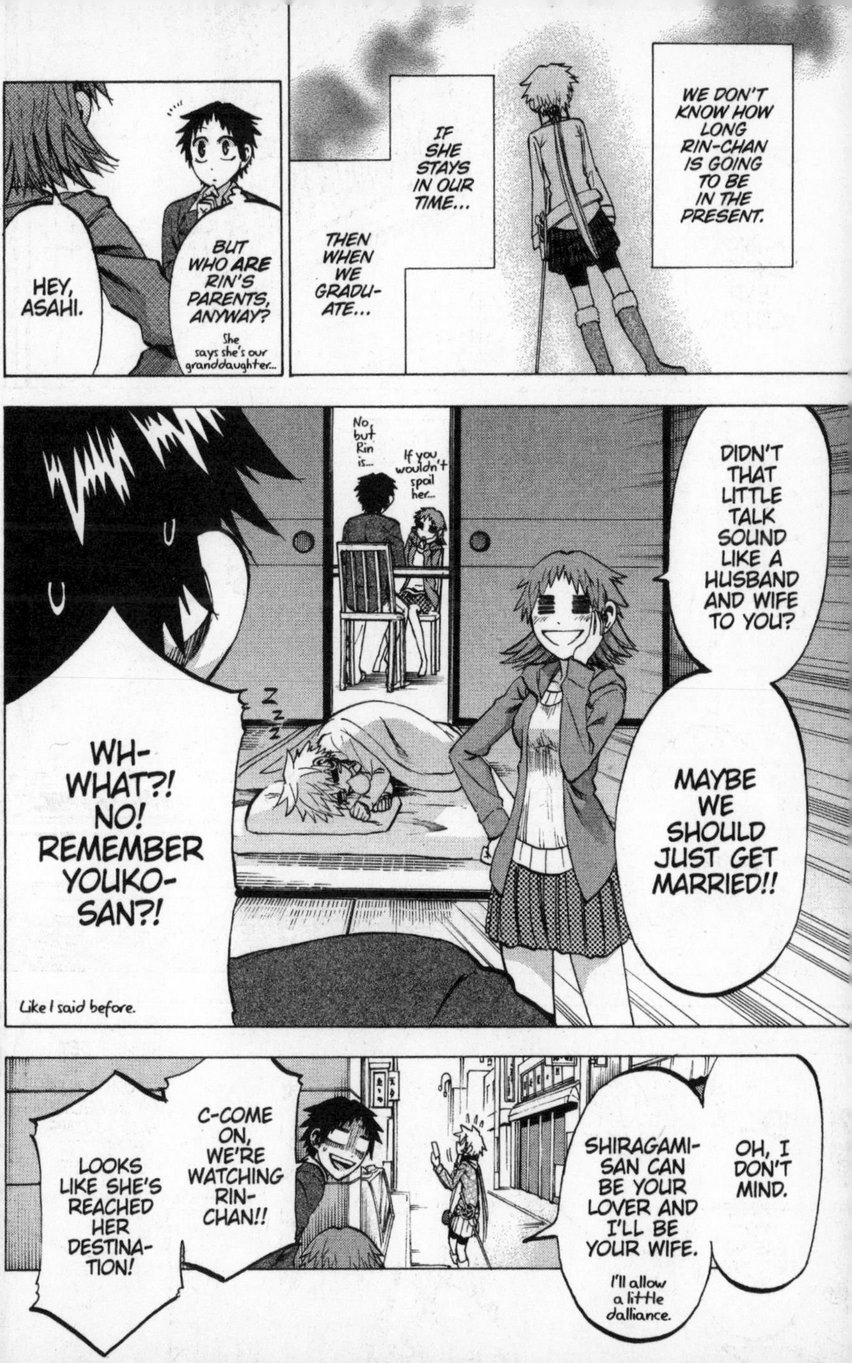
WE DON'T KNOW HOW LONG RIN-CHAN IS GOING TO BE IN THE PRESENT.
IF SHE STAYS IN OUR TIME...
THEN WHEN WE GRADUATE...
BUT WHO ARE RIN'S PARENTS, ANYWAY?
She says she's our granddaughter...
HEY, ASAHI.
DIDN'T THAT LITTLE TALK SOUND LIKE A HUSBAND AND WIFE TO YOU?
MAYBE WE SHOULD JUST GET MARRIED!!
If you wouldn't spoil her...
No but Rin is...
ZZZ
WH-WHAT?! NO! REMEMBER YOUKO-SAN?!
Like I said before.
OH, I DON'T MIND.
SHIRAGAMI-SAN CAN BE YOUR LOVER AND I'LL BE YOUR WIFE.
I'll allow a little dalliance.
C-COME ON, WE'RE WATCHING RIN-CHAN!!
LOOKS LIKE SHE'S REACHED HER DESTINATION!

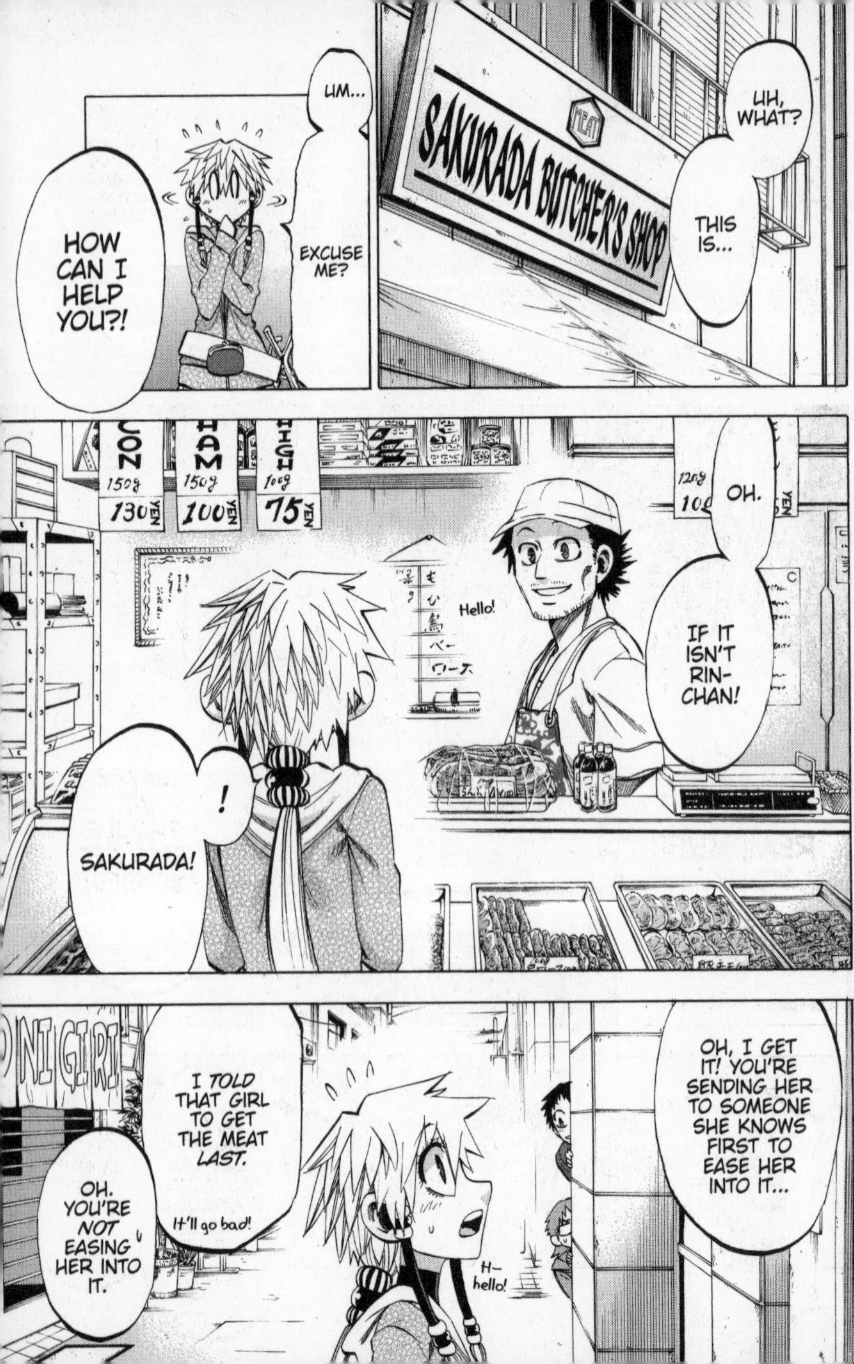
UH, WHAT?
THIS IS...
MEAT
SAKURADA BUTCHER'S SHOP
UM...
EXCUSE ME?
HOW CAN I HELP YOU?!
OH.
IF IT ISN'T RIN-CHAN!
Hello!
HAM 150g 100 YEN
!
SAKURADA!
OH, I GET IT! YOU'RE SENDING HER TO SOMEONE SHE KNOWS FIRST TO EASE HER INTO IT...
H-hello!
I TOLD THAT GIRL TO GET THE MEAT LAST.
It'll go bad!
OH. YOU'RE NOT EASING HER INTO IT.
ONIGIRI

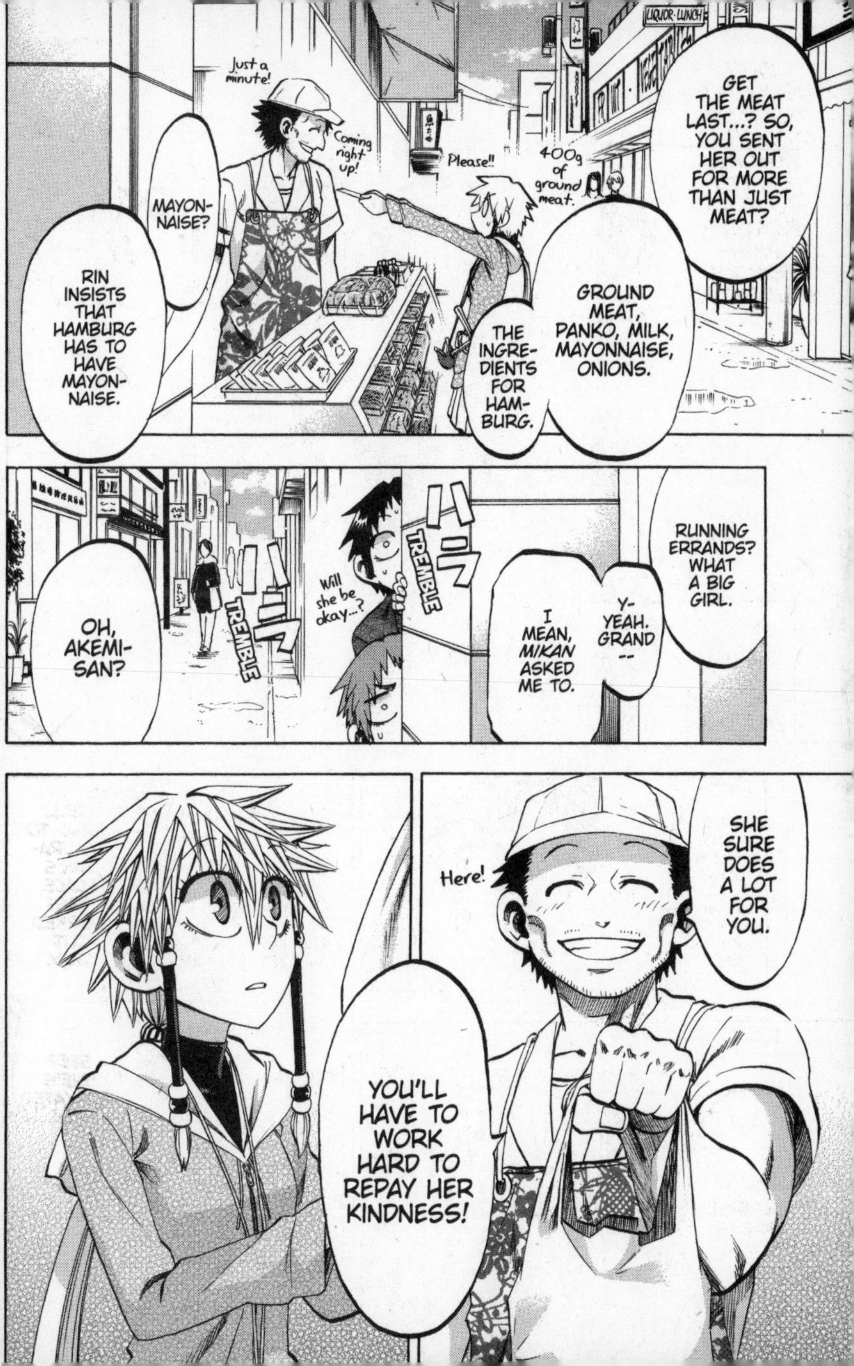
LIQUOR · LUNCH
GET THE MEAT LAST...? SO, YOU SENT HER OUT FOR MORE THAN JUST MEAT?
GROUND MEAT, PANKO, MILK, MAYONNAISE, ONIONS.
THE INGREDIENTS FOR HAMBURG.
400g of ground meat.
Please!!
Coming right up!
Just a minute!
MAYONNAISE?
RIN INSISTS THAT HAMBURG HAS TO HAVE MAYONNAISE.
RUNNING ERRANDS? WHAT A BIG GIRL.
Y-YEAH. GRAND--
I MEAN, MIKAN ASKED ME TO.
TREMBLE
Will she be okay...?
TREMBLE
OH, AKEMI-SAN?
SHE SURE DOES A LOT FOR YOU.
Here!
YOU'LL HAVE TO WORK HARD TO REPAY HER KINDNESS!

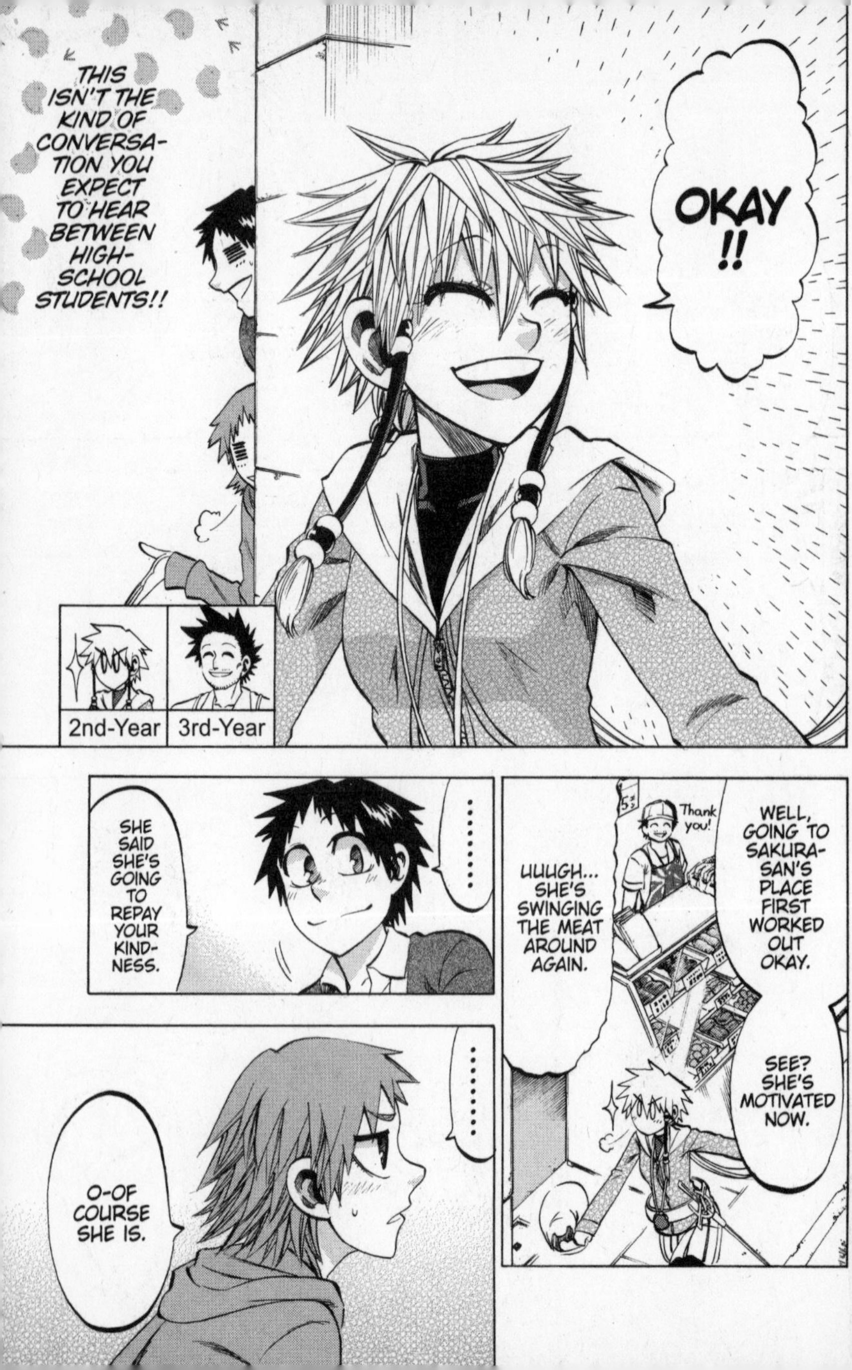
OKAY!!
THIS ISN'T THE KIND OF CONVERSATION YOU EXPECT TO HEAR BETWEEN HIGH-SCHOOL STUDENTS!!
3rd-Year
2nd-Year
WELL, GOING TO SAKURA-SAN'S PLACE FIRST WORKED OUT OKAY.
Thank you!
UUUGH... SHE'S SWINGING THE MEAT AROUND AGAIN.
SEE? SHE'S MOTIVATED NOW.
......
SHE SAID SHE'S GOING TO REPAY YOUR KINDNESS.
......
O-OF COURSE SHE IS.

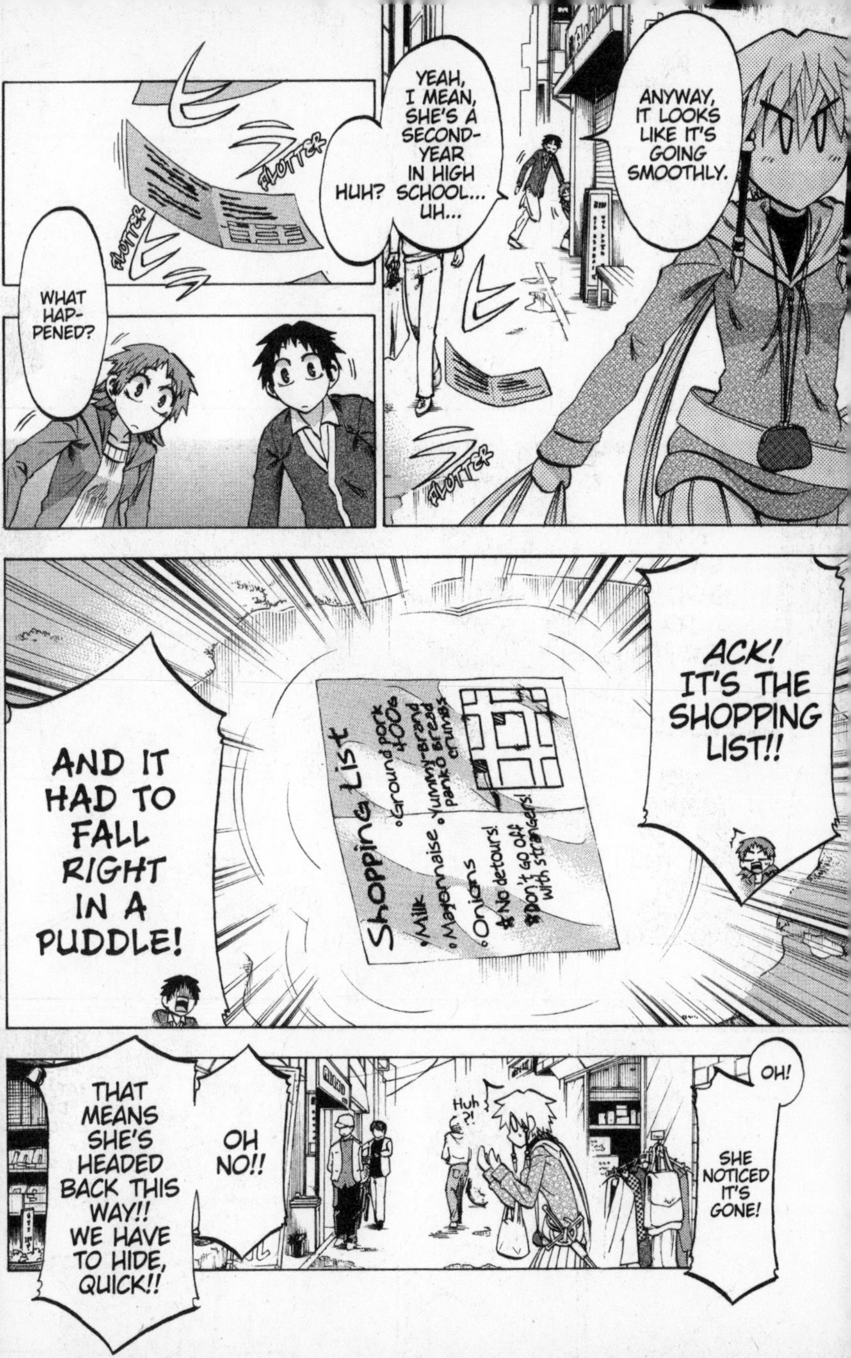
ANYWAY, IT LOOKS LIKE IT'S GOING SMOOTHLY.
YEAH, I MEAN, SHE'S A SECOND-YEAR IN HIGH SCHOOL... UH... HUH?
FLOTTER
FLOTTER
FLOTTER
FLOTTER
WHAT HAPPENED?
ACK! IT'S THE SHOPPING LIST!!
Shopping List
Ground pork 400g
Milk
Yummy-Brand panko Bread crumbs
Mayonnaise
Onions
No detours!
Don't go off with strangers!
AND IT HAD TO FALL RIGHT IN A PUDDLE!
OH!
SHE NOTICED IT'S GONE!
Huh ?!
OH NO!!
THAT MEANS SHE'S HEADED BACK THIS WAY!! WE HAVE TO HIDE, QUICK!!

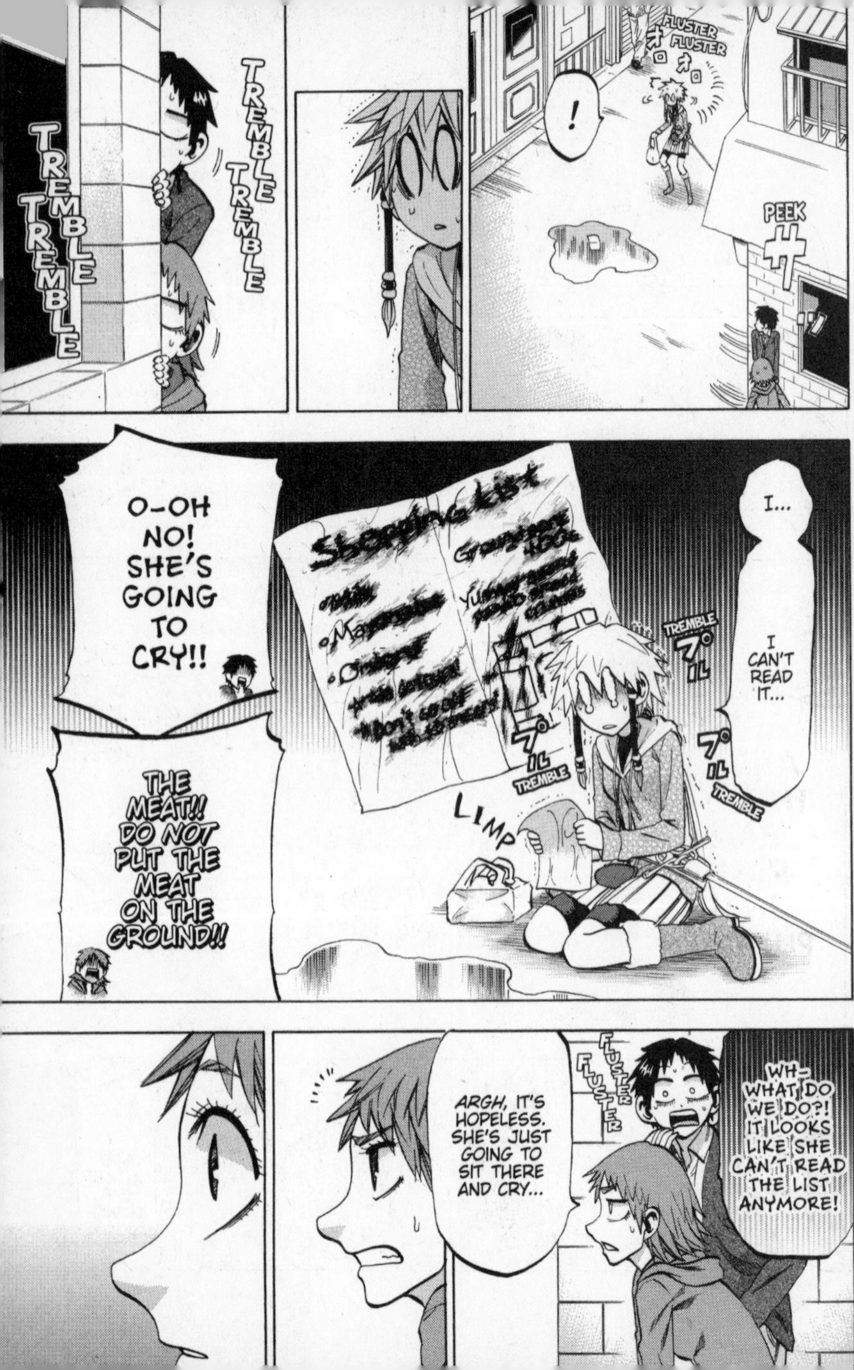
FLUSTER FLUSTER
!
PEEK
TREMBLE TREMBLE
TREMBLE TREMBLE
I...
I CAN'T READ IT...
TREMBLE
TREMBLE
TREMBLE
LIMP
O-OH NO! SHE'S GOING TO CRY!!
THE MEAT!! DO NOT PUT THE MEAT ON THE GROUND!!
WH-WHAT DO WE DO?! IT LOOKS LIKE SHE CAN'T READ THE LIST ANYMORE!
FLUSTER FLUSTER
ARGH, IT'S HOPELESS. SHE'S JUST GOING TO SIT THERE AND CRY...

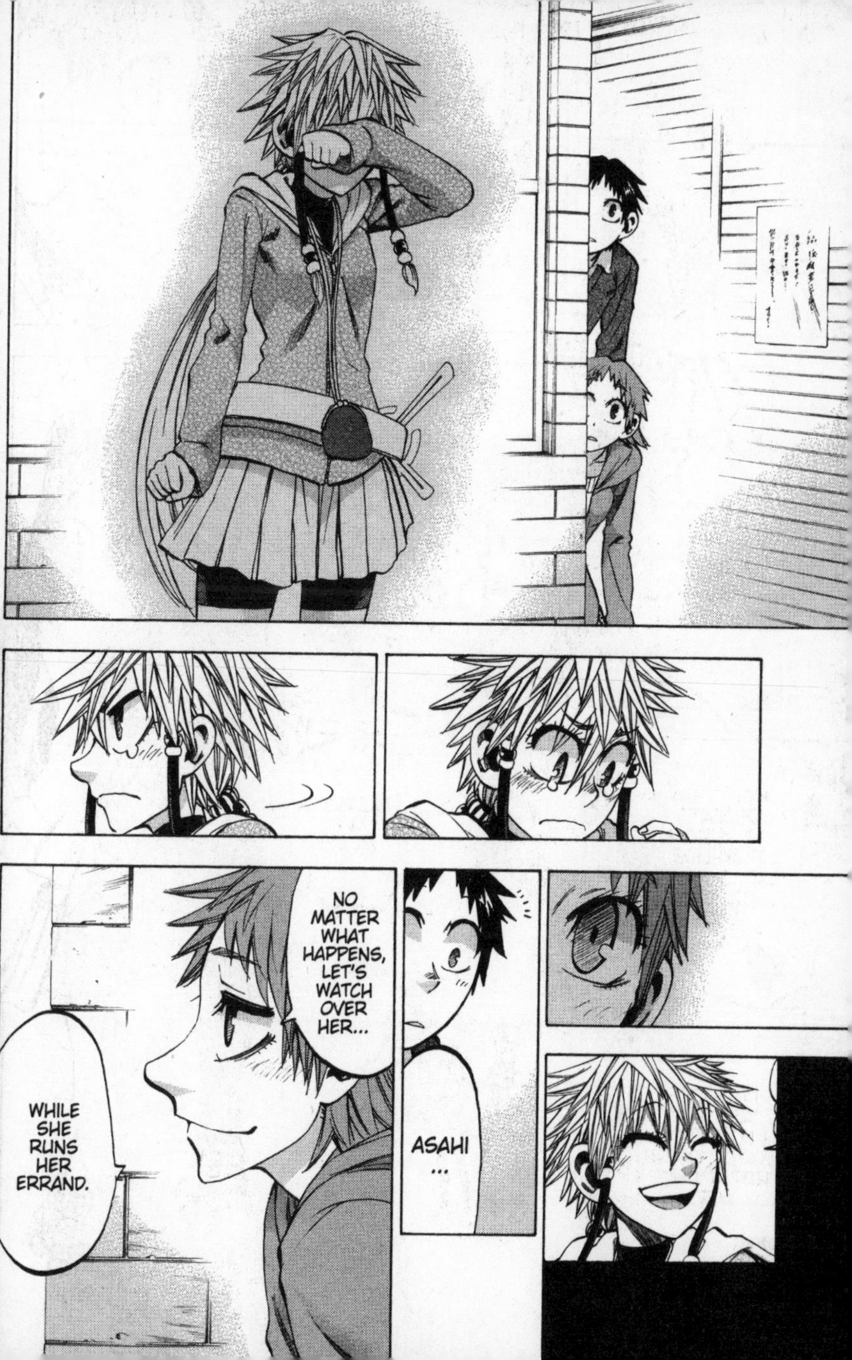
ASAHI
...
NO MATTER WHAT HAPPENS, LET'S WATCH OVER HER...
WHILE SHE RUNS HER ERRAND.

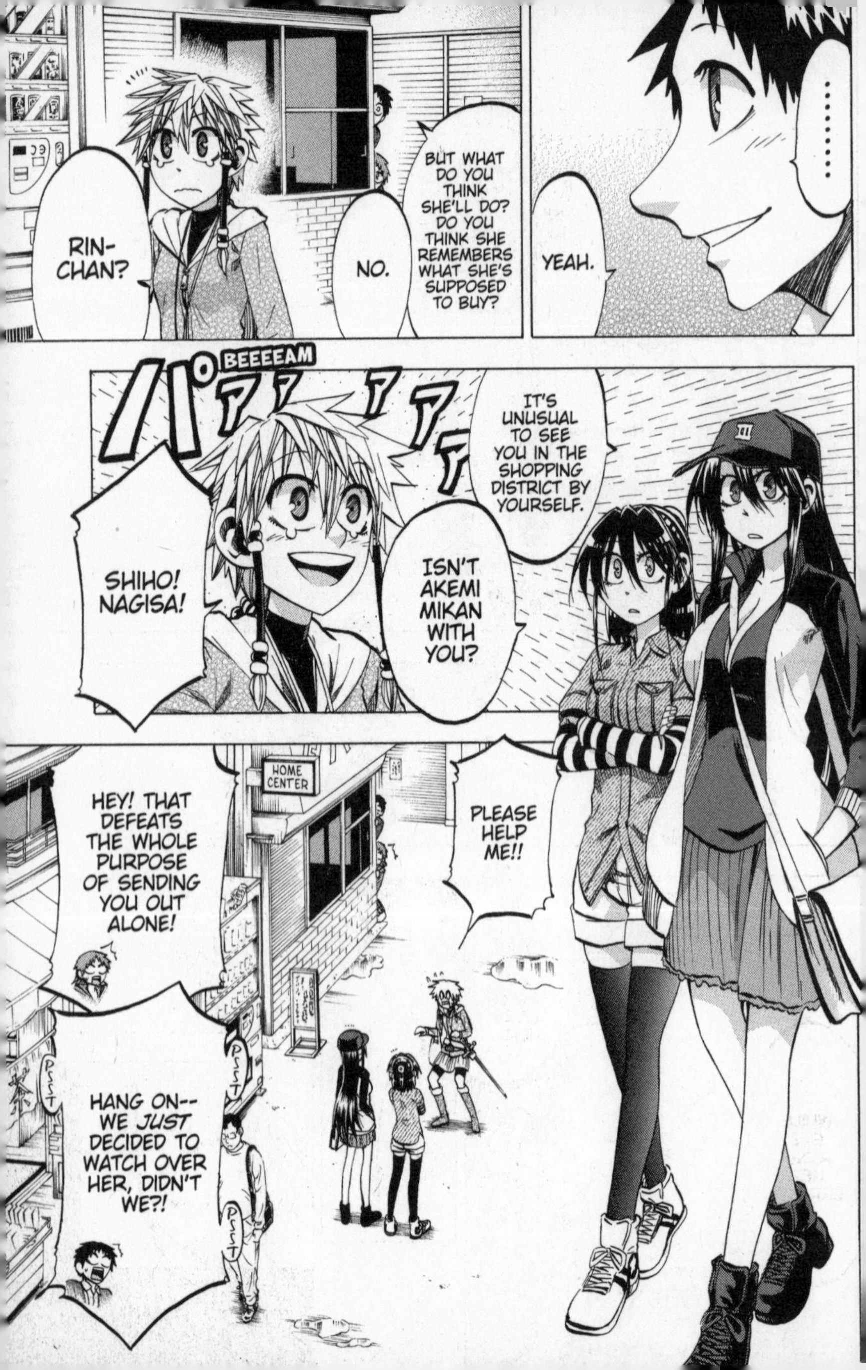
......
YEAH.
BUT WHAT DO YOU THINK SHE'LL DO? DO YOU THINK SHE REMEMBERS WHAT SHE'S SUPPOSED TO BUY?
NO.
RIN-CHAN?
IT'S UNUSUAL TO SEE YOU IN THE SHOPPING DISTRICT BY YOURSELF.
ISN'T AKEMI MIKAN WITH YOU?
BEEEEAM
SHIHO! NAGISA!
PLEASE HELP ME!!
HOME CENTER
HEY! THAT DEFEATS THE WHOLE PURPOSE OF SENDING YOU OUT ALONE!
PSST
PSST
PSST
HANG ON-- WE *JUST* DECIDED TO WATCH OVER HER, DIDN'T WE?!

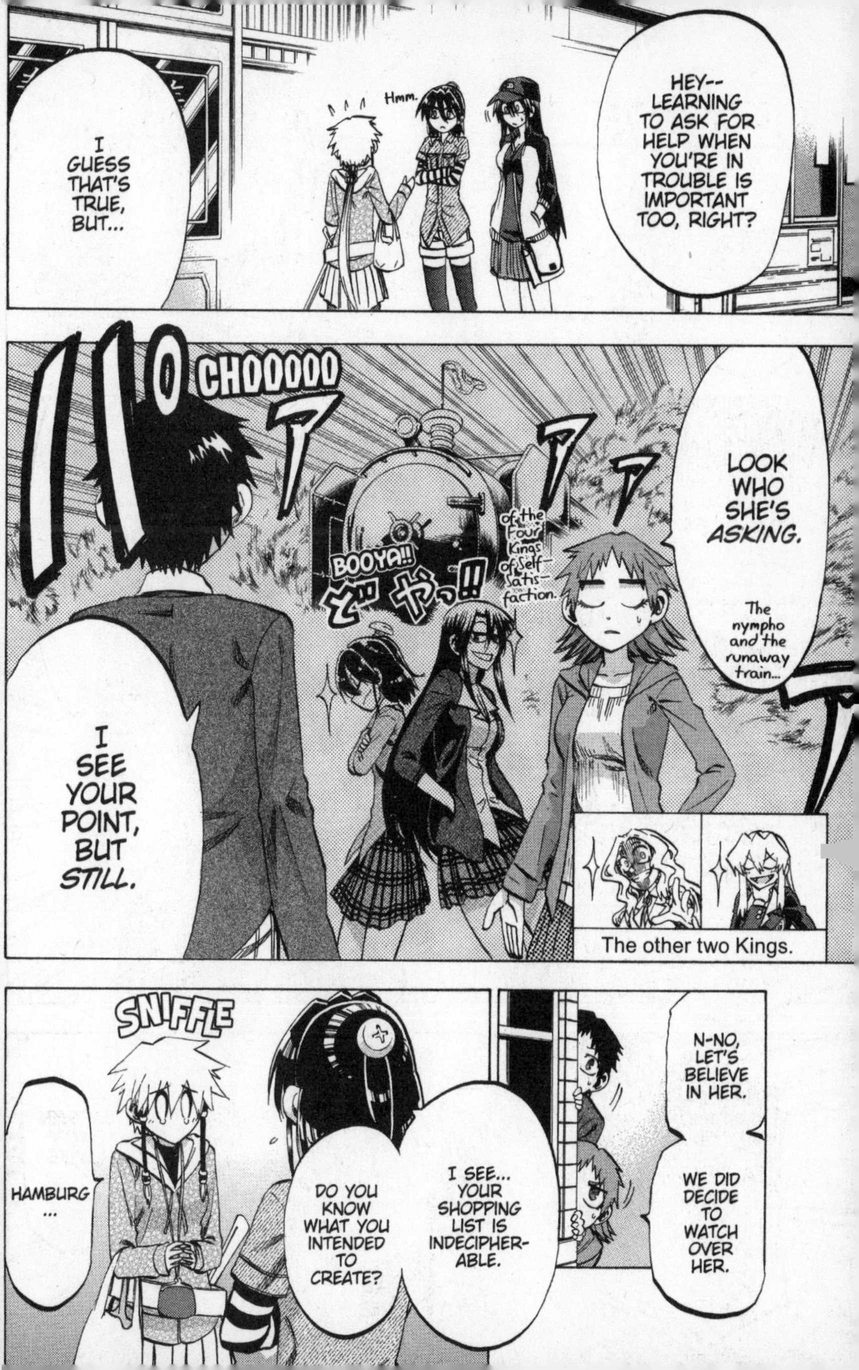
HEY-- LEARNING TO ASK FOR HELP WHEN YOU'RE IN TROUBLE IS IMPORTANT TOO, RIGHT?
Hmm.
I GUESS THAT'S TRUE, BUT...
LOOK WHO SHE'S ASKING.
The nympho and the runaway train...
of the Four Kings of Self-Satisfaction.
BOOYA!!
CHOOOOO
I SEE YOUR POINT, BUT STILL.
The other two Kings.
N-NO, LET'S BELIEVE IN HER.
WE DID DECIDE TO WATCH OVER HER.
I SEE... YOUR SHOPPING LIST IS INDECIPHERABLE.
DO YOU KNOW WHAT YOU INTENDED TO CREATE?
SNIFFLE
HAMBURG ...

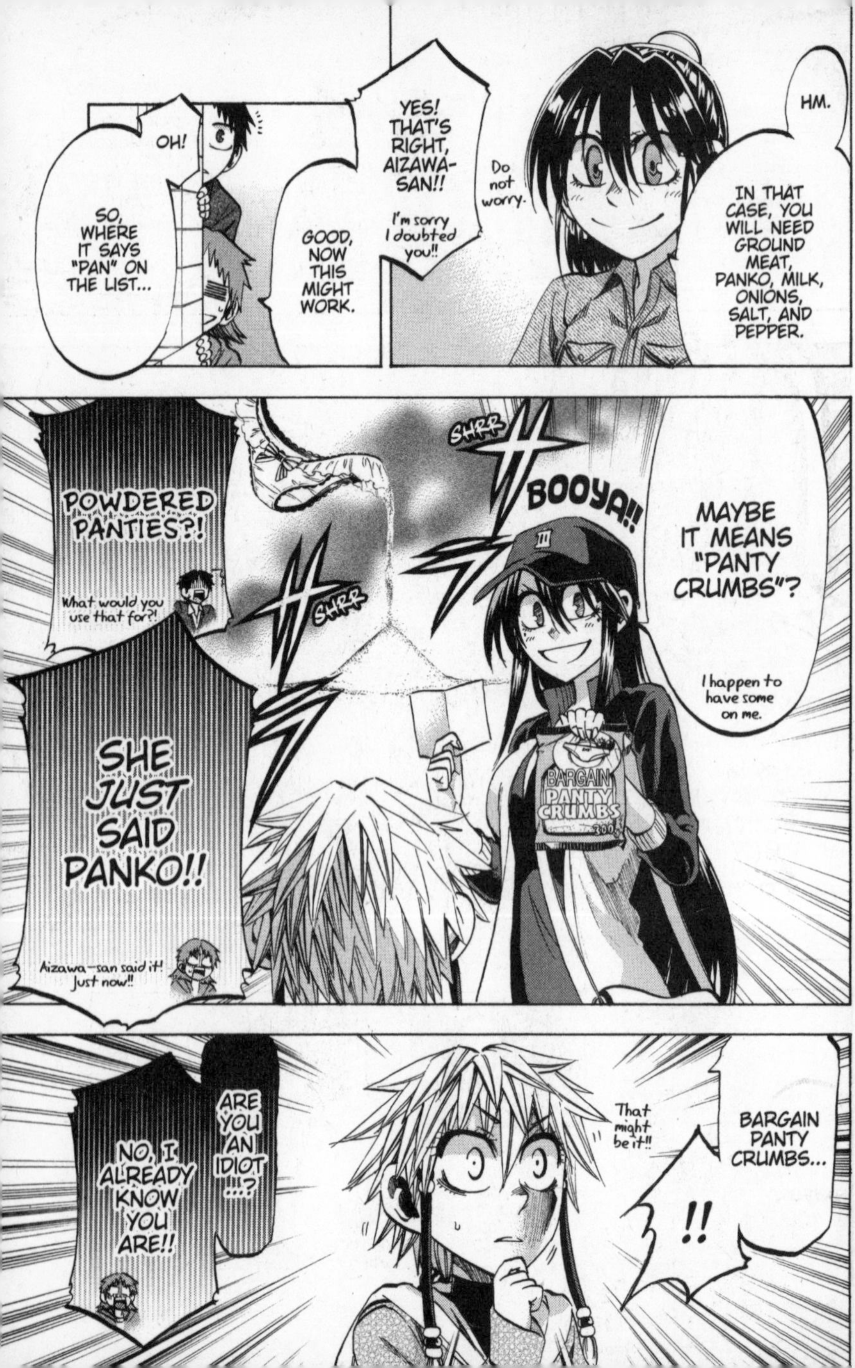
HM.
IN THAT CASE, YOU WILL NEED GROUND MEAT, PANKO, MILK, ONIONS, SALT, AND PEPPER.
Do not worry.
YES! THAT'S RIGHT, AIZAWA-SAN!!
I'm sorry I doubted you!!
GOOD, NOW THIS MIGHT WORK.
OH!
SO, WHERE IT SAYS "PAN" ON THE LIST...
MAYBE IT MEANS "PANTY CRUMBS"?
I happen to have some on me.
SHRR
BOOYA!!
SHRR
BARGAIN PANTY CRUMBS
POWDERED PANTIES?!
What would you use that for?!
SHE JUST SAID PANKO!!
Aizawa-san said it! Just now!!
BARGAIN PANTY CRUMBS...
!!
That might be it!!
ARE YOU AN IDIOT ...?
NO, I ALREADY KNOW YOU ARE!!

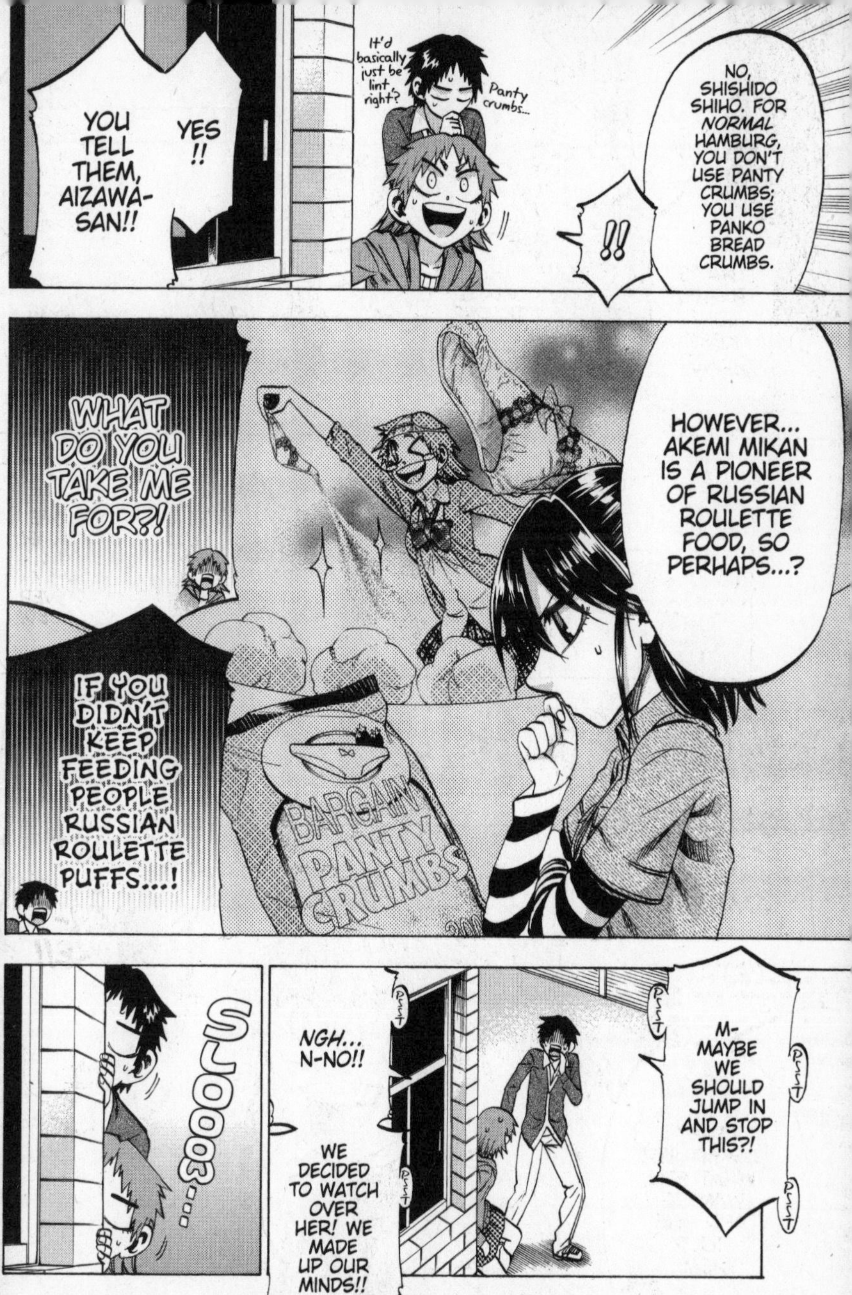
NO, SHISHIDO SHIHO. FOR NORMAL HAMBURG, YOU DON'T USE PANTY CRUMBS; YOU USE PANKO BREAD CRUMBS.
!!
Panty crumbs...
It'd basically just be lint, right?
YES!!
YOU TELL THEM, AIZAWA-SAN!!
HOWEVER... AKEMI MIKAN IS A PIONEER OF RUSSIAN ROULETTE FOOD, SO PERHAPS...?
WHAT DO YOU TAKE ME FOR?!
BARGAIN PANTY CRUMBS
IF YOU DIDN'T KEEP FEEDING PEOPLE RUSSIAN ROULETTE PUFFS...!
M-MAYBE WE SHOULD JUMP IN AND STOP THIS?!
NGH... N-NO!!
WE DECIDED TO WATCH OVER HER! WE MADE UP OUR MINDS!!
SLOOOOW...

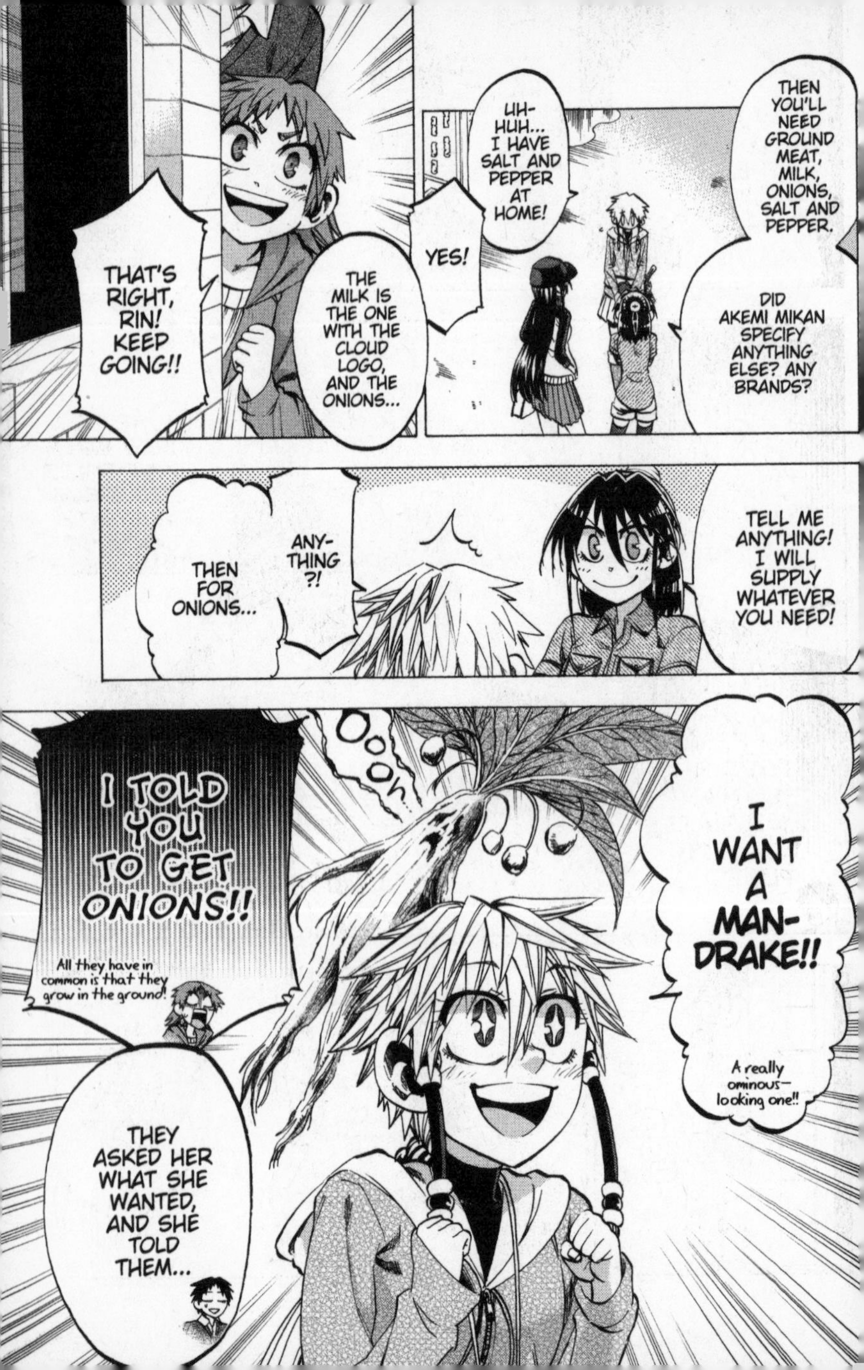
THEN YOU'LL NEED GROUND MEAT, MILK, ONIONS, SALT AND PEPPER.
DID AKEMI MIKAN SPECIFY ANYTHING ELSE? ANY BRANDS?
UH-HUH... I HAVE SALT AND PEPPER AT HOME!
YES!
THE MILK IS THE ONE WITH THE CLOUD LOGO, AND THE ONIONS...
THAT'S RIGHT, RIN! KEEP GOING!!
TELL ME ANYTHING! I WILL SUPPLY WHATEVER YOU NEED!
ANY-THING?!
THEN FOR ONIONS...
I WANT A MAN-DRAKE!!
A really ominous-looking one!!
Ooooh...
I TOLD YOU TO GET ONIONS!!
All they have in common is that they grow in the ground!
THEY ASKED HER WHAT SHE WANTED, AND SHE TOLD THEM...

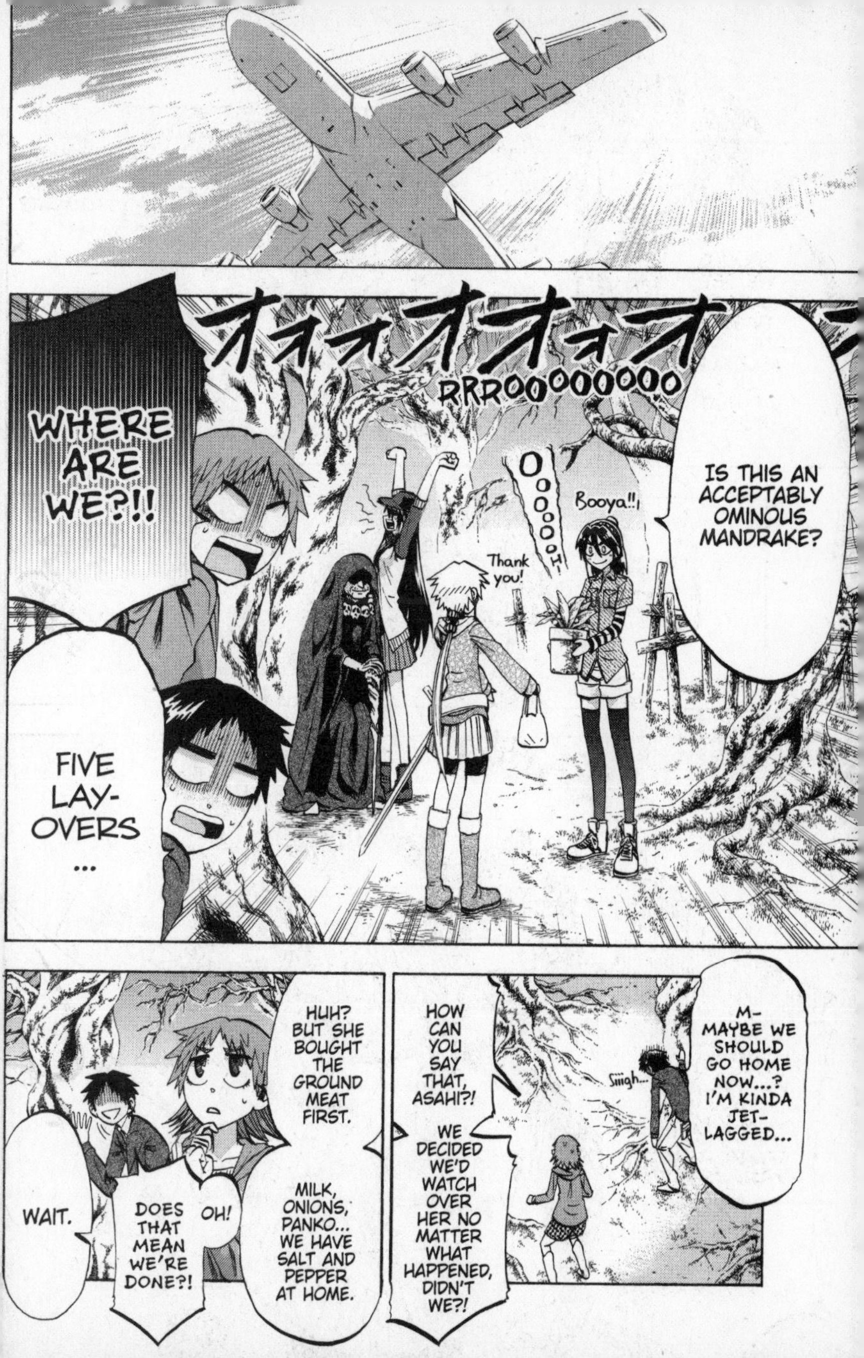

オォォオオォオ
DRRROOOOOOOOO
IS THIS AN ACCEPTABLY OMINOUS MANDRAKE?
Booya!!
OOOOOOOOH!
Thank you!
WHERE ARE WE?!!
FIVE LAY-OVERS ...
M-MAYBE WE SHOULD GO HOME NOW...? I'M KINDA JET-LAGGED...
Siiigh...
HOW CAN YOU SAY THAT, ASAHI?!
WE DECIDED WE'D WATCH OVER HER NO MATTER WHAT HAPPENED, DIDN'T WE?!
HUH? BUT SHE BOUGHT THE GROUND MEAT FIRST.
MILK, ONIONS, PANKO... WE HAVE SALT AND PEPPER AT HOME.
OH!
DOES THAT MEAN WE'RE DONE?!
WAIT.

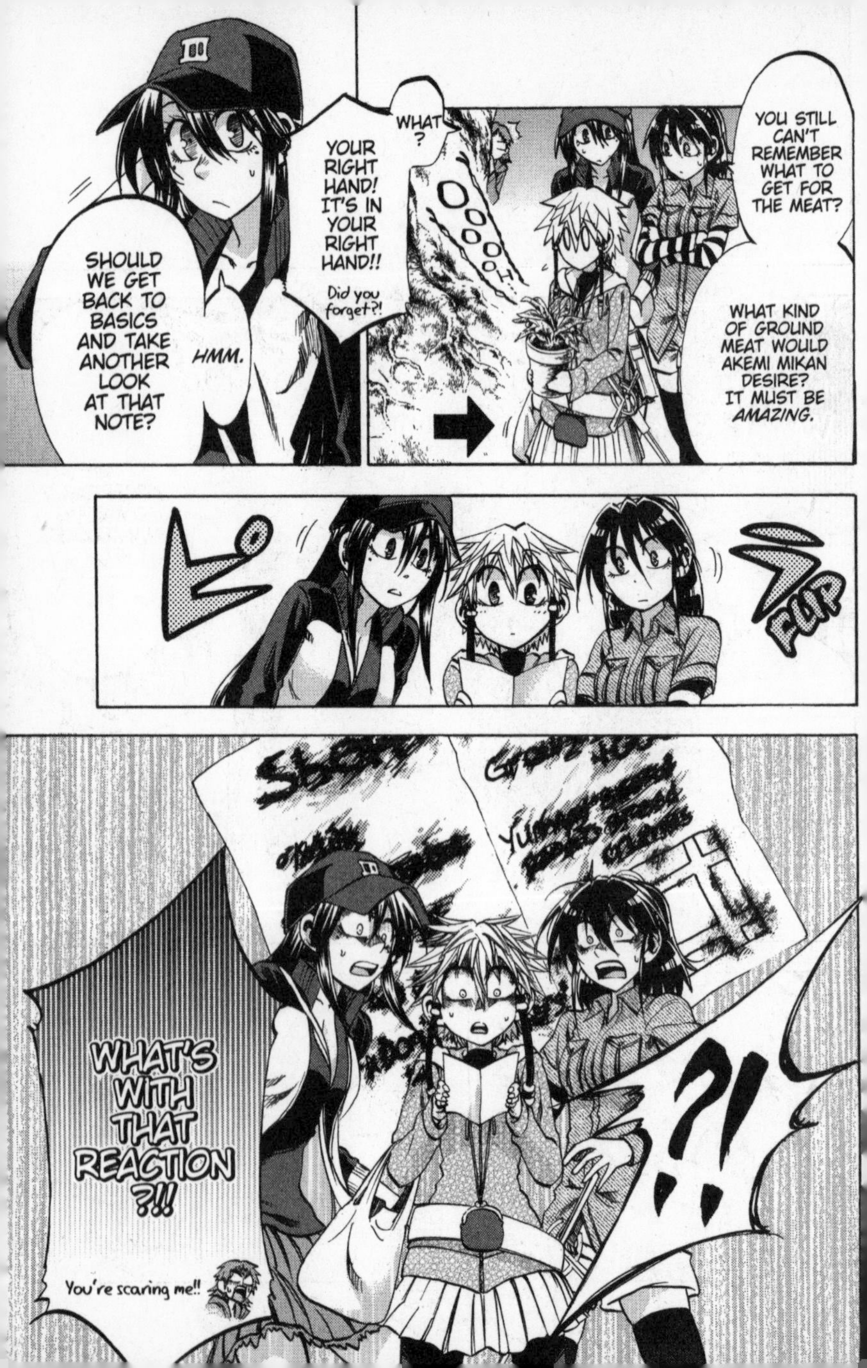

YOU STILL CAN'T REMEMBER WHAT TO GET FOR THE MEAT?
WHAT KIND OF GROUND MEAT WOULD AKEMI MIKAN DESIRE? IT MUST BE *AMAZING*.
WHAT?
OOOOOH
YOUR RIGHT HAND! IT'S IN YOUR RIGHT HAND!!
Did you forget?!
HMM.
SHOULD WE GET BACK TO BASICS AND TAKE ANOTHER LOOK AT THAT NOTE?
FLIP
?!
WHAT'S WITH THAT REACTION ?!!
You're scaring me!!

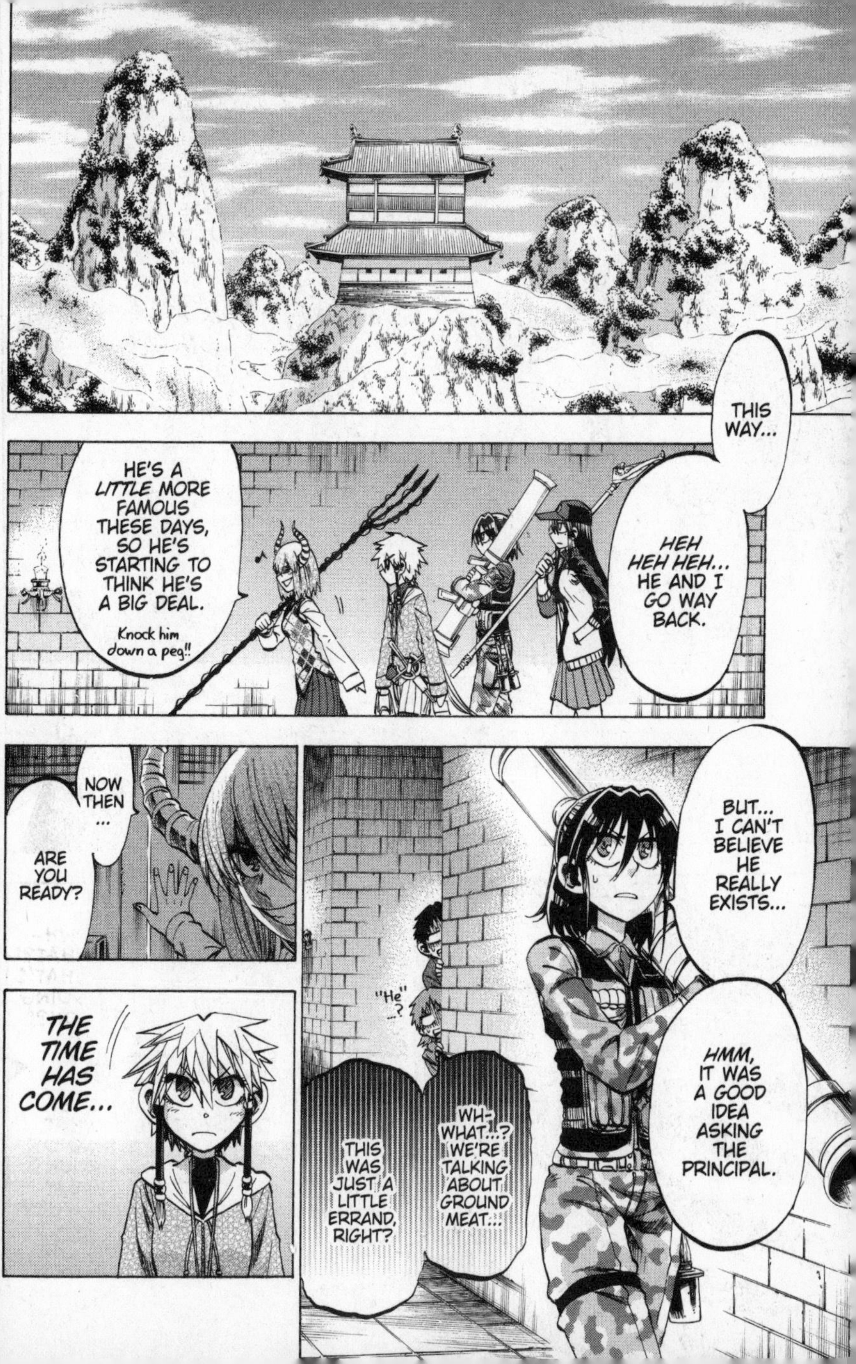
THIS WAY...
HEH HEH HEH... HE AND I GO WAY BACK.
HE'S A *LITTLE* MORE FAMOUS THESE DAYS, SO HE'S STARTING TO THINK HE'S A BIG DEAL.
Knock him down a peg!!
BUT... I CAN'T BELIEVE HE REALLY EXISTS...
HMM, IT WAS A GOOD IDEA ASKING THE PRINCIPAL.
"He" ...?
WH-WHAT...? WE'RE TALKING ABOUT GROUND MEAT...
THIS WAS JUST A LITTLE ERRAND, RIGHT?
NOW THEN ...
ARE YOU READY?
THE TIME HAS COME...

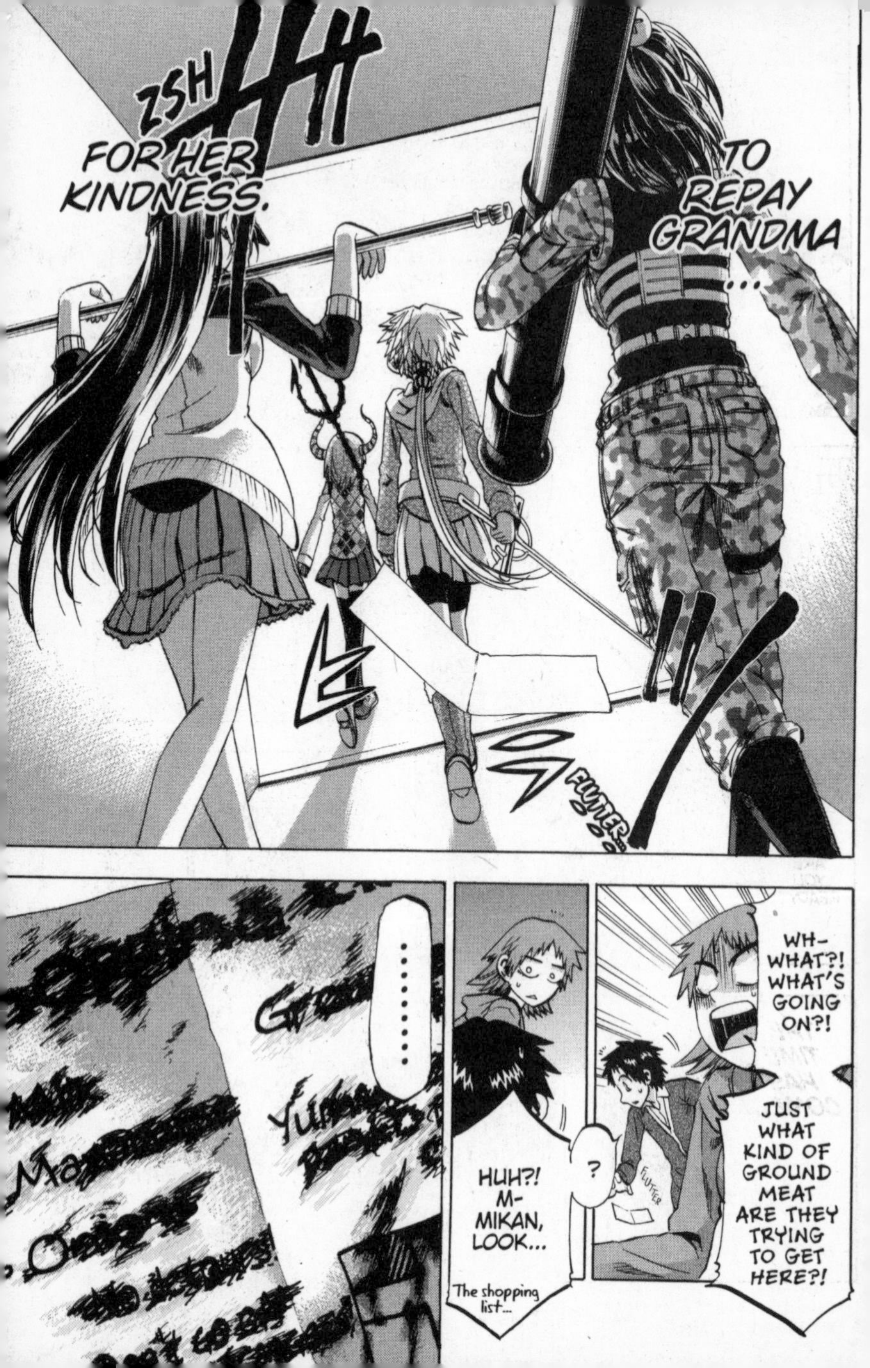
TO REPAY GRANDMA...
FOR HER KINDNESS.
ZSH
FLUTTER
WH-WHAT?! WHAT'S GOING ON?!
JUST WHAT KIND OF GROUND MEAT ARE THEY TRYING TO GET HERE?!
?
FLUTTER
HUH?! M-MIKAN, LOOK...
The shopping list...
....

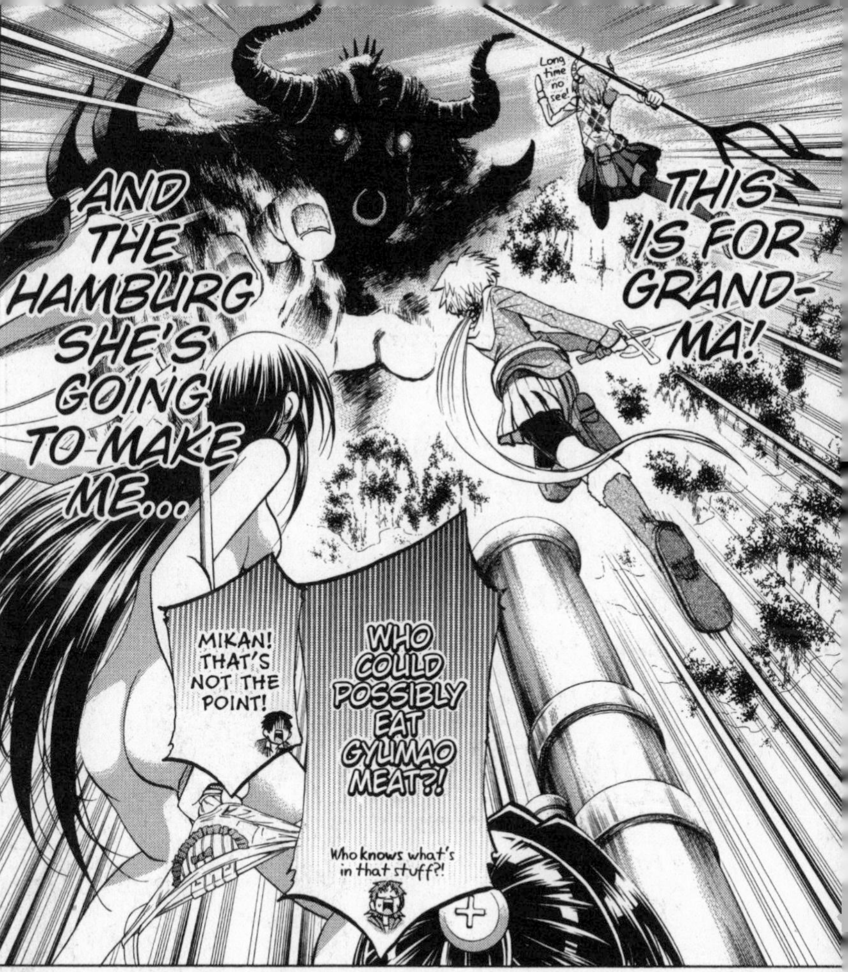
Long time no see!
THIS IS FOR GRAND-MA!
AND THE HAMBURG SHE'S GOING TO MAKE ME...
WHO COULD POSSIBLY EAT GYUMAO MEAT?!
Who knows what's in that stuff?!
MIKAN! THAT'S NOT THE POINT!

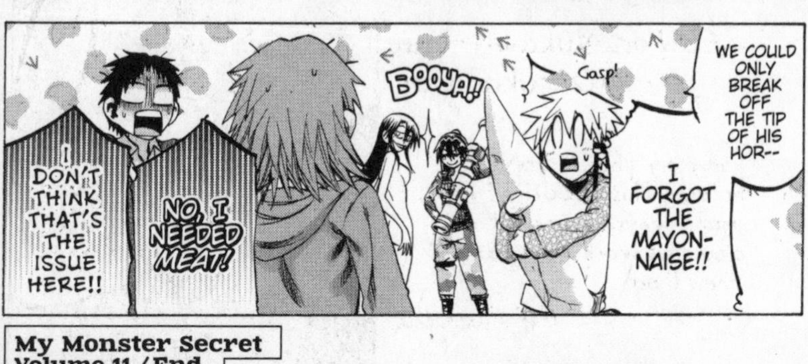
WE COULD ONLY BREAK OFF THE TIP OF HIS HOR--
Gasp!
I FORGOT THE MAYON-NAISE!!
BOOYA!!
NO, I NEEDED MEAT!
I DON'T THINK THAT'S THE ISSUE HERE!!

My Monster Secret Volume 11 / End

STAFF.

- Garage Okada-san
- Shuumeigiku-san
- Seijun Suzuki-san
- Daifuku Mochiko-san
- Nakamura Yuji-san
- Hayashi Rie-san
- Mana Haruki-san
- Hiroki Minemura-san
  (in syllabary order)

SPECIAL THANKS.

- Araki Nozomu-san
- Kawaji-san
- Yamada Jirou-san

Editor: Mukawa-san,
Otsuka-san

I give my thanks to you,
holding this book right now,
and everyone who let me
and this work be a part of
their lives.

Eiji Masuda

April Fool's

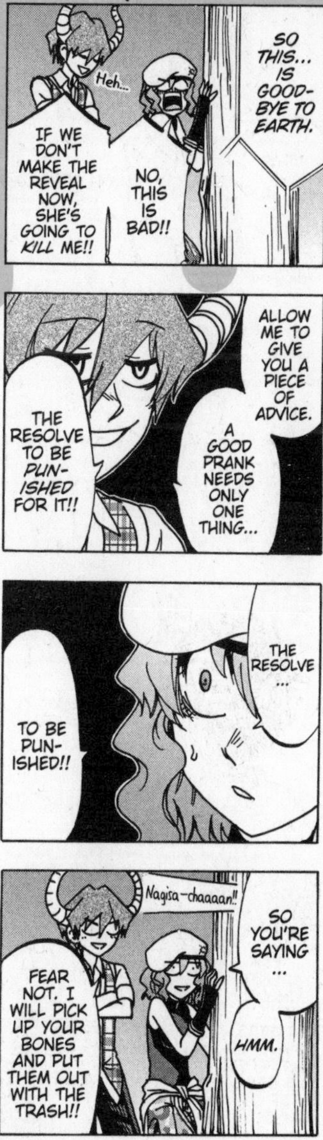
SO THIS... IS GOOD-BYE TO EARTH.
Heh...
NO, THIS IS BAD!!
IF WE DON'T MAKE THE REVEAL NOW, SHE'S GOING TO *KILL* ME!!
ALLOW ME TO GIVE YOU A PIECE OF ADVICE.
A GOOD PRANK NEEDS ONLY ONE THING...
THE RESOLVE TO BE *PUNISHED* FOR IT!!
THE RESOLVE...
TO BE PUNISHED!!
SO YOU'RE SAYING...
HMM.
FEAR NOT. I WILL PICK UP YOUR BONES AND PUT THEM OUT WITH THE TRASH!!
Nagisa-chaaaan!!

After Becoming Third-Years

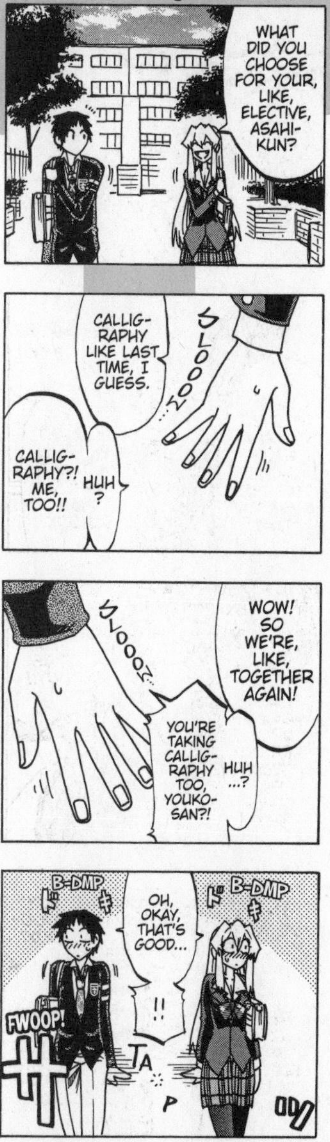
WHAT DID YOU CHOOSE FOR YOUR, LIKE, ELECTIVE, ASAHI-KUN?
SLOOOOW
CALLIGRAPHY LIKE LAST TIME, I GUESS.
HUH?
CALLIGRAPHY?! ME, TOO!!
WOW! SO WE'RE, LIKE, TOGETHER AGAIN!
HUH...?
YOU'RE TAKING CALLIGRAPHY TOO, YOUKO-SAN?!
SLOOOOW
B-DMP
OH, OKAY, THAT'S GOOD...
B-DMP
!!
FWOOP!
TAP

I am... 11

After the Family Chat

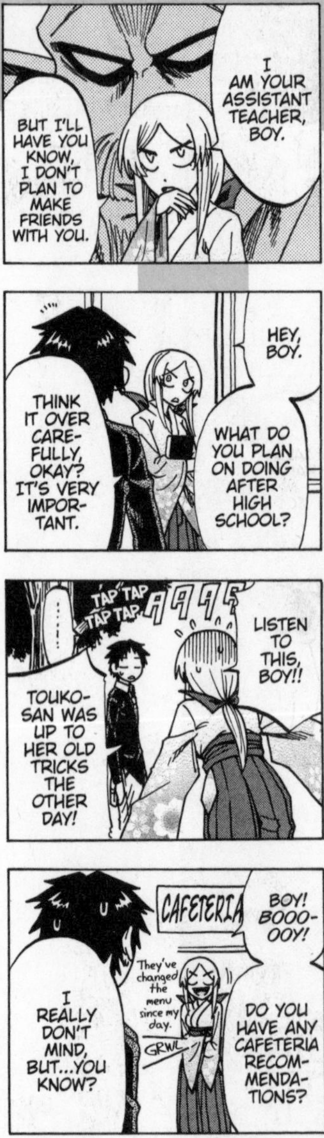
I AM YOUR ASSISTANT TEACHER, BOY.
BUT I'LL HAVE YOU KNOW, I DON'T PLAN TO MAKE FRIENDS WITH YOU.
HEY, BOY.
WHAT DO YOU PLAN ON DOING AFTER HIGH SCHOOL?
THINK IT OVER CAREFULLY, OKAY? IT'S VERY IMPORTANT.
LISTEN TO THIS, BOY!!
TAP TAP TAP TAP
.....
TOUKO-SAN WAS UP TO HER OLD TRICKS THE OTHER DAY!
BOY! BOOO-OOY!
CAFETERIA
DO YOU HAVE ANY CAFETERIA RECOMMENDATIONS?
They've changed the menu since my day.
GRWL
I REALLY DON'T MIND, BUT...YOU KNOW?

Flower Viewing

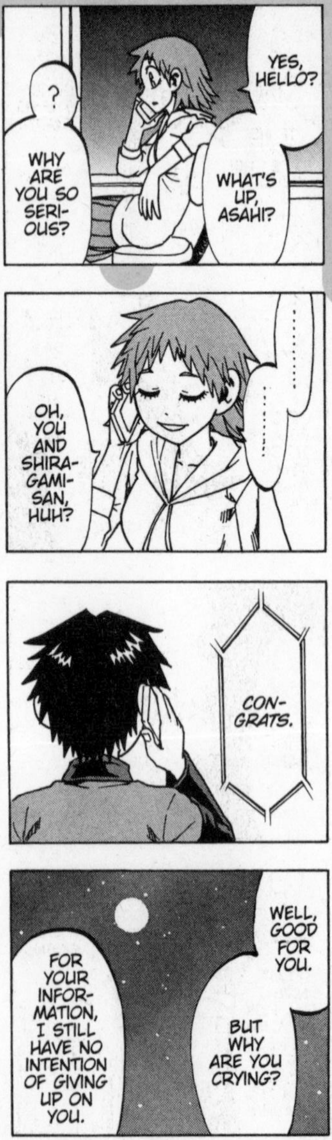
YES, HELLO?
WHAT'S UP, ASAHI?
?
WHY ARE YOU SO SERIOUS?
......
......
OH, YOU AND SHIRAGAMI-SAN, HUH?
CONGRATS.
WELL, GOOD FOR YOU.
BUT WHY ARE YOU CRYING?
FOR YOUR INFORMATION, I STILL HAVE NO INTENTION OF GIVING UP ON YOU.

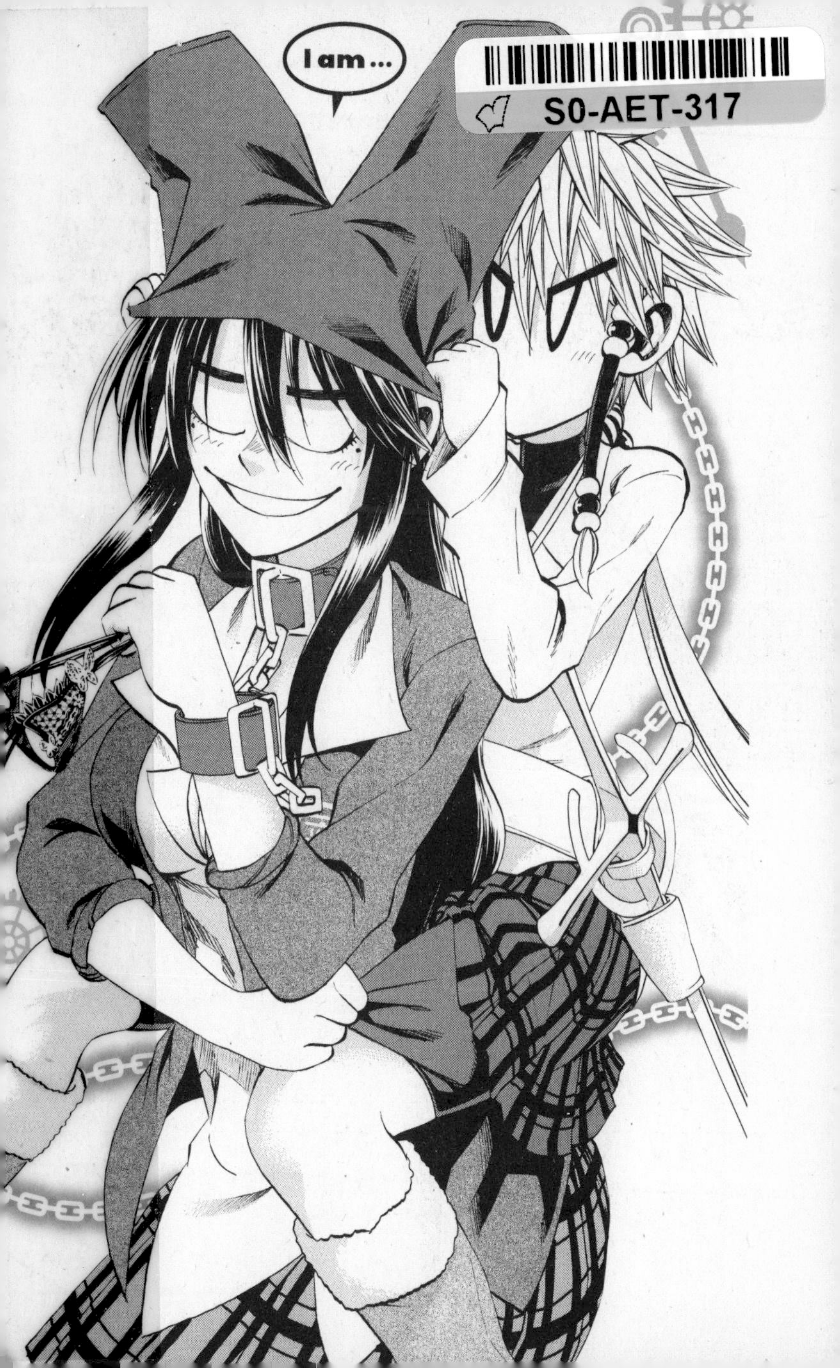
I am ...